By the same author:

The Influence of Hobbes and Locke
Trouble-free Travel: An Insider's Guide
Black Jenny (a novel about Shakespeare)
500 Destinations to Avoid

1000 TIPS+TRAPS FOR THE WORRIED WELL

ABOUT THE AUTHOR

Ian Wilson took his doctorate at Oxford University after seven years studying languages and philosophy. Since then he has spent a further year studying anthropology and three years training part-time to become a counsellor. He has briefly been an art dealer and is a qualified masseur.

After a short spell in advertising in London he founded WEXAS International (1970), the uk's lading club for independent travellers.

Ian Wilson was married for fifteen years and split up with his first wife at the age of 39. He remained in close contact with his son and daughter and they still form an important part of his life. He is currently re-married to a Master of Wine and has a two-year old son.

He has had a passion for surfing since the age of 20 and his position as chairman of a successful travel company enables him to travel widely, mainly to tropical destinations. Surfing was and still is one of his regular ways of keeping fit, seeing less developed parts of the world and exploring places on behalf of the 25,000 members of WEXAS. During this time he has never lost what he calls the 'philosophical perspective on life'.

Ian Wilson is currently researching a popular psychology book about love, marriage and divorce in the 21st century.

His other interests are sailing, skiing, scuba and free diving, parapsychology and collecting antiquarian maps on New Zealand, where he has a home on an idyllic offshore island.

1000
TIPS+TRAPS
FOR THE
WORRIED WELL

A GUIDE FOR MEN
IN MIDDLE LIFE

DR IAN WILSON

Foreword by
Dr Thomas Stuttaford

Osculum
Press

Published in 2008 by Osculum Press, 45-49 Brompton Road, Knightsbridge, London SW3 1DE

A catalogue record for this book is available from the British Library

ISBN 978–0–905–802–99–2
EAN 9 780905 802 992

Printed and bound in India by Nutech Photolithographers
Designed and Typeset in Janson Text by De-sign
Index by Susan Boobis

This book is dedicated to my two-year-old son Thomas Edward Mowat Wilson who will, I hope, live to see the twenty-second century

Ian Wilson

CONTENTS

FOREWORD

Everything Ian Wilson undertakes he does with passionate attention to detail. Whether he is writing on travel – he has been a traveller to remote spots since his student days at Oxford – or on health, the intensity with which he pursues a subject is apparent from the first chapter.

In *1000 Tips and Traps for the Worried Well*, Ian Wilson demonstrates his commitment to well researched detail. His writing is concise and easy to read. His approach to health and medicine sometimes differs from my own, but his ideas are so reasonably presented that readers cannot fail to be convinced. His easy but well crafted style ensures that this book will be read, while its advice will provide a framework for living for many of its readers. Ian Wilson has combed hundreds of sources in his hunt for the facts and they are all presented here, jargon-free. Unlike so many self-help books, this one does not partronize the reader. As a result, life led according to Ian Wilson's formula is likely to be healthy and active in life's middle and later years.

Ian Wilson trained as a counsellor, but in medical matters he is self-taught. His interest in medicine was fostered by the early death of his mother and his contact with the health problems that inevitably go with Third World travel. His advice on lifestyle, exercise and diet, as on much else, is sound. This book will tell you that physical fitness cannot be acquired from a bottle of tablets prescribed by a doctor, or from a bottle sold by the local wine merchant. The answers are more complex than that and Ian Wilson's book explores them all. His disciplined approach to an ordered pattern of living should be acquired by many of us if we aspire to a long life with a sound mind in a sound body.

FOREWORD

Everything Ian Wilson undertakes he does with passionate attention to detail. Whether he is writing on travel – he has been a traveller to remote areas since his student days at Oxford – or on health, the thoroughness with which he pursues a subject is apparent from the first chapter.

In 1990 *Tips and Traps for the Hurried Host*, Ian Wilson demonstrates his commitment to well-researched detail. His writing is concise and easy to read. His approach to health and medicine sometimes differs from my own, but his ideas are so reasonably presented that readers cannot fail to be convinced. His easy but well crafted style ensures that this book will be read, while its advice will provide a framework for living for many of its readers. Ian Wilson has combed hundreds of sources in his hunt for the facts and they are all presented here, jargon-free. Unlike so many self-help books, this one does not patronize the reader. As a result, life led according to Ian Wilson's formula is likely to be healthy and active in life's middle and later years.

Ian Wilson trained as a counsellor, but in medical matters he is self-taught. His interest in medicine was fostered by the early death of his mother and his contact with the health problems that inevitably go with Third-World travel. His advice on life style, exercise and diet, as on much else, is sound. This book will tell you that physical fitness cannot be acquired from a bottle of tablets prescribed by a doctor, or from a bottle sold by the local wine merchant. The answers are more complex than that and Ian Wilson's book explores them all. His disciplined approach to an ordered pattern of living should be acquired by many of us if we aspire to a long life with a sound mind in a sound body.

FOREWORD

Everything Ian Wilson undertakes he does with passionate attention to detail. Whether he is writing on travel – he has been a traveller to remote spots since his student days at Oxford – or on health, the intensity with which he pursues a subject is apparent from the first chapter.

In *1000 Tips and Traps for the Worried Well*, Ian Wilson demonstrates his commitment to well researched detail. His writing is concise and easy to read. His approach to health and medicine sometimes differs from my own, but his ideas are so reasonably presented that readers cannot fail to be convinced. His easy but well crafted style ensures that this book will be read, while its advice will provide a framework for living for many of its readers. Ian Wilson has combed hundreds of sources in his hunt for the facts and they are all presented here, jargon-free. Unlike so many self-help books, this one does not partronize the reader. As a result, life led according to Ian Wilson's formula is likely to be healthy and active in life's middle and later years.

Ian Wilson trained as a counsellor, but in medical matters he is self-taught. His interest in medicine was fostered by the early death of his mother and his contact with the health problems that inevitably go with Third World travel. His advice on lifestyle, exercise and diet, as on much else, is sound. This book will tell you that physical fitness cannot be acquired from a bottle of tablets prescribed by a doctor, or from a bottle sold by the local wine merchant. The answers are more complex than that and Ian Wilson's book explores them all. His disciplined approach to an ordered pattern of living should be acquired by many of us if we aspire to a long life with a sound mind in a sound body.

INTRODUCTION

Life begins at forty, the saying goes, but according to an article I read in a newspaper, life now begins at fifty.

It's sobering to know that according to doctors, middle age starts at 35 and old age at 65. And now the obesity epidemic threatens to reverse the increased longevity we keep being told we can expect.

Chronological and biological age are often very different. A 50-year-old might have the body of a 40-year-old or a 60-year-old. This book will show you how you might knock ten years off your biological age, especially if you are that biological 60-year-old. But be warned: staying young for your age is not for the lazy.

There are lots of books about how to exercise, eat better, drink less and quit smoking. This one is slightly different. I'm a doctor of philosophy, not medicine. I have qualifications in massage and counselling. I got my diploma as a gym instructor when I was 59 and became a father for the third time on the eve of my 62nd birthday. Now, at 64, my hobbies are free diving, sailing and surfing big waves in remote corners of the globe.

I've been one of the worried well since I read *Let's Get Well* by Adelle Davis in 1972. It's still sitting beside me on my shelf, accompanied by another hundred books on healthy living. *Let's Get Well* worried me enough to make me go and get a medical check-up – blood and urine tests, blood pressure, chest x-ray, ECG and so on. I've been getting an annual once-over ever since, mostly courtesy of BUPA, and tracking my performance on key indicators like cholesterol and blood pressure.

Am I a hypochondriac? I don't think so. Maybe just a bit obsessive. I take care of my health as best I can. I can't do much about my age, my sex or the genes I inherited, so there's three negatives for a start.

The inspiration for writing this book came from my mother. She smoked a lot, she didn't eat well, she hardly took any exercise and she ended up with clinical depression and osteoporosis. Then she fell and broke her hip at 58. The rest of her story is all too common. Within a year she was dead in hospital from a pulmonary embolism, a fatal clot on the lungs. This is why it is often said that depression can kill. It can lead to such self- neglect that the will to eat and exercise properly is lost.

Loss of the will to live so often accompanies depression that it's almost as if what Freud called libido in its broadest sense has gone and only death can follow. That is why the will live is so important and why depression, which affects about one man in three in the course of his life, is so dangerous.

Is looking after yourself neurotic, is it narcissistic, is it obsessive? I would say it's a little of all these things, but if it gives you a few happy and healthy extra years, it has to be worth it.

Go too far, though, and you could become a hypochondriac, someone who is concerned they have illnesses that aren't there. The worried well are not that person. The true hypochondriac is not a well person. They have imaginary illnesses and that is a serious psychiatric disorder. The worried well focus on preventing real disorders. They notice small symptoms and try to get to their cause so they can eliminate them. They believe in preventive medicine. They don't imagine maladies that don't exist. And above all they know their bodies very well, inside and out.

The term 'worried well' is often used negatively, not least by doctors, and apparently one quarter of all those who visit a doctor in the UK have nothing wrong with them. This upsets some doctors, who feel their job is to look after the truly sick, not have their time wasted. I think they are wrong. Doctors should be willing to encourage preventive medicine, even if this means having to deal with patients who are anxious and have symptoms that turn out to be innocuous. If the symptoms are there, who is to say that they are not indicative of disease if not the doctor?

So should your doctor welcome the worried well into their surgery. My answer is a definite 'yes.' The worried well are not hypochondriacs. They just believe in taking care of themselves and checking out any suspicious symptom – who knows, that headache could turn out be the sign of a cerebral aneurysm or malignant tumour and catching it early could make the difference between life and death.

I read not long ago that middle-aged men were more prone to depression than middle- aged women, and that people in middle age are less happy, on the whole, than the elderly. That may or may not be true. I have always believed that the elderly were the group most prone to depression, though there seems little doubt that men of working age who are poor and unemployed face a tough time mentally, especially if they are divorced or were never married. It's the elderly, though, especially men, who commit suicide when depression passes the point of no return.

Much of this book's contents will be found in other books or in newspapers, but not as comprehensively in one single volume. *1000 Tips and Traps for the Worried Well* goes beyond healthy eating and exercise. It answers questions about stress, work, sleep, lifestyle , relationships, ageing and finding meaning in life. It will teach you to look on the passing years as maturing and getting less young, not getting old.

A recent study showed that people were happier in 1953 than they are now. No one would deny that most people are better off materially now, which only goes to show that happiness and money do not necessarily go together. This has been brought home to me on my travels around Third World countries where I have seen some of the poorest people, so long as they are fed and in reasonable health, laughing and smiling far more than the faces I pass on the streets of London each day. The moral here is that if you cannot be both, it is better to be healthy than rich.

As Baby Boomers, maybe we are getting a bit tubby round the middle. Maybe we can't run like we used to, even to catch a bus. Maybe we're worried about our cholesterol. Maybe policemen are starting to look *terribly* young. Maybe we're looking forward to (and yet dreading) our kids leaving home. Maybe we're worried that coupled or not, we don't seem to catch the eye of the girls like we used to, or thought we did. Could it actually be that as we grow older we become invisible to the younger generation, despite still wearing jeans and driving a car that is twice as powerful as the one we drove in our twenties?

Do you catch sight of yourself in passing shop windows and wonder about a receding hairline, comforting yourself that you read somewhere that by fifty more than half of all men are showing visible signs of hair loss?

Middle life is the time when we grapple with a whole new bunch of fears – the fear that we cannot change the world, much as we would like to; the fear that we have not fulfilled our potential, let alone our ambitions; the fear that our kids are not turning out the way we would have wanted; the fear that we will never visit all the places we wanted to see at least once in our lives; and above all the fear that our bodies and minds are in decline and presage ultimate oblivion in death.

But it doesn't have to be all downhill after forty. There are pluses to getting older and entering what the Swiss psychotherapist Carl Jung called the second stage of life, when we are meant to grow into our mature selves and move further down the road towards what Jung called individuation. Life between forty and sixty-five is when most of us have the chance to grow into who we really are, and when, knowing ourselves better, we can turn to a less material outlook on life.

I would like to think of *1000 Tips and Traps for the Worried Well* as a practical road map to a healthy and happy life for the worried well going through middle life – a practical guide book covering issues that I have had to face myself over the last two decades.

Generally, for the sake of easy reading, I don't sidetrack to give the sources of things I say. This may make what I write seem opinionated at times. Please bear with me. Inevitably a book like this will generalise and treat people like statistics and averages, which, of course, they are not. I have tried to avoid being dogmatic as I find this a weakness in many books on health, as though the writer had all the answers. With much still to be answered by science in the future, surely it is better to err on the side of caution and express doubt where doubt is due. Where something like dietary supplements is concerned there is no such thing as an absolute authority.

The biggest problem in writing a book like this is deciding what to leave out. It could have been ten times longer. I have tried to focus on the tips and traps that are most useful, while avoiding the obvious. I want readers to find things in this book that they didn't know already, or say, 'aha, I thought so,' as old opinions, even prejudices, are confirmed.

Maybe 50 years from now, 'good' cholesterol will be 'bad' cholesterol, or vice versa, or maybe cholesterol levels won't matter any more. In the meantime, we have to live with the information we have, unable to know whether in 50 years many people will routinely live active and healthy lives to the age of 130, as some medical scientists predict.

If you take the stairs instead of the lift, and if you walk up escalators, instead of standing, this book is for you. If you would like to do these things, you aspire to join the ranks of the worried well and this book is also for you.

If you do not have time to read the whole book, read the chapters most of interest to you or use it as a reference book. But if you are so short of time, you are probably running your life too fast, and when that happens, your life is really running out of control. Read the chapter on sleep. If you are only getting seven hours of sleep each night because your life is so busy, you are probably damaging your health.

Does it worry you that time seems to go faster as you get older? Are the years rushing by, marked by birthdays and Christmases that seem to happen with ever increasing frequency? Does this make you think about death and does that worry you? It used to worry me a lot. I tried being busier and it made no difference. So I tried relaxing and hardly being busy at all, and it still made no difference. Then I read that this is something that has been studied and it's a phenomenon found in all walks of life and in all societies.

Conclusion: there's absolutely nothing you can do about time passing faster as you get older. Subjectively, life will speed by faster and faster until you die. So take the Zen Buddhist viewpoint: whatever is simply is. Accept it and don't worry about it. You cannot do anything about it, and if you worry negatively you may shorten your life. People who worry negatively rarely have a long life. Worry positively, on the other hand, and you may extend your lifespan. This book will, I hope, show you the difference and how to be positively worried well.

Make the most of your life. You only get one shot at it. Think of life as a river. Swim with the flow, not against it.

Ian Wilson

CHAPTER ONE
GROWING LESS YOUNG

'Ageing is optional', said a sign I spotted in the window of a beauty salon yesterday. And to an extent that message is right. No one can stop the clock or turn it back, but you can slow it down.

What most books about ageing don't tell you is that it's a mental as well as a physical process. Your mind ages along with your body, and by adopting the right approach to health, you can slow the mental process down as well. Whenever I see really old people being interviewed on television, those that I admire most are the people who are articulate, often into their nineties and beyond. You cannot fail to be impressed by a man or woman over a hundred years old who can walk without the help of a stick, and who can talk intelligently and not too slowly. Of course such people are a rarity, but perhaps a couple of generations from now there will be far more of them around.

One story always sticks in my mind. It dates from the Seventies. I read of the death of a man aged 112 in London. Such an age is rare in itself. But what struck me was that this man had worked for the same company for 100 years, from the age of 12 to 112 without retiring. What's more, he had walked to work every day for those 100 years. I'm not suggesting that we all work 100 years for the same company, but the fact that he always exercised by walking and that he never retired speaks volumes about his ability to live such a long and active life.

A paradox of old age is that the less future we have left, the more we worry about it.

For some of us it isn't enough to eat right and keep fit if we want to live to a ripe old age. In fact the term 'worried well' is almost an oxymoron because if you are too worried you are not truly well. Ideally, a well person is someone without a care in the world. Such a person, in the unlikely event that they exist, has a great advantage over the rest of us, for freedom from worry, like laughter, is a great therapy if only you can get some of it. Those who get closest are probably Buddhist devotees.

Stress, on the other hand, is said to be a killer. This is another paradox. How is it that some of the longest-living people in the western world seem to live moderately stressful lives? I'm not referring to the man who lived to be 112, as I suspect that his long life was probably due to his genes, a daily walk and a disciplined life that changed very little, rather than to stress, which was probably foreign to him.

We hear of centenarians and see them interviewed from time to time, but they rarely seem like leaders of government and captains of industry. On the other hand we often hear of famous people – TV personalities and sportsmen – who die young. Could ambition have something to do with it? Our lifespan is partly influenced by our genes and our sex, but what about other factors?

One study showed that men living in closed communities as monks tended to have a long life. Another study showed a similar pattern for nuns in closed orders. From this it was concluded that perhaps abstention from sex was the key to prolonging life. But maybe it has more to do with the personality types who dedicate themselves to that kind of life. Perhaps in a more worldly setting they would not have lived so long. We can assume that they did not smoke and drank little or no alcohol. Perhaps the rest of the world expends its vital forces in the act of procreation, after which, nature in the shape of our genes has no more need of us – we have become expendable and are free to wither and die like a plant. We simply do not know.

If I worry about getting older and dying one day, will my anxiety speed ill health and ultimate death? In other words, if I am one of the worried well, without being a hypochondriac, will this itself shorten my life?

The best cure for depression is probably exercise. A lifetime of physical exertion – maybe only gardening – will keep most of us happy enough and lengthen our lifespan at the same time.

If physical exercise is important for wellbeing and can affect our mood so positively, let's take a look at how exercise affects the way we feel.

Prolonged aerobic exercise produces beta-endorphins and beta-lipotrophins that circulate in blood plasma. These opioid peptides, also known as cannabinoids, have the ability to act like morphine and reduce pain in the body while inducing euphoria in the brain, the so-called 'exercise high'. In response to pain, the body also produces two opioid pentapeptides: methionine and leucine enkephalin, as well as the endorphin called anandamide and the powerful opioid: dynorphin. It's thought that other similar opioids will be discovered in due course. With their ability to mask pain and create a state of happy if slightly sleepy relaxation, they are probably nature's best option for those who are mildly depressed or anxious. Not for nothing is the sensation that comes from the endorphins and the beta-lipotrophins compared with being lightly stoned on marijuana, without the side effects. But the point I am making is that this is nature's answer to depression – and a way to stay fit at the same time. Few things shorten lifespan as much as depression.

The way in which these opioids inter-relate with lactic acid, cortisol, serotonin, dopamine, adrenaline and noradrenaline, amongst other neurotransmitters and hormones, during and following exercise is still a research field in its infancy.

If stress is a killer, it should follow that its opposite will be life-enhancing. What is the opposite of stress? You might say relaxation. I suggest happiness. If the source of happiness is pleasure, it may be that pleasure can extend life. An opioid peptide released when we are happy is enkelytin, and it just so happens that enkelytin works as a natural antibiotic that combats bad bacteria in the body. No happiness – no natural germ killer.

Prozac, Seroxat and other SSRIs (selective serotonin re-uptake inhibitors) produce an anti-depressant effect artificially by boosting serotonin levels circulating in the brain, but wouldn't you rather get your high naturally? The combination of various elements coming together thanks to exercise can produce a feeling of contentment that is the antithesis of stress and anxiety, and might take the 'worried' out of 'worried well'. Get enough aerobic exercise at the right level and you might be floating on Cloud Nine for the rest of your (longer) life. Just be careful if you drive a car in this state, though. You may not be illegally drugged, but the effect on your driving could have serious consequences.

What about the role of two hormones, tryptophan, and melatonin?

Tryptophan is found in some foods and is made by the body. It is said to be an effective anti-depressant, but as a supplement it's a banned substance in the UK, except in the form L-5-hydroxytryptophan. Melatonin as a supplement is also banned (see chapter 37 on sleeping). It's what makes us feel drowsy and go to sleep. Both are stimulated by exercise, as is cortisol, another powerful hormone regarded as 'bad' and as a free radical that may speed up the ageing process. Elite athletes produce large amounts of cortisol and need to eliminate this, along with a build-up of lactic acid (by warm-down exercise) to prevent the damage that may ensue in training and competition. Failure to get rid of cortisol may be a factor in the weakening of athletes' immune systems when they are at the peak of fitness. It's well known that fit athletes, in fact any of us who are very fit, catch viruses more readily than non-athletes. The explanation seems to lie in the fact that after strenuous exercise, our immune system is temporarily weakened, although when it recovers after a few days, it's stronger than ever. It's during those first few days that a virus is most likely to get the better of our defences.

Exercise is a two-edged sword and very little is currently known about the interplay of our hormones in the bigger picture of how much exercise is good for you. Not long ago I bought a fascinating book called *Overtraining in Sport*, which turned out to be the bible on this largely unexplored subject. Unfortunately it posed as many questions as it answered. It did, however, lead me to understand that a great deal of exercise can strengthen the heart, which is after all a muscle.

We live in an age when obesity is an epidemic disease. Already two-thirds of all adults are said to be overweight. Fifteen percent of 15-year-olds in the UK are clinically obese and the figures get worse every year. If you are between 40 and 65 and are super-fit already, you will have no problem working out at a satisfactory level. For many of the worried well, though, the love handles round the waist will have been growing steadily since their twenties, and exercise of the kind I am talking about will be alien territory.

Some say that a brisk walk for twenty or thirty minutes each day, five days a week, is all that you need to keep fit and stay young for your age. I say make that thirty minutes a day at three and a half miles an hour (three miles an hour is almost brisk), provided that this raises your pulse to between 60% and 70% of your heart rate maximum. And then do some resistance exercise as well. But consistency is essential. Nothing beats a lifetime of keeping fit, and if you start late, you may never rid yourself entirely of the damage done to your cardiovascular system at an earlier age. This was the reasoning behind the death at fifty-two of Jim Fixx, the self-styled guru of jogging. So be warned, though it is never too late to start getting fit, you will always be better off if you have stayed fit all your life. That's what I've always tried to do. For example, I started surfing at the age of 20 and am still surfing at the same level today at 64, though I do admit to short periods in my thirties and forties when I put on the extra inch around the middle. And I sail, ski and dive (especially free diving) to make life more interesting, though these do not provide the same aerobic workout that surfing does through all that paddling.

Together with eating right and freedom from anxiety and depression, exercise should be the basis of a long and healthy life. There are many different views on what constitutes the right type of exercise and how much of it you should get, just as there are different arguments for what you should eat to get the best of health. It has become almost a cliché that today's must-have food is tomorrow's no-no. Think of butter and margarine in the Seventies. However, consensus is starting to appear on many fronts.

We know that being overweight, considered a sign of good breeding in the eighteenth century, is now the biggest no-no We know that you can stop your hair falling out by getting castrated, but that there is nothing else out there yet that will achieve this, despite the trumpeting of finasteride, minoxidil and similar agents that claim to stop and even reverse male pattern baldness. We know that high blood pressure is a warning that should not be ignored. But should we eat eggs with all that cholesterol in the yolks, and if so, how many a week? If we drink too much fresh orange juice, will we get fat from all that excess fruit sugar that's maybe going to storage as adipose (fat) tissue, even though fructose (fruit sugar) has a low count on the Glycaemic Index? This book will answer questions like these that affect the ageing process.

Montaigne, the great French essayist, extolled the virtues of the Golden Mean – the middle course in life. The concept goes back to Greek philosophy and has much to recommend it today, where we live in a world of excess and instant gratification. The Golden Mean implies that in all things we should seek the middle road. We should not be ambitious beyond our natural abilities. We should aim for moderation instead of excess. We should even shun greatness and celebrity unless they are thrust upon us. In other words, we should abandon ego, in the way that a Buddhist monk tries to abandon ego and become selfless. Unfortunately, this path is too difficult for most of us. If we can find a spiritual path, so much the better. If we fail to do so, we score a few less points on the road to longevity.

I used to think at twenty that being old was the same as being young, only you looked different. We all know from experience that as we get older we feel the same person inside, and only wish others could see us this way too. We still feel twenty when we are sixty, but others see us as sixty and act towards us that way – unless they have grown with us over the years, as spouse and family do. But go to a school reunion and meet your friends of forty or more years ago, whom you haven't seen since school, and within minutes of talking to them it will seem as if it were yesterday that you were kicking a ball around together. On one level you will see them as they were back then and on another they will seem like the sixty-year-olds they really are. The more friendly and animated the interaction, the younger your former school friends will seem. I went to such a school reunion recently and I have to admit, the experience was surreal.

But being twenty and being sixty are not the same, and anyone looking at you objectively for the first time at sixty will see a sixty year old (or a fifty year old if you look really young for your age). Unlike your old school friends, they will act towards you as though you are sixty (or fifty). A number of things will have happened to your body, inside and out, in those fifty years.

You may have got shorter as the discs between your spinal vertebrae become compressed with the passing of the years. Your eyesight, hearing and sense of taste and smell will have deteriorated. You may feel stiff when you have to run suddenly to catch a bus. Above all, if you are like me and millions of other men, you may have experienced the need to make more frequent trips to the loo in the middle of the night, and in the day as well. As the comedian Billy Connolly is fond of saying, 'Never pass up the chance of a loo'. If you have passed your mid-fifties, you will probably know what I mean. Your prostate will have enlarged to the point where it becomes difficult to pee in a forceful stream, and impossible ever to empty your bladder completely. Fortunately this uncomfortable situation is now thought to be only marginally related to prostate cancer, the commonest cancer among men and still a killer.

So what is ageing? Is it programmed into our genes before we're even born? Is it something that can be halted or even reversed through gene manipulation, as some scientists believe? I find that hard to believe. My view and the thesis of this book is that ageing can be slowed. But it cannot be stopped altogether, making us immortal, as if that would be desirable anyway. I've heard it said that if we eat right and exercise properly all our lives we may be able to extend our lifespan by about three or four years. I think that is too pessimistic. I would make that ten to fifteen years, with the proviso that if the pursuit of a long life becomes obsessive to the point of fanaticism, the opposite may happen and life may end up being shortened. I cannot prove that, but I recall reading about a man in America who had adopted the well-known technique of Calorie Restriction (CR) as a way of prolonging his life. What he ate was healthy, but he only ate about 1200 calories a day. Tests have shown that it works in mice and few gerontologists – the scientists who study old age – now doubt that modest calorie restriction works in humans too. But 1200 calories a day was too extreme. This man looked like the worst victim of anorexia imaginable, and that is basically what he was. We know that anorexia is life-threatening. To make matters worse, the man admitted to constant hunger pangs. He had adopted a lifestyle that was without one of life's greatest pleasures: good eating.

If you lead a sedentary life, but still exercise enough – say for 45 minutes a day five days a week – you could do worse than eat 2000 calories a day of the right food, and make this 2500 –3000 calories a day if you have a manual job or you're extremely active all day, for example by gardening a lot. The normal recommendation of 2500 calories a day for a sedentary but fit man is sensible if you are happy with your life the way it is. But if you belong to the worried well, and are prepared to be a little bit hungry quite a bit of the time, 2000 calories a day will probably help you live a bit longer on the basis of a little calorie restriction. How much longer? I don't think anyone knows.

Let's take a closer look at calorie restriction, which for some men has become a way of life. These men are faddists aiming unapologetically to live longer. Their diet is usually a healthy one, but calorie intake is typically around the 1200–1800 a day mark. On the plus side, CR helps lower blood pressure and LDL (so-called 'bad') cholesterol level. Blood sugar and insulin level fall, along with insulin-like growth factor (IGF-1) (see below). On the downside, there may be an increased risk of osteoporosis and loss of brain cells and sexual libido, as well as a tendency to feel the cold. And, of course, there is a constant nagging hunger. There's proof that calorie restriction increases life expectancy in mice, but no one has yet been able to prove that the same applies to humans. To do so might involve a study lasting a hundred years or more.

It must be said that CR faddists who are not too extreme – those on say 1800 calories a day – do tend to be slim and to look younger than their calendar age, sometimes ten years younger or more. It's those on 1200 calories a day who look ill. There's no point in living longer if you're not healthy at the same time, but it does seem that on a moderate CR diet the two may go together – health definitely and an extended lifespan possibly.

As we live longer, cancer will increasingly become the disease we die from. It's currently in number two position between heart disease and stroke, but very soon it will be in number one position. Cancer is said to be the disease that kills us off when nature and natural selection no longer have any use for us and our reproductive time is over. According to CR theory, calorie restriction in men diverts the body's attention away from sex (the opposite is true in females) and towards maintaining the body's vital functions, speeding up metabolism. There seems to be a close connection between metabolic rate and life expectancy. The slower the rate, the closer you may be to dying. With a faster metabolism, the body is better prepared to avoid cancer and other diseases, and so life is extended. This does not explain, however, why women on a CR diet not only live longer but have more sex, as do mice fed a CR diet.

Just to complicate the picture, a colony of very special mice has been bred in a lab in Ohio. Scientists there have discovered that an enzyme known as PEPCK-C, which is found naturally in the muscles, as well as the kidneys and liver of all animals, has an extraordinary effect when the skeletal muscles of mice are induced to express the enzyme in massive quantities. The result is a supermouse that eats twice as much as ordinary mice, yet is leaner and more active, physically and sexually. It isn't proven yet that these mice will live much longer than normal mice, but it seems likely that they will as some of the females are giving birth at three years, the equivalent of the age of 80 in humans.

The supermouse can exercise almost endlessly, and wonder of wonders, it burns fat for energy, whereas we humans, like ordinary mice, burn glucose first, and have to stop exercising when lactic acid build-up in our muscles screams at us to stop. Losing fat by exercising is difficult for humans because we cannot burn fat first, much as we would like to. Our bodies have been too conditioned by the lean times of a million years ago, making us cling to fat as a defence against starvation. The super-mouse can lose weight while eating twice as much as normal simply because it burns fat first. This will not be lost on CR faddists. There is no calorie restriction here. A human exercising at the same level as the supermouse would need to eat 5000 calories a day. The supermouse likes to exercise, and with no lactic acid to say no, it can presumably enjoy all those endorphins and other opioids to the full.

Yet there are similarities between CR mice and the supermice, for all the differences in their diets. Both have larger numbers of mitochondria, the body's power cells. In other words, the magic enzyme in the supermice has produced the same effect as calorie restriction in the CR mice. If this were the same in humans – and it's a big if – we could live longer without the pain of a CR diet, since we too carry the PEPCK-C enzyme.

There's some way to go yet before playing with our enzymes will turn us into supermen, but large doses of resveratrol, the wonder ingredient found in red wine, may provide a similar shortcut (see chapter 3 on alcohol).

Calorie restriction is thought to 'work' by turning off human growth hormone (hGH) and IGF-1. If this is so, there may be a price to pay. If you want to become a sexually retarded dwarf with wasted muscles, just turn off hGH completely. Or cut your IGF-1 right down and see your insulin level rise 400%. It's true that these techniques may be risky, even if they work on mice. As with many drugs and hormone treatments, the side effects could outweigh the advantages. My personal view is that moderate calorie restriction – say 2000 calories a day for men – may be worth a try with little risk on the hGH and the IGF-1 front.

I take a closer look at resveratrol in the chapter on alcohol because a team led by a Harvard scientist, assisted by researchers in France, is claiming there's a promising approach to turning back the ageing clock based on another technique involving enzymes. They are experimenting with a drug called SRT501 derived from modified resveratrol, the alleged wonder compound found in the skins of red grapes and now produced from Japanese knotweed. Wonder cures that claim they will make us all into Methuselahs come and go and generally I don't pay much attention. But in view of the publicity given to red wine in recent years and the academic credibility of the American and French scientists, I think resveratrol may have a future, as may those who take it. The researchers are canny enough not to claim too much, though, emphasizing that their initial target is the metabolic disease diabetes and not life eternal.

Psychologists talk of an inner and an outer locus of control. What they mean by that is that some people – those with an inner locus of control – feel in charge of their lives and some people (the majority) do not. It will come as no surprise to learn that those who feel more in charge of their lives are likely to be self-employed or one of the bosses in the place where they work. People with this inner locus of control, all else being equal, tend to be more confident and happier than wage-earning employees working for others. I'm not trying to put down the role of being an employee, but being your own boss or at least having a lot of autonomy in your job definitely makes people happier, and in turn this is thought to prolong life, even if it means working longer hours. Money doesn't bring happiness, but as they say, 'it sure helps'. Maybe, though, it's not the money that brings happiness, but how it is acquired. If you are your own boss, whether your money is inherited or self-made, you are in a better position to influence your destiny, and it is this control of your own life that may make a difference in the ageing process.

Perhaps in this lies the key to the question of stress – the idea that there is good stress and bad stress. Good stress is self-inflicted stress where you are in charge and can control the stress. Bad stress is inflicted by others, such as your employer, and you have little if any ability to change that situation. So having an internal locus of control and being your own boss enables you to impose as much stress on yourself as you can handle and rein back when and if you feel the need. The positive feelings that come from such a position can help to slow the ageing process, partly by limiting potential depression. To put that another way, good stress combats depression and bad stress makes depression worse. That would explain why men who are employees are more prone to stress and depression than men who are self- employed.

I'm lucky to have been my own boss since the age of twenty-seven, and I can see, looking back at my working life, that there have been times when I have unconsciously engineered stressful situations in my life to alleviate boredom, in much the same way that I have sought a degree of danger on my holidays by surfing and diving in shark-infested waters. Could it be that such stress has been good for me? Yes, probably.

If you want to have a long and healthy life, you must work at your social life, for few things shorten life faster than loneliness, and the depression and anxiety that often go with it. This is why poverty is such a death trap, for the poor are in a weaker position than the well-to-do when it comes to maintaining a healthy social life with advancing years. But it isn't just a matter of keeping depression at bay. A good social life means a healthy brain. You will inevitably lose cerebral neurones and synapses as you get older, but brain exercise will slow this process and help delay or ward off completely Alzheimer's disease and other forms of dementia. Social interaction is a stimulant to healthy brain activity, which in turn keeps the brain younger. An active mental life from reading and creative activities will also make a big difference, though it is doubtful whether watching television, one of the great crutches of old age, will make much difference.

As we get older our immune system weakens. We cannot stop this process, but as with ageing generally, we can slow it down by eating well and keeping fit. How do we measure the strength of our immune system? There's always the results of the blood screen that comes with an annual check-up. But just see if you recover as fast from a cold as you did when you were twenty. Or how fast you recover from your daily bout of exercise. If it knocks you out and you have to lie down until the next round, you are definitely overdoing it and should slow down. Do you take ages to recover from an illness? Do skin cuts and abrasions take longer to heal? Do you catch viruses more easily? All of these things probably indicate an immune system that is weakening as you get older. Much of the advice in this book will help you live longer, not least because it will show you ways to strengthen your immune system. This in turn may help you to ward off the killer many of us fear most and from which many of us will die: cancer.

If you are already looking back on your life more than you are looking forward to the future, you are probably losing the battle of the libido in the sense of the will to live. To win that battle you must have ever-new challenges, however modest, in front of you. That might mean planning for retirement by turning your hobby into a part-time job from home, one in which money is not the main objective. I collect old maps for a hobby, and if I ever gave up my day job, I might become a map dealer, working from home and networking with dealers and collectors I have met over the last twenty years. Apart from making a small amount of money this way and keeping up with my hobby, I would have the social interaction that goes with the job. Have you ever looked at art or antique dealers at a local fair and wondered how they make a living at it? My guess is that many of the small-time players barely make a living at all. They have made a lifestyle choice and the main reason they do it is the enjoyment they get from talking to the collectors and other dealers that they meet as they do the round of fairs. In other words they are prolonging their lives through the brain exercise of social interaction.

Don't ever consider that all that is good in your life is behind you. Don't think Zimmer frames when you can think of a new life doing something you've always really wanted to do. It may be travel, it may be creative writing, it may be voluntary work, it may be learning to dance. I took up reeling at age 45 and apart from the aerobic exercise involved, I found that I had a new interest that stretched parts of my brain never stretched before as I struggled to master a variety of different and sometimes complicated steps.

There are scientists in the field of gerontology who make outlandish claims from time to time about the future longevity of mankind. Generally when this happens, the more serious majority among them are embarrassed and issue official denials to protect a branch of medicine that is sometimes accused of quackery. There is certainly no pill, monkey gland or snake oil around at the moment that will extend the human lifespan, except possibly resveratrol and the enzyme PEPCK-C (see above). However, the desire of some gerontologists to jump the gun with their claims has led the respectable American Society on Aging to bestow their Silver Fleece award each year on the 'product that makes the most outrageous or exaggerated claims about human ageing'. One of their recent judges, Jay Olshansky, believes that no matter what, the upper limit for the human lifespan is around 130 years.

Dominant males live longer and tend to have higher self-esteem, but whether having a higher testosterone level works for or against longevity is still debatable. The dominance trait should not be confused with anger – quite the opposite. The testosterone-driven dominant male, once displaced, may well live a shortened life. The male who is dominant through wisdom rather than brute force is likely to live longer.

Stand unsupported on your left leg on a hard floor with your right leg raised at 45 degrees and your hands on your hips. Shut your eyes and see how long it takes, in seconds, before you put your right foot down. Deduct this figure from 100 and that is said to be your biological age. I cannot vouch for this, but having tried it, I've found that with practice you can soon improve your score.

It used to be thought that the brain lost neurons (brain cells) steadily from about the age of six months. This has now been disproved and neuron loss and the related loss of synapses (brain cell connectors) vary widely from individual to individual and can be slowed considerably with a healthy lifestyle.

Ageing can be slowed by sound nutrition, exercise, plenty of sleep, sociability and strategies to limit all non-productive stress. Most other advice, as of now, is more in the realm of wishful thinking than hard science, including the recent idea that there is a gene or cluster of genes that is responsible for ageing and that once we can find the way to disarm these, Bob's your uncle and everyone will be immortal.

Social class, as defined by birth, income and job, affects life expectancy. Those higher up the scale live longer. While the gap in life expectancy between the top and bottom social classes is widening in women, it is getting slightly narrower in men, probably because obesity is more a women's than a men's problem. Women tend towards obesity the lower down the scale you go, while obesity in men is much less defined by class.

The further you go down the social scale, the more people drink and smoke too much and exercise too little. The only surprise is that while life expectancy was growing only slowly until fairly recently, it is now accelerating fast for those at the upper end of the social scale, and above all for professional women, thanks probably to the confidence and self-esteem that come from job status and having a considerable degree of control over one's own life.

Women live longer, on average, than men in all societies, but the gap has narrowed in recent years as more and more women adopt what would once have been considered rather masculine lifestyles. While life expectancy for men as a whole is now around 77 years of age, it's around 80 for professional men, those in the top social class. Unskilled workers are on the up too, but still trail behind at around 73 years of age.

Life expectancy normally means life expectancy at birth, though it is sometimes used to describe life expectancy at age 65. Official retirement age for men is currently 65, but in the UK, will be increased gradually to 68 by 2040. Not surprisingly, those who work for themselves often do not retire at the official age, but go on working and living for a good many more years, their increased life expectancy being directly linked to the fact that they have not retired and probably enjoy their work.

It's not just that nutrition and exercise make a difference to lifespan. It's also what money can buy. Whether it's preventive healthcare or medical treatment, the moneyed classes have more to spend and spend more. They are more likely to be well informed on health matters (and read books like this one) and more likely to take care of themselves. They are also more likely to have private medical insurance and annual health checks. For this reason they have sometimes been called the 'worried wealthy'.

························

More Tips and Traps

The idea that ageing can be regarded as an illness and somehow treated is frowned upon in some medical circles. If cancer, stroke and cardiovascular disease could be abolished altogether, it would not leave very much from which to die.

As people age, they feel heat and cold less. They should be aware of this and guard against heat stroke and hypothermia that they might not be aware of.

As you get older your sense of thirst declines, and it may be necessary to force yourself to drink enough liquid to stay properly hydrated.

To live a long life, it's best to be lean and fit, but fat and fit is better than lean and unfit.

Going to church regularly may lengthen your life, especially if you are a true believer. Contact with others and singing in a group enhances the effect.

Maybe the new name for middle age is late youth. Maybe 50 is the new 40. Maybe we should think of our 50s and 60s as the frisky fifties and the sexy sixties, as one journalist has suggested.

Men with a personality deemed 'hostile' are three times more likely than the average to suffer from cardiovascular disease. This is thought to be a long-term effect of the release of certain hormones. Such men are likely to live a shortened life.

In the UK there are around 2,000 men and 8,000 women aged 100 or more. By 2030 these figures will have risen to 7,000 and 28,000, and to 20,000 and

80,000 by 2050. By then there will be over 1 million centenarians in the US. According to serious gerontologists, the maximum human lifespan is somewhere in the 120–130 years range.

People with more moles on their bodies live longer on average. The reason is unknown.

You are born with about 10,000 taste buds. By the age of 80, this is down to 3,000.

The world's oldest man puts his long life down to not drinking alcohol. However, the previous world's oldest man, who died at 120, drank barley wine, took up smoking at 70 and retired from work at the age of 105.

Centenarians come from all socio-economic groups. Some are vegetarians and some eat fatty diets. Some drink alcohol and some are teetotal. Some even smoke.

Men living to 100 or more do tend to have some characteristics in common. They tend to be lean and have lower than average blood pressure. Most never smoked or gave up before the age of 60.

Around 30% of centenarians show no sign of dementia. Exercise, a healthy diet and sociability all seem to be related to keeping a healthy mind in later years.

Loss of brain cells can be slowed through adaptability and flexibility (not getting too set in your ways), for example by learning a new skill or taking up a hobby.

The following may accelerate neuron (brain cell) loss: chronic illness, extended grieving, excessive alcohol, high blood pressure, living alone without the mental stimulation of a partner.

Using the brain stimulates it to produce nerve-growth factor (NGF). This in turn prompts the brain to create new pathways (synapses) linking brain cells, and stimulates the myelin sheath in the brain. And exercise stimulates neurotrophins, nerve growth agents which increase production of nerve cells.

CHAPTER TWO
FLY NOW: PRAY LATER

Going abroad for business or pleasure or even having an away holiday at home can be stressful, especially as you get older.

I don't mind being in a plane so much, provided that it's a relatively short flight. But getting to the airport and checking in can be a nightmare. If you're driving to the airport, you stand a fair chance of running into gridlocked traffic or going through the stress of parking the car at a long term car park and then waiting around for a shuttle to the airport itself. If you can afford a valet parking service, you might have to take your chance that the chauffeur will not be there to meet you, even though your flight is due to depart shortly and check-in closes in ten minutes. It happened to me recently and I had to dump the car in the short-term car park at £44 per day, even though I was heading off on a month-long trip.

You may have access to a private airport lounge, which is one way to get your composure back and bring your blood pressure down after the stress of getting thus far. But increasingly the tribulations of check-in and security take up so much of your time standing in queues that there may be little time left to de-stress in an airport lounge and have a snack and drink before the boarding ritual.

All of which plays havoc with your blood pressure even before you get off the ground. Once in the air, even if you are lucky enough not to be flying at the back in cattle class, you have various challenges to face. While it's true that air is recirculated in the cabin, it is mixed constantly with fresh air drawn from outside the plane. This gives a combined circulation in most planes of about 20 cubic feet per passenger per minute. The effect of this is that the air in the cabin is completely replaced every two and a half minutes. The problem is that there is still a high chance that one passenger's virus will quickly become yours,

CARDIFF
CAERDYDD

ensuring a bad start to your holiday. On top of which, the oxygen level in the cabin air is only 80% of the level it would be at ground level.

The cabin pressure is kept at the equivalent of about 5,000–6,000 feet above sea level. This pressure is a compromise. It would feel more comfortable if it were higher, as it is at ground level, but the cost in fuel and consequent air pollution would be about 40% higher. This is because the outer shell of the plane, flying at say 35,000 feet for speed and efficiency, would need to be that much thicker and heavier. On the other hand anything over about 6,000 feet equivalent would lead to some degree of altitude sickness, the atmosphere being thinner. The equivalent of 5,000 feet is bad enough when you consider you have not had time to acclimatise to that altitude if you took off from a sea level airport. The oxygen component of the air you are breathing is reduced by 20% and your body suffers from this sudden attack, even though you may not be aware of it. The symptoms are bloating, perhaps a headache, dehydration and a long list of things that a scientist could measure in a lab. The older you are, the more susceptible you are.

Some airlines have a lot to answer for. The cost of aviation fuel makes for quite a high proportion of an airline's operating costs, so airlines will sometimes take shortcuts to reduce expenditure on fuel. One way is to slow the turnover of fresh air in the cabin. Another is to reduce the oxygen proportion still further. As if that wasn't bad enough, a recent report has shown that in many aircraft there is leakage of toxic fumes from aviation fuel getting into the air circulated in the cabin. This isn't another deliberate cost-saving measure, except that an airline can reduce costs by ignoring the problem, which gets worse as aircraft get older. I'm not suggesting that we are all being poisoned in every aircraft we fly in, but it seems that the problem is widespread. Expect new laws soon to force airlines to make their cabin air conform to more acceptable levels.

As if the risk of breathing polluted air, the chances of a virus or bacterial infection, altitude sickness and airport stress weren't enough, passengers have to contend with the risk of a deep vein thrombosis (DVT), sometimes known as Economy Class Syndrome. While you might not actually get one that is life-threatening, it's now thought that a long haul flight triples your chances of a DVT, and as many as 10% of all air passengers suffer some kind of circulatory problem on long haul flights, though most are never aware of this and the problem goes away once they are back on terra firma. Those most susceptible are people with varicose veins, smokers, the obese, those who have had a recent leg injury or undergone an anaesthetic for a hip or knee operation, those under the age of 30, and women on the pill or hormone replacement therapy. Very tall and very short people are also more susceptible as a result of calf pressure induced by aircraft seating. Each year a number of air passengers die from a pulmonary embolism resulting from a clot in a deep vein caused by long inertia in a cramped plane. To be fair to the airlines though, an embolism can equally occur as the result of travelling in a car for a long time without moving around to stir the circulation. My mother's cousin died of a pulmonary embolism after getting off a flight from Canada to the UK.

It has been suggested that the best thing you can do to counter DVT is take 65 mg of aspirin each day for ten days before the flight, and another before each leg of the flight. About one in five long-haul passengers takes aspirin for long haul flights. However, a recent study concluded that the risks from taking aspirin – gastro-intestinal bleeding, which can be fatal – outweigh the benefits of taking aspirin to prevent a clot. This reverses for those at high risk, especially if the flight lasts four hours or longer, in which case the relatively limited risks of taking aspirin are generally outweighed by the benefits.

If it's a long haul flight, you should wear compression stockings, which are widely available at UK airport shops. These stockings compress your calves, helping to keep your blood from clotting.

Some people are more prone to DVT than others, and about one in eight is particularly at risk. This risk can be detected by a simple blood test that measures Factor 5 Leiden, a clotting factor. Since I fly quite a lot, I had the test done a couple of years ago to see if I was susceptible. I wasn't. But older people are more at risk of DVT, as are those who travel a lot and take long haul flights. Other risk factors are a family history of venous thrombosis or other circulatory problems, suffering from cancer or having had treatment for cancer, having one of a number of blood diseases or heart failure, or having had recent surgery. Having had a travel-related thrombosis previously also puts you at increased risk. Eating rich meals on a flight may increase blood lipids (fats), raising the level of what is called Factor 7, another clotting factor.

If you have pain in one or both calves, or your legs remain swollen after a flight, even a month later, you should consult a doctor immediately or go to A and E. You may have a DVT which could lead to pulmonary emboli, small clots which break away from the thrombosis in the legs or pelvis and move to the lungs, often with fatal results. Heparin is the standard drug for thinning the blood, a risky procedure as it may cause further clots to break away. There is no effective treatment for sudden emergency pulmonary embolism, and heparin treatment is only effective in non-emergency situations. In fact heparin should only be taken for this purpose under a doctor's instructions. Pulmonary embolism causes 2% of all deaths in the UK and should be treated extremely seriously. Even if you don't fly, it commonly occurs following certain kinds of surgery, especially hip replacement surgery. It is also thought to be a risk factor after laparascopic abdominal surgery.

It is said that the class of travel that you fly in does not alter the risks of a clot. I would guess that the advantage of the extra space available in Business and especially First Class may sometimes be wiped out by the possibility that more alcohol will be drunk and more fatty foods eaten in the premium classes. It may seem a waste, but if you fly in First Class, try to say no to all alcohol and eat sparingly, avoiding any fatty foods.

To reduce the risk of DVT on a flight, move around as much as possible – something that's easier to do if you are lucky enough to be in First Class. Also try to wriggle your toes and stretch your legs frequently while seated. Again it helps to be in a premium cabin – expensive, but maybe it could save your life.

The reduced cabin pressure in a plane leads to bloating and this can be especially uncomfortable for people suffering from irritable bowel syndrome (IBS). Aspirin may well be a good antidote to circulation problems, but those who have had ulcers or chronic indigestion are at increased risk of internal bleeding if they take aspirin on a flight. Passengers with high blood pressure who might be at risk of a haemorrhagic stroke should also avoid aspirin.

An alternative to aspirin is said to be the anti-oxidant pycnogenol, derived from the bark of a pine tree. It combats the problem of swollen feet (plasma seeping into tissue) that plagues many air travellers. Like aspirin it reduces platelet stickiness that can lead to unwanted blood clotting. Pycnogenol combats thrombosis, oedema (swelling) and inflammation and also makes for a useful if expensive anti-oxidant to combat free radical damage, thanks to its content of procyanidins (see chapter 14 on supplements).

Seat pitch on a plane is the distance from the front of a seatback to the back of the seatback in front. A recent report recommended that this should be a minimum distance of 28.2 inches, up from the current minimum of 26 inches. This would make seating more comfortable and thereby reduce the incidence of DVT. It would also enable taller passengers to adopt the brace position in an emergency. The report showed that several UK airlines fell short of the recommended minimum seat pitch, and some even cheated by including the width of a seat back (about 2 inches) in their figures.

What about jetlag? Its effects are well documented. They include insomnia, irritableness, headache, mood swings, poor thought processes, reduced concentration and upset digestion. There have been numerous suggestions for defeating this very real negative effect of crossing several time zones in a short space of time. I do not subscribe to any of them. One is to allegedly 'reset' your body clock by taking the hormone melatonin as a supplement. Melatonin helps to regulate production of serotonin and dopamine, both of which engender feelings of wellbeing under normal circumstances. My experience of melatonin is that not only does it not work to reset the body clock, but it can leave you feeling quite bizarre if you are among those who are susceptible, which is probably why it is banned from sale in the UK, though not in the US. Melatonin will make you sleepy, but the boredom of a flight will often do that anyway. If you feel sleepy on a flight, try to sleep. If you don't feel sleepy, don't try. Sleeping pills for long flights are not a good idea. You may sleep, but you will not feel rested afterwards.

Viagra has been put forward as a cure for jetlag following experiments with hamsters. Body clock (circadian) rhythms are regulated in part by a compound called cyclic guanine monophosphate (cGMP). It was felt that if Viagra, better known for its function in dilating genital blood vessels, could disrupt circadian rhythms on the ground, it might be used to re-programme disrupted circadian rhythms following a trip in the air. In hamsters it appeared to work and might do so in humans, but with the proviso that it might only be effective for travellers moving across time zones from west to east and not east to west. Jetlag is known to be worse following travel in an eastwards direction, probably because this is into the sun and days are accordingly shorter. Recovery therefore takes slightly longer. Travel north to south does not affect the human body clock, since it is the pattern of daylight and darkness that is the problem in jetlag. Any major change can take the body up to two weeks to adjust to, although crossing three time zones or less is reckoned to have only minimal effect on your body clock. Viagra has a number of side effects, including eye and cardiovascular problems, and anyone trying Viagra for jetlag, even in a reduced dose, should be aware of the risks. It should never be taken by anyone taking nitrates for angina, nor by anyone with liver or retinal disease.

There is the suggestion that you try to keep to the routines of the place you have left when you get to the other end, and even during the flight itself. So you would go to sleep at your destination in accordance with your bedtime back home. Apart from the near impossibility of adopting home routines for meals and sleep on a flight, especially in Economy Class, the chances of being able to keep up such a routine at your destination make the whole idea fairly ludicrous. Better to just bite the bullet and live with jetlag on arrival. After a long flight across as many as twelve time zones, jetlag will wear off gradually over the next two weeks, though you may feel it has gone sooner than that, even if medical tests would show this not to be the case.

One of the main selling point of South Africa as a holiday destination is that its time zone is virtually the same as the UK's, which means that after a twelve hour flight you can get off at the other end and be in the same time zone, give or take an hour, as you would have been had you stayed home. You still have all the other negative effects of long haul air travel to contend with, but jetlag is not one of them.

In fact, travel to most of Africa has the advantage of zero or minimal time zone changes.

What you should be doing on a flight to help your body adjust to the cabin pressure, the poor air quality, the noise of the engines and any time zone changes is avoid alcohol before and during the flight, drink plenty of water or fruit juice to combat the dryness of the cabin air, eat as little as possible, wear loose clothing, get up frequently and walk around, move your arms and legs around from time to time to aid circulation, sit with your shoes off as your feet swell during a flight, and sleep if you can when tired. When you arrive at your destination, adopt the local time of day immediately. Try not to have important meetings within 24 hours of arrival. It's said that a hot bath can re-set our body's temperature control mechanism, which is often in a chaotic state at your destination.

A lot of people don't mind travelling like sardines on short flights, but when it comes to long haul – and that can mean as long as 30 hours from the UK to New Zealand – those who can afford it will generally try to fly in Premium Economy, Business or First Class, especially if that means the chance of a seat that turns into a completely horizontal bed. For most regular travellers the prospect of food and films offers little excitement, but a horizontal bed is a big plus. For years even First Class seats did not go back to a fully horizontal position. Then the seat wars started and now every self-respecting airline offers horizontal seats in Business as well as First Class, the wider the better. There is no doubt that lying horizontally is not only the most comfortable position but also the position that best helps circulation. Not surprisingly, it is older travellers who will tend to book more horizontal seats, provided they can afford it or their company is paying in the case of business travellers.

Think laterally about the discomforts of travel by air and the solution may be to travel by car, train or boat, all of which, even if slower, remove the feeling of being squeezed into a box and shot through the air with considerable discomfort, even in First Class. Think what you can avoid by using another form of transport. You might avoid the noise level that is high in a plane. By going slowly you can cross time zones without the jetlag problem. You may be able to avoid picking up the airborne diseases of others. You will certainly avoid altitude sickness unless you are taking a train from the coast up to La Paz, the capital of Bolivia, some 12,000 feet above sea level. And you are unlikely to get DVT unless you sit for hours non-stop behind the wheel of a car.

Best of all, you will not have to go through airport security, though you may still face the trials of departure and arrival officials, as well as alternative security checks.

Of course you could just stay home, saving yourself a lot of cost, the visa hassles, the packing problems and the traffic congestion getting to airport, station or port.

And that's just the problems of getting there and back in one piece. The insurance underwriters who look after travel insurance know that the risk of claims rises with age. Medical claims go up as our immune systems become less robust and our bodies become more vulnerable to breakage. After the age of 65, claims rise steeply and after 70 they rise exponentially. It's not only the medical claims that rise. Trips are cancelled as a result of poor health, rental cars crash as older drivers become less competent to drive, luggage and money are lost as the elderly become more forgetful and more vulnerable to robbery. The result of this trend is that now it has become almost impossible to find travel insurance at an acceptable premium if you are over seventy years old. For all that, travel overseas and in the UK has never been more popular with older people.

Which explains why cruising has become so popular with retirees and even younger age groups. Everything moves at a more genteel pace, while the cruise boat makes possible travel to far-flung places with the promise of a safe haven to return to at the end of the day ashore. No airport hassles. No jetlag. Perhaps there's a slightly increased risk of picking up an infection from the air conditioning or the food. I think we're going to see a lot more people of all ages turning to cruising as their favourite way to see what is increasingly a troubled world.

Anyone over the age of forty should not be complacent about the effects of air travel. There are studies which show that regular flying is bad for your health in a variety of ways, the most significant of which is that it raises blood pressure and the risk of cardiovascular disease. Airline pilots have to undergo regular medicals and few, as far as I know, live to a ripe old age. The position is no better for flight attendants, most of whom are women. Few stay in this job for more than a short spell, and they are wise to quit. Regular flying can play havoc with the menstrual cycle and may eventually affect fertility.

If you must travel by air, try to fly in the most comfortable class you or your company can afford. Take advantage of chauffeured parking or limousine service to the airport. Use premium class check-in, passport and security avenues where available. Give yourself plenty of time and use a private airport lounge if you can. Board the plane as late as possible. Don't touch the alcohol you are offered. Eat sparingly. Wear comfortable casual clothes for the flight. You'll still feel, after a long flight, as though you need a shower and a good sleep, no matter how old you are, but the younger you are, the more quickly you will recover and be ready to enjoy your holiday or make the most of your business trip.

A new more fuel-efficient generation of passenger aircraft is on the way. Passengers are promised better cabin humidity and lower noise levels. But how much oxygen is in the air and how frequently the cabin air gets turned over will still be down to the airline. Let's hope that airlines will be forced in future to stop taking shortcuts and put passenger and crew welfare first.

CHAPTER THREE
RAISE YOUR GLASS TO RED WINE

While most of us who drink alcohol are not alcoholic, especially if we belong to the worried well, it's a fact that this is another area where the jury has not yet returned a definitive verdict. There are books to tell you why alcohol in moderation is good for you, and a steady stream of newspaper articles praising the virtues of red wine.

You've probably read about the French Paradox. This is the fact that the French have one of the richest, fat-laden diets in the world and yet they have a relatively low incidence of heart disease. This has been put down to their habit of drinking wine, especially red wine, with meals. Red wine is rich in cardio-protective resveratrol, a compound found in the skins of red grapes (see below, and also chapters 1 and 14 on ageing and supplements). The resveratrol we get from wine may have been oversold, as the amount we get from a glass of red wine probably makes only a negligible difference to health. However, resveratrol supplementation at a level of 2 grams or more a day, although expensive, may make a real difference by producing the same effect as serious calorie restriction (see chapter 1 on ageing) without having to cut back to, say, only 1,500 calories a day. Resveratrol at this level may also be protective against the diseases that make up the metabolic syndrome and lead to diabetes.

Red wine also contains procyanidins, which are polyphenols high in anti-oxidant properties. Grape seeds are the best source of procynanidins and these can be obtained from grapeseed oil, readily available from health shops. Pycnogenol is another good source of procyanidins, though it tends to be expensive (see chapter 14 on supplements).

Allegedly French hearts, despite the rich creamy sauces, are also protected by the Mediterranean diet of fish, lean meat, fresh fruit and vegetables. But it's said that young French men and women now prefer beer to wine and junk food to traditional French cuisine. If the theory is correct, the incidence of cardiovascular disease in France should now be on the rise. France has had the highest rate of alcoholism in Europe for many years, so we should expect more heart attacks in addition to already widespread cirrhosis of the liver.

When I went for my annual BUPA check-up recently, the doctor I saw to go over my test results told me that as far as he was concerned, all alcohol was bad for you. 'What about the resveratrol and procyanidins – all those flavonoids?" I asked. The doctor didn't have a reply to that. I mentioned all the studies that seemed to be unanimous in concluding that red wine was good for the heart. What I didn't get a chance to tell him was that I partly agreed with him.

The current thinking in most medical circles is that alcoholic drinks in small quantities are good for you – that wine is the best form, that red wine is better than white wine, that either Cabernet Sauvignon or Tannat is the best red grape variety, and, depending on who you listen to, the best red wine for your heart comes from Bordeaux, or a handful of little known vineyards in Madiran in the Gers region of south-west France – or even from a certain vineyard in Chile, though generally it's thought that Old World wines are more healthful than New World wines. There's a grape variety found in Sardinia's Nuoro province that is thought to be up there with the best that Madiran can offer, and both are said to contribute to the longevity of the local population. It gets that specific. In fact it gets so specific that you wonder whether producers' PR hasn't got something to do with it. There's no doubt that for the wine industry, the news of wine's alleged health properties has been a blessing for sales over the last decade.

I used to think that maybe red wine was good for the heart, but surely it was bad for the brain, fogging it and mimicking early dementia if you took too much – and perhaps, over time, even inducing Alzheimer's disease. Then along came a study that said that red wine was good not just for your heart, but for your brain as well, and could keep normal age-related cognitive decline and perhaps Alzheimer's at bay. Then along came another study that 'proved' the exact opposite, especially in those over the age of 40.

As we age, our brains shrink. This process is accelerated in those who drink alcohol, especially those who drink excessive quantities. There appears to be a direct correlation. There is no evidence that drinking alcohol can slow or halt brain cell depletion, though it has been argued that we do not know whether a shrinking brain means shrinking cognitive function, especially in those parts of the brain linked to memory and learning. It's thought that it's the ethanol in alcohol which is the key to the shrinking process.

It has been said that the first drink of the day leaves you thinking more clearly and with faster reaction times than no drink at all. In other words, 'one for the road', provided that it is the only one. This sounds dubious at first glance. Yet one piece of research claims to show that one glass of wine a day, and one only, may slow the onset of Alzheimer's.

It has been known for a long time that calorie restriction of as much as 40% can considerably extend life expectancy (see chapter 1 on ageing). The problem has always been that at this level of dietary restriction, you are so hungry you feel you are starving -and you probably are. Apparently a single gene called SIRTI, linked to the sirtuin family of enzymes, controls the way in which calorie restriction extends lifespan. It does this by speeding up metabolism, thereby improving mitochondrial function and insulin sensitivity. But the gene has to be activated to produce this effect. If you cannot activate it by starving yourself, you can activate it with the magic compound in wine – resveratrol, which stirs the gene into action without having to restrict your diet. The trouble is that you would need to drink a huge quantity of wine to get enough resveratrol.

Now a modified synthesised version of resveratrol more potent than the natural version is on trial as a pharmaceutical drug in the US. If the results found in mouse trials translate to humans, the small molecule SRT501, as the trial drug has been called provisionally, will be in great demand, assuming that side effects are minimal. SRT501 is said to cut glucose level and weight gain, making it, theoretically, an effective weapon against Type 2 diabetes. It appears to make muscles stronger by increasing production of mitochondria, the powerhouses of our muscle cells. If humans perform like mice under the influence of resveratrol, they will not only lose fat and become leaner, but will be able to eat more at the same time. They will also find renewed interest in sex and live longer. It sounds too good to be true.

All of which leaves someone like me a bit confused when it comes to red wine in particular and alcohol in general, especially when I read claims that white wine is good for you too, but less than red wine, and that alcohol generally is good for you in small quantities. Does that mean that small drops of 100% alcohol are healthy? I doubt it. Here is another of those cases where there is no clear answer – yet. I don't drink much alcohol, but I'm not teetotal either. I drink a bit of wine and prefer red to white most of the time. A healthy intake of red wine is said to be two units (small glasses) a day, but that's about as much alcohol as I drink in a week. Am I missing the chance to bring some extra health to my heart and brain? I just don't know. Meanwhile I read that those who drink two glasses of red wine a day are 50% less likely to have a heart attack.

The standard pro-wine position is that the first two or three units are good for you and after that it's all downhill.

Alcohol is a depressant, not a stimulant. You feel good at first, but the euphoria quickly fades and turns to a negative feeling – even on a single glass, even though with this quantity you might not be consciously aware of the change. Alcohol, including wine, loosens inhibitions, which is why it's such a good catalyst for conversation at a dinner party. But what about the drive home, brewer's droop, falling asleep yet not being able to get a good night's rest, the headache and other symptoms of a hangover the next day? Of course you may not experience all of these effects after a glass or two, especially if you drink wine with food, but isn't it logical to assume that if alcohol can do that to you when you take more, it's going to do the same, but less noticeably, when you take less? If that's the case, wasn't my BUPA doctor right?

I'm sure that alcohol affects different people in different ways, and that if you are used to drinking more than two units at a time, you get used to its effects to the extent that you don't react to it as quickly as a light drinker like me. That doesn't mean that if alcohol is damaging, a given quantity must be less damaging to a seasoned drinker whose liver is more used to handling it. It just means that to an onlooker the effects will show more quickly in a light drinker. I am that light drinker and I joke that after one glass I am anybody's and that after two I am everybody's. From watching myself drink, I know that after two or three units, I am more talkative, briefly more amiable, slower thinking, less concentrated when I drive (and more cavalier), more likely to fall asleep, more amorous but less able to deliver, dehydrated and thirsty (and if I'm out, keen to get home and down large quantities of cold fresh fruit juice), slightly headachy and increasingly unwell. And that's just after a couple of glasses.

My reading of all this is that as I am reasonably fit, the effect of even small quantities of alcohol shows up more obviously in those who are fit – and of course in those who are older too, as it's undoubtedly true that younger people recover more quickly from the effects of alcohol.

Yet I am meant to believe that alcohol is good for my heart and brain and probably a lot of other parts of my body, despite making me dehydrated, tired and moderately hungover. Let's list what alcohol can do to you, though I don't expect many alcoholics to be reading this book. Alcoholics belong in the ranks of the worried unwell, after all, and worried they should be.

Here's list of a few of the things that alcohol, including the best Bordeaux, can do to you, to a greater or lesser degree, according to how much you imbibe:

Dehydrates
Impairs liver function
Leads to alcoholic fatty liver
Can lead to acute and chronic alcoholic hepatitis
Can induce hepatic fibrosis
Can lead to cirrhosis of the liver
Can lead to liver failure and death
Reduces good intestinal flora
Reduces absorption of vitamins (especially B and C) and minerals
Increases body's requirement for Vitamin B1 (Thiamine)
Induces neuropathy
Increases oestrogen (female hormone) level in males
Induces snoring

Induces sleep apnoea (snoring may be an early sign)
Weakens the immune system (lowered white blood-cell count)
May cause erectile dysfunction
Increases risk of pneumonia
Keeps you awake
Reduces REM sleep
Makes you tired the next day
Depletes zinc, potassium and magnesium
Destroys cells in the left brain, the so-called 'male' brain responsible for logic and language
Adds potentially fattening calories to your diet (alcohol contains 7 calories per gram of alcohol)
Increases blood pressure
May damage heart muscle
Raises triglycerides level
May damage the pancreas, causing pancreatitis
Increases the risk of some cancers, including cancer of the bowel, oesophagus, liver, mouth and larynx. As many as 6% of cancer deaths each year are attributed to alcohol. That's around 10,000 deaths. As little as one drink a day is said to increase the risk of bowel cancer by 10%. The risk of mouth cancer rises dramatically in drinkers who also smoke.

The proven benefits of wine are few. They come down to:

Less constricted blood vessels (heart and brain)
Improves blood circulation in the legs
Reduces risk of gallstones
Reduces kidney cancer in those who drink two units per day
Alcohol is calorific, therefore produces energy
May lower blood pressure

Red wine is said to reduce so-called 'bad' cholesterol (oxidated LDL cholesterol in the arteries) through the anti-oxidant effects of the polyphenols resveratrol (see above) and polymeric procyanidins, which will mop up free radicals and maintain healthy blood vessels. But non-alcoholic red grape juice, with the skins and pips, is also rich in these anti-oxidant flavonoids. The benefits are not in the alcohol, although it's thought that alcohol may promote vascular health by keeping blood vessels open. The anti-oxidants in red wine help circulation by blocking production of endothelin-1, a protein which can constrict blood vessels. Good red wine also contains the anti-oxidant flavonoid quercetin. Red and white wine contain the nutrient silica, which is important, like calcium, for bone density. Draft beer also contains silica and a number of anti-oxidants.

But this doesn't tell me why this package of positives has to come wrapped in alcohol, or why, as has been alleged, alcohol is a key goodie itself. It's clear to me that there are plenty of foods and juices I can turn to if I want free radical-fighting agents in my diet. I can even resort to capsules containing resveratrol (see above) and there's no alcohol in these. The reply to this is usually that alcohol is part of the secret curative power of red wine, and that all forms of alcoholic drink are good for your heart in moderation.

It seems to me that in this debate there are a large number of vested interests trying to justify a legal drug that brings the Treasury a fortune in tax, makes lots of profit for the drinks industry, brings a short-lived pleasure to many people and at the same time costs society untold misery and the NHS billions through the effects of immoderate drinking.

The recommended maximum intake of wine (or any alcohol) is about three units a day for men, which is about two bottles of wine a week if you count a bottle as 9–12 units. It may come as a surprise to learn that a standard 125 ml glass of wine contains 1.5 units of alcohol and not one unit, as a unit is based on 8% alcohol and most wine is 12% alcohol or more. A standard 175 ml glass of wine averages about two units. A 750 ml bottle of wine averages 9 units of alcohol. A large glass of wine will be a minimum of three units and could contain four units or more. The average small glass of wine contains 90 calories.

Spirits and fortified wines contain 1 unit of alcohol in a pub measure.

A unit of beer is based on a half pint, which is 300 ml at 4% alcohol, but some beers go up to 10% alcohol. So a pint of beer could add up to 2 units, or equally it could add up to 5 units. The average pint of beer probably contains about 2.5 units, or 3 units if it's cider or strong lager. One unit of alcohol contains 8 grams of pure alcohol. I would not be able to get out of bed, let alone go to work, if I drank even 2 units day in and day out. But studies show, I am told, that men who drink in moderation – two small glasses a day – live longer than those who do not drink at all, assuming that this does not lead to their death in a road accident. Four units in the blood is over the allowable limit of 80 milligrams per 100 millilitres of blood, which may soon come down to 50 milligrams per 100 millilitres to bring the UK into line with much of the rest of Europe. At this level, one small glass of wine would be permitted and two would not. Some 1500 road injuries would be prevented each year, 250 of them serious, even fatal.

Wines have become stronger in the last few years through the popularity of Australian wines, where alcohol level may reach as high as 14% Alcohol By Volume (ABV). Compare this with the typical level of German white wines – around 9%. If a wine goes to 15% alcohol or more, it is classified as a fortified wine. Now there is pressure on the government to reduce the tax on low alcohol drinks in order to combat binge drinking and alcoholism by providing a price incentive.

A small glass of Madiran wine contains between 100 and 150 milligrams of procyanidins. Fully extracting the procyanidins from the grape skins (and pips) is an expensive process making the healthiest wines relatively costly as well as fairly tannic. By contrast, mass market wines, especially those from the New World with the exception of some Cabernet sauvignon wines from Chile, tend to be low in procyanidins. If you want to get procyanidins from a non-alcoholic source other than a supplement, apples, cranberries and dark chocolate are options.

Resveratrol and procyanidins are polyphenols with anti-oxidant properties. (See above). Which is more useful to your health? The answer has yet to be found. In the meantime, you will get a good deal more of both, and at less risk to your health, if, instead of drinking alcohol, you take 2 grams of resveratrol a day, alongside a supplement of pycnogenol, while using procyanidin-rich grapeseed oil as an alternative to olive oil as a dressing and for cooking. It may be helpful to take a supplement of the anti-oxidant quercetin – 1000 mg – with resveratrol supplementation. They are said to work synergistically.

We are led to believe that the benefits of moderate drinking have been validated in scientific studies. I wonder. We are told that single men die younger than married men. But correlation is not causation.

I am not addicted to alcohol. I stay fit and this makes me feel the effect of alcohol more readily. I am not single. I am a light drinker. I enjoy, if only briefly and at the time, drinking a glass of good wine with a meal, though I prefer Burgundy – and Madiran – to Bordeaux. I am not about to become a teetotaller. But I remain sceptical about the benefits of drinking wine or any alcoholic drink. If it were proved tomorrow, once and for all, that alcohol in any quantity did more harm than good, the anti-oxidants notwithstanding, I would probably continue to drink moderately, not least on the grounds that to give up something that I enjoyed occasionally, though it might be slightly harmful, would take me into the domain of the obsessively worried well. I might live a little longer, but that would put me in the same league as the fanatic who went on a low calorie diet of 1200 calories a day, admitted to being constantly hungry, and consoled himself that he might live a few extra years by leading such a life.

What about hangover cures? Try bananas. Honestly. If you are hung over, you need to put back the electrolytes that alcohol has depleted, and bananas are rich in potassium, as are oranges. Before you drink, you might lessen the effects by taking milk thistle supplements. People in the wine trade swear by milk thistle. It's also said to help with a hangover.

For the moment, the pro-red wine lobby is in the ascendant, and their detractors are largely silenced. After all, most of our society likes a drink or three now and again and the majority are not alcoholic. The majority and the vested interests have a common cause. But I think the pendulum will swing eventually, as it has for tobacco products. It's a matter of time. I don't mean that alcohol is likely to be banned. I just think the medical research will give clearer answers and show that the negatives outweigh the positives.

It may take a while, though, as doctors are notoriously heavy drinkers.

Spending on alcohol in the average British household rose by 21% in the past five years.

CHAPTER FOUR
A SIMPLE GUIDE TO ALLERGIES

There are many reasons why it may be difficult to breathe easily, and allergic rhinitis, whether seasonal or perennial, is one of the most common. It's widespread and getting worse. The chapter on air pollution indicates some of the many things that can make breathing problems worse. If you are one of the many with an allergy problem and you happen to live in a city with heavy traffic, you will find that your allergic symptoms are made worse by the poor air quality.

Doctors divide allergic rhinitis, with its symptoms of runny nose, sneezing, eye irritation, throat irritation, huskiness and general malaise (and in more severe cases, headache, skin rashes and nausea) into seasonal and perennial. Seasonal rhinitis comes from breathing in pollens from grasses, flowers, trees and weeds. Year-round rhinitis comes from dust and food mites, and from dog fur and one or more proteins secreted from the skin of cats. Air pollution can not only make allergic rhinitis worse, but can also create an allergy in itself, as I have found. I have lived for a number of years next to a road busy with diesel taxis and buses, and perspiration tests have shown that my nasal congestion all year round is due, at least partly, to an acquired sensitivity to particulates from diesel fumes (see chapter 31 on air pollution). This is made worse in spring and summer by pollen sensitivity, which used to be worse when I was a teenager, so I tend to share the view that allergies can actually get better naturally as we get older.

But being bunged up all year round is not much fun. The symptoms, apart from those listed above, are varied and include being unable to breathe clearly through one's nose, which is made worse in my case by a slightly deviated septum, the divider at the back of the nose. I have been a partial mouth breather all my life, and mouth breathers tend to be snorers (see chapter 37 on sleep). A congested nose means a nasal cavity (the large cavity in the skull behind the nose) that gathers clear mucus. This can, if it becomes a chronic problem, lead to post-nasal drip. This in turn can lead to insomnia induced by frequent awakenings in the night as you try to clear your throat of mucus. Mucus that gathers in the nostrils, reducing your ability to breathe through your nose, turns into crusting and the temptation to pick your nose when this dried mucus can no longer be blown out with a handkerchief.

Catarrh is a general term doctors use to refer to nasal congestion. When this congestion is complicated by a virus, it can lead to bronchial problems, especially if the infection becomes a bacterial one and mucus that turns a yellowish-green colour is formed. This does not mean that an allergic rhinitis will turn into a common cold or lead to bronchitis. It means that sufferers from a rhinitic response to an allergen are going to be more predisposed to picking up a bug as a result.

An allergy that makes it hard for you to sleep at night is bad enough. But if, like many over the age of 50, you suffer from benign prostatic hyperplasia (BPH) as well, and need to take a trip to the loo frequently, you could be up and down like a yo-yo much of the night. It's often said that as people get older, they sleep more lightly and need less sleep. Equally, they are thought to need naps in the daytime. I am inclined to think that older people sleep badly because there is so much disturbing their sleep, and that they may need to take naps in the daytime to compensate.

Allergies are an immune system problem. They are an inappropriate response to a substance that is normally harmless. The immune system becomes sensitised to an allergen on first contact with it. The allergic reaction occurs on further exposure. Mast cells in tissue, mainly skin and nasal linings, are destroyed in an allergic reaction, producing swelling and release from the mast cells into the blood stream of a substance called histamine. This in turn further irritates tissue, producing the well-known symptoms of allergy.

The cleaner the environment in which we grow up, the more we are likely to react to external allergens. Allergic reactions are mostly redundant – they do not serve any useful purpose, and may be damaging by interfering with our lives and encouraging genuine infections. Allergic reactions are an exaggerated response by the immune system to a perceived threat from the environment. The link between allergies and asthma is strong, and is seen typically in the high incidence of asthma in households with cats. At least 15% of the population are known to be allergic to cats, and many of these people are asthmatic in some degree.

The recent rise in asthma is attributed to the growing cleanliness of the home environment, together with central heating, lack of proper ventilation and the degree to which the growing use of motor transport has led to an equal rise in poor outdoor air quality. If the present generation of children grows up spending more time indoors than previous generations, they will suffer more from the kind of reactions that the home induces, particularly asthma with its characteristic wheezing and the general breathing difficulties which go with an airway constricted in reaction to a variety of triggers and stressors.

As many as 3 million people suffer from hay fever in the UK and half a million sufferers seek medical help each year. Asthmatics tend to suffer more in summer when pollen counts are high. June is the worst month of the year, but the season lasts from March to July. There are many remedies on the market to mitigate the symptoms, but so far nothing in the way of a proven cure. Some palliatives are available over the counter, though the stronger and more effective ones are only available on prescription. Most take the form of pills or nasal sprays, and are based on either corticosteroids or antihistamines intended as anti-inflammatories. Personally I try to avoid anything with the word 'steroid' in it, and did not have much luck a few years ago with the most commonly prescribed of the corticosteroids. It has been suggested, however, that if you persist long enough with one of these drugs, you will eventually 'retrain' your nasal receptors and the message of foreign invasion will no longer be passed to the brain and the immune system. Personally I think the theory is doubtful and I am disinclined to take either corticosteroids or antihistamines for weeks and perhaps months to put it to the test.

If you have an allergy problem, or think you do (as the cause of the problem might be something you have not thought of), you can get allergy testing done. The most thorough examination also involves lung function tests to rule out the possibility of asthma and lung diseases such as bronchitis and emphysema, both common in smokers. The tried and tested skin test for pollen allergens, dust mites and animal hair is the RAST test.

Immunotherapy (desensitisation) is still the best form of treatment for pollen and dust mite allergies, and for mild asthma, though it is not easily available in the UK except privately. It doesn't work for eczema, dermatitis or food allergies. It involves a lengthy series of injections with ever increasing amounts of extract from the allergen to which you are sensitive. In this way you gradually build up tolerance and the auto-immune response that is an allergic reaction weakens. Results are usually long-lasting and effective, reducing symptoms by around 50%. Steroid treatments, on the other hand, are still the commonest type of therapy in the UK, even though they tend to be less effective than immunotherapy.

There isn't a lot you can do to stop inhaling pollen in the hay fever season, unless you stay indoors all the time and barricade your windows and doors with draft preventers, which also keep out airflow, but this would be a bad idea, as ventilation would suffer and poor air quality would become a hazard in itself. Nor would that do anything to deal with the problem of dust mites and pet hairs. You could get rid of your pets, though that might be a bit drastic. Not stroking them might be the best compromise.

A lot has been written about the problem of dust mites, also called house mites. They are typically about half a millimetre in length, so are not exactly visible to the naked eye. It's said that they infest our beds, carpets and soft furnishings in their tens of thousands, feeding off flakes of dead human skin. The problem is not the mites themselves, but certain proteins in their faeces. As far as carpets go, the answer may be to have bare wooden or stone floors, and this has become more fashionable anyway in recent design. Beds and bed linen, though, are a different matter. Regular washing of bed linen is advisable. Hypoallergenic mattress and pillow covers, which isolate you from the bugs, are available in many shops. But this may not solve the problem. A recent study suggested that hypoallergenic covers were not effective in reducing dust mite allergy. The reason does not seem to be clear. Either the covers do not isolate the bugs as intended, or perhaps there are so many bugs elsewhere in the house that this measure makes little if any difference. Note that anti-allergen bedding is a sales gimmick since the protective treatment is lost after two or three washes. If you use down or feather pillows and duvets, you could switch to synthetic materials instead, as these are less inviting as a home for dust mites.

Another allergen in the house may be part of the problem. This is mould spores, which thrive in a warm humid atmosphere, so turning the central heating down will help. In winter when outside air tends to be cold and damp, rather than warm and damp as it is in summer, there is a risk in opening the windows too much, especially for those getting on in years. The problem is that while the lungs need a certain degree of humidity, too much cold damp air produces an environment more conducive to disease, and at the same time too much damp encourages mould spores, an allergen. Getting the home environment right all year round is quite a challenge.

Household products can induce an allergic reaction, particularly cleaning products, but also deodorants (a big no-no) and perfume. Materials used in the making of modern houses, especially paints and flooring products, can give off allergy-producing fumes, though non-allergenic products are generally available.

As many as 40% of the UK population are believed to suffer from one or more allergies. This percentage is growing annually. No environment is completely free from allergens, but you can acclimatize to some degree.

Treatment for hay fever, which affects a quarter of the UK population, usually involves taking one or other of two classes of drug, the sedating or the non-sedating. Sedating remedies contain chlorpheniramine, which causes drowsiness. Anyone taking it should not drive while under its influence. The non-sedating remedies include loratidine, desloratidine, levocetirizine, fexofenadine, acrivastine or cetirizine.

It may be that a simple immunisation will solve the problem of allergies in the future. A Swiss biotech company, following on from the work of English scientists, is developing a drug which dupes the immune system into believing it is under attack from a form of germ, found in soil, called *Mycobacterium vaccae*. Experiments with volunteers found that hay fever sensitivity was almost completely eradicated, at least on follow-up eight months later. A similar experiment with the drug aimed at dust mite sensitivity was found to be equally successful on follow-up after a year. The bacteria are commonly found in dirt and soil, and the theory is that in the past people were much more exposed to these pathogens and developed immunity. Modern cleanliness has largely robbed us of this immunity. Exposure via the new drug, it is hoped, will mimic the natural exposure we might once have got in an earlier age. Until a medically safe dosage is approved (if ever), I would not suggest that it's a good idea for adults with an allergy to roll in the dirt. The age at which this is effective has probably passed.

The English scientists working on *M. vaccae* have found what they claim to be a further use for the bacterium. Allegedly when it is ingested it stimulates the production of serotonin in the brain. As serotonin is one of the body's principal natural anti-depressants, it has the potential to be a major mood enhancer without resorting to pharmaceutical drugs. This claim has aroused considerable interest but also scepticism.

Another suspect in household allergies is the food (food-storage) mite – or strictly speaking as many as 12 distinct species of food mite – commonly found in breakfast cereals, bread, flour, cakes and biscuits. A government study found 22% of samples to be contaminated. Like dust mites, they produce faeces containing proteins which cause an allergic reaction. If you are allergic to dust mites, you will be allergic to food mites. And if you have asthma susceptible to allergic triggers, you could find that a combination of food and dust mites makes your symptoms worse. Most houses today are ideal breeding ground for both mites.

The chances are that if you suffer from an allergy, you inherited a predisposition to the problem. Then suitable triggers in childhood – exposure to the allergens – sensitised you to asthma or allergy. There are 3 million asthma sufferers in the UK and around 2,000 of these die annually from complications of the illness.

As if the worsening picture were not bad enough, with 70% of UK homes now deemed to be a prolific breeding grounds for food and dust mites, there has been a recent infestation by another bug, a so-called superbug called *Blomia tropicalis*, a house mite from abroad with more damaging proteins in its faeces than the home grown varieties, to which some people at least have an inherited or acquired immunity.

So what is to be done about allergies while we wait to see whether a general remedy in the form of immunisation becomes available? I suggest alleviating the symptoms with antihistamines rather than corticosteroids. The old breed of antihistamines had a downside in that they made you drowsy, which made driving under their influence risky. A new generation is now available that does not have this side effect, though it's not clear whether they affect intellectual performance as much as the old drugs did. In more severe cases, the old solution is still available privately – a course of desensitising injections.

Another possible remedy for hay fever being tested is a tablet that dissolves under the tongue. It is aimed at grass pollen sensitivity, and will not cover flower pollen. Whether or not it works remains to be seen.

There's a lot still to be learnt about the immune system. In families with many children, the youngest often has the strongest immunity to infection, having had more chance than the rest to pick up immunity from the infections of older brothers and sisters. It may be that not only asthma and allergic rhinitis are attributable to insufficient rolling in the dirt in childhood, but also eczema and auto-immune diseases such as Type 1 diabetes and inflammatory bowel diseases such as Crohn's disease. Why else would a growing list of chronic inflammatory diseases become more and more common in the developed world if not as a result of improved hygiene and its impact on the immune system? In early life the immune cells, it's alleged, need to be challenged by harmless bacteria in order to learn how to deal with seriously threatening bacteria later in life. Yet this view of childhood cleanliness and exposure to dirt is currently being questioned.

There are food allergies as well, of course, and these respond, unsurprisingly, to withdrawal of the problem food. Easier said than done, as it is only by a slow process of trial and error that involves withdrawing one food at a time and seeing what happens that a food allergy may be identified. The most common culprits tend to be wheat and dairy produce, but nuts and peanuts in particular are well known for their life-threatening properties if you happen to be one of the few thousand in the UK who is susceptible to anaphylactic shock, a sudden and sometimes fatal narrowing of the windpipe. The good thing about food allergies is that you can do something about them if you can identify the source of the problem. Food allergies should not be confused with food intolerance. Because you may be intolerant of gluten, for example, that does not mean you are allergic to gluten.

Most common allergies belong to what is called the Type 1 hypersensitivity group. They derive from a specific antigen fitting with a specific IgE antibody. To this group of allergies belong red eye (allergic conjunctivitis), hay fever (allergic rhinitis), eczema (eczematous dermatitis), asthma and the food allergies.

Let's hope that the most interesting research area, that of immunisation using a bacterium, comes to a positive conclusion in the next few years, making the lives of millions of sufferers more tolerable.

CHAPTER FIVE
ALTERNATIVE AND PHYSICAL THERAPIES

I am not a great believer in the more unconventional (complementary) forms of therapy, and I draw a line at the likes of colonic irrigation, psychic (faith) healing, crystal healing, reflexology, aromatherapy and diagnosis of disease through the iris of the eye (iridology). Having said that, I believe that alternative therapy can be helpful in effecting what might be termed psychosomatic or placebo cures, using the power of the mind (psyche) over the body (soma) to cure illnesses, or at least alleviate symptoms. Needless to say, no amount of alternative therapy will re-grow a missing limb, but in true believers with bodily complaints which have a hysterical element, 'miracle' cures are undoubtedly possible. Those who have thrown away their crutches on visiting Lourdes are testimony to the power of the mind over the body.

Physical therapies such as osteopathy, chiropractic and podiatry have each been broadly accepted as a useful adjunct to mainstream medicine. And physiotherapy is an absolutely necessary part of many treatments. However, my experience with podiatry has not been particularly successful. I have had two foot problems, a strained tendon in one foot and a synovitis (inflammation of the sheath around a joint) in the other and both have been treated by reputable podiatrists who produced made-to-measure orthoses to fit inside my shoes and take the strain off the tender spot. The second podiatrist, who treated the synovitis and had every diploma in the book, told me that I would have to wear orthoses for the rest of my life. They felt uncomfortable, as you would expect in shoes that were not designed to take an extra thickness. They were not intended to make the synovitis go away, only to make the pain bearable. I hated wearing these plastic moulds in my shoes and gave them up after two weeks. Instead I bought a good pair of running shoes and within ten days the synovitis had disappeared forever. Look around and you will see quite a few men over sixty these days walking around in running shoes. If you have foot problems, this is the cheap and quick solution to try first.

Two alternative therapies popular for many years have had well documented confrontations with orthodox medicine. Acupuncture has become widely accepted for local anaesthesia. However, its curative powers are still mainly attributed to psychosomatic effect, as is the power to heal of the sister therapy, acupressure. But it is homoeopathy that has endured the toughest battle with the mainstream, and homoeopathy has been the clear loser. Trial after trial, including double blind placebo-controlled prospective trials, have all shown that homoeopathy does not work. Any seeming cures are put down to placebo effect. In other words, homoeopathy has about as much basis in scientific reality as astrology.

Biofeedback is based on sound science and has its followers. I have tried it and find that used in conjunction with meditation, it can be a significant way of tackling stress. It involves using a device which measures brainwaves and sometimes blood pressure and heart rate. It's a good way of showing the extent to which the mind can control the body. Peace and serenity are particularly associated with alpha brain waves. Biofeedback training and learned meditation techniques can produce positive results for a number of problems such as anxiety disorders, migraine, high blood pressure, irritable bowel syndrome, insomnia and urinary incontinence. As a way of tackling stress without taking pills, biofeedback has much to recommend it and is a form of therapy accepted by most doctors who know anything about it.

Naturopathy is a term that covers the practice of a range of alternative therapies, such as homoeopathy, herbal medicine and acupuncture, from a single clinic. Some clinics and practitioners are more alternative than others and may offer treatments like colonic irrigation and reflexology.

Herbal medicine is an area about which I have mixed views. The chapter in this book on supplements lists the alleged benefits of a number of remedies that are herbal, and I have explained in the chapter on the prostate how I am trying a regime of herbal remedies in an attempt to deal with an enlarged prostate typical of benign prostatic hyperplasia (BPH). That doesn't mean I am a believer when it comes to herbal medicine, and I readily admit that this is a minefield awash with unsubstantiated hype.

There are practitioners of what is now called Individualised Herbal Medicine (IHM) keen to prescribe Ayurvedic, Chinese or western herbal remedies allegedly tailored to the precise needs of an individual and their ailments. Most of this is hogwash, and there is a risk that some remedies may be harmful. If you embark on the herbal road, take small quantities to start with to test whether you are likely to have a problem. I have never consulted a herbal medicine practitioner, but I do believe in using the internet to research very thoroughly any supplement I take, herbal or not, and I tend to be extremely sceptical about some of the reports that I read, as I hope I have shown in this book. We tend to think of pharmaceutical drugs as something totally modern because they are synthesized, while many are in fact concentrated versions of natural substances, some of which are herbal remedies used for centuries. The distinction between herbal remedies and pharmaceutical drugs is a modern and slightly artificial one. Just as pharmaceutical drugs can have side effects, so can herbal remedies, though as a rule of thumb, herbal remedies will have fewer side effects and be less effective.

The risks with herbal supplements include possible chemical contamination, especially if the remedies come from China, and negative interaction with other herbs or drugs. Almost no trials on herbal remedies are conducted using proper randomised methods with placebo controls, so when you read on a website selling such remedies and quoting from trials, bear this in mind. Reliance on herbal remedies that do not work may delay or prevent more orthodox treatment that could be life-saving.

The UK herbal remedy market is worth about £200 million a year, and involves the sale of several hundred products, of which only some 10–20 are judged by the medical world to be effective.

CHAPTER SIX
WHEN PERSONALITIES FALL APART: ALZHEIMER'S

There can be few diseases that arouse more apprehension in men as they get older than what used to be known as senile dementia. We've all heard phrases like 'he's lost his marbles' and 'he's in his second childhood' to describe people slipping down the road to losing their minds, along with their identities. To an extent, this will happen to everyone in some degree if they live long enough, but this may be a result of the brain's inevitable decline with age (those 'senior moments') and not necessarily the disease known as senile dementia, the commonest form of which is Alzheimer's disease (AD). For most men of 40, Alzheimer's isn't yet on the horizon, but there can be few men over sixty to whom the thought has not occurred: am I losing it now and then? For the unfortunate 700,000 in the UK who have dementia, the first symptoms may not show until a decade or two after the deterioration has actually begun, perhaps as early as their forties or fifties.

The number of people with dementia in the UK will grow to 1.7 million by 2051, putting the dementia epidemic on a par with the diabetes epidemic.

There are several types of dementia, all of which are classed as degenerative diseases. Alzheimer's disease accounts for about 60% of cases. Another form of dementia known as vascular dementia results from a series of mini-strokes, each of which affects the brain and intellect. There may be a mixture of these symptoms together with Alzheimer's, in which case the condition is classed as mixed dementia. Parkinson's disease is a form of dementia, and when there is a combination of Parkinson's disease and Alzheimer's, the condition is called Lewy body dementia.

Alzheimer's presents researchers with a dilemma. It has been shown conclusively that progressive deterioration in brain function as we get older – usually after one's late twenties – may be slowed through diet, exercise and other lifestyle interventions. Alzheimer's, on the other hand, may be quite distinct from this process and develop erratically. One may mimic the other to some extent as there is a degree of overlap in the symptoms. At present the disease is incurable and leads ultimately to death. Nevertheless some forms of treatment do appear to slow development of the disease.

The good news for men, if you can call it that, is that Alzheimer's is much more common in women. At first glance, the reason for this may simply appear to be that old people belong to an age when women were less inclined to hold mentally stimulating jobs or to work at all. The old rule about 'if you've got it, use it' appears to apply to the brain as much as the muscles of the body. But I think that this is again to confuse normal mental decline with the disease that is Alzheimer's. A more likely explanation is that women, since they live several years longer than men on average, have more years in later life when Alzheimer's may occur.

What is certain is that as the population ages, Alzheimer's will become more and more widespread.

AD is normally diagnosed through a combination of cognitive tests, the taking of a family history, the noting of behaviour changes, and scans looking for signs of brain atrophy. The onset of AD is not sudden, so if symptoms such as loss of coordination and problems with vision appear suddenly, Alzheimer's is unlikely to be the diagnosis.

The symptoms of Alzheimer's in its early stages include indecisiveness, avoidance of responsibility, depression, lack of concentration, moodiness, confusion, forgetfulness and irritability. Those who are more intelligent and highly educated are likely to take longer to be diagnosed and to feel frustration at their mental decline more keenly. Sufferers in the middle stage of Alzheimer's find it difficult to follow what others are saying, may be unaware of time and date, and may be unable to identify where they are.

One line of research shows that men with higher levels of oestrogen in the blood are twice as likely to develop Alzheimer's disease as those with normal levels. Enzyme activity in the brain accelerated by higher levels of female hormones appears to increase the incidence of the neurodegenerative changes and cognitive decline that are Alzheimer's. The principal oestrogen in men and women is oestradiol and this is the form which is involved and may be a causative factor.

What causes raised levels of a female hormone in men? It's not so much a case of the female hormone level rising as of the male hormone level falling with age. Conversely in women, as they age, the female hormone declines, leaving their testosterone level more prominent as a result. This leads to the often-observed fact that as a married couple get older, they generally become more alike. Sexual distinctiveness declines and the men become more 'old womanish' and the women more 'masculine', though of course this is more likely to be a feature of old age than of middle life.

In recent years there have been news items in the press suggesting that a male's oestrogen (female hormone) level can rise above the normal either from drinking too much water that contains minute residual traces of the contraceptive pill, which contains female hormones, or because they have eaten too much food derived from soybeans, which contain phyto-oestrogens (plant oestrogens).

However, I would not rush to conclude from this that soybeans and tap water with traces of contraceptive hormones are the main cause of Alzheimer's. What about taking testosterone supplements (see chapter 14 on supplements)? Unfortunately, most hormone supplements are bad news and in the case of testosterone, supplements are said to be capable of inducing prostate cancer among other undesirable effects. Soybeans and female hormones may play a small part in Alzheimer's, but scientific evidence suggests that the main factor is heredity.

Various studies tend to support the view that a diet rich in anti-oxidant micronutrients can combat AD. What is more likely is that a dietary approach can mitigate the effects of normal ageing on the brain. Again it's a matter of whether researchers aren't perhaps confusing normal decline with Alzheimer's. The following claim to have been linked to improvements in brain function, or a slowing of normal degeneration: taurine (an amino acid) and the vitamins A, B12, C and E. Flavonoids in cocoa are claimed to improve intelligence, though there is no definitive evidence at present. It all depends on how much you want to believe the test results. Even caffeine, found in coffee, tea, cola drinks and chocolate, is said to help, as are carnitine and alpha-lipoic acid. A healthy diet may provide plenty of carnitine without the need for a supplement.

Just to complicate matters, cholesterol is said to be involved in Alzheimer's as well, along with a lipid (fat) called ceramide. Oxidated LDL cholesterol and ceramide together are said by one research team to trigger a 'neurodegenerative cascade' that destroys the brain cells of those with AD. Antioxidants in the diet may limit this process, but much more research needs to be done.

There is one study that shows that a modest amount of red wine each day (say 2 units) can help keep Alzheimer's at bay, but I am inclined to treat this particular finding as suspect until it is conclusively validated as alternative research suggests the opposite (see chapter 3 on alcohol).

An interesting recent finding is that there exists a group of men classified as the 'elite old'. These are men over the age of 70 who keep fit and who, as a result, appear to have an IQ score that is increasing with age rather than declining. The message seems to be that regular exercise, physical and mental, is crucial to defeating age-related cognitive decline. So is the avoidance of negative stress. One thing I have found in writing this book again and again is that the key to a long and healthy life, physically and mentally, is a healthy vascular system. That means healthy blood that flows freely through arteries, veins and capillaries that are free from damage and obstruction. This applies not just to the heart but to the brain as well.

While there is no doubt that the brains of most people go downhill after their late twenties, this is compensated by what might be called wisdom. The brain cells might be dying off, but life experience can make up for this in many ways. As a result, verbal skills go on improving up to about age forty, thanks to sheer practice, and arithmetic skills remain good even longer.

In its terminal stages, sufferers from Alzheimer's may become too weak to speak, move or eat, and with lowered immunity, may contract an infection such as pneumonia, from which they die. In a case like this, Alzheimer's proves fatal but is not recorded as the direct cause of death, the death certificate being more likely to record death from pneumonia.

Some research suggests that cortical thinning, associated with mental decline, may be halted and even reversed by meditation, which may thicken the pre-frontal cortex. Since meditation is usually very healthy and can be sociable as well, I find this a wise suggestion. But it's worth repeating that the impairment of the brain that is Alzheimer's is not the same thing as normal mental decline, and while the two may be related, and certainly have some symptoms in common, it would be over-optimistic to suggest at this stage that various approaches, while effective in slowing normal age-related cognition, could also do wonders in the battle against Alzheimer's.

General pollution, too, particularly air pollution, may play a role in age-related mental decline, but whether it is a causative factor in Alzheimer's has not been demonstrated. It was once thought that aluminium derived from cooking pots was a cause of AD, but this theory is now discredited.

Alzheimer's is often seen to run in families, and genetic science has recently identified five genes which are linked to a higher risk of Alzheimer's. The most recently discovered is known as SORLI. It's thought that this gene causes beta amyloid proteins to accumulate in the brain, causing the symptoms we identify with Alzheimer's: progressive loss of memory, (particularly short-term memory), disorientation, mood changes, poor concentration, language impairment, nerve cell impairment and eventually loss of individual identity and death. Anger, grumpiness, confusion, aggression and paranoia may be symptoms of advancing AD.

Let's look at these proteins a bit more closely. Their full name is amyloid beta-derived diffusible ligands. These are sticky protein plaques which accumulate in the brain and contribute ultimately to the large fibres characteristic of Alzheimer's. Identifying the ligands early on before too much damage is done currently offers the best promise of an effective treatment in the future.

Other genes are already identified as contributing too: apolipopro-tein E (ApoE) is found in three forms, one of which, Apo4, increases the disposition to Alzheimer's tenfold. However, this gene is not carried by 60% of Alzheimer's sufferers, therefore further genes and gene clusters, yet to be identified, are certain to play a part. As genes are inherited, most of the answers to the puzzle that is Alzheimer's will probably be uncovered by further DNA research.

Genes are not the only factor implicated in Alzheimer's. A head injury, perhaps caused in a car accident, may trigger the onset of the disease, and lack of education and intellectual stimulation are thought to be contributory factors.

A study in the US recently claimed to show that the incidence of AD could be cut by 68% simply by following a classic Mediterranean diet of fresh fruit and vegetables, olive oil, whole grains, fish and moderate quantities of red wine. And of course this diet has also been shown to reduce the incidence of cardiovascular disease, strokes and diabetes. It's no surprise, therefore, that further research reveals that smoking, obesity (which can cause high blood pressure) and lack of exercise may all contribute to Alzheimer's, as to so many other illnesses. In other words, lifestyle affects health including the health of the brain.

In my view this type of research, with its claims for combating AD, has yet to demonstrate that the results are not confusing Alzheimer's and normal age-related mental decline. That lifestyle, especially diet and exercise, can slow the process of brain degeneration is not in dispute. Whether it can delay the onset of Alzheimer's or prevent it altogether is another matter. It certainly cannot cure it once significant degeneration is established.

A picture is emerging of who is most likely to escape normal mental decline. That person is sociable and committed to the notion that a healthy mind goes with a healthy body. It is now thought that the way you live can make a difference of as much as 10% to your cognitive ability. Another finding is that psychotropic drugs taken to treat depression can impair the brain.

An interesting theory, but one yet to be proved once and for all, is that the Omega 3 oils EPA, DHA and ALA, together with the Omega 6 oil GLA, while undoubtedly important for cognitive function as we get older, may help to ward off or prevent Alzheimer's (see chapter 14 on supplements for more on the essential fatty acids).

It used to be thought that our fate lay in our stars. Now it lies in our lifestyle and our genes. You may feel that there isn't a lot we can do about the genes we inherited, and while this may no longer be the case years from now, in the meantime we are stuck with the DNA that our mothers and fathers gave us. But we can always try to improve the odds. In the case of Alzheimer's, it seems that the best thing we can do (until it's confirmed or disproved) is assume that Alzheimer's might be linked to lifestyle factors in the same way as age-related mental decline.

So try to keep an active mind as well as an active body – not just by reading books, for example, but by really exercising the mind by problem-solving in some way, or by pursuing a creative activity such as painting or writing, or even involving yourself in some type of research. I'm well aware that I am writing this book to keep my brain in tune. And above all it's important to be sociable. Living alone makes this harder, and loneliness is to be avoided if mental decline is to be warded off in those susceptible. About 60% of people who live alone regularly feel lonely. Depression and poverty, sadly, do not help.

The drugs currently in favour for treating mild to moderate Alzheimer's are Exelon (rivastigmine), Reminyl (galantamine) and Aricept (donepezil), while Ebixa (memantine) is the drug of choice for advanced cases. Exelon is available as a skin patch, thereby reducing side effects. Aricept and Exelon are aimed at prevention rather than cure and are designed to improve memory for a short period. The object of these drugs is the preservation of levels of acetylcholine, which aids communication between brain neurons. Alzheimer's sufferers increasingly lack acetylcholine. These drugs do not reverse decline, but they can postpone it for some months, provided that diagnosis and treatment are early enough.

The drugs are expensive and there is much controversy about who should get them on the NHS, with those in the moderate stages most likely to be given them, but not those in the mild or the advanced stages. This has led to anger when moderate cases have progressed to the advanced stage and NHS-funded treatment has then been withdrawn.

Another drug said to be showing promise is known simply as CX717. It sharpens the mind of anyone who takes it, not just those suffering from Alzheimer's.

The micronutrient known as phosphatidyl serine, a phospholipid, is thought to improve cognitive processing, but as yet, despite being available as an expensive dietary supplement for several years, it has not been proved to be of benefit. Neither has supplementation with Ginkgo Biloba, ginger, garlic, chilli or curcumin (the active ingredient in turmeric). Homocysteine, best known as a signal for cardiovascular problems, can also, with high levels, cause brain atrophy. The best natural antidote to homocysteine is folate, found in dark green leafy vegetables, citrus fruits, liver and nuts. Folate may also be taken in supplement form as folic acid. However, folic acid has a known downside in that it may stimulate histamine production (see chapter 4 on allergies).

Foie gras, enjoyable as it is to eat if you aren't counting calories, has been found to be rich in amyloid proteins which may, according to researchers, trigger Alzheimer's, as well as Type 2 diabetes and rheumatoid arthritis. These are classified as amyloid-related disorders, diseases in which normally soluble proteins change shape and form insoluble clusters in organs, blocking their capacity to function correctly. If you eat foods with these rogue proteins, you may encourage their development in your body, which is how BSE spreads from animals to humans, with sometimes fatal consequences.

Meat and the soy product tofu contain the protein L-tyrosine, an amino acid which synthesizes the catecholamines noradrenaline (which can function as a hormone) and dopamine (a neurotransmitter). These biogenic amines may improve learning, memory and alertness, increasing synapses (the cell connectors) in the brain's hippocampus. Exercise stimulates the hippocampus to produce new brain cells, countering the old belief that no new brain cells are created after the age of about six months.

Now neurologists are working on ways of regenerating brain cells. Some of this research takes the form of deep brain stimulation (DBS) and transcranial magnetic stimulation (TMS). DBS is a partially invasive technique aimed at treating Parkinson's disease and multiple sclerosis. In those suffering from Parkinson's, electrodes implanted in the brain reduce or eliminate tremors, though not other symptoms. Currently around 30,000 Parkinson's sufferers have electrode implants in their brains to reduce symptoms. TMS is completely non-invasive. It stimulates non-active brain cells in the hippocampus with the aim of lifting depression, and it may prove to be effective in the treatment of some types of epilepsy, as well as schizophrenia, stroke, obsessive compulsive disorder (OCD), post-traumatic stress disorder and migraine. If DBS and TMS turn out to be successful in these areas, this may open up the possibility of their use in the treatment of Alzheimer's.

Parkinson's is also being treated experimentally with gene therapy. Sufferers typically have reduced amounts of gamma-aminobutyric acid (GABA) in their brain. This deficiency results in the lack of movement coordination typical of the disease. Now trials involving the injection, directly into one side of the brain, of the gene responsible for making glutamic acid decarboxylase (GAD), which in turn produces GABA, have shown that the excessive brain cell activity that characterises Parkinson's can be reduced by as much as 25–30%, and by as much as 65% in one exceptional case.

Chewing gum improves brain performance (and heart rate as well) by getting more oxygen and nutrients to the brain. The chewing action also stimulates insulin release, which is thought to improve memory. New experiences stimulate the brain to produce neurotrophins. These potentiate nerve cell dendrites, which process information. One line of therapy for Alzheimer's is playing a musical instrument, which improves verbal memory.

Alzheimer's is not the only form of dementia, but it does account for 60% of cases and is the fourth most common cause of death in the developed world (after heart disease, cancer and stroke). As we live longer, the diseases from which we die tend to change, hence the growing prevalence of cancer and now Alzheimer's in modern times. One in twenty of those over 65 is afflicted with Alzheimer's, from which we can conclude that it is already affecting a number of those under the age of 65.

Magnetic resonance imaging (MRI) scans are now able to identify at an early stage the degenerative changes in brain cells and consequent changes in brain wiring that come with Alzheimer's. Should an MRI scan be undertaken as a preventive measure? To do so as a matter of routine screening for the entire population over, say, 60 would not be practicable, but to wait until the first obvious signs appear might be leaving it too late. As happens so often, it might be the rich who get the earliest diagnosis as well as the best treatment. Perhaps, if you can afford it, you should have a scan, however expensive, at the age of 65 and periodically thereafter, even if you are not showing any symptoms beyond the general failing of memory that comes with age. Radiation exposure with an MRI scan is low.

Be aware, though, that the brain does shrink with age. Your brain, however mentally healthy you are, will be smaller at 60 than it was at 20. In the average man it will be only 80% of what it was. What science does not know yet is whether a gradually shrinking brain necessarily equates to a brain functioning less well. Many older people would judge themselves to perform as well cognitively at 60 as they did at 20.

All of which does not add up to a cure for those who are found to have Alzheimer's. If there is no cure yet, and drug treatments are all still very experimental, is it better to know sooner rather than later that you have the disease? I have implied that this is the case, but I admit that I am not entirely sure that it helps to know early on that you have what is still an incurable disease. As I write this, I am stuffed up with a bad cold, which has fogged my brain, and I wonder to myself whether this is what Alzheimer's feels like in the early stages. What scientists involved in research in this field have concluded with some certainty is that Alzheimer's and the general cognitive decline that comes with age are distinct from each other, and that you should not panic yet if you find yourself losing your memory now and again.

A test called the Cantab test is a simple cognitive test developed by Cambridge scientists. It runs on a touch screen computer and is designed to look at short-term memory with tests of visual recall and spatial working memory. It identifies those with a failing short-term memory, and aims to spot Alzheimer's earlier than scans. It also aims to differentiate between symptoms of Alzheimer's and other forms of dementia and brain disease. However, the test can also produce false positives, the occurrence of which is as high as 12%. The reason for this is clear – if failing short term memory is common to those with Alzheimer's and to those who are simply ageing normally, the test will sometimes pick up the latter as well as the former. It would be unfortunate for someone without Alzheimer's to be told that they might have the disease when all that they suffered from was the absent-mindedness that comes with advancing years. To confuse matters more, Alzheimer's often masquerades as apathy and depression, which may delay proper diagnosis.

In most cases, the Cantab test can also detect pressure hydrocephalus, a potentially fatal build-up of pressure on the brain which looks like Alzheimer's and can kill within two years if left untreated. The test can pick up this illness before it appears on a brain scan.

Alzheimer's as I have described it is usually called late-onset Alzheimer's disease. There is also a version called early-onset Alzheimer's, which can strike men as young as thirty or forty. This is invariably an inherited version of the disease and a great tragedy for its victims in view of their age. Let's hope that before long the researchers working on the disease – either version – will come up with answers that will lead to a cure. This means more experimental drugs – to start with, at least. Later there may be hope in the shape of DNA therapy.

Currently undergoing trials is a blood test which, if successful, will identify Alzheimer's in its earliest stages and much sooner than any other test available. This could be good news as the earlier treatment begins, the more chance there is of holding Alzheimer's at bay.

....

More Tips and Traps

Old people in care homes often have Alzheimer's in addition to a variety of behavioural problems. It has been found that treating them with neuroleptic tranquillisers shortens their life, while reducing verbal fluency and cognitive function.

From Japan comes news that onions contain an anti-oxidant sulphur compound capable of ridding the brain of harmful toxins which impair memory and may contribute to both Parkinson's and Alzheimer's disease.

CHAPTER SEVEN
THE BASICS OF BACK PAIN

It's sometimes said that the widespread incidence of back pain, especially lower back pain, is a sign that we have not fully evolved as animals designed to walk upright on two legs. Back pain is one of the commonest reasons why patients visit doctors, and the problem gets worse with age. There are several underlying reasons why back pain occurs and a large medical field has developed around this difficult area. The commonest form of back pain is lumped under the general name sciatica, which is a term descriptive of the symptoms rather than the cause of the problem. Sciatica involves lower back pain which radiates from the lumbar spine through the sciatic nerve to the buttocks and legs.

More than half of all adults will suffer from lower back pain at some stage in their lives, and a sizeable proportion of these will be keen gardeners, in the habit of constantly bending over. Back pain is often experienced as acute muscle spasm or as an achingly stiff back. It's a disease that costs the economy large sums of money in healthcare and lost productivity, and when it's chronic, it brings misery to millions.

Sudden severe back pain is commonly attributable to a so-called slipped (prolapsed) disc, a herniated intervertebral disc. Osteoarthritis of the spinal joints can also produce excruciating pain and is fairly common. When back pain persists, it is best investigated with an MRI scan first. If pressure on nerves from an intervertebral disc and osteoarthritis are ruled out, the next most likely cause is a problem within a vertebra itself, and the best way of looking at this more closely is a CT scan.

I had problems with mild lower back pain a few years ago. It came on mainly when I sat driving my car for several hours on end. It helped to add a lumbar support to the car seat, but the problem did not go entirely. I went to see a doctor specializing in sports medicine. He looked at me for a few minutes, made my stand on my toes in bare feet and then pronounced that I needed to do some exercises to strengthen my abdominal muscles. I was a bit sceptical but I did as he suggested. Not only did I get a better looking six pack (well, let's be honest, to me it looked like a six pack), but the pain in my lower back disappeared in two weeks and has never come back, not even on long drives. So I would suggest that if you get lower back pain that seems to be associated with a lack of lumbar support, do a lot of sit-ups (but only go part way up or you could damage your back) and make sure that seats that you use offer plenty of support in the lumbar region. If you sit at a desk, spend money to get a good chair with an adjustable lumbar support and sit in the chair the correct way. Having written that, I have a proviso to add, since one study suggests that a slumped but comfortable sitting position may be better for your back and less painful in the long run than sitting in the traditional correct position – upright with shoulders down, stomach in and head straight. Another case where the jury is still out.

As far as gardening goes, don't give up. What you probably need is plenty of stretching exercises to lengthen the spine. Think about yoga, Pilates or Alexander technique, all of which could help, though there's a school of thought that says that yoga and Pilates don't help much and could even make things worse for some people. Bending over should not leave you with an aching back afterwards, but it may do so if your spine isn't used to such stretches. Gardening is a wonderful way to get exercise and should be on every older man's list of ways to look after their body.

Treatments for back pain are many. Research shows that contrary to previous thinking, softer rather than harder mattresses are good for the back, so long as they are not excessively soft. Acupuncture is believed to help some, though the cure may be largely psychosomatic in my view. Sessions with an osteopath work in many cases, or at least relieve the symptoms.

Being overweight or obese causes many physical ailments and lower back pain is one of them. Weight loss is the obvious solution here, though as anyone who has tried to lose weight knows, this is no easy thing.

Supplements of a herb called Devil's claw, and bromelain, derived from the pineapple stem, are said to work as muscle relaxants and pain killers respectively, and to help those suffering from certain types of back pain. But the best supplement for joint health generally, including the lower back, is said to be glucosamine sulphate. I have taken it on and off for years, unable to make my mind up whether it really does work (see chapter on supplements), in my case to help bursitis and synovitis around joints. Of all the supplements on the market, this is probably the one most recognized by orthodox medicine as being effective. On balance I would like to give it my vote and say that it works. As things stand, I have been taking it regularly for some time now and will continue to do so. It is said that chondroitin supplements work equally well, and chondroitin is often found combined with glucosamine sulphate in capsule form. However, there is no need to use chondroitin. It is expensive, while glucosamine sulphate is cheap, and using the latter on its own is just as effective.

Pain reduction is the first objective of most treatments for back pain and while this is only dealing with symptoms and not causes, it is important as a starting point. Stronger painkillers may be necessary in some cases, but for most sufferers a painkiller that is combined with an anti-inflammatory will usually suffice, and the favourite anti-inflammatory these days is ibuprofen. With the right painkiller, sufferers can sleep better and are more mobile. Increased mobility itself may help the problem as the immobility that is usually associated with severe back pain can actually make the problem worse through lack of exercise of the muscles, tendons and ligaments surrounding the lower spine.

CHAPTER EIGHT
BAD BREATH

Halitosis, which affects at least half of the British population to some extent, has many causes. It may be caused by food you have recently eaten. The problem may come from the stomach or throat, or equally from the mouth and surrounding area, such as the sinuses and nasal cavity. The tongue is a frequent source of bad breath (see chapter on teeth), where it can harbour billions of bad bacteria, as can the teeth and gums. A narrowing of the oesophagus, sepsis in the lungs, untreated diabetes, sinusitis, liver failure and tonsillitis can all be a cause of the problem. Smokers and heavy drinkers tend to have bad breath, especially when the two go together.

The best way to tell if you have bad breath (since even your best friends will probably not tell you) is to lick the inside of your wrist hard with your tongue, count ten seconds and then have a sniff. If the odour is unpleasant, you have bad breath. The most likely cause for most people is dental plaque, and the best cure is good dental care and oral hygiene. A trip to the oral hygienist may be called for, followed by some dental work and then a lifetime of brushing and flossing properly.

A good cure for oral bad breath may be chewing gum sweetened with xylitol, a natural sweetener derived from the birch tree. Studies suggest that xylitol counters acidity and oral bacteria responsible for plaque formation. Xylitol enhances the flow of saliva, and saliva is one key to reducing bad breath as it contains good bacteria. If you skip meals or breathe through your mouth, you will have less saliva in your mouth and your mouth will be drier. This encourages the growth of bad bacteria.

Regular hydration – drinking liquids, particularly water – helps to keep saliva levels in the mouth up, and drinking green tea is even better, not just for the anti-oxidants it contains, but also for the way it improves the health of your gums. On the other hand, mouthwashes are probably a waste of money, except short term. Some herbal remedies, though, may improve mouth freshness by tackling bad bacteria while enhancing the good. Into this category, for their chlorophyll content, fall parsley, wheatgrass and spirulina seaweed tablets. Other aids to fresh breath are said to be peppermint oil (a few drops on the tongue), fennel, anise seeds and cloves (chewed).

Though garlic and onions may be good for health and essential to some kinds of cooking, they do not go down well when eventually they find their way to our lungs and come out as an odour that is unpleasant to some people. Eating sugary foods between meals is another no-no if plaque build-up is to be avoided. It only takes half an hour for plaque formation to begin, so unless you are prepared to brush your teeth within half an hour of eating, you could have a breath problem as well as helping dental decay to form.

It's hard to say what supplements might help. Co-enzyme Q10 has been touted, as have foods rich in vitamin C. I would suggest that general dietary health, along with exercise, is likely to help the problem of bad breath, but not enough research has been done to suggest that any particular supplement might help. Were it not for the chlorophyll factor, I would say the same for the foods suggested above. What is probably true is that a healthy digestive tract is important for fresh breath, and that means avoiding constipation by eating lots of roughage in your diet. If you have ulcers, get treatment. Most ulcers are caused by the bacterium *Helicobacter pylori* and can be cured with antibiotics in a couple of weeks.

If you have reflux of stomach contents and stomach acid caused by a hiatus hernia, that is harder to treat properly, and the benefits may be outweighed by the downside of what is still a clumsy and unsatisfactory operation. The same may be said of a cricopharyngeal diverticulum, which is a pouch in the upper throat which may catch mucus and food. This may cause the growth of oral bacteria and bad breath if not surgically treated. However, this is an operation rarely performed well, and it may be better to forego it and live with a small degree of bad breath instead.

CHAPTER NINE
THE C WORD: CANCER

In the UK, one in three people will get cancer and one in four will die from it. Putting that another way, only one in four who contract cancer will not die from cancer, but from something else. On a brighter note, there is hope that within ten years it will be possible to diagnose many forms of cancer early from a simple blood test. The earlier cancer is diagnosed, the more chance there is of beating it. There are around 200 known types of cancer. The ten-year survival rate for a group of common cancers is now about double what it was thirty years ago, and is getting close to 50%.

Cancer is not just something that happens and over which, like the weather, you have no control. You can do a lot to limit your chances of getting it. Many forms of cancer are strongly influenced by lifestyle and prevention is always better than cure. As rates of cardiovascular disease decline with better healthcare, rates of cancer rise. Cancer has now overtaken stroke as the second commonest killer of men in the UK. We have to die of something someday, and as we live longer, cancer has inevitably become more prevalent as a cause of death. I remember my father saying he would rather die suddenly from a heart attack than slowly from cancer, as his mother had. As a young medical student he had administered the morphine that saw her through her final days, including the shot that finally took her out of her misery – dead from breast cancer at the age of forty-two.

Most of us would rather die from a heart attack than cancer and my father's wish came true when he died suddenly from a heart attack at the age of seventy. Now we have the seeming paradox that more people are dying from cancer than previously, yet your chances of being cured of cancer or living longer with cancer have never been better. The explanation lies partly in the fact of better cancer care, increased longevity and the reduced incidence of heart attack and stroke. But it also lies in the fact that more of us are eating badly, drinking too much alcohol, exercising too little and lying in the sun too long. Just as lung cancer rates are starting to improve as fewer adults smoke (see chapter on smoking), rates for mouth and kidney cancer are climbing, and above all skin cancer, the fastest growing, though not the most prevalent cancer in the UK.

How you live makes a big difference to your chances of getting cancer. In a few words, if you want to avoid cancer, eat healthily, exercise moderately, don't smoke, drink alcohol lightly or not at all, be happy, have lots of friends and family around you, avoid negative stress and pollution, laugh a lot, have a religious faith, do voluntary work and meditate regularly. You may still get cancer, but the chances will be greatly reduced, or if you do get one of the many forms of the disease, it will probably be at an advanced old age. It seems, too, that cancer is less likely than your heart to be influenced by the genes you inherited.

It has been known for some time that stress can increase your chances of getting cancer. Now it seems we know the reason why. Stress releases the adrenal hormone epinephrine, which in turn makes cancer cells – at least those found in prostate cancer – resistant to apoptosis or cell death, the means by which lethal cells are normally prevented from multiplying. We know that in people who are anxious or depressed, epinephrine levels remain abnormally elevated. Men who take blood pressure drugs are less prone to prostate cancer, and this, it seems, could be the result of epinephrine suppression brought about by the drugs. Being stressed could make cancer more likely and also make treatment less effective, though it must be admitted that those with cancer are likely to be more stressed knowing they have a potentially fatal disease.

High fat diets increase the risk of cancer, though in one study of women suffering from breast cancer it was found that eating fruit and vegetables beyond the normal recommended allowance gave no additional protection. Many plant foods contain sterols, substances classed as anti-carcinogenic, something that cannot generally be said of animal source food. Link that with the fact that on average vegetarians live longer than omnivores and you might conclude that eating animal protein was actually bad for you, until you reckon with the fact that vegetarians are more likely to look after themselves, in which case it may well be that omnivores who eat healthily have the best diet of all. That still doesn't answer the question of whether a healthy diet can help fight cancer and reduce your chances of getting it or suffering a relapse. For want of better information at this stage, it is wise to assume that a healthy diet does help. If it doesn't work against cancer, at least we know that it works against cardiovascular disease. One thing is certain, though. If you are obese, you are considerably more at risk of getting cancer. In fact, obesity is now thought to be on a par with smoking when it comes to cancer risk.

One study has shown that at least four types of cancer in men can be linked to obesity or even just being overweight. The cancers in question are throat (oesophageal), bowel, pancreatic and kidney cancer. This is alarming when you consider that by 2050 as many as 60% of all men could be obese if the present trend continues. Apart from keeping weight down, the most important message from this study was that red meat consumption should be severely limited to no more than 500 grams a week. Sugary drinks should be avoided and all smoked, cured and pre-salted foods, such as salami, bacon, ham and smoked salmon should be avoided completely if you want to limit your chances of bowel cancer. Grilled and barbecued foods increase the risk of stomach cancer. We are likely to see bacon become a major target of healthy eating campaigns in the next few years. What we eat is now reckoned to account for about one-third of all cases of cancer generally, so the message is clear: cancer is a disease that you may be able to avoid or postpone if you adopt a healthy lifestyle.

Red wine may help to reduce your chances of a coronary event (see chapter 41 on cardiovascular disease), but the evidence now suggests that alcohol increases the risk of cancer. Caffeine consumption doesn't seem to be related to cancer. Milk may reduce your chances of bowel cancer, but too much calcium could increase the chance of cancer of the prostate.

According to one oncologist, the right diet helps in the prevention of cancer, but if you already have cancer, it is too late for what you eat and drink to make a difference, and he includes in that both food and supplements, including herbal supplements. A review of the literature on cancer shows how far away we still are from knowing once and for all what food and drink can influence prevention and possibly treatment. In the past many foods have had their advocates: chillis, turmeric, lycopene (concentrated in cooked tomatoes), vitamins D and E, grape-seed and rice bran. Sugar converted to glucose feeds cancer, so those with cancer are generally advised to cut down on sugar.

Cancer prevention and treatment breakthroughs appear from time to time in the press. One that looks promising as a preventive measure and alternative to chemotherapy is based on eating nuts, cereals, and pulses. Foods such as nuts, lentils, peas, wheat bran and beans contain the water-soluble phosphate compound inositol pentakisphosphate (InsP5). When these foods are cooked, the effect of the InsP5 is enhanced, making them even better cancer-fighting agents. The compound inhibits the enzyme phosphoinositide 3-kinase, which plays a significant part in tumour development. Unlike chemicals used in cancer treatment, there are no toxic side effects, no matter how much is ingested. InsP5 also boosts the effect of cancer- fighting drugs in the treatment of lung cancer. It's found in beans generally, and as beans are a rich source of fibre and contain useful anti-oxidants, it makes sense to follow the US dietary recommendation and eat at least three cups of beans a week. Amongst the richest in anti-oxidants are pinto beans, black beans, small red beans and red kidney beans, while navy beans – the beans used in baked beans – are another everyday source, best taken in the form of sugar-free baked beans. Colon cancer has been shown to respond positively to a diet with plenty of beans.

Men in middle age, if they think about cancer and do not smoke, are likely to think of colorectal cancer and prostate cancer first (see chapter 43 on the prostate). Cancer of the rectum used once to cause panic as operating on the rear end of the digestive canal usually involved a colostomy and therefore a bag. Of colorectal cases, about one-third involve the rectum and two-thirds the colon (the large intestine). Cancer of the small intestine is unusual, and cancer of the stomach or the oesophagus, while not unusual, is not as common as colorectal cancer, the incidence of which peaks around age sixty.

Treatment of colorectal cancer is indebted to developments in MRI scanning and recent research on the lateral as well as the longitudinal spread of the carcinoma. Treatment is typically with radiotherapy before surgery, followed by more radiotherapy and drugs after surgery. Recurrence rates and five year survival rates for this form of cancer are now at levels which would have been unthinkable twenty years ago. Radiotherapy in the bowel region is not without its long-term risks and these include faecal incontinence, bladder damage, testicular damage and impotence. If anal surgery is involved, a colostomy bag may still be an inevitable handicap for the rest of the patient's life.

It may seem an embarrassing topic, discussing your bowel with your doctor or undergoing a digital examination of your rectum, though this will more probably be to look at the size of your prostate rather than to determine the presence of a cancer of the rectum. If the quality of your life and your life itself are at stake, it makes no sense to be coy about such discussions and the investigations which may result if there is any suspicion of a cancer. Where the prognosis for treatment is poor, it is generally in cases where detection has occurred too far down the line. Early detection is essential in the battle against cancer of any kind.

In the case of cancer of the colon and rectum, the starting point is a faecal test looking for occult (hidden) blood. If traces of blood undetectable by eye are found, this may be nothing more sinister than a sign of piles or perhaps diverticula in the walls of the colon. More serious are polyps, which are always classed as pre-cancerous. That means that they might become cancerous, and should therefore be removed. This is done simultaneously with the colorectal examination by colonoscopy. Many cases of colon cancer stem from polyps which went undetected. Cancer that is limited to the mucosal lining of the bowel is generally treatable provided that it has not spread to the nearby lymph glands.

A recent breakthrough in colon cancer is the discovery of a small group of abnormal stem cells that are responsible for the formation and growth of tumours. Therapy with a clearly identifiable target such as this has far more chance of success.

What are the classic signs of possible colorectal cancer? The following may be indicative of cancer, but could also be signs of something else:

unexplained loss of weight; unexplained tiredness and breathlessness, which may result from anaemia caused by internal bleeding; mucus, blood or pus in stool; a lump that can be felt in the rectum or abdomen; constipation that has grown worse over a four to five week period; changes in bowel habit such as looseness and frequency, with changes in stool shape from normal to thin.

Some minor cancers can be treated with a form of light therapy called Photodynamic Therapy (PDT), in which a bright laser light activates a drug applied to the cancer. The light activates a form of oxygen which destroys the cancer. PDT has been used to treat stomach, oesophageal, mouth and bladder cancer using an endoscope. But PDT is most effective in treating skin cancers where the cancer is not too big or too deep. It won't work for all cancers, and there are side effects, though these are likely to be less severe than the side effects from radiotherapy and chemotherapy.

In few medical fields are so many breakthroughs announced with such regularity as in the field of cancer (oncology). Some discoveries fall by the wayside, others take years to become viable and available options for patients. But one way or another, identification and treatment inches forward year after year, so that having cancer is no longer the automatic death sentence that it was in previous generations. However, in the UK, 1.2 million people have cancer at any one time, and of these about 150,000 will die each year.

One of the most promising areas of cancer research is in the field of DNA. At present, around a dozen drugs aimed to work on cells at a genetic level have been approved for various cancers and another hundred are in trial or awaiting approval. As it becomes increasingly less expensive to produce an individual's DNA profile – the complete genome – it may become possible to match cancer therapy precisely to the requirements of that individual. The same will be true for other diseases as well, not just cancer.

Scientists have discovered a gene called Trop-2 that is thought to be actively involved in tumour growth in around three quarters of all cancers, including colon, breast, prostate, stomach, lung, pancreatic and ovarian cancer. No other marker for cancer is found across such a broad spectrum. In colon cancer, Trop-2 is particularly associated with aggressive and fatal tumour development. Targeting Trop-2 specifically with drugs tailored with appropriate antibodies may make it possible to slow or even halt a variety of cancers, especially cancer of the pancreas, for which there is currently no treatment that works.

Antibody research is now one of the most popular areas for cancer research. Antibodies form part of the body's own defence system against attack. Harnessing antibodies in the fight against cancer, one research team has found that the key may be to inject antibodies into a tumour 'cloaked' in an organic oil that makes them ineffective until they are activated by ultraviolet light, enabling them to link up with T-cells and trigger these natural killer cells to attack and destroy the surrounding cancerous tissue. Because the body has difficulty in recognizing a threat from itself in the form of cancer cells, the body's immune system needs encouragement to go into action. This is the premise on which this antibody therapy is based. The objective of such therapies, as of all cancer therapy, is to destroy cancer cells without harming surrounding healthy tissue. The risk in activating a T-cell response is that the killer cells will not only attack cancer cells but also go on to attack healthy cells as well. It may be several years before any treatment based on T-cell activation is on the market.

Around twenty cancer drugs that use antibodies to shrink tumours are currently on the market. The best known are Herceptin and Avastin. Many more such drugs are on trial or awaiting approval.

It has been found that cancer is commonest in those with a high fat diet and a low consumption of fruit and vegetables. Flavonoids from fruit and vegetables (see chapter 17 on nutrition) are protective against cancer, as are the plant oestrogens (phyto-oestrogens) such as lignans and isoflavones. The main lignans are enterolactone and enterodiol. Flaxseed is the best food source of lignans, while soy products are the best source of isoflavones.

CHAPTER TEN
THE CHOLESTEROL CONUNDRUM

Cholesterol is implicated in 45% of all deaths from cardiovascular disease. It may also be involved in cases of kidney failure, dementia and limb pain resulting from a lack of oxygen in the muscles involved. One in three deaths in the UK is attributed to heart disease.

Cholesterol has been a major point of debate in health matters for over fifty years. We now routinely talk of 'good' (high density lipoprotein: HDL) and 'bad' (low density lipoprotein: LDL) cholesterol, as if the body somehow has not evolved enough over millions of years to get rid of the latter. This ignores the fact that both forms of cholesterol serve a positive function, and it is only when there is too much oxidised LDL cholesterol in the vascular system that it has a negative effect. Contrary to popular belief, cholesterol is a lipid (fat) which cannot be measured. When we talk about blood cholesterol levels, we are actually referring to LDL and HDL levels, that is, lipoprotein levels. For simplicity's sake I have adopted common if erroneous usage and refer to LDL and HDL as cholesterol.

So we talk routinely about HDL and LDL as though they were cholesterol though they are not. Lipoprotein particles are what transports cholesterol to every cell in the body, just as they transport the fats that are known as triglycerides. Cholesterol helps to make bile and some hormones, and it strengthens cell walls and membranes throughout the body. The synapses in the brain that connect brain cells are almost entirely made from cholesterol. LDL contains a higher fat level and fewer proteins than HDL. So-called bad cholesterol is carried in LDL and so-called good cholesterol is carried in HDL, when actually the cholesterol itself is the same – only the lipoprotein carrier is different. 'Bad' cholesterol, which is cholesterol carried by LDL, attaches itself to the endothelial walls of arteries, particularly the coronary arterial system, forming plaque. 'Good' cholesterol, which is cholesterol carried by HDL, is so-called because, so the theory goes, it transports 'bad' cholesterol from the artery walls back to the liver for disposal from the body.

If we all lived a healthy life, eating the right things and getting enough exercise, there would still be LDL cholesterol, but for most of us it would now be good cholesterol, like HDL, with a positive role to play. It is not 'bad' cholesterol as such that is bad, but excessive 'bad' cholesterol. The excess oxidizes and sticks to arterial walls forming part of the atheroma, the sticky substance which solidifies into plaque (atherosclerosis) and may either rupture and block the artery (stenosis) or break away in the form of a life-threatening clot (thrombosis). A recent study suggests that the more dangerous form of plaque is not hard plaque, but semi-hard plaque which is more likely to burst, especially if the artery walls are inflamed, forming a clot that leads to a heart attack. There is clear evidence of the role of 'bad' cholesterol in the process of plaque formation.

Half of all deaths in the UK are said to be avoidable if cholesterol level, and LDL level in particular, is within normal limits. The fact that deaths from heart attacks, despite growing obesity, have come down in recent years is credited to the arrival of statin drugs (see below). It is said that 70% of men over 45 have a high cholesterol level, and this figure rises to 80% in men over 55.

Cholesterol is a light-coloured waxy fat about 10–25% of which comes from diet and 75–90% from production by the liver using dietary saturated fats. It is essential for the efficient running of every cell in our bodies. Cholesterol attached to LDL and HDL is transported round the body in our blood, and also goes into and out of the digestive tract, from where some of it is eliminated in the faeces by plant sterols (phyto-sterols) contained in our diet. The remainder is absorbed back into the bloodstream. In this way our diet can play an important part in keeping our cholesterol level within healthy limits. Phyto-sterols are plant compounds found in soluble viscous fibres, the best sources of which are oats, barley, rice bran, apples, pulses (peas and beans), soybeans, hoummos (made from chick peas) and vegetables such as okra and aubergine.

Soluble fibres are so called because, unlike most fibre found in vegetables and grains, they are soluble in the gut. A particularly good form of soluble fibre is pectin, good sources of which are grapefruit and apples. Plant stanol esters are another compound that has the same effect on cholesterol as phyto-sterols. These have been introduced into food products in the last few years, notably spreads, yoghurt and drinks produced under two well-known brand names. These products do appear to reduce LDL and raise HDL to some extent. Sterols are found in most vegetables and fruits. Nuts and seeds are rich sources, and contain monounsaturated fats which will help to keep LDL levels down, as will their fibre content. Most nuts are also important sources of vitamin E, and Brazil nuts are rich in selenium.

What other foods are thought to encourage LDL reduction? Soy products are believed to cut down LDL, though only minimally. Tofu and soy milk are two of the most widely available soy products in the UK. Some of the general foods that you will find covered in the chapter on nutrition will probably help too. These include oily fish, flaxseed and hempseed for their Omega 3 oils, fresh garlic and wholegrain bread, as well as milk and eggs fortified with Omega 3. Avocados are particularly useful as they contain beta-sitosterol, which blocks LDL absorption through the wall of the intestines. Pomegranates contain nutrients which boost the level of the enzyme paraoxonase, one function of which is to break down cholesterol patches on arterial walls.

It used to be thought that we should avoid foods rich in cholesterol such as liver, eggs, prawns and shellfish. We now know that eating foods like these, which are healthy, has very little effect on our blood levels of cholesterol. To the extent that diet does play a part, HDL levels are thought to be more susceptible to diet than LDL levels, which, if true, is good news, particularly as HDL is believed to also be subject to the positive influence of exercise. HDL appears to be influenced positively, also, by a high fibre diet, which may also lower LDL.

Dietary cholesterol should not be avoided unless you suffer from hypercholesterolaemia (see below). I remember reading Adelle Davis thirty years ago on the subject of eggs and cholesterol. She was ahead of her time, pointing out that eggs were one of the most complete foods we could eat, and that they would have almost zero effect on our cholesterol count. How right she was. Now we know that cholesterol from egg yolks is only very minimally absorbed in the intestines. Eggs provide iron, protein and vitamin D, and help to build strong bones. They also contain choline, an essental part of the brain chemical acetylcholine, which is vital to memory. Regularly eating eggs will boost blood levels of lutein, which, ironically in view of the former bad reputation of eggs, helps to reduce inflammation of the artery walls, and in that way limits build-up of LDL in the form of fatty plaque. Because eggs are mainly protein and protein is more filling, calorie for calorie, than fat or carbohydrates, eating an egg every morning for breakfast can help reduce hunger pangs. Meanwhile, the lutein, which gives egg yolk its yellow colour, is good for our eyes, helping to protect them from age-related macular degeneration.

There are certainly foods that are bad for your cholesterol level and these tend to be the usual suspects – excessive amounts of saturated fat and, worse still, trans (partially hydrogenated) fats, to be found in a variety of processed foods and especially in cakes, biscuits, pies and the like. These fats stimulate the liver to produce more cholesterol than your body needs, with the resulting high levels that we discuss below. However, some of your daily fat intake should come from saturated fat, (see chapter 17 on eating right), which is not the big bad wolf it was once thought to be. It seems that whether a low fat diet is good for you or not depends a lot on your genes. People with what has been identified as pattern B LDL have an increased risk of heart disease and diabetes. About one-third of men carry this genetic trait and are those who would benefit from a low fat diet. The remaining two-thirds have pattern A LDL and do not benefit from a low fat diet. In fact if they go on a low fat diet, as many as one-third may become pattern B and acquire its attendant risks.

Older people who take a daily supplement of EPA Omega 3 fatty acid (see chapter 17 on eating right and chapter on supplements) have been shown to reduce their chances of a heart attack, and this positive outcome is increased if statins are added. The addition of grapeseed oil was found in another study to increase the level of HDL cholesterol and lower the level of triglycerides. Grapeseed oil is rich in anti-oxidant procyanidins, found also in pycnogenol.

A Canadian research group, in a carefully controlled study, found that a well balanced diet could reduce LDL cholesterol by 29%. They matched this against the results with a control group on statin drugs, and when all extraneous factors had been eliminated they found that the improvement with statins was 30.9%. The difference was not statistically significant. I am sure that many people with high LDL would prefer the dietary route to the statins route. The group on the diet ate large quantities of soluble fibre, almonds, soy protein and plant sterol-fortified margarine.

The optimum level of LDL and HDL cholesterol has been much debated over the years, and the tendency in the last few years has been to lower the LDL threshold in particular, as well as the overall cholesterol level, while reducing concerns about the HDL level and HDL as a percentage of total cholesterol (which includes VLDL – very low density lipoprotein, incidentally). As with blood pressure and BMI, there has been a tendency to relax the limits as you get older. I'm not sure there is a good case for this. Averages may rise with age, but that is generally because older people are less active and have a slower metabolic rate. This does not make higher levels acceptable. If your overall cholesterol level is higher at 60 than it was when you were 30, age is not an excuse.

Cholesterol is measured in millimoles per litre (mmol/l). I'm looking at my cholesterol level in 1978 when I was 34 years old. Back then it was: 4.30 mmol/l (total cholesterol including VLDL); 0.88 mmol/l (HDL); 3.42 mmol/l (LDL and VLDL combined); HDL percentage 20.46%. In my last BUPA check-up at the age of 63 it was 3.40 mmol/l (total cholesterol including VLDL); 0.80 mmol/l (HDL); 2.60 mmol/l (LDL and VLDL combined); HDL percentage 24%. The average man in the UK has a total cholesterol count of 5.5 mmol/l.

My HDL figure may seem low in both sets of figures, and ideally, so it is said, it should be over 1. I've looked back over my track record on HDL and it looks as though it is usually about 0.9. In fact it has never been higher than 1. I've done all the things you are supposed to do to raise HDL. I've eaten lots of pectin and other forms of soluble fibre, I've taken niacin (vitamin B3) supplements, I've never stopped exercising all these years. The result is that my overall cholesterol count is better at 63 than it was at 34, and so is my LDL count. My conclusion is that there is little I can do about my HDL level. More to the point, I don't think it matters as long as the other figures are OK, which they are.

So what is an acceptable level for a man – at any age? The books will say that total cholesterol should be under 5. My view is that this should be between 4 and 5. The books say that LDL (including VLDL) should be under 4. I would make that between 3 and 4. If you can achieve these targets or better them, I don't think that it matters if your HDL level is over 1 (the recognized target) or under 1. The books say that your HDL should be at least 20% of your total cholesterol score. I used to think that mattered. I'm not so sure now. More and more experts now seem to agree that getting the HDL proportion higher is not that important. I'll be happy if my total cholesterol stays around 4 and my LDL stays around 3.

It's not generally appreciated that total cholesterol level can be too low as well as too high. Let's say that the optimum is 4.5 and the ideal range is between 4 and 5. The more you go above the optimum range, the more your chances of cardiovascular disease rise. However, the opposite also appears to be true – the more you go below 4, the more your chances of CVD rise, along with the risk of haemorrhagic stroke. Low cholesterol is not a problem facing many people, but it does happen.

Statin drugs have made a big difference in the last twenty years to the way in which high LDL cholesterol is tackled. Statins work by blocking the enzyme in the liver which produces LDL cholesterol. It's also claimed that they stabilize the lining of blood vessels by reducing inflammation. Statins are not only effective when they are taken. One report suggest that they may still be effective as long as ten years after they have stopped being taken, though the best results appear to be in those who take them for life. Some doctors have even advocated that all men over the age of 60 should take these drugs, regardless of their LDL cholesterol level. I don't go along with that.

Three and a half million people in the UK are now on statin drugs to control their cholesterol level, and as many again are thought to be in need of them. Statins not only lower cholesterol levels, but are also thought to relieve inflammatory conditions. They stabilize the endothelial lining of the arteries, thin the blood, stabilize arterial plaque and cut the risk of heart attack and stroke in those with high cholesterol levels. A quarter of all male deaths in the UK are attributable to heart disease, and for the medical profession and the NHS, statins have proved a life-saver. Yet one cannot help but get the feeling that these drugs are over-prescribed. While undoubtedly their effect is enhanced for many men by a healthy diet and plenty of exercise, for many others, it seems that they may be regarded as an excuse for continuing a lazy lifestyle, rather like a diet pill which might serve as an excuse to continue with junk food and zero exercise. If many people on statins ate well and exercised sufficiently throughout their lives, I am sure they could make a difference to their LDL and total cholesterol scores and perhaps have no more need of drugs.

The list of benefits attributed to statins seems to grow constantly, with Alzheimer's disease now added to the list of diseases which might benefit – by improving circulation in the brain. It's also suggested that stains might slow age-related macular degeneration (AMD) in the eyes, again by improving circulation. It has even been proposed that the whole population should take a so-called polypill, a combination of statin, aspirin and drugs that tackle high blood pressure. Supporters of this pill point out that it would reduce deaths from heart attacks and stroke, saving the NHS billions of pounds. What this ignores is that if more people live longer as a result, more people will be left to die from cancer, and ultimately the cost of treating cancer is higher than the cost of treating circulatory disorders.

There is no doubt that statins have saved many lives, some of which could not have been saved without the drugs. I'm not a great believer in pharmaceutical drugs. Generally, the more effective they are, the more side effects they have, and this is equally true of statins. They are known to cause muscular inflammation, pain and wasting in a small minority of people taking them. This is called rhabdomyolysis and in a few cases has led to kidney failure and death. There is some as yet limited evidence that statins may encourage the onset of Parkinson's disease, which suggests that LDL cholesterol may do good by influencing the uptake of the neurotransmitter dopamine, which is lacking in those with Parkinson's. There is limited but growing evidence that those taking statins may be at a slightly increased risk of cancer. There is also a risk of eyesight problems and even blindness as evidence suggests that statins may affect the amount of pigment in the retina called the macula lutea. This is interesting in view of the claim that statins may counter macular degeneration.

Further side effects are abdominal pain, skin rashes, insomnia, nausea and diarrhoea. And statins may interact negatively with other drugs. They are also alleged to block the body's ability to make the important anti-oxidant co-enzyme Q10.

There is a drug on the market called Ezetrol (ezetimibe), designed to be taken with statins to reduce the side effects, or even taken on its own if statins cannot be tolerated or are not effective enough. This drug is taken with a smaller dose of the statin, and it is this reduction in dosage which reduces the statin's side effects. Ezetrol works at the same time to boost the effectiveness of the statin.

Statins can cause changes for the worse in liver function, the liver being the organ in which cholesterol is formed. It is known that an exceptionally low LDL cholesterol score, generated for example by starvation (ketosis), can compromise the immune system, and it may be that the cholesterol-lowering effect of statins carries the same downside risk. This begs the question: Does this risk come from a lowered level of LDL or is this a side effect of the statin drugs? As yet, nobody knows. We do know that the lower the level of LDL achieved by statins, the higher the cancer risk, although this increased risk is relatively limited. Where liver damage is concerned, the greater the statin dosage, the greater the risk. However, dosage does not appear to make a difference to the degree of muscle wasting, if it occurs at all.

About 7,000 lives are said to be saved by statins each year. They don't tend to have much effect on HDL, but they do lower LDL, which is more important. As I've said, they reduce arterial inflammation and thus the risk of plaque rupture, as well as plaque formation in the first place. They reduce the risk of stroke as well as heart attack. It has been suggested that they are cardioprotective even for people whose cholesterol scores are normal, though as with taking aspirin as a preventive measure when there is no high risk of a heart attack, I would suggest that this is a measure too far. If cholesterol is high, though, taking statins regularly will cut the risk of a heart attack by a quarter. The drugs may be for life, however, which is the other reason why I am not too enthusiastic. And recent research suggests that if you quit taking the drugs, you are at more risk of a cardiovascular event than if you had never taken them in the first place. One study has demonstrated that about half of those on statins have stopped taking them within two years out of laziness and boredom. This is a common problem with any long term drug treatment, especially if there is no visible outward sign by which to judge a positive outcome.

Five percent of men over the age of 70 suffer from atrial fibrillation, an irregular heartbeat that can occasionally be life-threatening. The condition can induce fatigue, palpitations, shortness of breath, as well as increasing the possibility of a stroke. Statins have been found to help the condition.

Another study has suggested that statins may cut the risk of Alzheimer's disease by as much as 79%, and reduce the risk even in those not genetically susceptible to Alzheimer's. About 700,000 people in the UK suffer from dementia, of whom about two-thirds have Alzheimer's. Guidance from the National Institute for Health and Clinical Excellence (NICE) suggests that as many as 7,000 lives could be saved each year from cardiovascular disease and stroke if everyone who could benefit from statins were to take them. This would increase the number of people on statins in the UK to over six million. For many people, unfortunately , their introduction to statins comes only after they have suffered a heart attack, angioplasty or bypass surgery.

It probably sounds as though I am saying that no one needs statins if they are prepared to eat right and exercise enough. That would be to deny the fact that cholesterol levels may have a genetic component. About 100,000 people in the UK suffer from hypercholesterolaemia, a hereditary disease marked by a cholesterol level that is life- threatening in youth and middle age. This is normally tackled with statins and in some cases by removing the patient's blood, filtering two-thirds of the cholesterol out of it and putting it back again. As you would expect, this is expensive and not very practical, though it does work.

For those who have marginally high cholesterol (say a score between 5 mmol/l and 6 mmol/l) I would say statins should not be prescribed unless every attempt to bring the level down by diet and exercise has failed. However, for those with a score over 6 and especially if it is over 7, I would recommend a combination of diet, exercise and statins. Statins on their own without healthy eating and exercise should not be an excuse for anyone. Those with elevated cholesterol scores already have one of the factors that define the metabolic syndrome, the group of symptoms considered predictive of Type 2 diabetes (T2D). Most sufferers from this, the commonest type of diabetes, are said to be insulin-resistant, and one of the benefits of statins not directly related to cholesterol is that allegedly they reduce insulin resistance (see chapter 15 on diabetes).

Research has come up with a product said to be on its way to being introduced into yoghurt, an ingredient that will grab cholesterol in the gut and ensure its removal from the body. This sounds risky to me. Cholesterol has a job to do in every cell in the body and if this process is disturbed, the outcome could be worse than a furred artery.

With all the focus on cholesterol, it is easy to forget about triglycerides, the other blood fats that are usually measured in an annual check-up or a general blood screen. A high level tends to go with a high cholesterol level. The ideal should be a level less than 1.9 mmol/l. Someone with high blood fat levels is three times more likely to suffer from cardiovascular disease than someone whose levels are normal. If there is high blood pressure, the risk rockets. Statins do not bring down triglyceride levels. In fact, in one study of statins, they actually went up as cholesterol levels went down. It turned out that this was because, relying on the statins to lower their cholesterol, the patients had relaxed and eaten more fattening foods than ever before, thinking that they were protected by the drugs. This clearly shows one of the risks, albeit an avoidable one, of prescribing statins to an increasingly exercise-averse and self-indulgent population.

Various foods are believed to raise HDL cholesterol level. These include rice bran oil, oat bran, apple pectin and psyllium fibre. The lycopene in tomatoes is believed to lower LDL cholesterol level, though to get the maximum benefit, the tomatoes should be cooked and the seeds crushed, as the most lycopene is found in the seeds. Exercise raises HDL cholesterol level slightly, as does vitamin B3 (niacin), which allegedly lowers triglyceride level at the same time.

Low strength statins are now available without prescription. Self-administration of statins without advice from a doctor is probably unwise unless you are extremely well informed about what you are doing. Those in need of statins are said to be those deemed to have a 20% or greater risk of a cardiovascular event within the next ten years. Routine health screens such as the BUPA screens normally assess this risk.

....

More Tips and Traps

The causes of raised cholesterol levels are not always genetic or related to diet and exercise. An underactive thyroid, diabetes, and liver and kidney disorders can all be responsible for a raised level of LDL.

Most foods of animal origin contain cholesterol, including fish, especially shellfish.

CHAPTER ELEVEN
FIGHTING COLDS AND FLU

The many cold and flu viruses mutate constantly, which is why it has never been possible to pin them down with a successful vaccine to prevent them, or with anti-viral drugs to get rid of them the way that antibiotics can control bacterial infections. The body is still more sophisticated than medicine when it comes to viruses, but the search for working vaccines, whether for HIV or the common cold goes on. There are flu vaccines available, but the trouble is that they only work to a limited extent. By the time that the vaccine is triggering production of sufficient antibodies in our blood, the antigens in the virus will have moved on by a process of mutation called antigenic drift (or antigenic shift in the case of Type A viruses) and our antibodies will no longer be a perfect match for the antigens in the virus. If there is an outbreak of bird flu on a pandemic scale, as expected, any vaccine produced will benefit by being manufactured as fast as possible to get a better match of antibody and antigen.

People over 65 are advised to get a flu jab at the beginning of each winter. This is because older people have a weaker immune system than younger people. At the same time their response to any vaccine declines with age. In the old and infirm, flu can be a fatal illness. The vaccines on the market are produced as fast as possible each year, based on the latest known strains of Influenza A, which have pandemic potential, and Influenza B, which are limited to humans and have epidemic potential, but even so, they will come too late to be a perfect fit for any virus they encounter. The point of such vaccines is that they will afford some protection as the fit may not be perfect but hopefully there will still be a partial match. Fewer people will get flu and those who get it will have milder symptoms.

Those in the 50–65 age range as well as the elderly would be well advised to get a flu jab each autumn, especially if they have asthma, a heart condition, chronic liver, kidney or lung disease, or diabetes. Those whose spleen has been removed or who live in care homes where there is increased risk of flu being passed on are also advised to have the flu vaccine, as are those on immunosuppressant drugs, including steroids, and those who are immune-deficient from HIV. The most important thing is to avoid bronchial pneumonia (pneumococcal pneumonia) that can be the most serious secondary consequence of catching flu. If you do have a damaged spleen or no spleen at all (asplenia), if you have sickle cell disease, or if you have impaired kidney function, it can be advisable to have a second dose of the flu vaccine. However, the annual flu vaccine, given to 15 million in the UK, has its critics who say that because viruses mutates so rapidly, the vaccines are not effective and therefore a waste of money. The balance of evidence at present suggests that the vaccines do have some positive effect, and anyway, it's better to be safe than sorry.

Flu jabs are not without their problems since the discovery that they increase by 150% the risk of getting Guillain–Barré syndrome, a neurological disease in which the immune system attacks part of the nervous system. The symptoms may be only a tingling in the limbs, but in the worst cases there may be paralysis. About 1,500 people get this illness each year in the UK. However, the risk to any one individual is still so low that the upside of having the flu jab makes it worthwhile. It takes 10–14 days to become fully effective, so it's wise to get it done early on, say in October. Flu epidemics usually occur in December, January and February, and protection from the immunisation lasts up to 12 months.

False flu is the name given to a virus which many sufferers from the winter blues assume to be flu. In fact it's a particular cold virus which reaches into the chest, causing bronchitis. The technical name for this virus is respiratory syncytial virus (RSV). It is on the increase in the UK each winter, and when summer weather conditions mimic those of winter, it can appear in summer too. It produces slight aches and shivers, as well as a lot of mucus, and it can take several weeks to disappear. A secondary (bacterial) infection is common and the sufferer can be left feeling weak and fairly helpless. RSV is common among infants, most of whom catch it before the age of two. However, if, like me, you become a father in your sixties, you are prone to catching this virus from your child along with several others.

A recent discovery is that some obesity may be triggered by or made worse by a virus, strictly speaking an adenovirus known as Ad-36 which can change adult stem cells in fat tissue into fully developed fat cells. Researchers emphasize that obesity has multiple causative factors, of which this is only one, and only affects some obese people. They also emphasize that not all people who have the virus will necessarily become obese.

Influenza is a serious illness and shares many of its symptoms with the common cold. There are three broad types of flu virus, divided into A, B and C. Type A is the most dangerous.

With flu you are more likely to experience shivering, aches and pains and a raised temperature than you are with just a cold. The search for an antiviral drug to treat those with flu has led an American team of researchers to unravel the structure of a nucleoprotein (NP) found in all the most dangerous forms of the flu virus, including H5N1, which is avian flu, better known as bird flu. The main flu antivirals presently on the market are Tamiflu, Relenza and Peramivir, and these are still the best line of defence against a bout of flu, not just bird flu, once it has been contracted. If you keep a stock just in case – and the government has stocked enough Tamiflu for 25% of the UK population – you should be aware that their shelf life is about five years. However, it's not likely that any of these drugs will give more than limited protection against bird flu in the event of a pandemic. They might, however, make the difference between a bad attack and death. In the meantime it is hoped that the nucleoprotein unravelled in the US will lead to a more effective antiviral drug for flu.

Tamiflu has the advantage over Relenza that it penetrates the brain, thereby, in theory, giving it protection. The risk is that those protected by Relenza in an avian flu pandemic might survive with brain damage, while survivors who used Tamiflu as an antiviral will recover completely.

Is it worth wearing a mask if there is a bird flu pandemic? The answer is maybe if you are in close proximity to others who might have caught the virus. Various masks are available for a variety of purposes, but none is totally effective against the airborne particles that constitute a flu virus. That said, there is nothing to lose by wearing one if the time comes, and the best bet would be a surgical mask, the most effective being marked N-95.

Finding a working vaccine against colds and flu has been one of the Holy Grails of medical research for decades. There have been many false starts. Now there is renewed hope for a vaccine that the makers believe may give protection against Type A influenza, which includes bird flu. It's called Acam-Flu-A, and it claims to work by training the immune system to recognize and target a peptide called M2E that is found on the surface of all A-strains of flu, and that doesn't constantly mutate, thereby overcoming the main problem with cold and flu vaccines. The vaccine is stable, can be manufactured from a cell culture (not fertilised chicken eggs) and can be stockpiled for years, rather than having to be produced at the last minute once a new strain of flu has been identified, by which time it is usually too late to attack it with a vaccine. The important point about the M2E peptide is that it doesn't mutate at all, or, at worst, only minimally, therefore any minor mutations could be taken care of with matching vaccine. The makers hope that by adding an adjuvant called QS-21 to boost antibody production, and possibly also a further vaccine to tackle B-strains, they will have come up with an effective replacement for the current annual flu vaccines, as well as a reliable protective measure in the event of a bird flu pandemic. If the vaccine fails to work by preventing infection, it is still hoped that it will reduce the severity of a virus in people who are infected, thereby working with antibodies already generated and so becoming an antiviral.

To avoid winter flu and colds, here are a few tips: While it's good to leave the bedroom windows wide open at night in summer, close them except an inch or two at the bottom in winter. This leaves a small amount of moist air getting in for ventilation, but prevents too much damp and cold from getting in. Viruses thrive in cold damp conditions, but do not like cold dry air. Your lungs will function best in slightly warm slightly moist air, which is what they are likely to get with the windows open in summer. But in winter central heating can be a problem, since it dries the atmosphere. This is why it's best to leave the windows open slightly to let in a degree of damp – and some cold, for that matter, as a room that is too stuffy and too warm is not healthy either. The air in your bedroom in winter should be slightly damp and not too warm. If it's too cold though, you could be inviting angina or an asthma attack if you are susceptible. Turning the heating down and leaving the window slightly open should give you optimum conditions for a good night's rest in the months when you are most at risk of picking up a cold or flu virus.

....

More Tips and Traps

One way to distinguish flu from a cold, apart from the level of severity, is that flu usually strikes suddenly whereas a cold develops slowly.

Influenza doubles the risk of a heart attack

CHAPTER TWELVE
CONTRACEPTION AND THE OLDER MALE

Most men in middle life are likely to be beyond the age when they wish to father children, though many will do so in their forties and some at a later age. Men have been known to father children in their eighties and even in their nineties in one or two rare cases. A willing and younger partner may, however, not always be available. Chances are that you are still fertile and if your female partner is under fifty, contraception is still a relevant subject, unless you have abandoned sex altogether, which some couples will have done at some stage of middle life.

The easy solution for men who want to run no risk of an unwanted pregnancy is to have a vasectomy. This is an easy and relatively painless operation which can, with difficulty, be reversed at a later date, as sometimes happens when there is a subsequent relationship, usually with a younger woman who wants a family. My concern with vasectomy is that it may lead to loss of self-image as a man. This is a psychological matter and whether it happens or not will depend a lot on the individual. While vasectomy does not affect erectile function physically, it could affect it psychologically, causing impotence. Fertility is normally unimpaired, but obviously the ability to impregnate has been removed if the vasectomy has been correctly performed. Drugs like Viagra and Cialis can solve the erection problem and have only minor side effects.

Many men have heard women complain that it should not just be the woman who takes care of contraception. Women who may have taken some form of the contraceptive pill in their twenties and thirties are unlikely to extend its use beyond about ten to fifteen years for fear of long-term side effects. Many who have taken the pill go on eventually to use a diaphragm, a well-known passion-killer since it spoils the spontaneity of sex and has a fairly high failure rate. On the other hand, for men, using condoms year in and year out can feel like a life sentence and also serve as a passion-killer. It is often the problems associated with contraception that lead to sex becoming less frequent and eventually drying up altogether.

Both sexes find that their libido declines with stress, and stress often translates as long hours at work. That is one reason why it is estimated that men and women are not as sexually excitable as they once were. More women are working and both sexes now put in longer hours than ever before. When you are worn out at the end of the day, sex is often the least appealing option for something to do. It's usually easier to reach for the TV remote. Often the problem can be more clearly defined than that. It may be that the man is stressed by work to the point of suffering from hyperprolactinaemia, an excessive output of prolactin from the pituitary gland, the result of which is reduced testosterone, libido and fertility. The woman in his life may also suffer from an excess of circulating prolactin with the result that she too loses her libido.

However, one piece of research concludes that in only 1% of cases is hyperprolactinaemia responsible for low libido. Prolactin level is now a routine part of an assessment for male erectile dysfunction. In some cases a high level is accompanied by male breast formation. Hyperprolactinaemia in mild form is likely to be a stress reaction, but in more severe form it can be linked to an overabundance of the glandular tissue prolactinoma, which produces prolactin in the pituitary gland. The larger the prolactinoma mass, the greater the production of prolactin. A micro prolactinoma is less than 10 mm in diameter, while a macro prolactinoma is over that size. A macro prolactinoma may produce over ten times the upper end of the normal scale for prolactin. There may be other non-sexual effects, such as pressure on cranial nerves like the optic nerve. When this happens, vision may be double or blurred. Intracranial pressure may rise, causing headaches. There are a number of drugs on the market for lowering prolactin levels, the newest of which have few side effects. If hyperprolactinaemia is identified as a problem in your sex life, at least there is a cure. However, the disease, if it can be called that, is not a reliable form of contraception. Should intercourse ensue, despite the low testosterone level, hyperprolactinaemia will not prevent conception. For that, a contraceptive will still be needed.

Condoms to prevent STIs (sexually transmitted infections) are important at any age. Apparently STIs are on the increase in older age groups as a result of the erroneous assumption that only young people catch diseases like gonorrhoea, herpes and Chlamydia. Even syphilis is making a comeback. And many travellers of all ages will be putting themselves at risk of STIs and even HIV by indulging in sex with prostitutes while away on holiday or business.

This is not the place for a discussion of contraceptives for women but I'll mention long-acting reversible contraceptives (LARC), which are implants lasting up to three years, and the intrauterine system, which can last up to five years. The downside of these is mainly the long time required for normal fertility to return after withdrawal of the device. But look out one day in the future for a new non-hormonal contraceptive for women that is likely to become available in about a decade. It relies on what is called RNA interference. RNAi will target the ZP3 gene, switching it off so that the zona pellucida coating on the outside of a maturing female egg is not formed, thereby preventing sperm from binding to the egg and fertilizing it. If that sounds complex, it is. But maybe, as hoped, it means that one day there will be a reliable female contraceptive applied in a monthly patch, and there will be no more risks and side effects. What's more, contraception should be easily reversible, making conception readily available again at fairly short notice.

A male contraceptive pill has been talked about for years, but none trialled so far has proved reliable and successful. If all else fails and you want absolute spontaneity, there is still the old fashioned solution of last minute withdrawal. Be aware that there is a small amount of seminal discharge prior to male orgasm and this may contain sufficient sperm to cause conception.

CHAPTER THIRTEEN
COUNSELLING AND PSYCHOTHERAPY

It used to be said that when women got depressed they went to a counsellor or psychotherapist, but that when a man got depressed he started drinking more alcohol. In the medical world the general view is that men are just as likely to be depressed as women, but women are twice as likely to seek professional help. Fifteen percent of men still attach a stigma to the idea of any form of mental illness.

There are tens of thousands of counsellors in the UK and several thousand psychotherapists. As our standard of living has risen in the last sixty years, our level of happiness has declined according to a number of reports. On in four of us will suffer from depression at some time in our lives and at any one time it's said that one in six of us is depressed. However, only one in four of this number is receiving treatment. Social class doesn't appear to make any difference. Mental illness accounts for 30% of visits to doctors and 40% of those on incapacity benefit have a mental illness. The annual cost to the UK economy is estimated at £12 billion.

It gets worse. Eighty percent of GP's admit that pressure of time and work leads them to write more prescriptions for anti-depressant pills than they know they should, and the volume is growing. There are now fewer unemployed people seeking job seeker's allowance than there are people on incapacity benefit.

You could say there was a mental health crisis, and if you look for reasons, they are not hard to find in our fragmented society with its ever-accelerating drive towards material things, which have come to masquerade as our 'standard of living'. When people had fewer luxuries fifty years ago they were generally happier. But then society and the family had not been torn apart by the decline in authority, self-discipline and responsibility that is the unfortunate result of an over-bountiful welfare state.

Why does anyone need to see a counsellor or therapist and will it do much good, compared with just taking pills? I spent three years training part-time as a counsellor and I hope I am qualified to answer. Most people who seek counselling are suffering from depression and anxiety resulting from stress, psychological and/or physical trauma, bereavement, relationship problems, job loss or general dissatisfaction with their lives, low self-esteem, loneliness or the problems of facing old age, declining health and death.

Counselling tends to be short-term, goal-oriented and typically involves talking to an empathic listener who will reflect back what the client has said in a way that will lead the client to insights and hopefully a degree of relief. A counsellor's job is not to offer advice. The client must find their own way in the end, with the counsellor acting as catalyst. A typical counselling process might last from ten to twenty weekly sessions.

A therapist tends to take on deeper and more complicated problems. Therapy may be open-ended and last for weeks, months and sometimes years, and goals may be only vaguely defined, but emerge more clearly in the course of the treatment. Therapists may or may not have medical qualifications, but, in the UK, are unlikely to be medically qualified, whereas in the US, it may be a prerequisite for some governing bodies, and many therapists will be qualified psychiatrists. In the UK, few psychiatrists practise psychotherapy, though they may refer patients to a therapist where they feel this is appropriate. Not surprisingly, GP's and psychiatrists are seen by many in the UK as relying too heavily on pills to cure the problems of the mind.

Therapists who follow in the footsteps of Freud and his many derivative schools are said to practise a psychodynamic form of therapy, which means broadly that they look for a 'cure' through the exploration of the client's past and present relationships with others, including the therapist. Psychodynamic treatments tend to be lengthy and may involve any number of visits per week for an indeterminate length of time. The client may sit facing the therapist or lie on a couch, the latter being encouraged on the grounds that it improves the quality of free association and the therapeutic insights which result.

The other widespread approach is known as the humanistic. It tends to focus on the 'here and now' rather than the past, and treatment normally tends to be shorter.

A third approach that doesn't really fit either category is a school on its own called cognitive behaviour therapy (CBT). Treatment tends to be short (generally between ten and twenty sessions) and goal-oriented, and to target specific problems by confronting negative mindsets in an attempt to turn them, progressively, into a positive position. Its critics would argue that it tackles symptoms rather than underlying causes. CBT has become very popular in recent years, especially as it is often effective in treating milder cases of depression, as well as anxiety and obsessive-compulsive disorders.

No form of therapy is considered effective in the treatment of the psychoses, and only modest results have been achieved with the group of mental illnesses classified as personality disorders, though these may improve spontaneously over a period of many years.

Freud believed he could analyse himself and did so. Self-therapy isn't for everyone, but if you are particularly well informed, by reading, for example, it may work for you, but I suspect that most people will have more luck by sharing their problems with another human being. In fact it is this sharing process that is part of the reason why therapy can and often does work, and why talking to some-one, even if they say little or nothing in return, often produces change for the better. To that extent, a 'cure' may be said to be brought about psychosomatically, though critics of psychotherapy are inclined to take a sceptical view and suggest that a cure would have occurred anyway over time. Studies on the effectiveness of therapy have been inconclusive.

One problem with therapy, though, is getting someone to 'see someone'. Men are especially difficult to convince, despite the breaking down of masculine stereotypes and associated prejudices in recent years. It's often those who are half-way to being cured anyway who see someone, while those most in need remain resistant and 'in denial'. Research shows that if you pay for your treatment yourself and this requires some degree of financial sacrifice, the chances of a positive outcome are greater. Perhaps this is one reason why free counselling on the NHS would not be a good thing for everyone.

Within the framework of humanistic therapy lies group therapy, in which people with a common problem (for example, alcohol or eating disorders) discuss their issues with the help of a facilitator, who will tend to be a trained therapist. Couples, usually with relationship problems, may go through couples counselling or therapy.

Within the psychodynamic and humanistic approaches are many schools. Breakaways from Freud gave us the schools of Jung and Adler, among others, and later Melanie Klein, Anna Feud and D.W. Winnicott. In recent decades in the US there has been great interest in the object relations school, whose main proponent is Otto Kernberg. A simplified version of Freudian analysis is transactional analysis, made famous by the book *Games People Play*.

The humanistic approaches have not always had a good reputation, many being too outlandish for some people. The more orthodox humanistic approaches have included, in particular, Gestalt, client-centred therapy, transpersonal therapy and psychosynthesis.

There is now a whole range of what might vaguely be called holistic therapies to choose from, though some are better termed 'treatments'. There are many kinds of meditation, some of which appear to be excellent ways of training the brain to function better, focusing our lives in the present rather than the past or future. Meditation also calms and relaxes by stimulating the parasympathetic nervous system, countering its opposite, the sympathetic nervous system, which is stimulated by stress and the stress hormones cortisol, adrenaline and noradrenaline. Meditation, in this way, strengthens the immune system. Hatha yoga, with its emphasis on breathing and postures, can have the same effect.

Transcendental meditation (TM) was made popular by the Beatles in the Sixties. Since then, western interest in meditation practices derived from Hindu forms of worship has declined somewhat, but interest in Buddhism has grown, not least because of the advantages that come from Buddhist meditating techniques. Whereas TM aims to balance the left and right hemispheres of the brain and produce more alpha rhythms, Buddhist meditation aims to move brain activity from the right to the left frontal cortex and calm the amygdala, the forebrain structure that is activated by fear and other negative emotions. This process produces happiness rather than anxiety and depression and can be objectively measured. With enough meditation, the brain's 'set point' can be changed in favour of a more permanent positive outlook. Production of serotonin, the 'happy' neurotransmitter is increased and there is some evidence that the immune system is boosted.

The spiritual message from Buddhism is that it's what's inside our heads, not out there in the world, that makes us happy or sad. If we are happy, negative thoughts and feelings such as greed and envy are displaced by wisdom, compassion and generosity.

Other therapies include hypnotherapy, music therapy, dance therapy and art therapy, all of which will work for some clients, if not for all, simply because the mind/body relationship is so powerful that belief in the efficacy of a treatment is enough to produce a cure. Without it we would not have the placebo effect whereby inert substances are able to produce a cure simply on the basis of conviction.

In the last century and a half, the power of the mind to influence the body has been increasingly recognized. Doctors are well aware that many of the symptoms presented to them by patients are a direct conse-quence of stress, anxiety and depression. These can take many forms visible on the outside, such as skin complaints like hives and psoriasis, or breathing difficulties triggered by, for example, a panic attack. Internally there may be a wide range of symptoms measurable by tests of blood, urine, saliva and hair. Symptoms betoken illness and some illnesses produced by mental problems can be every bit as debilitating as any with a more physical cause. Heart disease can be triggered by stress, and we now know that cancer isn't just something that happens to you – what we eat, how we exercise and how happy or unhappy we are all play a part.

Psychosomatic illness is a branch of medicine that goes right back to the great French alienist Charcot, who demonstrated the power of the mind over the body with exhibitions of hypnotism using 'hysterical' women patients who would produce so-called conversion symptoms on demand, usually a paralysis of arms or legs that was all too real.

Psychosomatic illness is illness that produces real bodily symptoms. These should not be confused with the imaginary symptoms which are the delusional belief of the true hypochondriac. Often the cause of symptoms will be a crossover between psychosomatic and purely somatic (soma: the body in Greek), in which case doctors speak of a psychological overlay. Unsurprisingly, depression is often at the root of psychosomatic disorders. Unfortunately, not enough counsellors and therapists in the UK are medically trained.

Nowadays many counsellors and some therapists are generalists who do not belong to any 'school', and for many the lines between the psychodynamic and the humanistic have become blurred, the emphasis being laid on whatever works, no matter where it comes from. Hence many counsellors and therapists would describe their approach as eclectic. It's generally acknowledged that the 'fit' between therapist and client is more important than the therapist's 'school'.

The grounds for seeing a counsellor or therapist are usually stress, anxiety, depression and often intense feelings of anger and guilt, especially following a bereavement.

If you think you need counselling or therapy, where do you start? There are good and bad therapists and counsellors, just as there are good and bad doctors, and even the good ones are never perfect. You can turn to friends and family for recommendations, or you can call one of several governing bodies. Your doctor may be able to refer you to someone, though this is not a guarantee you will find the right person. The governing organisations may refer you to someone in your area to either become your counsellor or therapist, or to refer you on to someone they recommend in the area. The latter process is more likely to occur if it's a therapist you are looking for, and not a counsellor.

Which raises the question: counsellor or therapist? There's no easy answer, but as a rule of thumb, a counsellor is probably a better bet for a specific problem such as a bereavement or a medical trauma, while a therapist may be a better option for a more generalized (and probably deeper) problem such as long term depression. Depression is often accompanied by anxiety. You may feel your life is stressed to the point where you can no longer cope. You may even feel suicidal. It's important to realize that depressive tendencies run in families. Your depression may be endogenous, that is, you may have inherited a tendency to be dour and depressed, regardless of the vagaries of life. Or your depression may be exogenous, that is, it is a response to an identifiable outside problem. In fact, the two types of depression are not nearly as distinct from one another as some text books like to make out. You my react to a divorce by becoming depressed and that would be classified as an exogenous depression, with a good chance of a successful outcome to treatment (which might well include anti-depressant drugs and therapy or counselling in combination). More difficult to treat is long term chronic depression which is likely to be endogenous, or may be exogenous depression that failed to dissipate even though the trigger that caused it is only a memory. When depression verges on the psychotic, as it sometimes does, therapy is often unsuccessful, though the fact of seeing someone and being listened to may be enough to save the depressed person from suicide.

Knowing how to deal with feeling anxious and low is a complicated matter. If you have not got a clue about where to turn for help, your doctor will be the best starting point. If friends tell you that a stiff upper lip is the answer, ignore them. Just because you cannot see depression in the way that you can see a broken arm doesn't mean that it isn't a serious illness. Indirectly, depression can kill. It can lead to self-neglect which in turn can lead to a litany of illnesses, such as osteoporosis, which can lead to a hip fracture, which can be the root cause of a fatal pulmonary embolism. I know from experience, as that is how my mother died at the age of fifty-nine, twelve years after a divorce which set in train a chronic depression from which she never recovered. She did not have counselling or therapy, and the tricyclic antidepressant drug that she was given, apart from changing her personality, only postponed the inevitable. It's my view, with the benefit of hindsight, that good therapy might have saved her.

I say good therapy because therapy can be good, bad or indifferent and you will never be absolutely sure which is the right description for what you received. No counsellor or therapist will tell you that they are bad at their job. If you get a bad counsellor they may not help you, but in ten or twenty sessions it's unlikely they will do you a lot of harm either. Not so, however, with therapy that lasts for months or longer and digs that much deeper. Some research studies appear to show that most successful outcomes from therapy would have resulted positively anyway over the course of time, without any intervention. That may be so, but my own view, having been a client with three therapists (all psychodynamic) is that a good therapist can make a difference.

Only you will be able to judge if your counsellor or therapist is good for you. There is no really objective way of measuring the outcome. You should be able to tell after a few sessions whether you and he/she have a good 'fit', as they say in the trade. That doesn't mean someone who indulges you to make you feel good. Often they will practise 'tough love' in their role of surrogate parent and there will be times when you may feel quite hostile to them. Your judgment of whether the treatment is working or not is best guided by your sense of whether there is what is called 'movement' in your treatment. Are you stuck or is there movement?

Clients always wonder how they can possibly judge their therapist. You don't question the quality of the work done by your brain surgeon, at least not from a position of superior knowledge, so how can you do so when it comes to your therapist? In the end, you can't, you can only trust your intuition, read a few books on the therapeutic process, and quit if you think the treatment is not moving forwards or is even going backwards. Bear in mind, however, that therapy can get stalled for lengthy periods and this doesn't necessarily mean you should quit. If you are going through a lot of emotional pain as your buttons are pushed, that is a good sign, more often than not. Your therapist will probably see any wish to quit as part of your problem. Either way, my advice is to become as well informed as possible about therapy and then follow your instinct. There are not a lot of bad therapists, but one who is bad for you is not worth sticking with. Quit and find another.

I have tended to use counselling and therapy as interchangeable terms. They are not, though often the difference is only one of degree. Therapists tend to have trained for longer, and as I've said, they tend to dig deeper and the treatment will probably last longer, with sessions that are more frequent in the week. Therapists may also be slightly more expensive. Counsellors and therapists are more likely to be women, especially counsellors. Does it make a difference? In theory it doesn't. In practice I think it does, and whether you should see someone of your own sex or the opposite sex will depend a lot on you and your problem, and, just to make things more complicated, it will also depend on the particular counsellor or therapist. In other words, the particular counsellor or therapist may, in many cases, be more important than what sex they are. I have had one female therapist and two male therapists. The woman was, I thought, excellent, and so was one of the men, but not the other, whom I quit after two months.

One thing we can be sure of – as the western world we live in gets more materialistic, and technology makes greater demands on our psyches, demand for therapeutic services that heal the mind will continue to grow. If the answer lay only in a pill, pills would have taken over by now. But pills always have side effects and the current generation of anti-depressants is no exception. Some may even be dangerous. There is an important place for the talking cure and there is a place for the pill, and very often there is a place for a combination of the two.

DIETARY SUPPLEMENTS: FADS AND FACTS

The question is often asked: 'Are supplements necessary at all if I eat a healthy diet?' As far as I am concerned, the jury is still out. Until we know what makes for a perfect diet, we won't know whether we might benefit by supplementation or not. In the meantime, I take the position that even the healthiest diet might benefit from well-informed supplementation. In the UK, 43% of the population take supplements at some point in the year, many if not most on a regular basis.

While some men will take dietary supplements as a general health insurance, others will take them to treat, hopefully, a specific medical condition. For example, glucosamine sulphate is widely taken to treat stiff and achy joints, and Saw Palmetto (see chapter 43 on the prostate) is used to treat benign prostatic hyperplasia (BPH). These two supplements are possibly the most widely taken in the western world after general 'multi' supplements containing vitamins and minerals. However, both, according to authoritative recent reports, fail to achieve their intended results. It's this kind of finding that leads me to say that the jury is still out. If we are healthily sceptical, who do we listen to, who is the authority, what dose should we take and of what? Do we need more selenium as we get older? Can we get all we need from what we eat and drink? How much is too much and might it be dangerous?

There are plenty of books and websites claiming to know just how much of supplement X you need to cure ailment Y. Ask yourself how they know this. When you read this chapter, note that I have tried to be careful about the supplements I mention. I'm relying on some of the best authorities I can find, and I'm often quoting my own experience, but I've been careful never to sound like an authority, because I'm not one, and neither is anyone else when it comes to supplements. So what I write usually comes with a proviso or a 'maybe'.

Recently a study came up with the news that by taking supplements of vitamins A and E, and beta carotene, you could shorten your life, even if you only took the recommended dosage – not megadoses. Vitamin A was reported to increase the risk of death by 16% (by 7% in the form of beta carotene – the body converts beta carotene to vitamin A) and vitamin E by 4%. Considering that billions of pounds are spent worldwide on supplements, mostly vitamins, this was worrying news. The only good news was that contrary to other reports, the trace mineral selenium was no longer deemed a threat in reasonable doses. (See below).

Confused about supplements? If even the experts can't agree, what chance has the consumer? So one in three of us take supplements of this and that, not clear what they might be doing for us, but as 'insurance'. If they work, so much the better, and if they don't, at least, we assume, they won't be doing us any harm – we'll just be a bit poorer, that's all. Which is great news for the supplement manufacturing industry, which delights in adding a new ingredient every so often to the long list already appearing on the back of their multi-vitamin packaging, though many of these ingredients come in such small quantities that you have to wonder if they do us any good, even if they are absorbed. Anything I say in this chapter should not be taken with a pinch of salt, but a dose of scepticism, because the scientific data currently available to the multi-billion pound supplements industry is still sketchy and all too often biased by commercial interest.

Absorption is one of the biggest problems facing those who take supplements, even if they are in chelated or ester form (see below). According to one study, only 15% is absorbed on average – less if you are elderly. Pills kept for months or even years, even in a fridge, lose some of their potency over time. When you absorb nutrients naturally from food, they have the assistance of phyto-chemicals, natural bio-active substances, many of which have not yet been identified by science. (Phyto-therapy is treatment with natural remedies of plant origin). Synthesized supplements lack this advantage of nutrients absorbed directly from food. Polyphenols are anti-oxidants, natural substances that are examples of phyto-chemicals.

Taking megadoses of supplements as a cure for a disease not only won't work, but may prove to be dangerous. If you take supplements at all, take them in preventive doses, which are usually fairly small. For example, do not take more than 1000 grams of vitamin C a day. The idea that you should take 10,000 grams a day if you catch a cold has been disproved. It can help a bit, it has been found, but only in those under extreme stress, such as marathon runners. For most people, a large amount is more likely to leave you feeling bloated and give you diarrhoea, on top of your virus. According to one study, consistent megadoses of vitamin C may increase the risk of heart attack and stroke. Some vitamins can definitely be toxic in very large doses, and megadoses of vitamins A and D have been known to be fatal.

Older people may get too much manganese from a multi-vitamin and mineral supplement, and this may result in depression, nervous complaints and general fatigue. If they have a healthy diet, they will not need extra potassium or boron either. In fact the elderly should avoid supplements containing potassium as too much may trigger nausea, diarrhoea and stomach upset. Today's diets often lack enough of the trace mineral selenium, but correcting this dietary deficiency is easy without taking supplements. Selenium is a mineral which acts as an anti-oxidant and is said to boost the immune system, slow prostate cancer and Alzheimer's disease, support a healthy heart and fade liver spots. Don't take my word for it. If you have the choice between a dietary source of a nutrient and a supplement, always choose the dietary source. Selenium is found in Brazil nuts, a delicious addition to muesli and a rich source of healthy saturated and monounsaturated fat. You have to get some fat in your diet and since some of it should come from these two types of fat, why not from nuts and seeds, along with selenium if you eat Brazil nuts? Just don't eat too much if you're watching the calories. Nuts and seeds are calorie-dense.

There have been scare stories about excessive intake of vitamin B3 (niacin), vitamin B6, zinc, calcium, iron, chromium, and the herbal supplements Echinacea and St John's wort. Vitamin B6 in excess, for example, can cause peripheral nerve damage, leading to loss of feeling in the arms and legs. You can get plenty of vitamin B6 from cereals, bananas, potatoes and spinach, while broccoli, salmon, spinach and milk provide lots of calcium without the need for supplements. For chromium, you can rely on lentils, meat and whole grains, and for zinc, you'll find plenty in chicken, dairy products, beans, shellfish and pumpkin seeds. Don't worry about the cholesterol in shellfish. The food will do you a lot of good, just as eggs will, without you having to worry about a small amount of cholesterol.

Echinacea, which comes in nine varieties from North America, has gone through a popularity high in recent years before dipping on the discovery that maybe it isn't all it's cracked up to be, and may trigger an allergic reaction. The three key ingredients in Echinacea are chicoric acid, polysaccharides and alkamides. In combination they allegedly boost the immune system. As a preventive, though this is disputed, Echinacea can halve your chances of catching a cold, and once you have caught a virus, it does appear that Echinacea can shorten the duration and lessen the impact. As a preventive it seems to work for those with a weak immune system rather than those with normal to strong immunity. More research is needed to test the theory that Echinacea can do more harm than good.

Osteoporosis is a worry for men as well as women as they get older. For men, exercise that strengthens the bones is the best antidote, followed by dietary commonsense. Calcium and boron strengthen the bones, and plenty of boron is found in a normal diet. However, calcium may be lacking, especially if dairy products are avoided. Calcium supplements in moderation, alongside plenty of load-bearing exercise, may help to prevent osteoporosis, in which case vitamin D supplements (also in moderation) should be taken at the same time to aid absorption. Soy products like soy milk, tofu and tempeh are rich in isoflavones. On the one hand these help to build strong bones and are much favoured by post-menopausal women. The downside is that isoflavones mimic oestrogens, the female hormones, and that may reduce 'maleness' in men when, as they age, their testosterone level is already losing out to their oestrogen level (see chapter 20 on fertility and erectile function, and chapter 43 on the prostate).

Aspirin has been around for a very long time in the form of salicylic acid, a natural pain killer and anti-inflammatory. There are hints that it may help to prevent colon cancer, and its ability to help with cardiovascular complaints is well known (see chapter 41 onthe heart). How salicylic acid may help with colon cancer is still being teased out. Taking an aspirin won't help, but it seems that taking salicylic acid in a natural form can alter enzymes that are linked with the development of cancer in the colon. Salicylic acid is found naturally in some spices and in curry powder in particular. The dosage from food is small compared with taking an aspirin, but it may be enough, in food form, to build up a protective effect over time.

This effect may be produced in conjunction with capsaicin, which is the hot stuff in chilli peppers. It appears to cause apoptosis, which is cell death, including the death of cancerous cells in the early stages. Chilli capsaicin and mustard isothiocyanates also have the ability to speed up metabolism and therefore calorie burn rate, making them another addition to the array of possibilities for losing weight. Capsaicin and isothiocyanates dilate blood vessels and boost levels of the hormone ephedrine, which burns fat. Ginger, also spicy, is good for calming an upset stomach and reducing nausea. It boosts digestive juices and can neutralize stomach acid.

For a few years now, there has been a great deal of publicity surrounding probiotics, the so-called 'good' bacteria found naturally in the gut. Manufacturers have produced a wide range of probiotic drinks, mostly in the form of drinking yoghurt, as a panacea for a range of stomach complaints and as a way of restoring balance in intestinal flora following a course of antibiotics. They can also help tackle *Clostridium difficile* (*C. difficile*), the superbug which, along with MRSA, has acquired a reputation as a killer of the infirm and elderly in British hospitals – up to 10,000 a year. It's true to say that up to a quarter of hospital patients taking antibiotics fall victim to the gut infection *C. difficile*, though fortunately it's only fatal in a small proportion of cases and most sufferers will escape with a bout of diarrhoea. Nevertheless, treatment with appropriate probiotics as a preventive would probably cut the rate of infection considerably. The key probiotic is *bacteria Lactobacillus* in a strain that matches the disease.

For stomach ulcers, yoghurts containing *Lactobacillus acidophilus* and *Bifidobacterium Bb12* work most effectively. In particular they are an effective preventive against *Helicobacter pylori* (*H. pylori*), the cause of up to 85% of ulcers. Once the *H. pylori* bacterium has become established, however, the answer lies in a cocktail of antibiotics taken over two weeks, then ideally four weeks or more on probiotics to restore intestinal flora to balance and health. Another preventive against *H. pylori* is *Lactobacillus johnsonii*, marketed as LC1. It also works to prevent gastritis, which is inflammation of the stomach lining. For irritable bowel syndrome and bloating, try *Lactobacillus acidophilus*, *Lactobacillus plantarum* or *Lactobacillus casei*. The latter especially is found in a popular yoghurt drink available in supermarkets. Another probiotic that does a similar job, but seems better at strengthening the killer cells of the immune system, is *Lactobacillus casei Shirota*. It's also widely available in a one-shot container.

If intolerance of dairy foods is a problem because you lack the enzyme lactase and cannot digest lactose (milk sugar), two probiotics which come in soy yoghurt are the answer. These are *Streptococcus thermophilus* and *Lactobacillus bulgaricus*. It's been suggested that probiotics can even ward off cold viruses and the product on the market that can allegedly do this contains a combination of *Lactobacillus gasseri*, *Bifidobacterium bifidum* and a variety of other bifidobacteria.

Probiotic yoghurts and drinks should be kept in the fridge, and should be drunk completely once opened. After a course of antibiotics, it's a good idea to take probiotics every day for four or five weeks, though you could take them for the rest of your life and be the better for it. You don't have to take probiotics in the shape of yoghurts and drinks and this can be expensive. Taking a sachet of probiotics is cheaper and just as effective. You'll find that a quantity of 10 billion good bacteria per day is about right. If you take more than 20 billion, there is no added benefit. Don't take hot or cold drinks before or after taking probiotics, as this will make them ineffective.

One problem with probiotic drinks and yoghurts is that they do not contain enough good bacteria to make a difference. As I've suggested, there should be at least 10 billion to be worthwhile, and the most important bacteria for most people are lactobacilli and bifidobacteria. Even then there is another problem. Most of these good bacteria may be killed off on the way down your digestive tract. Good bacteria formed in the gut do not have to run this gauntlet. Another problem is that the bacteria you swallow may not be the right kind for the problem that you are taking them for.

Prebiotics are types of fibre, such as inulin, on which probiotics depend. They enhance the absorption of calcium, bolstering bone density while improving the health of the digestive tract. There are healthy natural sources of prebiotics in the form of fructo-oligosaccharide fibre, found in bananas onions, leeks, chicory, asparagus, chickpeas, peas, corn and whole wheat products. Prebiotic fibre is already being added to some types of bran-based breakfast cereal.

Bones are also strengthened by vitamin K, which activates proteins in our bones so that they take up calcium. Trans fat, the really 'bad' fat in many diets today, denatures vitamin K, preventing it from assisting in calcium absorption. Dark green vegetables such as spinach and broccoli are good sources of vitamin K. Silica, found in many foods, is essential for healthy bones once it is metabolised as silicon. There's no need for supplements as enough is found in most diets.

An anti-oxidant enzyme called glutathione, important for eye health, is synthesized in the body and can be found in whey protein. It contains the non-essential amino acid cysteine (not to be confused with homo-cysteine). It appears to be a very good indicator of biological age. The higher the level, the lower the age, when correlated with blood pressure, cholesterol level, BMI and body fat, along with incidence of heart disease, arthritis and diabetes. However, glutathione supplementation is ineffective as glutathione is poorly digested in the intestinal tract. It therefore serves as a guide to how young and healthy you are, rather than as something you should take to make you younger by warding off the ageing process. Grow fat on unhealthy foods or fall victim to airborne pollutants and your glutathione level will drop.

A journalist or supplement manufacturer invented the word 'super-food' and suddenly everyone was clamouring for the latest must-have food, usually one touted as having even more anti-oxidants than its predecessor. Thus we have goji berries (wolfberries), pomegranates, açai, guarana, mung bean sprouts, dulse, kombu, nori seaweed, Arctic wrack, wheatgrass, barley grass, chlorella, bee pollen, maca and spirulina. We've got cranberries, strawberries, papaya, blueberries, hempseeds, flaxseeds, cocoa nibs and argane oil. Then there's aloe vera, apple and grapefruit pectin, rice bran oil and many others, including the Omega oils. It seems as though another superfood comes along every month. One of the latest is coffee berry. One gram of coffee berry extract is said to contain as much anti-oxidant capacity as a pound and a half of blueberries.

How do you separate the science from the science fiction? It isn't easy. There are dozens of books about which supplements to take and what they will do for you? How do the writers know? Some are doctors and nutritionists (often in the field of alternative therapy) who prescribe them. Others are biochemists conducting scientific investigations. Some are journalists simply repeating what they have heard, often without much discrimination so long as it makes a good story.

What supplements do I take regularly myself, if any? Well I do take some – about sixteen at the moment – for insurance. I like to think that with the healthy diet I eat there is no need for supplementation. But I take the following just in case:

I take one multi- supplement with a list of ingredients as long as your arm. It's expensive. I do not know if the quantities of most of the ingredients are optimum. But then nobody does know. I do know that these supplements make my pee bright yellow, and I put that down to the turmeric which contains the ingredient curcumin, believed to be a strong anti-oxidant. Turmeric is a major ingredient in curry. Curcumin turmeric is said to be cardioprotective, to raise insulin level, to maintain joint health and to improve blood circulation in the brain.

Supplements like these tend to sell, after all, on how many ingredients they contain, rather than how much of each ingredient. The quantity of each ingredient may only be a token one. The longer the list, the more such supplements can sell for. Do I sound cynical? But unless someone can tell me that these supplements are doing me harm, I will take them 'just in case'.

Niacin (vitamin B3). Books have been written about this vitamin alone. It comes in various forms, some of which are probably more effective than others. However, some forms are 'denatured' (for example nicotinamide and nicotinic acid) and no longer have the magic ingredient that does what niacin is meant to do – act like a powerful anti-oxidant and raise HDL cholesterol (the so-called 'good' cholesterol) that will help to clear the LDL cholesterol (the so-called 'bad' cholesterol) from our furred-up arteries. Niacin, unless denatured, is notorious because it gives you a hot flush – a hot prickly sensation round the face and head. I didn't know this the first time I tried some – a double dose – and the ensuing reaction led me to believe I was having a stroke. I called an ambulance and they took me to hospital where they quickly (well actually not so quickly – I could have died by the time they got round to seeing me) concluded that it was a niacin reaction. Today the general view is that niacin is safe and that the hot flush is unthreatening. In fact, as you get used to niacin, the flush tends to disappear. Some say niacin is the best way of all, short of taking statins, to raise your HDL proportion – better even than exercise. However, niacin has its critics and some say it can cause liver damage if taken too long in large doses. The jury is still out on this. Natural sources of niacin are wheat flour, maize flour, chicken, pork, beef, milk and eggs.

Folic acid (folate). Folate is the natural B vitamin and folic acid is the synthetic form that comes as a supplement. It's well known as the must-have supplement for pregnant mothers if they want to make sure their babies do not have spina bifida. However, it's less well known that it works, allegedly, to lower the level of homocysteine (a metabolite of the amino acid methionine), which is good news for your arteries given the established link between raised homocysteine and cardiovascular problems. Folic acid supplements are often taken by elderly people based on claims that it may slow cognitive decline and Alzheimer's. However, there is now compelling evidence that this is not true. There are those who contend that folic acid is dangerous for the elderly and may cause neurological damage. It has been pointed out that the elderly often lack vitamin B12, and that taking folic acid supplements may mask this deficit, which is why it is always safest to take folic acid in combination with vitamin B12. Men with bowel cancer or leukaemia or a history of either, and men with rheumatism or blocked arteries are advised not to take folic acid supplements Natural sources of folate are broccoli, Brussels sprouts, peas, yeast extract, chickpeas, bananas, oranges and brown rice.

Glucosamine sulphate. Of all supplements, this is probably the one most often believed to work and to add something that your diet cannot give you. I take two grams a day and I can honestly say that I've had no bursitis and synovitis problems since. That isn't proof of anything, not scientific proof anyway, but I would not be without this supplement and neither would millions of others as they get older and their soft tissues become more vulnerable to tears. The supplement known as chondroitin does the same job. It's no better than glucosamine, yet costs several times as much. Glucosamine is probably the most widely taken non-vitamin/mineral supplement in the world and is widely endorsed by doctors. Despite the faith of so many people, there is one reasonably reliable study that suggests that glucosamine simply doesn't work.

Omega oils. These are the essential fatty acids. Omega 3 and Omega 6 are mainly polyunsaturated fatty acids (PUFAs), while Omega 9 (oleic acid) is mainly monounsaturated. I take a highly purified Omega 3 fish oil capsule daily in the ratio of four parts eicosapentaeinoic acid (EPA) to one part docosahexaenoic acid (DHA), these being the essential fatty acids that are metabolised from Omega 3 along with alpha linolenic acid (ALA). Where do the fish get their DHA and EPA? These fats that have become so popular originate in algae that come up through the marine food chain until eventually they are found in the flesh or liver of the fish that we eat. It's not surprising, therefore, that higher levels of DHA or EPA are found in wild fish than farmed fish. Very little DHA or EPA is found in tinned oily fish like salmon and tuna, but tinned fish, on the other hand, is likely to contain less mercury than the fresh equivalent.

The problem with wild tuna is the risk of mercury poisoning (see chapter 31 on pollution) and it seems that it's bluefin tuna, the largest of the tuna species, that's the worst offender. Smaller tuna like albacore and yellowfin are safer. But when you buy tuna in most UK food outlets, you're unlikely to know what kind of tuna you are getting. The good news is that if you don't eat too much, you are unlikely to be harmed in any measurable way, unlike small children, who are much more vulnerable.

It's said that the weekly requirement for DHA and EPA is 450 mg. However, the average UK consumption is only 244 mg. Seventy percent of the UK population eat no oily fish at all. One portion a week of oily fish would provide the necessary 450 mg.

When you eat foods containing ALA, metabolism converts it to DHA and EPA. Foods rich in ALA are English walnuts, canola oil and soybean oil. However, it's not all good news with ALA. According to research, it's possible that ALA may contribute to Age-Related Macular Degeneration (AMD) in the eyes (see chapter 19 on eyesight). Equally worryingly, it may also promote prostate cancer.

I also take gamma linoleic acid (GLA) (Omega 6) in the form of Evening Primrose Oil. However, the Evening Primrose Oil capsules generally available only contain about 10% GLA. Be aware that borage oil will do the same job and may cost less. The problem is that it's harder to find, as are starflower oil and blackcurrant oil, which also do the job. Hempseed oil and flaxseed (linseed) oil, on the other hand, are readily available. Broadly the Omega 3 and Omega 9 oils are anti-inflammatory and therefore aid vascular health and improve circulation. Some Omega 6 oils, in contrast, are inflammatory and therefore may damage blood vessels and increase the risk of clotting. Nuts are one of the best sources of Omega 3 and Omega 6 oils.

EPA is said to enhance positive mood. DHA is particularly associated with better blood circulation to the brain and is considered a useful weapon against age-related cognitive decline and even dementia, including Alzheimer's disease. There is some evidence that doses of Omega 3 following heart attacks or angina may reduce the chances of a re-occurrence. Broadly, EPA and DHA are said to support the immune system, keep the blood thin and possibly keep blood pressure down. GLA is said to benefit the heart, ward off Alzheimer's disease and some forms of cancer, and to lessen the symptoms of arthritis. You can get ALA and GLA from a single source if you take flaxseed or hempseed oil supplements.

The optimum dietary ratio of Omega 6 to Omega 3 is said to be between 4:1 and 2:1, but in most diets in the west, it varies between 10:1 and 30:1. It has been suggested that this imbalance may contribute to the high incidence of prostate problems and Benign Prostatic Hyperplasia, in particular in the west (see chapter 43 on the prostate).

I avoid the Omega 6 oils found in polyunsaturated cooking oils like sunflower, peanut, rapeseed and corn oil. Most people get too much Omega 6 in their diet, largely from the common cooking oils. They may also, in this way, get too much vitamin E, which is plentiful in these oils. Omega 6 oils contain alpha linoleic acid (not to be confused with linolenic acid) and gamma linoleic acid (GLA). Alpha linoleic acid is metabolised in the body as arachidonic acid, which acts as a precursor to 'bad' eicosanoids. These raise blood pressure by constricting blood vessels and causing blood platelets to become sticky, raising cardiovascular risk. Taking Omega 3 counteracts this inflammatory effect by dilating blood vessels. The best solution to the Omega 6 dilemma is to use foods containing linoleic acid sparingly, apart from gamma linoleic acid, which does not produce arachidonic acid and eicosanoids.

I get Omega 9 from cooking lightly with olive oil. I use this as a salad dressing too, but if I use the Omega 3 that is walnut oil instead, I get ALA, the Omega 3 oil that doesn't come from fish. ALA is also found in flaxseed and hempseed oil and soy lecithin (a good source of phosphatidylcholine), as well as in some types of algae. An Omega 9 oil that's the equal of olive oil when it comes to cooking and salad dressings is hazelnut oil.

Which foods contain which Omega oils can be confusing, as some foods contain two and sometimes all three oils. Flaxseed, for example, contains the omega 3 oil alpha linolenic acid and the Omega 6 oil alpha linoleic acid in the ratio 3:1. As I've suggested above, alpha linoleic acid is not particularly healthy. However, it should not be considered a problem when combined with three times as much alpha linolenic acid. While Omega 9 is mainly associated with olive oil, some is found in flaxseed oil, as well as in hempseed oil, blackcurrant oil, borage oil and evening primrose oil. You will see from this that the one source of all three oils is flaxseed oil.

Omega 3 polyunsaturates from fish are different from Omega 3 polyunsaturates from plant sources, and of the two, fish Omega 3 is the more beneficial, being made of long-chain fatty acids, while Omega 3 from plant sources such as nuts and seeds is made of shorter-chain fatty acids. The amounts of Omega 3 added to foods like yoghurt, baked beans, fruit juice and bread may not be enough to be effective, may not match the stated quantity, and whether the added oil comes from fish or plant sources is unlikely to be shown.

Dozens of manufacturers tout added Omega 3 on their packaging. As the Omega oils are classed as essential fatty acids, it's often said that they are a necessity for health, but must be taken as supplements as the body does not synthesize them. This is not entirely true. The body does manufacture them in small quantities. The point is that for a healthful intake, you need to find them in food or supplements or a combination of both. We should get most of our Omega 3 from eating oily fish, though one recent report has cast doubt on the nutritional value of the Omega oils generally.

The main oily fish are: herring, mackerel, sardine, anchovy, salmon, trout, eel, tuna, barracuda and swordfish. There are dangers in eating farmed salmon, though, given the kind of food that the fish are fed on (mainly cereal grains, whereas wild salmon eat mainly algae and wild shrimp), and the conditions in which most are kept. They don't get enough exercise penned in mini-lochs in Scotland. Even organically fed farmed salmon swim in water polluted with their own excrement, though organic farmed salmon have to be healthier than non-organic farmed. Try wild salmon instead. The taste is much better, but unfortunately it costs twice as much. And it carries the risk of methylmercury contamination, as do the other ocean predators on the list: tuna, barracuda and swordfish. Some fish also contain small quantities of the pollutants PCBs and dioxins (see chapter on pollution).

Zinc and magnesium. These are the only two mineral supplements I take, apart from the minerals contained in a multi-supplement. Zinc is reputed to be good for fertility, but high doses are alleged to reduce bone density and cause anaemia. Some people swear by boron supplements (more usually fed to cattle), while others would not be without extra iron or chromium. Iron, though, is a mineral supplement best avoided unless you are anaemic. You should be getting enough from healthy eating. Some supplements are best taken with other supplements for full effectiveness, allegedly, and while I don't dispute that this is probably true, this is an area that is in its infancy. I think it's a serious area for research, though – something that cannot be said for the pseudo-science of food combining that was a fad a few years ago and which some people still believe in. That craze involved only eating certain foods with certain others and at its most basic, meant not mixing proteins with carbohydrates.

Glutamine. This is an amino acid, which means that it is one of the building blocks of protein. Almost all the amino acids have their aficionados who will tell you how wonderful say taurine is, or that you should take arginine for your sex life. Arginine went through a big craze in the US a few years ago, but like many of the supplements of the moment, it fell out of favour, supplanted by an even more fashionable must-have. I take glutamine because it is said to help you fight sugar cravings and because there is a reasonable degree of evidence showing that when you exercise hard, it will help repair muscles more effectively. This can also be done by taking a supplement of creatine powder, but I gave this up after a few weeks as the taste was awful. However, creatine is believed to be effective and it doesn't have any known side effects. Many athletes swear that it helps to improve muscle bulk as part of a training regime. It has the advantage over anabolic steroids of being safe and legal.

Lutein. Lutein is an anti-oxidant that I take as a safeguard to protect my eyesight. It's found naturally in bright yellow and dark green leafy vegetables, and is closely linked with zeaxanthin, another anti-oxidant. Together they combat age-related macular degeneration (AMD). I eat a healthy diet, so probably a lutein supplement isn't necessary. It's another instance of 'just in case' (see chapter 19 on eyesight).

Saw Palmetto and Stinging Nettle Root Extract. These are both, like Pygeum Africanum, herbal remedies that in theory will shrink the prostate enough to reduce the problem of benign prostatic hyperplasia (BPH), which involves frequent trips to the loo for a pee. I'm not convinced that any of these supplements work on their own, but I have taken Saw Palmetto for a long time. Recent trials suggest that it doesn't work. See chapter 43 on the prostate for more on Saw Palmetto and other supplements targeting BPH.

CHAPTER FOURTEEN: DIETARY SUPPLEMENTS: FADS AND FACTS

Green tea extract. This is another anti-oxidant, and as I don't drink tea but would like some of the benefits, this may be the next best thing. I am sure that drinking say four daily cups of green tea that has brewed for five minutes (see chapter 17 on nutrition) would do me more good. Green tea is better for you than the black tea usually drunk in the UK, and white tea, if you can find it, is said to be better still when it comes to anti-bacterial properties. Let's look at green tea in more detail, as to its many fans it's a superfood. It can allegedly protect the heart and prevent strokes, though the theory that it can also help prevent cancer has been disproved. There is no doubt that green tea contains abundant anti-oxidant polyphenols and flavonoid catechins, especially epigallocatechin gallate, which has a mildly sedative effect. The average British cup of black tea contains twice as many anti-oxidants as an average-size apple. In green and black tea, the anti-oxidants come in the form of bioactive compounds, the theaflavins, especially theanine, and a variety of other polyphenols.

The catechin anti-oxidants in tea are thought to work by improving circulation, by relaxing blood vessel walls, by making it harder for plaque to form on these walls and by reducing the clotting agents in the blood known as platelets. In the colon, the polyphenols in tea may reduce the presence of 'bad' bacteria and act as a source of nutrition for 'good' bacteria. They are also alleged to improve the proportion of 'good' (HDL) cholesterol by reducing 'bad' (LDL) cholesterol. The flavonoids (the catechins) in tea are believed to strengthen the immune system. When we drink green tea, cortisol level drops. Cortisol is a stress hormone that raises blood pressure and heart rate. Contrary to popular belief, it has been established that tea is not a diuretic – it doesn't make you pee or become dehydrated. On the contrary, it is an excellent source of hydration. However, it does contain caffeine, and the longer the brew time, the higher the caffeine level. Three cups of tea a day are probably fine, but more than that and the caffeine content will start to affect blood pressure and may cause insomnia and anxiety, even if concentration is improved. On the other hand, if you drink six cups a day, you may speed up your metabolism and boost daily calorie burn rate by 80-100 calories. The average British cup of tea contains about

40 mg of caffeine, compared with about 75-100 mg per cup of real coffee. Caffeine prevents iron absorption.

Carnosine. I take a carnosine capsule each day. Carnosine is a dipeptide – a kind of mixture of two amino acids. It is said to be the only supplement that will actually reverse oxidative damage to muscle tissue caused by free radicals, and for this reason it is popular with professional athletes.

Carnitine. This is an amino acid that is not to be confused with carnosine, though it has a similar role in rebuilding the small tears in muscle tissue that follow resistance exercise. It's synthesized from the essential amino acids lysine and methionine. Most men get enough from their diet, so a supplement should not be necessary. I mention it here as I do, I admit, take it as a supplement. Carnitine is found naturally in meat, dairy products, avocados and tempeh, which is made from fermented soybeans and is delicious seared in olive oil. Strict vegetarians are unlikely to get enough carnitine from their diet. The alleged benefits of carnitine include: slowing the development of dementia, including Alzheimer's disease; improving insulin sensitivity in Type 2 diabetics; lowering LDL cholesterol; enhancing exercise performance; improving lipid (fat) metabolism. However, a word of caution – as a treatment for any condition, it may be that carnitine will only be effective in large doses, not the small doses that come in supplements from the local health shop.

Vitamin C (ascorbic acid). I used to take 1 gram of vitamin C each day, but I decided eventually that although this was doing me no harm, I was probably getting enough vitamin C from my plentiful daily intake of fresh fruit and vegetables – well, fresh fruit mainly as I consume a lot of mangoes, strawberries, raspberries, blueberries, pomegranates, peaches and nectarines. Not that the latter two have a lot of food value compared with the others – I just like the taste of them. Papaya would be a good bet too, but I have given up on it simply because I find it boring and not very tasty. When it comes to vegetables I eat mainly broccoli and spinach, the latter either cooked or raw as salad. And for straight salad, I like watercress, rocket or spinach. In an ideal world we would eat everything raw as cooking can remove so many of the goodies, especially vitamin C, which is also depleted by exposure to sunlight.

However, I can think of two foods that benefit in food value when cooked. Tomatoes contain lycopene, a useful anti-oxidant. When you cook them, the lycopene becomes more accessible, which is why the kind of tomatoes that come in tins and tubes and are used a lot in Italian cooking are very healthy. The other food is baked potatoes. The goodies in potatoes are in the skins, which is why you should never peel potatoes, but if you bake them the goodies are enhanced. Potatoes are a good source of vitamin C.

Co-enzyme Q10. This supplement comes up again and again. It's a useful anti-oxidant that the body produces, but not in sufficient quantity, so the supplement manufacturers tell us. It's found naturally in oily fish, spinach, pork, walnuts, sesame seeds and soy oil. It is said to keep the gums healthy, increase the ability to exercise, look after your heart and possibly help to lower blood pressure.

Quercetin. This is a powerful anti-oxidant and does much the same job as pycnogenol, an anti-oxidant derived from the bark of a pine tree (see below). Quercetin is thought to support the immune system and to boost the effects of resveratrol (see chapter 1 on ageing) when they are taken together.

Alpha Lipoic Acid. This is another powerful anti-oxidant which, unusually, is both water-soluble and fat-soluble. It's involved in glucose metabolism and insulin function and therefore may be helpful to Type 2 diabetics, as well as reducing their symptoms of neuropathy, which is usually characterized by pain and tingling in the feet and fingers. Food sources of alpha lipoic acid include spinach, broccoli and the organ meats kidney, heart and liver.

Vitamin B12 is especially important as you get older, and like selenium, is often recommended for those over 60. It's associated mainly with cognitive ability and is therefore recommended as a way of slowing normal age-related mental decline. It helps in red blood cell formation and in keeping the nervous system healthy. The elderly should not take selenium supplements without taking vitamin B12 supplements as well.

There are supplements that I used to take and take no longer, mostly herbal remedies. It's not that I think that they did any harm or that they were a waste of money. It's just that there wasn't enough convincing evidence that they did any good either, despite numerous claims in their favour. There was hawthorn extract, which I took to get my blood pressure, which is reasonably good, down a little bit more. There was the pine bark extract that is pycnogenol, which is an undoubted anti-oxidant, but I felt there were so many other anti-oxidants already on my menu that this was one I could skip, especially as it's expensive. Then I discovered how rich it was in anti-oxidant procyanidins and went back to it.

Phosphatidylcholine is a phospholipid usually found in soy lecithin. I take some in my morning muesli (see recipe at end of this chapter). Commercial lecithin varies in how much phosphatidylcholine it actually contains, but the normal range is between 10% and 55%. What does it do? Allegedly it will reduce triglycerides and LDL cholesterol, but to have this effect, very large quantities are required. Allegedly it will also help to reduce liver damage from alcohol abuse.

Choline itself is an important B vitamin which is made in the body from the amino acid methionine. Choline is an amine precursor for acetylcholine, which is a neurotransmitter.

Phosphatidyl serine is meant to be great for the brain and warding off Alzheimer's disease. It's derived from soy phospholipids, and while it is found in small quantities in soy lecithin, food sources are usually insufficient for those wishing to get a good dose and therefore supplements are the only answer. But how do you know if it's working or not? I read that you should take 300 mg a day for a month then go on to a maintenance dosage of 100 mg a day to treat the early stages of Alzheimer's. But how can anyone know how much you should take, when it's still far from proven that it helps tackle Alzheimer's or any other disorder? At least there don't appear to be any long-term side effects, though that's true of most supplements. This is the reason, of course, why supplements find favour with people who are sceptical about the side effects of pharmaceutical drugs.

As with many of the supplements, there just aren't the prospective long-duration randomised double-blind placebo-controlled trials around that might convince me. Yet to read some of the books, you would think that the writer knew precisely what supplements would have what effect. The truth is that some may be beneficial, but for most supplements we simply do not know what they do for us, if anything. At one time or another I have tried (and no longer take): astragulus, cat's claw, oregano, licorice root, hawthorn extract, bilberry, fenugreek, milk thistle (said to be good for hangovers), extract of aged garlic, pantothenic acid, ginseng, ginkgo biloba (claimed to be good for preventing macular degeneration), feverfew, goldenseal and brewer's yeast. I haven't tried valerian (to treat stress and insomnia – see chapter 37 on sleep) or lyprinol, the active compound found in green lipped mussel extract and said to reduce joint swelling and pain. Nor have I tried astaxanthin, an allegedly powerful anti-oxidant, or rhodiola rosea, said to be an effective anti-depressant. Your local health food shop will have dozens of other supplements on offer and probably an eager assistant who will give you a long list of ailments that they will cure. Ask for scientific evidence, though, and they will be flummoxed.

Taking a combination supplement of vitamins A, C and E used to be popular. This is less so now that their benefits are no longer as impressive as they once seemed. Many people get too much vitamin E from their cooking oils, enough vitamin C from a healthy diet and enough vitamin A if they eat plenty of fish. The body converts carotene, especially beta carotene into vitamin A (retinol), much loved by women's skin cream manufacturers. It takes 6 micrograms of beta carotene to produce 1 microgram of vitamin A. Vitamins C and E, along with beta carotene and selenium are all anti-oxidants that worsen the health of people with heart disease who are taking statins or niacin to lower 'bad' LDL cholesterol.

As I don't drink much red wine, or very much alcohol at all, but do not want to miss out on the anti-oxidants in red wine, I take a resveratrol supplement which contains 98% pure resveratrol (500 grams per capsule – four capsules a day). That way I'm getting many times the benefits of red wine without the hangovers and other negatives. At least I may be getting these benefits. Then again, maybe I'm not. In the meantime, I look at it as insurance and take a deep breath when I think about the cost. (See chapters 1 and 3 on ageing and alcohol for more on resveratrol).

A supplement that you should not try is chromium picolinate. It metabolises sugar and is said to be carcinogenic by damaging DNA.

It may also cause kidney failure. It has been used in the past by people seeking a shortcut to losing weight on the grounds that it increases lean body mass. The amino acid tryptophan, which is available in the US and sometimes used as an anti-depressant, is also not recommended as a supplement. It is said to have unpleasant side effects and is banned in the UK except in the form L-5-hydroxytryptophan.

It has been suggested that most supplements simply end up as expensive urine. Some vitamins are chelated, which means they are produced in a form that is more soluble in the gut, but now doubt has been cast on whether chelation makes any difference to absorption. It's often said that supplements extracted from natural sources are better for you and more easily and fully absorbed than those that are synthesized. If you see 'ester' in the name of a vitamin such as ester vitamin C, this is vitamin C from a natural source. What is certain is that the vitamins and other micronutrients we take as supplements would be better for us consumed as part of a healthy diet. This is because these nutrients work better in conjunction with other nutrients, though for the most part science is still years away from knowing just how that works and what goes best with what. There are many micronutrients in food still to be discovered.

Even the experts do not know what is the optimum amount we should take (or absorb). Should we take supplements before meals, with meals or after meals? I take about sixteen supplements each day and though it would be ideal to spread them over the day, I take them all at once after breakfast. If you don't know whether something is making a difference to your health, you are not going to know how much of it is right for you. Nonetheless almost every expert out there has a view on the right quantity to take, starting with the government's own Recommended Daily Allowance (RDA) of vitamins and minerals. These quantities have traditionally erred on the side of caution and most promoters of supplementation will recommend higher doses, sometimes megadoses, as did the late Dr Atkins of diet fame. Needless to say there are few serious nutritionists today who recommend megadoses of vitamins and other supplements as a cure for ailments. I say serious nutritionists as there are still alternative therapy practitioners who believe that for a cold, for example you should take 10 grams of vitamin C a day. That quantity won't hurt you, but it could send you rushing for the lavatory. On the other hand megadoses of vitamin A, once recommended for a long list of ailments by Dr Atkins, are now known to be harmful.

Without doubt there are limits to how many supplements you can or should take each day. It isn't just the quantity or cost that matters, but also the fact that it simply isn't practical to take say 50 different micronutrients if each is a separate capsule. Multi-vitamin and mineral supplements ease the problem a bit, but only go part of the way, and generally contain only small quantities of each ingredient, which is why the worried well in the US are often encouraged to take as many as six (or nine in one case) of a multi-supplement daily. Dr Atkins himself popped 50 tabs a day according to his wife, only to fall over on an icy pavement and die of a brain haemorrhage – or a heart attack – depending on whom you believe.

Most of us, myself included, don't pay enough attention to the quantities of the supplements we take. In fact, how many of us even understand the way quantities are measured for micronutrients. Here's how:

1000 micrograms (mcg) = 1 milligram (mg)
1000 milligrams = 1 gram
And for liquids measured by volume:1000 millilitres = I litre. This can be written as 1000 mll = 1 l. If we want to say, for example, 5 millilitres per litre, this is written as 5 mll/l. Cholesterol is measured in millimoles per litre (mmol/l). Testosterone is measured in nanomoles per litre (nmol/l).

Knowing how to read such figures is not only important for under-standing the labels on the back of supplement jars, but also when trying to understand the various blood and urine readings that you get back from a medical check-up. But how much you actually need of any supplement is not helped by simply knowing that your daily multivitamin, for example, contains 10 mg of co-enzyme Q10. It may help you to understand, though, that the quantities you are getting are only a token amount, included so that the manufacturers can say they've put it in. A multi-supplement may seem convenient, but bear in mind this weakness in most of them. The US multi-supplement that I used to take daily and that appears to contain everything under the sun tells you in the packaging that you should take six a day. Anyone who goes that far is leaving the ranks of the worried well and joining the army of hypochondriacs that, in America especially, account for the fact that virtually every supermarket has rows devoted to nothing but supplements, sometimes in giant containers. Four times as many supplements are consumed per head in the US as in the UK.

Does all this leave you feeling confused? I'm cynical about supplements and yet I take some every day. All I can say in my defence is that this used to be about two dozen before I cut out most of the herbal remedies and several others, some of which were extremely expensive.

But my most important source of micronutrients is my diet, and with that I can be reasonably sure of absorbing most of the goodies in what I eat, in quantities that are probably acceptable to my system (or else my body simply expels any surplus), and in coordination with other enabling nutrients that get the best out of everything. With all that fruit, for example, I get more than enough vitamin C. True I may also get more than enough fruit sugar as I drink about a litre of pure fruit juice each day, when I ought to limit myself to about 300 millilitres (see chapter on nutrition).

I wish I could say with authority that this is what you need by way of supplements and these are the quantities you should take. That is how it will be one day, and perhaps the recommended additions to our diet will be tailored to our age, sex, state of health and metabolism, and perhaps even to our personal DNA profile. But that is still years away, and if anyone tells you otherwise, they are probably trying to sell you something you do not need. Today we are only at the beginning. We can safely say that all pregnant women should take folic acid supplements and even that everyone over the biological age of fifty should take glucosamine sulphate supplements and think of it as I do, as insurance.

I'm going to round off this chapter by disclosing my recipe, a secret until now, for what I believe to be the healthiest and tastiest muesli in the world. However, if you are interested in trying it out, I'll leave it up to you to work out the proportions for each ingredient.

That way you can suit your own taste. Here are the ingredients in no particular order:

Organic whole oats
Organic wheat germ
Dried goji berries
Dried cranberries
Brazil nuts
Walnuts
Almonds
Macadamia nuts
Pine nuts
Hazelnuts
Cashew nuts
Shelled pistachio nuts
Cocoa nibs
Maca powder (sparingly)
Shelled hempseeds
Flaxseeds

Pumpkin seeds
Sesame seeds
Soy lecithin granules (25%
phosphatidylcholine)
Apple pectin
Grapefruit pectin
Psyllium fibre
Fresh strawberries
Fresh raspberries
Fresh blackberries
Fresh blackcurrants
Fresh blueberries
Fresh mango
Fresh apple
Fresh pomegranate

Add on top: skimmed organic goat's milk, live organic plain goat's yoghurt, dark honey (the darker it is, the more micronutrients it contains).

CHAPTER FIFTEEN

THE DIABETES EPIDEMIC

Diabetes is a metabolic disorder, a disease of the pancreas and its insulin-producing beta cells, the islets of Langerhans. The pancreas also produces glucagon, a hormone which, like insulin, is a glucose regulator. The two commonest types of diabetes are known as Type 1 and Type 2 diabetes. Type 1 diabetes, the onset of which is usually rapid, is characterized by a shortage of insulin that is an autoimmune response triggered in someone who is susceptible. It is often described as insulin-dependent diabetes as insulin supplements are required, applied by injections or inhalers, or, more recently, experimentally, by patches. It usually affects young people, but can sometimes strike suddenly in middle age. Around 10% of diabetics suffer from Type 1.

Insulin is a hormone important to all cells in the body. Without insulin to metabolise glucose, the muscles lack energy and the fat cells are unable to store triglycerides and other fatty acids. Insulin also controls glucose levels in the blood. We usually refer to glucose as sugar, a carbohydrate that is the basis for energy production in the body.

Type 2 diabetes occurs when the beta cells are in short supply or absent, causing an absence of insulin production, or when, as a result of too much insulin production (see below), the body becomes resistant to insulin, with the result that glucose metabolism fails. Insulin resistance is a common feature in the development of Type 2 diabetes. Most Type 2 diabetics do not require treatment with insulin.

Type 2 diabetes is growing at an alarming rate as a result of the obesity epidemic which shows no sign of slowing. Obesity and Type 2 diabetes are often connected and most new cases of Type 2 diabetes, which more usually strikes after the age of 40, are in the overweight and obese. About 90% of diabetics have Type 2 diabetes.

In both types of diabetes the inability of the body to optimally use glucose for energy results from either a shortage of insulin or a loss of adequate sensitivity to insulin (insulin resistance).

Insulin reduces levels of glucose in the blood by stimulating body cells to absorb glucose. At the same time it stimulates the liver to store glucose as glycogen, and fat cells to convert glucose into fatty acids. Insulin's function, and that of its sister hormone glucagon, to a lesser extent, is to stabilize the body's glucose level. This level is influenced not just by food consumption but also by, for example, stress. Physical and emotional stress trigger a reaction in the adrenal gland which then produces the corticosteroid hormones cortisol and aldosterone. Exercise, especially strenuous exercise has this effect too. Cortisol in the blood raises glucose level, calling for release of insulin to bring the level down again to a healthy and stable level.

Recently the Glycaemic Index (GI) has proved a useful way of scoring carbohydrates by how fast they are converted to sugar to be burnt as fuel for our bodies, or are otherwise stored as fat in the body's fat cells. The lower a carbohydrate is on the index, the more likely it is that, rather than being stored as fat, it will be burnt, with oxygen, as adenosine triphosphate (ATP) in the mitochondrial cells that are the tiny power-houses of our muscles. Sugar requires insulin as a part of this process. The carbohydrates most likely to be stored as fat, those high on the index, tend to be pure sugars such as glucose, and refined carbohydrates such as those found in biscuits, cakes and a long list of processed foods. The healthiest carbohydrates are those with a low GI factor such as those found in unprocessed foods, mainly fruit, nuts, seeds and vegetables, in whole cereal breads, and in foods like museli, wholewheat pasta, basmati rice and porridge oats.

Carbohydrates high on the GI will readily raise the blood sugar level, triggering a response from the pancreas which produces insulin to take the sugar out of the bloodstream. In some individuals, possibly those predisposed since they carry a gene called the FTO gene (see chapter 44 on weight loss), this rise in blood sugar triggers too much insulin production with the result that blood sugar falls dramatically. It goes from being too high to being too low. The result of this sudden drop is a rise in appetite and the person may then find themselves unable to resist further eating of more high GI carbohydrates. The pattern is repeated. More insulin is released and so the blood sugar level goes up and own without stabilising in between.

Meanwhile a large surplus of insulin is circulating in the body. This in turn makes the body's cells insulin-resistant and the knock-on effect from this is that even more insulin is produced as the pancreas attempts to overcome the resistance. In the end, the pancreas is exhausted from so much insulin production and can no longer function properly. Its insulin production goes into decline. This is Type 2 diabetes. It produces a variety of problems which may include kidney failure, blindness, depression, heart attack, stroke, hypertension and heart failure. Diabetes is associated with high levels of LDL 'bad' cholesterol with the result that men with diabetes are four times more likely to suffer from peripheral arterial disease and twice as likely to fall victim to coronary arterial disease. In men found to have diabetes, one in six already has cardiovascular disease. In men, there is the likelihood of several extra inches around the middle, the area where dangerous fat accumulates and some highly undesirable hormones may be produced. In extreme cases, where blood circulation is affected, diabetes may result in the need for amputation.

Insulin resistance is increased by excess abdominal fat, which is fat that adheres to the mesenteric tissue around the stomach and guts, and around the lungs also in extreme cases of obesity. The cells of this visceral fat, when they become overextended, produce adipokines, which are biochemically active molecules that induce insulin resistance and therefore diabetes. Visceral fat is the hardest fat of all to get rid of.

Statin drugs (see chapter on cholesterol) have been shown to help diabetics reduce their chances of dying from strokes and heart attacks. In one trial, deaths fell by a fifth for every millimole per litre drop in LDL 'bad' cholesterol. The results were equally successful for non-diabetics with raised LDL.

Damage to eyesight is a serious problem for those who have had diabetes for many years without getting treatment. Most men who go blind before the age of 65 do so as a result of untreated diabetes. There are now drugs, however, which can save the eyesight of those at risk.

Fenofibrate works by modifying blood lipid (fat) levels, which in turn reduces damage to the arteries feeding blood to the retina in the eye. Damaged eyesight cannot be restored, but further decline in vision can be slowed, and the treatment may save the eyesight of diabetics not yet showing signs of vision loss.

Type 2 diabetes may run in families, but environmental factors, especially diet, are thought to be as important as hereditary factors. It is unlikely to strike before the age of about forty unless you are seriously obese. It can be controlled to some extent through weight loss and diet, but most sufferers will eventually need drugs. Type 2 diabetes develops slowly and many people don't even realize they have it until the symptoms can no longer be ignored. Early identification of what is sometimes called glucose intolerance (easily determined from a blood sample) and early treatment offer hope of a more favourable outcome. I don't particularly like the description of diabetes as glucose intolerance as this is only a symptom, and the core of the problem is not sugar levels, but insulin production.

Since two million people in the UK know they have diabetes and over a million people are thought to have Type 2 diabetes without realizing it, it's important to be aware of the symptoms. These include: fatigue, weight loss, wasted muscles, blurred vision, recurrent boils, dry skin, raised blood pressure, unusual thirst, irritability, weight loss that cannot be explained, itchy skin, especially in the genital area, poor circulation and loss of sensitivity to pain in the fingers or feet (neuropathy). (If you are a Type 2 diabetic, it is important not to step into a hot bath without carefully testing the water first with hand or elbow as you may scald yourself). More frequent urination can be a symptom of both diabetes and benign prostatic hyperplasia (BPH) (see chapter 43 on the prostate). A simple blood glucose test will usually identify whether diabetes is involved.

The symptoms of Type 2 diabetes are sometimes referred to as signals of glucose intolerance because they are caused by the body's inability to control the glucose it derives from food, since what remaining insulin the pancreas can produce is inadequate for the job. The challenge is therefore to boost, with drugs, the ability of the pancreas to produce insulin, while restricting diet in a way that will lower circulating sugar levels. One problem with insulin-boosting drugs is that they can some-times lead to weight gain. When the pancreas finally produces no insulin at all, the only solution is insulin supplementation, and in this way Type 2 diabetes resembles Type 1 diabetes, where dependence on injections (or other forms of application) begins much sooner.

Diabetics who drive must inform the DVLA if they are taking drugs or injecting insulin. Diabetes can lead to kidney problems and the evidence for this is usually cloudy urine and/or a burning sensation when urinat-ing. There may also be a raised temperature. An annual blood test will normally include a creatinine score which shows whether your kidney function is healthy. Diabetes can damage blood vessels and nerve cells with the result that, in men over 50 or thereabouts, there may be erectile dysfunction. Needless to say, both types of diabetes weaken the immune system.

The prognosis for men with coronary arterial disease – atheromatous plaques blocking their arteries – is better these days than it used to be with one exception: Type two diabetics who have had a heart attack. Here the outlook is no better than it ever was. The reduction in life expectancy for those with Type 2 diabetes, all else being equal, is 15 years. However, for those who have had a heart attack it is even more.

There is now a drug available which, it is hoped, will give a longer life expectancy to diabetics who suffer from coronary arterial disease. Actos pioglitazone added to standard diabetic medication of statins, blood pressure drugs and the like appears to have a booster effect by tackling arterial plaques while going some way to stabilising blood sugar levels. Coronary arterial disease is implicated in the death of 80% of diabetics.

The following are a few of the ways recommended for a healthy lifestyle aimed at preventing diabetes: reduce stress, drink moderately, do not smoke, eat healthily, take exercise regularly, keep an eye on your blood pressure, get your eyesight tested regularly, have a blood sugar (glucose) and kidney function (creatinine) test annually. A high choles-terol score may indicate Type 2 diabetes, as well as increased risk of heart and stroke problems. Diabetics should be careful to avoid a raised temperature during hot summer weather as they are more prone to suffer in such conditions, and global warming means increasingly hotter weather in most summer months.

The so-called metabolic syndrome is a group of symptoms which together may indicate serious trouble ahead, from Type 2 diabetes through to cardiovascular disease. The most obvious symptoms are obesity, insulin resistance, raised cholesterol, raised triglycerides and hypertension.

Diet is important in handling Type 2 diabetes and one recent study found that a diet the researchers described as Palaeolithic was successful in restoring and maintaining normal blood sugar levels in a test sample of Type 2 diabetes sufferers. This is essentially a primitive hunter-gatherer diet and is notable for several differences from what we now think of as the typically healthy diet, sometimes called a Mediterranean diet. It contains no dairy products and no farmed grains, since farming had not been invented in Palaeolithic times. The basis of the diet is seeds, nuts, fruit, vegetables, lean meat and fish. The few remaining people living a hunter-gatherer existence around the world are notable for their lack of cardiovascular problems and diabetes. It has been suggested that the Palaeolithic diet could also benefit those with coeliac disease, which affects the alimentary canal through a reaction to gluten proteins. A simpler solution is thought by some to be megadoses of vitamin B1 (thiamine), though whether this will turn out to be a wonder treatment remains to be seen.

Diabetics are advised to lose weight. Many find this difficult to do, if not impossible, without the help of drugs. One drug approved for this purpose is Rimonabant, which produces a feeling of satiety, while also turning off some of the hormones responsible for insulin resistance. Like many drugs, this should be a last resort. Another approach is still awaiting approval. The incretins are a class of drugs that utilize artificial hormones in the gut. These suppress appetite and work on the pancreas to cause more insulin production than would normally occur, since those with Type 2 diabetes are usually still able to produce at least some insulin.

However, injections of a hormone called GLP1 are likely to be a more effective option if current trials work out and problems of interference by an enzyme called DPP4 can be overcome. Those with Type 2 diabetes who live to a ripe old age will almost certainly need insulin injections in the end. Exercise and the right diet can do a lot to protract the period before injections become necessary and treatment with drugs to boost insulin production by the pancreas is no longer sufficient.

Since weight is such a big factor in the Type 2 diabetes epidemic, here are a few facts that should act as a wake-up call. One in four adults and children in the UK is obese – not just overweight but obese. (In the US, one on three adults is obese.) The obese are at risk of a litany of illnesses, not just diabetes, but cardiovascular problems, deep vein thrombosis and pulmonary embolism, which is frequently fatal. Those affected by obesity are to be found disproportionately in the less affluent. However, much research has suggested that obesity is not a disease of poverty. It is possible to eat healthily on a low income, just as it is possible to exercise adequately. Some critics have suggested that the real problem is not income or education, but a lack of willpower to eat well and exercise enough.

Here's another fact. Half of all children in the UK eat zero fruit and vegetables in a week. On top of that, as many as 65% of all adults do not take the minimum required amount of exercise – 30 minutes, five days a week. Most Type 2 diabetes can be prevented, yet by 2020 one fifth of all NHS resources will be going to the treatment of Type 2 diabetes. The current expenditure on the disease is £5 billion per annum. It's little wonder that the government is in panic mode over the crisis. You could say that obesity is to diabetes what smoking is to lung cancer.

Since diabetes is an incurable if manageable disease, it isn't surprising that depression is found to be two to three times higher in diabetics than in the general population. In fact diabetes is a major cause of mental illness as well as being a physical illness. Everyone over 40 should have an annual check-up which includes a blood screen for the signals that might indicate diabetes. Most of those who are diagnosed with Type 2 diabetes have had the disease for several years. If they had been diagnosed sooner, they would have benefited from being able to manage the condition sooner.

A recent discovery is that a peptide (a cellular building block similar to an amino acid) that comes from the skin of a South American frog called

Pseudis paradoxa or the 'paradoxical frog' can stimulate insulin production. The peptide, called pseudin-2, has now been synthesized in a more powerful form than its natural counterpart. The expectation is that pseudin-2 will join the class of drugs for Type 2 diabetes known as incretin mimetics, which are the resort of diabetics clinicians when all else has failed. Already a drug in the incretin mimetics class called Byetta, which comes from the saliva of the Gila monster lizard, is on the market, but the expectation is that pseudin-2 will prove more effective. Meanwhile the search is on for other amphibians that may help in the search for effective drug treatments.

....

More Tips and Traps

There is one piece of dietary advice for treating Type 2 diabetes that may be worth a try. Each day, eat half a teaspoon of powdered cinnamon mixed with food. This is said to help control blood sugar levels.

Type 2 diabetes is known to be linked to a number of genetic markers, and so far ten or more of these have been identified. Using these markers, it will be possible, in the future, to identify those most at risk.

Crash dieting can trigger diabetes.

CHAPTER SIXTEEN
YOU ARE THE GENES YOU INHERIT

Your genes say a lot about you and will say even more in the future, thanks to the unravelling of the human genome and ongoing research in gene therapy. Before long we will be able to get a full personal genetic profile and from it, assuming we want to know, we will be able to tell what our strengths and weaknesses are and what aspects of a healthy lifestyle we should therefore concentrate on if we want to live longer. Such possibilities are likely to revolutionize the assessment of risk in the insurance industry.

When I studied anthropology in the Seventies, it was fashionable at the time to see nurture as dominant over nature in the age-old debate. Since then the pendulum has swung and there is now general acceptance that our genes dominate, even though nature still has a big part to play. If you are middle-aged and start to think you are looking quite like your father at the same age, you probably are, right down to some of his mannerisms.

It is currently very expensive to sequence a personal genome, but in ten years or so this should be relatively cheap and easy to do. When that happens, the opportunities that diagnostic genetics will open up for identifying and treating a wide variety of diseases will be enormous. Just as we now routinely run blood and urine tests to check on a patient's state of health, a genome report will become routine eventually, with susceptibility to specific diseases highlighted. Cancer treatments will not be decided until such a genome had been produced. It will also be easier to accurately choose drugs that are matched to the patient and their specific illness. The ethical issues that will be raised by this advance will be considerable, especially as it will be possible to analyse the DNA of a baby in utero, raising the possibility that the identification of dozens of potential diseases may lead to pressure from one or both parents for a termination. Already Huntington's disease can be identified from foetal chromosomes.

One of the most interesting fields of DNA research relates to the way in which the body can correct errors in its own DNA. This is a fascinating area for cancer research. If the body can detect and wipe out genetic mutations that possibly occur at a rate of several per day, we must be playing a key role ourselves in warding off potential cancers. Possibly it is those mutations which escape this elimination process which are responsible for cancer and even the ageing process itself. One research team working on a DNA mutation caused by smoking called the oxoguanine mutation determined that a critical enzyme involved in the process, OGG1, had a lower value in those suffering from non-small cell lung cancer. Further research appeared to suggest that the enzyme could ward off cancer when there was a high level present, but could no longer always provide this line of defence in smokers, who generally had a lower level. It is early days and the possible role of DNA in cancer therapy is in its infancy.

A recent study made an important breakthrough by determining the genetic profile involved in six diseases: heart disease, bipolar disorder, rheumatoid arthritis. Type 1 and Type 2 diabetes and Crohn's disease. Genetic variants for high blood pressure also seem close to discovery. These findings explain why different people are susceptible to different illnesses, opening up better targeted options for treatment. The discovery of a predisposition to any of these disorders does not mean that an individual will inevitably succumb to one of them. The emphasis is on predisposition. As often as not it will be an environmental trigger that may produce the disease, if at all. The genetic variants identified for the six diseases are carried by between 5% and 40 % of the population, depending on which of the diseases we are considering. If genetic variation is present, the risk of an individual with one copy of the variant acquiring one of the six diseases rises by 40%, and by around 100% if they carry two copies of the variant. That means the risk doubles. Obesity is strongly linked to Type 2 diabetes. The FTO gene, for example, is the gene found to be most associated with obesity and to have a link to the gene cluster denoting Type 2 diabetes.

CHAPTER SEVENTEEN
EATING RIGHT

I almost called this chapter Eating Well. But eating right and eating well are not the same thing, and therein lies the problem. What we like to eat and what is best for us can sometimes be the same, but often isn't, as any meat-eater invited to lunch in a vegetarian salad bar knows, no matter how often we are told that vegetarian meals can be delicious. True, vegetarian food can be delicious, but a life without meat and fish, if you like meat and fish, would be less than satisfying, and a life with only the proteins found in chickpeas, soybeans and some vegetables would leave you without the many other proteins found in meat and fish. I believe, though, that a little indulgence in the food you like from time to time doesn't do harm and may improve the quality of life simply through the pleasure it brings, even if that means sneaking out for a hamburger once a year.

What you eat and drink and how you exercise go together. If you eat right and don't exercise, or vice versa, you are doing yourself no favours. Fortunately most people who take care of the one take care of the other.

Science has come up with a lot of the answers to what makes for a healthy diet, but there is still much that is unknown, which explains why this year's fad is often next year's no-no. If you are over forty, you will remember when, in the Seventies, it was fashionable to debunk butter in favour of margarine: saturated fat versus polyunsaturated fat. We now know that butter is good for you in moderation, while margarine is not so good as we already get too much polyunsaturated fat from the vegetable oils that are widely used for cooking. The new good fats are said to be the essential fatty acids, in particular Omega 3, which most of us don't get enough of, and monounsaturated Omega 9 such as olive oil.

Trans fats, beloved of processed food manufacturers and fast food outlets have replaced saturated fats in the hunt for a new food to demonize, in this case with a good deal of justification. Trans fats lower 'good'

(HDL) cholesterol and raise 'bad' (LDL) cholesterol levels (see chapter 10 on cholesterol). We know that saturated fat, previously the enemy, does raise LDL slightly, but raises HDL too to compensate. The problem with saturated fat is not that it is bad for you, but that it is calorie-dense, like any fat, and can lead to weight problems if too much is eaten.

'Fat' has become a dirty word in our language, thanks to its association with obesity. But some fat in the diet is essential. Our diet is made up of fat, protein and carbohydrates, together with fibre, water and micronutrients (principally vitamins, minerals and amino acids). What the body doesn't need it excretes. Some people have fast metabolisms and tend to excrete more readily, while others have slower metabolisms and are more prone to constipation. Ironically it is the latter group that probably extract more food value from their diet, even too much. This means that those with a slower metabolism may excrete less of what they eat and tend to put on weight, which is why more radical approaches to weight loss often focus on speeding up the passage of food through the body. Unfortunately the drugs that produce this effect by aiming at a faster metabolic rate tend to produce side effects.

However, it's true that your metabolism will slow down increasingly as you get older. You probably cannot reverse this trend, but you should, with good nutrition and exercise, be able to slow it down.

Your weight isn't necessarily a constant if you burn say 2000 calories a day and eat 2000 calories a day. Your body will naturally seek a homeostasis – a fixed weight if you eat and exercise according to what your body thinks it needs in line with its pre-programmed metabolic rate. Eat too much and you may simply excrete more. Eat too little and you may excrete less. This is part of the weight problem and one of several reasons why dieting is usually such a failure. Added to which around 70% of the calories you burn have little to do with what we think of as exercise. They are burnt as your body performs the functions essential to life, including digestion itself. (See the chapters on weight and metabolism). Even when you are asleep you are burning calories.

How much fat, carbohydrate and protein should there be in a healthy diet? The general view is that an adult male should eat about 2,500 calories a day if they lead a sedentary life and about 3,000–3,500 a day if they pursue a manual job. My view is that this is too much and that 2,000 calories a day are adequate for a sedentary man and 2,500–3,000 for a man working in a manual job, depending on how manual it is. You would expect manual workers to be fit, so it's surprising how pot-bellied a lot of men in physical jobs are, until you see how little physical work many of them actually do. On the other hand, look at a young man working on scaffolding, rigging and dismantling it, and you will see how a physical job can still keep someone fit, despite the tendency of older manual workers to spend time standing around.

My current view is that about 15% of calories should come from fat, about 15% from protein and the remaining 70% from carbohydrates. Most recommendations will be for more fat (up to 30%) and less carbo-hydrate, and also for more protein, with recommendations normally in the 15–30% range. While I think 15% of calories from fat is about right, I would suggest that no more than 7.5% should come from satu-rated fat, with the remainder coming from polyunsaturates and monounsaturates, some in the form of essential fatty acids. A diet alto-gether free from fat, including saturated fat, can lead to ill health. Vegetarians need fat like anyone else, and will tend to rely on nuts and seeds, and on dairy products if they are not purists.

One gram of fat contains 18 calories, whereas a gram of protein or a gram of carbohydrate contains only 8 calories. Volume for volume though, fat is only half the weight of protein. Imagine a cubic centimetre of fat weighing 1 gram and a cubic centimetre of protein weighing two grams. The fat cube will contain 18 calories while the protein cube will contain 16 calories. It's little wonder that in past centuries the rich got fat and displayed their extended bellies as a sign of wealth and good health, as if to say, looks at me – I can afford the best food and eat lots of it. The result was that the poor often ate mainly carbohydrates and this combined with a manual occupation ensured them better health and a longer life than their social superiors if they were lucky enough to live in a rural area and avoid communicable diseases. For the poor their one big disadvantage in this situation was lack of hygiene, not poor diet or lack of exercise.

What kind of fat are we saying is healthy? Saturated fat, the kind that we get in butter and cheese, has been over-demonized in recent times. Fat gives flavour to food. We would all prefer to drink full cream milk rather than skim milk if flavour was the only difference. Just as it would be damaging to eat no fat at all, it would be impossible to eat a healthy diet while avoiding eating any saturated fat. Nuts are one of the healthiest things you can eat, and yet they contain a high proportion of saturated fat, alongside healthy levels of monounsaturated fat. I recommend Brazil nuts for their selenium content, as our bodies produce less and less selenium as we get older. Yet Brazil nuts contain a high level of saturated fat. A handful of Brazil nuts each day will do you more good than harm.

The big no-no in the fat department is trans fats (trans isomer fatty acids) – usually unsaturated vegetable oils which have been chemically altered by a process called partial hydrogenation whereby the oils are heated and then subjected to process in which hydrogen is bubbled through them so that their molecules become solid at room temperature. Trans fats are a favourite of food manufacturers because they are cheap and because they prolong the shelf life of foods You are unlikely to find cheap biscuits on a supermarket shelf that do not contain trans fats, though now that it is becoming better known that such fats can be bad for you (and make you fat), there is a tendency for manufacturers to find alternative, albeit more expensive substitutes, and perhaps add the allegedly wonder fat that is Omega 3 oil. Other foods that are still to be found with trans fats are: ice cream, artificial cream, pastries, cereals, snack bars, breakfast cereals, doughnuts, pizzas, pies, pasties and most deep-fried food from fast food outlets. The best way to avoid trans fats is to avoid processed foods and fried foods that you have not fried at home. Better still, avoid fried foods altogether (see chapter 44 on weight loss). Though we trail behind the Americans, we British are the fattest nation in Europe. Saturated fats, unlike trans fats, are healthy in small quantities. The problem with saturated fats is simply that as with trans fats, we eat too much of them.

Expect to see trans fats either banned altogether or labelled distinctly as such on food labels rather like government health warnings on cigarette packets.

One study calculated that for every 2% rise in trans fats consumption the risk of cardiovascular disease doubled, whereas it took a 19% rise in natural fats to have the same effect. The principal natural fats used in food production are butter, lard and palm oil, all of which are saturated fats.

We find foods marked 'low fat', 'reduced fat' and 'zero fat' on supermarket shelves. That doesn't tell you a great deal, which is why the law requires the content of processed food to be described in detail. A food might be 'low in saturates' but high in trans fats, which is worse than the reverse. The description (if you can read the small print and have not forgotten to take your glasses to the supermarket) should tell you what kind of fats you are considering eating.

The essential fatty acids, of which Omega 3 is one (see chapter 14 on supplements), are so-called because they are essential to a healthy diet and yet are not manufactured by the body in sufficient quantity or at all. They have to be consumed in food (see chapter 14 on supplements for more on the Omega oils). There are three types of Omega 3 oils – eicosapentaenoic acid (EPA) (from fish), docosahexaenoic acid (DHA) (also from fish) and alpha linolenic acid (ALA) found in foods like lecithin, walnut oil, flaxseed (linseed) oil and hempseed oil, for example. The virtues of EPA and DHA are widely extolled for a variety of benefits including their blood-thinning properties, while DHA is said to do wonders for the brain. Omega 6 is found in abundance in corn oil, sunflower oil and safflower oil, all widely used in cooking. Most people get too much of these polyunsaturates. They are also found in margarine and low fat spreads, which may contain trans fats to give them a longer shelf life. (A spread like Benecol contains plant nutrients that may slightly lower your 'bad' cholesterol, as advertised, and raise 'good' cholesterol very slightly. It doesn't contain trans fats, but it will deliver a heavy dose of calories and more than enough Omega 6 oils).

The one Omega 6 oil most people do not get enough of is gamma linoleic acid (GLA), made by the body in small quantities and found in evening primrose oil, borage oil, starflower oil and blackcurrant oil. Some GLA is also found in flaxseed and hempseed oil. GLA is only usually taken as a supplement and works as an anti-oxidant. My advice is to avoid the Omega 6 cooking oils altogether and cook in hazelnut or olive oil (both Omega 9), while taking EPA, DHA and GLA supplements.

The saturated fats are natural fats found in food of animal origin such as meat, butter, cheese, yoghurt, and also in seeds and nuts, especially coconuts. Poultry contains a little saturated fat, but less if it is free range. And wild game has less still, thanks to a healthy outdoor life far from the mass production pens in which much of what we eat is reared. There are arguments in favour of a small amount of saturated fat each day in your diet. You should eat saturates in moderation and limit polyunsaturates. Steer clear of trans fats, which will probably be banned altogether one of these days as part of the war on obesity. Some of the fast food chains, in fact, have already jumped the gun and switched away from trans fats to avoid bad publicity and earn Brownie points.

Olive oil has become a staple of the British kitchen in the last twenty years as the so-called Mediterranean diet has grown in popularity. As a salad dressing, this Omega 9 monounsaturated fat is a valuable source of an essential fatty acid, though it should not be used too abundantly if calorie limitation is called for. It's also a favourite when it comes to cooking, in which case it should be used at a low temperature as any oils heated to the point of burning alter in molecular structure and may become carcinogenic. If the oils are polyunsaturates, they may also produce free radicals, causing oxidative damage. Monounsaturated oils like olive oil and hazelnut oil may slightly lower LDL levels and may even very slightly raise HDL. They are found in nuts and seeds alongside saturated fat, and some monounsaturates are present in eggs, fish, meat and dairy products, which also contain the eight essential amino acids (found also in soybeans, but not in any other single vegetable source). Protein is made from 22 amino acids of which eight are essential, meaning that the body cannot make them and they must therefore be eaten.

Soybeans are regarded by many vegetarians as an all-round staple for protein and carbohydrate. Soybeans and products derived from them such as tofu and tempeh contain phyto-oestrogens (including isoflavones – see chapter 43 on the prostate). These are natural substances which mimic the female hormone oestrogen and produce some of the same effects as oestrogen. Too much soy is thought to be implicated in certain feminising characteristics seen in some men in middle age, especially the development of male breasts, though the more likely explanation is a natural age-related fall in testosterone without a matching drop in the male's natural oestrogen level. Phyto-oestrogens aren't only found in soybeans, though they are probably the best source. All pulses (beans, peas and lentils) contain some phyto-oestrogens.

Protein comes from animal and vegetable sources. Too much animal protein in the diet is almost certainly bad for you, and has been implicated in high blood pressure. Animal protein is different from vegetable protein and a healthy diet should contain some of each. I count fish protein as animal protein in the same way that a piece of lean turkey or steak is animal protein. Some vegetables are rich in protein and probably more healthful than others. Two obvious examples are broccoli and spinach, each of which is almost 50% vegetable protein. While potatoes, whole wheat pasta, brown rice and whole grains are good sources of complex carbohydrates, it also turns out that they are a source of vegetable protein, though we should be aware that we digest vegetable protein less well than animal protein.

Cheese is something that most of us like but may eat with a guilty conscience if we are careful about our diet. A hard cheese like cheddar is 25% protein and 75% fat, of which almost two-thirds is saturated fat. As we know, saturated fat is not the enemy it once was. The problem with cheese is the number of calories it packs per mouthful. Low fat cheeses like cottage cheese don't come with the same flavour appeal. The only solution when it comes to cheese is to eat it sparingly, and perhaps opt for a tasty cheese with a lower level of fat, such as Brie.

Is there a hierarchy of what is good protein? I tend to think that weight for weight, fish protein is better than meat protein, but here there is a proviso. Fish from fish farms may contain elements that reflect the cheap feed that is often used. Farmed salmon has had a lot of bad press in recent years and for good reason. Taste wild salmon and compare it with farmed salmon. You will see immediately why wild salmon tastes better. It's firmer, less fatty and costs twice as much. Organic farmed fish comes somewhere in between wild and non-organic in the pecking order, though some would argue that well farmed organic salmon, for example, avoids dioxins and mercury on the one hand and the feed problems of non-organic farmed salmon on the other. But beware of farmed fish passed off as wild. With prices for wild fish so high, it's not surprising that it happened with Greek sea bass. It is bound to happen again.

Farmed salmon are fed mainly on cereal grains whereas wild salmon mostly feed on wild algae and shrimp. As a result of their diet, farmed salmon develop high levels of a bad form of Omega 6 oil – arachidonic acid. When we eat it, it can cause cell inflammation. Wild salmon has 30% more good Omega 3 oil than farmed salmon. While we're on the subject of the Omega oils (see chapter 14 on supplements), cattle are generally fed on grains whereas their natural feed is grass. This produces meat that contains too much Omega 6 oil and not enough Omega 3. Two hundred years ago, the balance between Omega 3 and Omega 6 in most diets was about right. Today there is a huge imbalance in favour of Omega 6, and we are only just beginning to find out how damaging that can be.

Most of us do not eat enough fish and the reason is partly the cost. Fish from the sea are getting scarcer and more expensive, and some say that this source of protein will be lost forever in another fifty years as a result of global warming and overfishing. The other reason why eating more fish may cause some hesitation is that there has been widespread advice in the media saying on the one hand that oily fish are good for you because of its Omega 3 content, which is true, but that you should only eat oily fish from the sea – salmon, swordfish, tuna, sea trout, mackerel, herrings, sardines and anchovies - no more than twice a week in case of mercury (and sometimes cadmium and dioxin) poisoning, especially the big predators in the food chain like tuna and swordfish.

I have a problem with this advice because what it is saying is that Omega 3 from fish is good for you, but the methylmercury that may be found in the liver and fat of some fish is bad for you, therefore you should limit your mercury intake, or at least limit your risk of ingesting mercury. That is about as logical as saying that if you have to cross a minefield to reach safety, you should hop on one leg to reduce your chances of being blown up. Either wild salmon is good for you or it isn't.

You decide if it's worth the risk of a build-up of mercury inside you. But the answer does not lie in hedging the risk by eating it twice a week instead of more often. And don't give up on the so-called non-oily fish, provided that they are not farmed. They contain Omega 3 oils too. Oily fish hold the Omega 3 oils in the flesh, whereas so-called 'white' fish hold them in the liver, which we tend not to eat.

Vegetarians notoriously do not get enough protein since animal sources are different from vegetable sources and in an ideal diet the body needs both. Vegans start at even more of a disadvantage, since vegetarians who are not pure vegetarians may at least get some animal protein from eggs and dairy products. I have never favoured vegetarianism let alone veganism, though I would be the first to admit that a good vegetarian diet is preferable to a bad non-vegetarian diet. The best answer is an omnivorous diet where animal protein is eaten in moderation and comes mainly from fish rather than meat and dairy products. No more than about 500 grams of red meat should be eaten weekly, all of it lean meat. I'm guilty of getting most of my non-protein food from fruit. The healthiest omnivorous diet, however, leans towards vegetables rather than fruit. Eat at least eight (not five) fruit and vegetables a day, and try to make vegetables predominant.

As far as vegan diets go, I am reminded of a former friend I last saw 16 years ago. She was then in her mid-thirties, but thanks to several years on a macrobiotic diet, she looked about ten years older. Her eyes had sunk into her head prematurely and as far as I could tell, the main part of her diet was soybeans.

Some attribute the longevity of the Japanese to soy products, but that may only be a part of the picture, given that the Japanese diet is well known for its dependence on fish rather than meat. Soy products contain a lot of salt and may score negatively for another reason – they tend to be high in natural oestrogens (see above) and an excess of oestrogens in a man's diet can lead to various problems (but see chapter 43 on the prostate). Nowadays many soy products are from GM (genetically modified) sources and we still don't know what risk GM foods might expose us to.

When the body requires energy, it can take it from fat, protein or carbohydrates. Our bodies are made up of fat, protein, a little carbohydrate, minerals, micronutrients and most of all, water. The body turns food into energy in the form of glycogen, a carbohydrate which is stored mainly in the liver. Glycogen is a sugar derivative and can be made from fat, protein or carbohydrates. It can come from food passing through the body, from reserves in the liver, or from energy stored as fat or as protein.

Anyone who keeps up with research in sports physiology will know that over time, opinion has gone backwards and forwards over what and when athletes should eat to maximize their performance. When I was at university, the college rowing team were fed vast quantities of steak each day in the belief that this would maximize muscle strength. Since then coaches have swung towards carbohydrates as the most important source of immediate energy. Hence we have the expression 'carb load-ing' which we tend to associate with marathon runners trying to get past the 'wall' at the 18-mile mark. The arguments for what to eat and when, before and after competing, go on and on. One that sounds plausible says that we should exercise in the morning on an empty stomach and then eat a protein- rich meal thirty minutes after the workout.

For what purpose? To get fitter? To lose weight? To win a race? To live longer? I don't think it's necessary to distinguish objectives like these. If the intention is to be fit and healthy for as long as possible in your life, what is good for the marathon runner ought to be good for everyone. That doesn't mean that what is good for the bodybuilder will be good for everyone, but that is because what makes a sculpted body that will win competitions like Mr Universe and leave you looking like Arnold Schwarzenegger in his Terminator days is not healthy. The middle road is the healthy road. I personally think that marathon running goes beyond what is healthy and normal, and that the diet and training that go with it are excessive. Yes, it may win marathons, but have you ever noticed how athletes and sportsmen at their peak often look exhausted (see chapters 18 and 37 on exercise and sleeping)?

How much carbohydrate should you eat and what happens to it? Carbohydrates come in two forms. They are either starches, in which case they are slow-release complex carbohydrates, or they are sugars, in which case they are simple carbohydrates. Complex carbohydrates are broken down into sugars. Sugars provide energy. That energy is measured in the calories we burn by using our muscles and even by thinking.

Examples of starches are potatoes, bread, pulses, pasta, rice and grains. There is some starch in most vegetables, but none at all in most fruit. An exception is bananas, which are also rich in potassium chloride. Fruits and vegetables contain what are called intrinsic sugars (extrinsic or free sugars are sugars that are added to a food, with the exception of lactose, which is an extrinsic sugar, even though it is not an added sugar). Since fruits are mostly composed of sugar, while vegetables are a mixture of sugars and complex carbohydrates, vegetables are generally a more rounded source of nutrition than fruit, particularly as many vegetables are also good sources of vegetable protein.

Carbohydrates that are not used quickly are stored as fat for future use. We burn glycogen with every move we make. As the saying goes, eat more calories than you burn and you put on weight. Eat fewer calories than you burn and you lose weight. Sounds easy. Let's say you've decided you need to lose a pound a week for the next four weeks. You go on a diet and start restricting calorie intake. In theory your body will start using up your fat store to provide the calories it is not getting from food.

But consider this. A team of four cold climate explorers recently made a film in which they simulated Captain Scott's rush to the South Pole in 1912, pulling sledges behind them. They used Greenland instead of the Antarctic, but the principle is the same. At the end of the trip, cut prematurely short as the men were getting weak and exhausted, they were examined and weighed. As expected, their strenuous efforts pulling sledges in freezing conditions and burning 8000 calories a day while getting a slightly less than adequate diet had led to severe weight loss over a period of a few weeks. What came as a surprise and has still not been explained was the fact that most of the weight loss came from muscle protein and not from body fat, as had been expected. It is well known that the body can eat its own protein for energy, but it has always been held that it will only do so when there is no readily available fat as an energy source. So why had protein gone first?

The answer is not at all clear and the TV programme that covered the expedition could not offer an answer. Sports physiologists know that when marathon runners load with carbs, it is these carbs that they are planning to use to see them through the race. Marathon runners do not have high body fat percentages. One that I know has a body fat percentage of about 10%, whereas the norm for a healthy middle-aged man should be between 17% and 22%. Needless to say, marathon runners do not expect to draw on fat reserves for energy during a race. Nor do they expect to draw on muscle protein. In fact they know that they need to provide an alternative to protein and this is where the carbs come in – complex carbs rather than refined carbs before the race and drinks rich in protein and simple carbohydrates (sugars) during the race to ward off dehydration and keep energy levels up.

What the polar explorer and the marathon runner have in common is a very high level of calorie burn. The evidence to date suggests that it is quite hard for a man to burn fat, especially visceral fat, which is found round his middle and is slightly different from the fat in the rest of the body. When we exercise hard and talk of burning fat at the gym, we may actually be burning protein as well, and while we may think it a good thing to burn fat, we may not be so keen to burn up our muscle tissue.

But the picture is more complicated than that. Different types of exercise burn calories in different ways. Resistance training such as exercising with weights will tend to speed up the metabolism a bit, fat will be burnt and muscles will enlarge as the tiny tears that come from exercise heal as expanded tissue. With aerobic exercise, the burning of fat is different. It's my view that every body has an inbuilt optimum weight for that individual, and that the body will always attempt to come to a standstill at that weight if it is optimally fed and exercised. When that optimum is reached, the body fat percentage will probably be in the 17–22% range. Aerobic exercise at the right pace and resistance training at the right level for the right duration will optimize the body's fat to non-fat ratio and that ratio will differ to some extent between individuals according to their genetic make-up.

What is the optimum aerobic rate to achieve such a result and how do you know when you have reached it? I am a great believer in listening to your body. It will soon tell you when you are overdoing it. Some sports physiologists write about how, if burning fat is our objective, this can be achieved by exercising for longer in the middle of the aerobic zone rather than for a shorter period high in the zone. For example, I work out on a rowing machine at home. If I want to burn fat, is it better for me to work out for 30 minutes at say 65% of my heart rate maximum or for say 20 minutes at 80% of my maximum, assuming that in both examples I burn the same number of calories? According to one theory, I will burn more fat in the first instance, and the nearer I get to my anaerobic threshold (about 90% of heart rate maximum), the more I will tend to burn muscle protein. Is this true? I have heard the opposite, and it seems to me that until there is more research, we simply do not know. In the meantime, my advice remains the same: listen to your body. If it's telling you that you are overdoing it, rest more and push yourself less. If your body fat is in the right zone, do not go overboard trying to lose weight. The chances are that you are already the right weight.

If your Body Mass Index (BMI) is between 18 and 26, you are probably doing fine. If it is over 26 but under 32, you may need to lose weight or you may just be another Brad Pitt, all heavy bones and solid muscle. That's where your body fat percentage comes in. It's better to have a BMI of 26 and be built like Brad Pitt than to have a BMI of 26 with body fat at 30% (see chapter 18 on exercise for why BMI is a flawed method for assessing fitness). If you are very fit and well muscled, don't be dismayed if you find your BMI suggests you are overweight or obese. BUPA in their medical screenings are beginning to wake up to this seeming paradox. However, if you are on the chubby side and have a BMI of 30, it may be that you are no Brad Pitt and really are on the starting line for obesity.

There's another factor affecting BMI to a lesser extent. If you exercise a lot throughout your life, especially if you do a lot of load-bearing exercise using your legs – running, rowing and cycling would be the most obvious examples – your leg bones will strengthen and thicken. At the same time as you are protecting yourself from osteoporosis, where bones are typically light through lack of density, you are building up a heavier weight relative to your height. This dawned on me when I was checked over by the doctor on my annual BUPA medical. The doctor picked up one of my legs as I lay on the couch and commented on how heavy it was. I replied that that was probably because I had been a walker all my life. I walk about twenty miles a week and my leg bones are probably quite heavy. I am not concerned that I might get the osteoporosis that afflicted my mother. While I could do with getting my body fat percentage down to say 17% from its current 19%, I am not concerned that my BMI is slightly over 25. In fact I would prefer it to stay around the 26 mark, though I cannot compete with Brad Pitt. For one thing, I could not put in the long hours of exercise that this would require, as I now get tired too quickly to be able to reach the fitness level of an athletic man twenty years younger than I am.

I would not advise that you become a calorie counter as that amounts to being obsessive and obsessive people are not the worried well. With a little practice it soon becomes possible to guess roughly how many calories a day you are eating and what the approximate percentages are between the three components. Aim for protein from fish, poultry and lean meat, especially game. Aim for carbs from plenty of fresh fruit and vegetables, but out-of- season food-miles-laden fruits and vegetables flown in from far away only if your conscience will allow and you have found a way to pay for the carbon footprint left behind. Eat complex carbs like brown rice, whole wheat pasta, wholegrain bread, wholegrain muesli and baked potatoes (the best way to eat potatoes, especially sweet potatoes, which are rich in anti-oxidants – potatoes and tomatoes are exceptional in that their food value actually goes up rather than down when they are cooked). Avoid refined carbs if you can – things like white bread, white rice, pies, pasties and virtually all cakes and biscuits. And for fat eat plenty of nuts and seeds. Use walnut oil for dressings and olive or hazelnut oil for cooking, and you will get a little extra fat anyway from your lean protein sources.

Should you limit saturated fat by consuming fewer dairy products? The best solution, until science tells us more, is to eat cheese in moderation, and buy low fat milk and yoghurt. For a few years I have been drinking semi-skimmed goat's milk (2% fat). I am hopeful of finding micronutrients in it which have escaped the process of fat removal and pasteurisation. The calcium is still there, and that is important. However, the ideal would be whole milk, sadly something that is hard to find in this age of too much Health and Safety. Whole milk herds have to be certified as tuberculosis-free. Otherwise the milk is pasteurised, which is what we normally buy at the supermarket. This heating process destroys much of the vitamin content. Whole milk from goats would be about 8% saturated fat, but as long as this fitted with an over-all daily limit of 7.5% of calories from saturated fat, I think this would be healthy – so long as you could find whole goat's milk from a source cer-tified as TB-free. Quite a challenge.

Hydration (drinking enough liquid) is vital for health. Water is the best source of liquid, though you will also get some from the food you eat and from other drinks. Water helps to control body temperature and contains no calories. It is lost through sweat, urine and breathing. It is hard to be precise about how much water we should consume each day. The amount will vary according to temperature, calorie expendi-ture and individual metabolism, but as an average in the UK, think of about four pints per day. However, it's important to know that as we get older, it becomes possible to need water without feeling thirsty as our internal thermostat starts to function less well. A parallel to this is the way in which people feel the cold less as they get older. Thus the elderly in particular are at risk of becoming dehydrated and of not keeping warm enough. Go without water for three or four days and you will die.

Drink plenty of liquid, preferably water, during the day, even when not feeling thirsty. Some weighing scales will tell your water percentage relative to body weight. It should be in the 50–55% range, ideally closer to 55%.

Defeating bone loss (osteoporosis) is a matter of load-bearing exer-cise and eating right. Women are four times more prone to the disease than men. If there is not enough calcium in your diet, you may need supplements, though too much calcium can be as bad for you as too little. Calcium supplements should be taken with vitamin D for better uptake. To fight osteoporosis with nutrition, you should also have adequate magnesium, vitamin K, folic acid, niacin (vitamin B3), zinc, vitamin C, potassium and possibly also the mineral boron. Healthy bones need calcium, and too much salt in your diet may cause bone loss through the excretion of too much valuable calcium. An excessive intake of alcohol will reduce calcium absorption.

To get as many micronutrients in your diet as possible, vary what you eat as much as you can. This is a good reason not to rely too much on supplements. Food contains hundreds of trace elements and phytochemicals (biologically active non-nutrients of plant origin), most of which are not found in supplements. We still know very little about the majority of these, let alone how they work in synergy with each other. Any synergistic effects are usually reduced or lost when we get nutrients from supplements, since they do not have the natural advantage of being part of a complex spectrum of ingredients put together the way nature intended.

Processed food, especially in the form of ready-made meals, is normally extensively denatured and may be high in trans fats (see above), salt or sugar. Denatured means that the processes that it has gone through have removed much of its food value, especially vitamins and minerals. All food is denatured to some extent unless eaten immediately on being harvested. From that moment on it starts to lose freshness and 'die'. Exposure to sunlight after harvesting denatures food and the inevitable process of oxidation enhances this effect. Buying fresh will provide more nutritive food on the whole than buying processed. Many 'fresh' foods on the supermarket shelves have been bred (though not extensively genetically engineered, at least in the UK at present) to last longer and look more appetising, and often fresh fruit and vegetables have been treated with sprays to give them a longer shelf life. These processes have usually passed Health and Safety checks, but you cannot help feeling that organic might be better. The trouble with organic food, however, is that it wilts very quickly and unless it is sold quickly, you may think twice about buying it. For this reason, foods that are typically frozen soon after harvesting, such as peas, will have more food value than fresh peas, organic or not, bought off the shelf. And frozen foods will generally have more food value than tinned. An exception is tomatoes. Heating and/or cooking tomatoes to produce tinned tomatoes or tomato paste enhances their valuable lycopene level.

Most foods are better raw than cooked – the so-called Evo or caveman diet that is said to be the healthiest of all. However, tomatoes and baked potatoes are an exception (see above). Some foods are safer cooked, for example chicken, which carries a certain risk of salmonella poisoning. Uncooked food should be kept well away from cooked food in a fridge. The temperature should be kept low and the fridge uncrowded to reduce the spread of bacteria. Uncooked meat and fish should be wrapped to reduce oxidation, and cooked food should only ever be reheated once.

The so-called Evo diet is interesting in that it harks back to an age before agriculture had been discovered. In other words, there are no cultivated grains in the Evo diet. Yet if you take unrefined whole grain cereals, including whole grain bread, out of the diet, you remove what is regarded as an important source of healthy nutrition. One of the results is thought to be a thickening of the carotid artery and resulting increased risk of stroke.

Some forms of cooking cause more damage to the molecules in protein food than others. The healthiest ways to cook meat and fish, as well as cheese-based dishes, are steaming, boiling and stewing rather than roasting, frying or grilling, which may trigger the formation of damaging toxins called advanced glycogen endproducts (AGEs) linked to hypertension, arthritis, Alzheimer's disease, heart disease and diabetes. If AGEs accumulate in the body faster than it can get rid of them, they can damage skin collagen, leading to premature sag and wrinkles and other signs of premature ageing. The effect over the long term doesn't stop there. The toxins can trigger tissue inflammation and precipitate a variety of diseases. If experiments on mice are anything to go by, avoiding AGEs by steaming, boiling or stewing could actually lengthen your lifespan. Best of all, you could eat everything raw. This might be too much of a challenge for most of us, but there are certainly plenty of foods that are delicious raw, not just salads. Think of sashimi, carpaccio or steak tartare. AGEs do not occur when you cook vegetables or fruit, so the way that you cook these doesn't matter.

One solution to the AGE problem might be to microwave more as microwaving has been shown in one test to be the least destructive form of cooking. When cooking broccoli, you will preserve 82% of vitamin C by microwaving, compared with 72% when you steam, 67% when you pressure cook and only 35% when you boil.

Fruit juices are high in sugar content (fructose) and also in calories. However, fructose is low on the Glycaemic Index, making it a more acceptable form of sugar than sucrose. The main types of sugar are glucose, dextrose, fructose, glucose syrup, lactose, maltose and treacle. Most are high on the GI, including sucrose, which is what basic white table sugar is.

Fibre is an important part of a healthy diet. Fibre is found in complex carbohydrate foods and mostly comes in the form of cellulose (roughage) and pectin, beta-glucens and arabinose. The former is insoluble in water and the latter is soluble in water, and therefore soluble in the digestive tract. Most plants contain soluble and insoluble fibre in varying proportions. A high fibre diet is important. Lots of roughage, accompanied by lots of liquid, helps speed stool passage and keep weight down. It may also make you feel full and so prevent overeating. Soluble fibre comes in several forms – pectin is found in apples and citrus fruits, beta-glucens in oats, barley and rye, and arabinose in pulses (lentils, peas and beans). Soluble fibre helps to keep 'bad' (LDL) cholesterol levels down and control blood sugar by slowing sugar absorption. Resistant starch is a fibre-like substance which helps to bulk stool. It is found in potatoes and cereals and goes through the intestines undigested.

The neurotransmitter acetylcholine is vital for brain performance and levels of acetylcholine are affected by blood glucose levels. A modest amount of glucose at breakfast is therefore a good idea, but the effect can be lost if acetylcholine is blocked by drugs, including pharmaceutical drugs. The glucose you eat in the morning should come from complex carbohydrates such as those found in whole grain cereals and bread, or from fructose-rich fruit or fruit juice, rather than from sucrose (table sugar) or other kinds of processed sugar that are added to many processed breakfast cereals. A strong burst of energy from too much sugar at any time can leave you feeling drained afterwards.

Coffee has it promoters and its detractors. Seventy percent of British adults are coffee drinkers and drink between three and four cups a day on average. Seventy million cups a day are drunk.

Coffee may cause the following:
nausea
itchy skin
joint pain
fatigue
anxiety
depression
raised blood pressure
osteoporosis (by depleting calcium)
inhibition of calcium and iron uptake from food (therefore coffee should not be drunk with food)
increased heart rate
an overstimulated nervous system,
raised cortisol
reduced dopamine level in the brain
a craving for carbohydrates, especially sugar
heart arrhythmias
irritable bowel syndrome
migraine headaches
insomnia
caffeine addiction
raised triglycerides and LDL 'bad' cholesterol

However, coffee has also been argued to be good for you if you keep your caffeine intake below 450 mg a day (average UK consumption is 280 mg). That doesn't just apply to coffee, but to tea, cola drinks and chocolate, all of which contain caffeine, though coffee is likely to be the one which may take you over the limit. On the plus side, coffee provides some anti-oxidants, improves concentration and keeps you alert.

Coffee has been shown to cut levels of uric acid in the blood and therefore the incidence of gout. In alcoholics, it delays the onset of cirrhosis of the liver. In fact it has the same preventive action in cases of non-alcoholic cirrhosis. Coffee, according to one study, also reduces the risk of Type 2 diabetes, which I find difficult to believe if it raises the level of blood fats (see above). It may also protect against gallstone formation. It used to be thought that coffee raised the risk of heart attack and stroke, but it has now been found to be neutral in this respect, which seems strange in light of the fact that it has been shown to raise blood pressure. The same view holds for cancer generally, and rectal cancer in particular, which used to be thought to have a strong link with caffeine.

The charge sheet against caffeine seems to grow with every new report. Drinking five to six cups of cafetière coffee each day raises LDL cholesterol by around 7%, increasing the risk of obesity. Many of the coffees sold in the UK's 3,000 coffee shops contain as much as 500 calories, which will come as surprise to those who see coffee as part of a weight loss programme. Cream on top of a coffee can add up to a further 120 calories and contain as much as seven grams of saturated fat. One line of research claims that fat from drinks is not the same as fat from food and is not as easily metabolised. If you must drink coffee from a high street outlet, it's worth knowing that the options lowest in calories (but not necessarily caffeine) are a single-shot espresso and what is called an Americano (an espresso with water added). Either should be drunk black or with the addition of skim milk to keep the calories down. One other advantage to espresso is its tannin and anti-oxidant content, though I can think of much better sources of both. A latte coffee is of course bad news if you want to keep the calories down.

Nor is decaffeinated coffee the answer. It has been found that decaf may be worse than some caffeinated coffee at raising the level of fats in the blood, including LDL cholesterol. The problem seems to be two ingredients in coffee called cafestol and kahweol, which raise blood lipid levels in drinkers of decaf and those who prefer cafetière or espresso to filtered coffee, where these ingredients are removed by the filter. Coffee boiled Scandinavian-style is also likely to raise triglycerides and LDL cholesterol.

Decaf coffee is not caffeine-free either. On average about 30% of caffeine is retained, making it a bad option for anyone with a caffeine intolerance. And the process of decaffeination removes useful flavonoids found in coffee beans.

Coffee easily becomes addictive, even if you only drink 100 mg of caffeine a day, the amount found in half a cup of instant coffee, and only one-third of the average daily intake in the UK. Different individuals have different tolerance levels and therefore vary in how easily they become addicted. As with alcohol, caffeine addiction means needing more and more to get the same kick the more habituated you become. Meanwhile it's clear that the UK is not just a nation of heavy drinkers, but a nation of caffeine addicts as well.

Caffeine should not be consumed at the same time as paracetamol as this can cause liver damage. Many commercial versions of paracetamol have added caffeine and these should be avoided. Heavy alcohol consumption can make taking many drugs dangerous and this applies to paracetamol too, so the worst combination is all three together: paracetamol, caffeine and alcohol. Men on anti-epileptic drugs or taking St John's wort as an anti-depressant should be particularly careful about taking paracetamol.

Cola drinks not only contain caffeine, they contain phosphoric acid which reduces bone density by blocking absorption of dietary calcium. They are therefore a recipe for osteoporosis. Many drinks contain the preservative E211 (sodium benzoate). Check the label.

Many cordials contain artificial colourants. If they say 'sugar-free' on the label, this is often a sign that they contain an artificial sweetener (see below). Sweeteners like these are suspected of being carcinogenic in the long run. Better safe than sorry. Avoid drinks like these or stick to those with regular sugar added. But no added sweetener at all is best.

We've touched on trans fats, the vegetable fats which are partially hydrogenated to give foods a longer more stable shelf life. Trans fats have no safe consumption level. They raise the level of LDL 'bad' cholesterol. My advice is that you avoid ready-made meals and processed foods altogether. If you must eat such foods, read and understand the label and see whether they contain any trans fats. They have already been banned in Denmark. The main reason why such fats are bad for you is that they are believed to block the passage of messages in the brain via the synapses, the pathways that link neuron to neuron. Three fats that may well be used widely in the future to replace trans fats are grape seed oil at the top end of the market, and rapeseed oil and soybean oil at the lower end. If you are wondering what foods commonly contain trans fats, think hamburgers, margarines, vegetable shortenings, biscuits, snacks, crackers, French fries, pies, pastries, crisps and baked goods.

Vitamin C, which is found aplenty in fruit and vegetables, is essential to a healthy immune system and to supporting the adrenal gland, responsible for producing adrenaline in response to stress. The benefits of vitamin C found in oranges and grapefuit is enhanced by a flavonoid called hesperitin.

A study shows that tea brewed in a pot for five minutes gives maximum benefit in the form of the anti-oxidants known as polyphenols. A shorter brewing time is not as effective, and brewing for over five minutes adds no extra benefit. Adding milk to tea has no added anti-oxidant benefit. The anti-oxidants in tea (especially green tea) can help reduce the risk of some cancers, including skin cancer. Another study suggests that four cups of tea a day can reduce the risk of heart attack, strengthen bones and help prevent tooth decay. The risk of stroke and diabetes is also thought to improve with tea drinking on a regular basis.

Many alcoholics are clinically depressed. Their depression often responds well to high doses of niacin (vitamin B3), folate and ascorbic acid (vitamin C). Depression is helped too by doses of Omega 3 oils, though no research has yet been done with this essential fatty acid in alcoholics.

Watch out for food fraud – food that is not what it purports to be or comes from a country that is different from the one on the label. One of the biggest scandals in recent years was the importation of millions of eggs that were passed off in the supermarkets as organic when they were anything but. There have also been Thai chickens sold as locally produced, Angus beef that was South American, rice from the US that was partially genetically modified (GM) and honey claiming to be from a single source that actually had a mixture of sources and added sugar.

Labels may disguise contents (see below) and the supermarkets have worked hard to block government moves for a traffic light identification system on the front of food packages to show high levels of salt, fat and sugar. The problem is that people are often not well informed enough to work out these things for themselves from the information on the back of the pack, if the information is there at all, as nutritional information is voluntary, unlike ingredient information. This is largely compulsory on processed food, the order being a clue to quantities, with the ingredient with the highest quantity by weight being at the top. You may not be able to interpret, say, 20 grams of sugar per 100 grams weight, but if you see sugar listed first on the ingredients list, this will be a clue to a high level of sugar.

The problem with sugar is that it comes in many forms and many manufacturers cheat if they list ingredients by gram weight per 100 grams by breaking sugar into different types to fool the consumer and avoid giving the total of all types of sugar combined. Sugar may be listed as fructose, invert sugar, honey, sucrose, glucose, treacle, glucose syrup, golden syrup, maple syrup, dextrose, maltose, lactose, hydrolysed starch, molasses or corn syrup. A product might have three or four of these sugar ingredients, each listed separately rather than together as 'sugar'. One well known muesli bar is guilty of doing this, though they would no doubt argue that educating the consumer is not their responsibility and the information given is correct. The ill-informed, and that is most of the population, will be misled, if they even bother to read the label at all. High sugar content in a processed food can strain the pancreas as the extra sugar in the blood drives up insulin production. This does not cause Type 2 diabetes directly, but may do so indirectly over time. There is evidence, however, that men with higher than average blood sugar levels are very slightly less at risk of prostate cancer. I don't think this is a reason, however, to push up your blood sugar level. There are too many factors on the downside.

This kind of deception is less of a problem with salt and fat, where there is less scope for cheating. However, not every consumer will understand that sodium chloride refers to salt, or understand the difference between monounsaturated, polyunsaturated and saturated fat, let alone what partially hydrogenated fat is.

Some high fat products are low in sugar and vice versa. So a product advertised as 'low fat' or 'low sugar' may be deceptively unhealthy.

Many sugar-free products contain artificial sweeteners such as aspartame, acesulfame-k and saccharin. These are believed to be safe to eat, but I have always avoided them, and personally I would rather eat sugar in moderation.

Most major UK supermarkets have embarked on a programme of reducing or eliminating foods and drinks that contain a long list of additives that colour, enhance flavour or preserve, especially benzoate preservatives. Where food is claimed to be organic, only 39 additives are permitted, compared with some 300 for non-organic foods. Organic producers can only use any of the 39 additives if they can demonstrate that their food would not be safe or could not be preserved without them.

More and more foods now come with RDA (Recommended Daily Allowance) or GDA (Guidance Daily Amount). I tend to agree that it's time that more consumers took the time and trouble to understand food labelling. Currently the majority of the population is deeply ignorant when it comes to understanding labels, and I cannot help feeling that some of this ignorance is deliberate as many of the population are afraid of talking themselves out of deeply fattening diets if they understand too much.

Drinking water is likely to reduce hunger pangs: drinking fizzy drinks less so. Tea, coffee, sports drinks and some fruit juices do not give satiety to the extent that water can. Many drinks act like foods and in this way can make you less hungry. This is true of milk, which becomes a semi-solid in the stomach. Soups and juices like tomato juice can have this effect too. In this way, soups, especially low calorie soups, can be a useful addition to a serious weight loss plan. Even looking at a bowl of soup can send a satiety message to the brain in a way that looking at water or fruit juice cannot. This reaction is reinforced by the smell and then the taste of the soup. A soup with chunky bits to chew is even more effective in getting the brain to receive a message that you are feeling full.

Smoothies are very popular, but most commercial brands are packed with sugar and calories. If you like smoothies, make your own with fresh fruit, skimmed milk and low fat plain yoghurt – and don't add any sugar. But the best drink of all is water, followed by diluted fresh fruit juice, then tea, including herbal tea. The problem with straight fresh fruit juices is the high level of calories and fructose. Fruit sugar is low on the GI, but even though that makes it 'slow release', in the same way that complex carbohydrates are slow release, it's still likely that if you drink too much, some will end up getting stored as fat. About 300 ml of pure fruit juice per day, diluted or not, is probably enough. Avoid fizzy drinks, even diet varieties and especially cola varieties. They don't quench appetite or thirst, and most contain more sugar than is good for you. Cola drinks may cause osteoporosis and are linked with obesity.

Sugar is sometimes referred to as hidden sugar because so much of it is unwittingly eaten or drunk. A low sugar product should have no more than 2 grams of sugar per 100 gram serving. Many products come with 10 grams or more per 100 gram serving.

Chocolate makes you feel good. It releases the feel-good hormones serotonin and dopamine. The cocoa in chocolate contains load of anti-oxidants, and chocolate would be a great food to eat lots of if it weren't for the sugar and milk fat that it contains and without which it would taste bitter. Chocolate with 70% or more cocoa will tend to be slightly bitter, but for that reason, will contain more of the goodies and less fat and sugar. Chocolate is said to improve blood circulation thanks to the flavonoids in cocoa. It also contains phenylethylamine (PEA), which releases the same hormones as sexual intercourse, thereby inducing a feeling of well-being. However, there is also a kick from a substance called theobromine, and another called oxytocin. Theobromine is also found in coffee and tea. The copper found in chocolate helps to pigment the skin, protecting it from too much sunlight. It also helps to slow the process of depigmentation whereby hair turns grey.

Four thousand flavonoids have so far been identified in food. All work in one way or another as anti-oxidants to combat free radicals, which are claimed by some to be the basis for the ageing process. The other main function of the flavonoids is to keep blood circulation healthy by reducing 'stickiness' in the blood and ensuring undamaged blood vessels. In other words, they have a key role to play in the never-ending battle against what might be generally if unscientifically termed 'inflammation'. In the progress of many diseases, there appears to be an increase in blood vessel inflammation, and the number and stickiness of platelets in the blood.

High protein diets can be dangerous. If there is not enough carbohydrate in the liver in the form of glycogen, the body will look elsewhere for energy. Protein is a poorly metabolised form of energy and a high protein diet may lead to ketosis, another word for a metabolic disorder that is a kind of starvation. Muscles looking for an energy source may consume themselves rather than draw on the protein eaten. Marathon runners will load with carbs before a race rather than run short at the 18-mile mark, the notorious so-called 'wall', and find themselves cannibalising their own muscles. A carbohydrate diet can induce release of the feel-good hormone serotonin and at the same time produce feelings of satiety to counter food carvings. A carbohydrate-dominant diet is good for everyday nutrition, even if you are not trying to lose weight, but if you are trying to shed a few extra kilos, it is still the best diet to follow.

Some people think that skipping meals is a good way to lose weight. It isn't. And neither is fasting or 'detoxing'. Contrary to popular belief, snacking is good for you, provided you eat the right foods and provided that overall calories are at the right level. It's when you stop and start with too big a gap in between that you get problems with your blood sugar. Low sugar levels one minute are followed by soaring levels the next if the gap between meals is too long. This in turn plays havoc with insulin production (see chapter 15 on diabetes).

It's often suggested that those on a lower income eat badly because of the higher cost of eating a healthy diet. However, one study found that the extra cost of a healthy diet was less than 1% more. The explanation is not hard to find. Bad diets usually involve ready-made meals and processed food. The extra labour involved in the production of such foods adds to cost, cancelling out any gain in the lower cost of cheap ingredients. The over-riding factor in poor diets appears to be the decline in willingness to cook meals starting from scratch with fresh ingredients. The combination of laziness and the pleasure that comes from eating many foods of poor nutritional value is enough, combined with lack of education, to explain the current obesity epidemic. Readymade meals tend to be high in salt, fat and sugar. It was found in one study that 44% of healthy eaters were graduates, whereas 39% of unhealthy eaters had left school at the age of 16.

Spinach is not as rich in iron as used to be thought, but it is rich in beta carotene, a form of vitamin A and an important anti-oxidant. Only carrots contain more. It is relatively low in vitamin C compared with some fruit and vegetables, but is high in vegetable protein, potassium and folate. Iron deficiency is associated with anaemia, depressed mood and low energy levels.

Each year, 4.5 billion litres of pesticides are used on British farms. And 350 types of pesticide are permitted. But are organic foods really better for you? The demand is said to be growing so fast that organic farmers cannot keep up, with the result that there is an increasing incidence of fraud and false labelling. At the same time, organisations like the Soil Association have witnessed a decline in the original strict standards in defining what is organic or free-range. Organic and free-range produce certainly costs more – up to twice as much. That might seem a high price to pay for food that has not been denatured with pesticides and fertilisers.

A lengthy study on tomatoes showed that organic really was better. Levels of anti-oxidant flavonoids were almost twice as high, reducing blood pressure and thus cardiovascular risk. High levels of flavonoids are also thought to help protect against some forms of cancer and perhaps dementia. According to one study, levels of the flavonoid quercetin have been found to be 79% higher in organic tomatoes, while levels of another flavonoid, kaempferol have been found to be 97% higher. Plants make flavonoids as a defence mechanism, so that if that defence is no longer required, as when a plant is protected by fertilisers, its flavonoid level will be lower, while the corresponding organic version, unsullied by fertiliser, will have a higher level, as well as more beta carotene and vitamin C.

There is much publicity given to the recommended diet of five fruit and vegetables a day. Flavonoids found in fruit and vegetables are seen as the key to healthy eating, yet the average person in the UK eats only two a day. Examples of flavonoids are catechin (found in tea), quercetin (found in good quality red wine), resveratrol (see chapters 1 and 3) and rutin (also found in red wine). All flavonoids work as anti-oxidants by limiting oxidative damage at the cellular level. Grapeseeds are rich in the flavonoids known as procyanidins. Other anti-oxidants include the carotenoids lutein and zeaxanthin, and beta carotene, found in carrots and other vegetables and fruits.

It's claimed that free radical damage is what makes us age, and that if we could only stop the oxidative damage to cells caused by free radicals, the ageing process itself could be halted and perhaps reversed. This seems like a tall order. The usual counter argument is that free radicals are natural oxygen-related reactive molecules that do impair cell function, but that the body produces anti-oxidants naturally to limit this process. In fact, it may be that if anti-oxidants are provided in the form of supplements, the body will respond by producing fewer anti-oxidants itself. So the body may be able to take care of oxidative damage itself without outside help if the diet is healthy and there's plenty of exercise. That may be an argument against taking anti-oxidant supplements in addition to a healthy diet. In any case, conquering free radicals and conquering ageing are probably not the same thing.

Exercise produces free radicals and cortisol, both potentially damaging to body cells. However, the body takes care of these itself provided that it is healthy and the immune system is in good shape. Admittedly, though, as we age, the body's defences will be less able to deal with the threat. But we can slow the process of decline by doing all we can to stay healthy.

Vitamin C from fruit and vegetables appears to have strong protective qualities as an anti-oxidant when it comes to air pollution and its impact on our lungs. When present in the lining of our lungs, it can reduce the impact of pollutants that serve as allergens, and reduce the chemical reaction that may cause itching, sneezing, wheezing and inflammation of the bronchioles associated with histamine production as the body defends itself against a perceived threat by producing mucus. Vitamin C may therefore also protect against asthma. Quercetin assists vitamin C in this role, especially when it comes to reducing histamine release, mucus and inflammation. Foods like raspberries, apricots, tomatoes, onions, bananas and apples are good sources of quercetin, which also has powerful anti-oxidant properties. Garlic and all forms of onions are also good for the lungs, though garlic is best eaten raw, something that may not be to everyone's liking. Garlic from a tube is less healthful, whereas aged garlic, available as a supplement, is said to be the best form of garlic. There are claims that garlic can lower blood pressure, though this currently remains unproven.

Vitamin E has been associated with a reduction in asthma levels. A rich source is dark green leafy vegetables. Sweet potatoes, almonds and blackberries are alternative sources. The Omega oils found in oily fish in particular are anti-inflammatory and therefore good at keeping the lungs healthy, preventing chronic obstructive pulmonary disease (COPD), which embraces illnesses such as emphysema and bronchitis. They are also believed to improve cholesterol levels, avoiding the need for statins in some cases. Clearly the lungs are best served by the so-called Mediterranean diet of fresh fruit, vegetables and fish. It has even been credited with reducing the risk of Alzheimer's disease.

Fresh berries are among the healthiest of foods. They tend to be rich in fibre, and potassium, which helps to regulate blood pressure. Blueberries can improve eyesight by boosting circulation in the tiny blood vessels in the eyes. The polyphenols in berries can keep bad bacteria in the digestive system under control and reduce the risk of diarrhoea. Raspberries are good at tackling the bacteria salmonella and staphylococcus, while strawberries and raspberries can deal with *Campylobacter jejuni* (a frequent cause of diarrhoea) and candida. For dealing with urinary tract infections, cranberries are called for. They also tackle mouth and gut infections quite effectively. Stomach ulcers and tooth decay are also said to respond to the anti-oxidants in cranberries. Strawberries can reduce atherosclerosis in the arteries, pigments in raspberries may help keep weight down, memory may be improved by eating strawberries and blueberries, and berries generally may add to your threescore years and ten.

Berries contain resveratrol, a bioactive phyto-chemical and one of the magic ingredients in red wine that is credited with making it a drink for good health, along with procyanidins and polyphenol anti-oxidants (see chapters 1 and 3 on ageing and alcohol). Resveratrol is also found in some fruits. Experiments with mice have shown that this anti-oxidant can have the same effect as a calorie-restricted diet and prolong life – at least in mice. The problem is that to imbibe the same amount as the mice received to prolong their lives, we would need to consume between 750 and 1500 bottles of red wine each day. If resveratrol is to be taken in sufficient quantity to make a difference, supplements are the only answer.

Blueberries contain powerful anti-oxidants and have been shown experimentally to be able to improve memory. Like red wine, they contain resveratrol. They also contain pterostilbene, an anti-oxidant said to protect the heart by reducing 'bad' LDL cholesterol.

Tomatoes contain lycopene, a powerful anti-oxidant that may have the ability to reduce the size of prostate tumours and strengthen the immune system, possibly raising the level of protection against cancer. The healthful qualities of tomatoes are enhanced by cooking, which is why tomato pastes from tubes and tins are actually very good for you. Ignore suggestions that you should not eat tomatoes if you suffer from osteoarthritis. Lycopene is also found in pink grapefruit, guava, papaya and watermelon and is said to protect the skin against damaging ultraviolet rays from the sun.

Vegans do not eat any food of animal origin. That's 'no' to fish, eggs, dairy products and honey. This makes it difficult for vegans to get sufficient Omega oils, the essential fatty acids which we mainly get from our diet. Minerals may be hard to get from a vegan diet too, especially iron. A vegan who does not take supplements of vitamin B12 will suffer brain nerve damage eventually, as there is no vegan source of this essential vitamin.

A vegetarian, on the other hand, if they are careful, can get a sufficiently varied diet to provide the necessities of a balanced intake without recourse to supplements. However, being a vegetarian has a pitfall that often isn't recognised. Though many vegetarians will wisely make their own meals using fresh ingredients, if they resort to ready-made vegetarian meals, they may unwittingly eat large amounts of calories. Many ready-made meals contain considerable quantities of fat of non-animal origin. Lasagne and moussaka are classic examples. Too many nuts may be another high calorie problem for vegetarians. Nuts are a healthy source of protein, minerals and non-animal fat, but they tend to be high in saturates and monounsaturates, pushing up the calorie count, even if some of those fats are essential fatty acids – the Omega oils. On the other hand, nuts like Brazils are good for selenium, necessary for male fertility as well as being cardioprotective. You get calcium for bone strength from almonds, while cashews are noted for their zinc content, also vital for fertility as well as a strong immune system. Walnuts, which contain the amino acid arginine help blood circulation though the release of nitric oxide in the walls of the arteries in much the same way as Viagra. They can work as a natural anti-inflammatory and reduce 'bad' LDL cholesterol oxidation in the arteries.

There are three allegedly wonder ingredients often added to fashionable fruit drinks. These are wheatgrass, barley grass and spirulina, which is blue-green freshwater algae containing proteins, vitamins and minerals. The problem is that the algae have been shown to encourage certain types of neurological disease, including Alzheimer's. Wheatgrass, which is 70% chlorophyll, is said to produce all kinds of benefits, but a recent study was unable to validate any of these. Most everyday dark green vegetables have as much or more food value, according to the study. The same appears to be true of oat grass (avena sativa) and barley grass. Nor are various substances, many of them touted as detox additives to fruit and vegetable drinks, effective for that purpose. The whole concept of detoxing, though fashionable, lacks scientific merit, given that the liver and the lymphatic system are perfectly capable on their own of getting rid of elements that are harmful or surplus to requirement.

Drinking juice from a fruit or vegetable is not as healthful as eating the fruit or vegetable in question. Of the five (make that eight) daily portions of fruit and vegetables widely advocated, no more than one should come from fruit or vegetable juice, where one glass can be deemed to be the equivalent of one of the five. The trouble is that the juice of ten oranges is not the same as eating ten oranges. The fibre is missing, even in orange juice with 'bits' in it, along with other goodies. People who drink too much fruit juice may suffer negative effects. The concentration of fructose (fruit sugar) will be higher. The acid in fruit juices can be bad for tooth enamel. There may be bloating, abdominal pain and the symptoms of irritable bowel syndrome, especially diar-rhoea, which is also a sign of excessive vitamin C intake.

Table salt is sodium chloride. Most men get too much salt in their diet. It's the sodium that's harmful. It pushes up blood pressure. Six grams of salt a day ought to be enough, and on a healthy diet there is no need for added salt, either in cooking or at the table. Some foods have a high salt content – foods like soy sauce and tinned anchovies. Eat them in moderation.

Healthy as fruit juices seem to be, they come with a warning. Too much fruit juice or too many fizzy drinks and you increase your chances of getting gout, the formation of painful crystals in the joints that derive from too much uric acid in the blood. In the case of fruit juices, natural fruit sugar (fructose) appears to be the problem.

When it comes to meat, the terms organic and free range become confusing. As much as 98% of imported pork products, including bacon, comes from intensively bred animals. And fully 70% of home-grown British pork is from indoor-bred animals. The labelling stan-dards for pork are much less strict than for chicken and eggs. Only 5% of our UK-reared pigs are free-range and only 2% are organic. Free-range and outdoor-reared are not the same thing and many outdoor-reared pigs are not free-range.

Additives and preservatives have always been a problem for those of us trying to read food labels in the supermarket. If they are listed, they tend to blind with science and for most people are incomprehensible gobbledegook. Now an increasing number of foods are being labelled 'additive-free' and/or 'preservative-free', which solves the problem. Thanks to labelling with 'low fat', 'low sugar', 'low salt', 'calcium added', 'organic', 'high fibre', 'no trans fats', 'free-range' and so on, it may soon be impossible to see the package for the health claims written all over it. Labelling for food colourants still has some way to go though.

Trans fats (see above) are gradually being removed from spreads, margarines, biscuits and baked goods. Some sly manufacturers, instead of calling trans fats just that, refer to them as 'hydrogenated vegetable oil' in the belief that most of their consumers can be fooled with big words. Just to make things more complicated, not all trans fats are vegetable fats that have been partially hydrogenated. Small amounts of trans fats are found naturally in beef, lamb, and dairy products. And not all hydrogenated vegetable oils produce trans fats as a by-product. Only partially hydrogenated vegetable oils do this. Fully hydrogenated vegetable oils don't. And remember that those Omega 3 fish oils that are so popular are polyunsaturated fats. They don't get hydrogenated, partially or fully. Just the vegetable oils. It's that complicated.

Nuts and seeds are rich and healthy sources of saturated and unsaturated fats. The nuts highest in saturated fats include coconuts and palm oil nuts. Nuts like pine nuts are almost 50% fat. Nuts and seeds provide a good mix of fat and protein, and should be included in a healthy diet. If you're watching calories, though, don't overdo it, as these foods are high in calories.

Avocados are rich in monounsaturated fat, alongside olives, olive oil and hazelnut oil. While the cooking oils made from safflower, corn and sunflower oil are becoming a no-no (see above), the polyunsaturate that is grapeseed oil is worth using as one of the richest sources of the antioxidant procyanidins, provided you don't damage its food value by overheating or burning it if you use it as a cooking oil. Polyunsaturated oils have been linked to colon and skin cancer, depression, asthma, Alzheimer's disease, obesity and diabetes, and to cardiovascular disease.

There are a number of organisations and agencies which monitor aspects of food quality, source, content and safety. Some indicate a Fairtrade source or sustainability, others organic or free-range, often with a political or at least a politically correct agenda. Many of these organisations put their mark on food packaging as a guide. In the UK, the following may have put their mark on something you buy:

The Soil Association
The Vegan Society
Fairtrade Labelling Organisations International
Leaf Integrated Farm Management
Marine Stewardship Council
OEKO-TEK 100
British Union for the Abolition of Vivisection

MBDC Cradle to Cradle
The RugMark Foundation
The European Union Energy Label
The Energy Saving Trust
Forest Stewardship Council

....

More Tips and Traps

Although we can get vitamin D from oily fish, we can get enough from 10 minutes exposure to sunshine. For this reason, it is the only vitamin that we do not need to get from our diet.

Vitamins B and C are water-soluble, while vitamins A, D, E and K are fat-soluble. Excess water-soluble vitamins are therefore excreted in urine, while fat-soluble vitamins are stored in the body. Without fat, the body could not transport the fat-soluble vitamins.

Tea contains catechin, an anti-oxidant which strengthens the cardiovascular system and may even raise levels of 'good' (HDL) cholesterol. Green tea may help prevent tooth decay and gum diseases.

You can buy some foods already enriched with Omega 3 oils – orange juice, milk and eggs.

The pectin found in apples helps to maintain stable blood levels of glucose.

Camomile tea is thought to be an effective destressor.

Vitamin K is essential for strong bones and the avoidance of osteoporosis. It's plentiful in soybeans and dark green leafy vegetables.
Iron is important for mental concentration and a deficiency may lead to depressed mood. A lack of folate can have the same effect. In fact all the B vitamins play an important part in maintaining the nervous system.

Most men in the UK do not get enough of the trace mineral selenium in their diet. A long term selenium deficit has been linked to infertility, cancer, cardiovascular disease and cataracts.

Broccoli is one of the healthiest vegetables we can eat. Not only is it almost 50% vegetable protein, but it contains isothiocyanate and sulphoraphane, nutrients important in preventing cancer.

Many foods have been suggested to help keep skin elastic and younger looking as we get older. The skin's elasticity depends on collagen and elastin and benefits from a diet rich in flavonoids. Raspberries and strawberries are among the best of these.

One study indicated that eating red meat slightly raised the risk of some cancers of the digestive tract, while eating white meat reduced the risk of the same cancers.

Well-intentioned dietary plans are often upset for the worse by major life events such as bereavement, illness, divorce, moving house, a wedding, losing a job, being promoted or the birth of baby. The ensuing pressure often leads to a return to unhealthy eating.

Anti-oxidant levels in foods can be measured scientifically using what is called the Orac Scale. This is one way of checking for yourself whether claims made for certain foods are valid.

Whole grains protect the heart. In one study men eating whole grain cereals were found to be 30% less likely to suffer from heart failure.

Seeds are full of goodies, but also dense in calories. We can get plenty of calcium from sesame seeds and tahini, made from sesame seeds, and also from hoummos, made from chickpeas.

Mushrooms are a useful source of anti-oxidants and are the best source of one in particular, L-ergothioneine. They are also a good source of selenium, vitamins and some unusual enzymes.

Some foods may be carcinogenic: smoked foods such as smoked salmon, foods cooked in oil that has been heated to burning point, and foods cured in salt such as Parma ham and bacon. It's probably safe to eat foods like these in small quantities.

CHAPTER EIGHTEEN
EXERCISE OR DIE

We think of exercise as aerobic, resistance or stretching, or a combination of these. Within these groups there are different types of exercise. You can work your heart aerobically by, for example, running, but also when it beats faster from fear or passion. The most basic types of resistance exercise are either isotonic or isometric. Isotonic involves moving weights, flexing and extending the muscles involved. Isometric involves tensing the muscles against a static object or simply clenching them. Stretching a muscle involves lengthening it, usually as part of a warm-up to prepare muscles for more strenuous exercise, or as a warm-down after exercise.

In recent years there has been a revival in resistance exercise. For a long time, pumping iron was associated with body-building of the Mr Universe variety, and this gave it a bad image among health professionals, especially as a result of bodybuilders' perceived association with anabolic steroids. We now know that moderate resistance exercise is good for you, provided that it is combined with aerobic exercise and preferably a stretch workout as well.

When you lift heavy weights to the point of muscle fatigue (overload), you produce minute tears in the muscle fibres. These heal over the next day or two, producing slightly larger muscles. Therefore, it might appear at first glance that resistance exercise is not a good idea. Tearing the muscle to make it bigger may produce a great six pack, but at what price?

For one thing, a well-planned and executed resistance programme will burn fat. I have read that because the process of healing those tiny muscle tears goes on for hours after a workout with weights, you will actually burn more fat with say an hour of weight training than you will with an hour of aerobics, where fat burning is said to occur mostly during the actual period you are doing the exercise. I believed that when I read it, but my own experience doesn't validate that claim. I have found that resistance workouts help to burn some fat, and of course they give better muscle definition, but they don't burn as much fat as you will get rid of with an aerobic session of the same duration.

Also controversial is the theory that if you do, say, an hour of aerobic exercise, you will burn fewer calories in this first hour than you would burn in a second hour, and so on. For example, you might burn six hundred calories in the first hour, seven hundred in the second hour and eight hundred in the third hour – assuming you could exercise that long and the intensity level is the same throughout.

It's well known that a good resistance programme, if you're quite fit already, will put on weight – muscle weight. You don't convert fat to muscle, though it's sometimes expressed that way. About 70% of our body weight is muscle. About 60% of this is protein and 40% is water. Exercise with weights will burn some fat and, depending on your fat/protein/carbohydrate make-up, some protein and carbohydrates as well. (If you're wondering where there is carbohydrate stored in our bodies, the answer is mainly in the liver). But protein is twice as heavy as fat, measured by volume. So you may lose fat each time you bench press that weight, but you put on muscle – heavier muscle – over the next day or two. Those Olympic weight lifters you see looking rather round are not fat. They just have bodies looking for somewhere to put all that muscle. Don't be fooled though. A paunch on most men is not muscle – it's fat of the most dangerous kind: abdominal fat.

Exercise is not all about losing weight or maintaining the right weight. It should be about having a healthy body, and the right weight should be incidental to that objective, rather than an end in itself. Yet men exercise to look good, to live longer and to lose weight or maintain a healthy weight. Many do not appreciate how different kinds of exercise will produce different body shapes and sizes. Progressively heavier weights in shorter and shorter repetitions will build bulk and increase weight, while longer repetitions with lighter weights will give tone and eventually reduce weight in those who are fit. Exercise with lighter weights is therefore more like aerobic exercise, and to some extent that is what it is. Muscles become used to the same exercise over and over, and with any specific exercise, the body reaches a plateau beyond which it makes little progress. It makes sense to vary exercises, therefore, and get all-round fitness by not focussing on just one muscle group.

We know that protein, fat and carbohydrates can all be burnt as fuel. But we're still learning how, when and why the body chooses which to burn first. Usually we want to burn fat, and failing that, carbohydrates, as every marathon runner knows. What we don't want is to burn protein, the body's fuel of last resort. Burning protein is like our body eating itself.

Exercise physiology still doesn't have all the answers. There are plenty of theories. One thing is clear. The body is not designed for too much exercise – resistance or aerobic, or for that matter too much stretching (look at what some ballet dancers do to their bodies and how they end up). Moderate exercise, we should conclude, is good for you. Too much is bad. Listen to your body and in time you should learn how much is right for you.

Weight loss fanatics will boast of how many pounds they lost in six months and so on. True, if you're grossly obese and start dieting and exercising, the pounds will fall away at first, though much of this will be water loss. However, if you're a relatively fit 13 stone and want to become a very fit 12 stone, the task is much more difficult. At this level you will tend to put on weight with resistance training, adding muscle with each piece of iron you pump. It's your controlled diet and aerobics that will overcome this weight gain, if you persevere, and oh-so-slowly, you will lose weight to the point where weight loss in fat will outbalance the weight gain in muscle mass. Your body fat percentage will fall and you should go from looking good to looking great. Slow the routine, though, and you will quickly go into reverse, with 13 stone looming on the horizon again. The older you are, the harder you will find it to lose weight and keep it off, no matter how fit or unfit you are. A lot of willpower will be required. This is because your metabolism will be slowing down as you get older.

Membership gyms and public gyms are fine provided you have the willpower to go regularly. Most men don't. They often sign up in

January and then drop out completely after a few weeks. Gym companies know this and plan accordingly. If all their members trained there every day, they would soon go bankrupt or get closed down by Health and Safety on grounds of overcrowding. If you have the space and can afford it, set up a home gym. Put in say a multigym, a few free weights, a mat, a treadmill, a rowing machine (my first choice for home aerobic equipment), a bike and maybe a cross-trainer. Buy second-hand from, for example, Loot, Exchange and Mart or e-Bay and you could get all of that lot for under £1,000. Then in winter when you're not in the mood to go to the gym, you could work out at home, maybe going to the membership gym in the warmer six months of the year if you can get a six-month membership – but choose a gym that is properly air-conditioned.

For men over forty I recommend a forty-five minute workout five days a week. That should be 30 minutes of aerobics (even brisk walking at 3.5 miles an hour might fit the bill, but more vigorous exercise than walking is ideal) and fifteen minutes on weights, plus maybe five minutes of warm-up and stretching beforehand and five minutes of cool-down at the end. Try substituting two of the weights sessions for fifteen minutes of stretching. Keep the weekend entirely free for rest and recovery (see chapter 37 on sleeping). If you find the thought of a home gym too daunting, consider the fact that you can do several resistance exercises, such as press-ups, using your body to provide the resistance.

It has been found that people with dogs get more exercise than those who don't have any. This is because dogs need to be taken out for exercise. People with dogs average at least 70% more exercise than people without dogs. Exercise like this, with a purpose behind it, other than exercise for its own sake, is likely to go on for years, whereas very few people will have the willpower to stick with going to the gym for years and years on end.

Exercise should not be judged in terms of whether weight is being lost. Exercise with no weight loss or which puts on weight is better than no exercise. In the fit and healthy who are already the right weight, exercise is more likely to put on weight than take it off, whereas weight loss is likely in those who are overweight or obese.

A lot of us who keep fit skimp on the warm-ups, the stretches and the cool-downs. In fact there's a body of research that suggests that warming up and stretching before exercise is unnecessary and, if you're competing in something like sprinting, may actually reduce your performance by stretching muscles that would perform better by going into action unstretched. The jury is still out.

The more general view is that you should do your aerobic exercise first. Or start with aerobics and then do some weights, then some aerobics and so on.

Your aerobic workout will be more effective the larger the muscle groups you bring into play – in other words, your legs and your arms, especially your legs, which explains why rowing, running, cycling and cross country skiing are such effective aerobic exercises. These involve an element of resistance workout as well. Elite rowers have been recorded consuming as much as seven litres of oxygen per minute, about twice the maximum of the average reasonably fit adult male. Running is almost all aerobics, which is why runners don't tend to bulk up to the same extent as rowers, whose sport is a cross between resistance (strength) and aerobic (endurance) exercise. At extreme levels of exertion in combination sports like rowing, the body may find it is losing coordination as it goes into what is known as oxygen debt, a reaction triggered by soaring levels of lactic acid.

If you run, it's important to wear the right footwear. However, contrary to popular wisdom, running on a hard surface does not damage the knees, feet, ankles and hips. Recent research suggests that running on a hard surface actually strengthens the ligaments and tendons that were thought to be vulnerable to hard surfaces. However, it's possible that your brain does not benefit from sloshing back and forth inside your cranium when you run, whatever the surface. This can be a problem for some rowers too, especially the older rower.

When you pump iron, your heart rate goes up, and it isn't difficult to get into the aerobic zone (say 60–70% of heart rate maximum) when you're really working hard on weights, though probably nearer the 60% mark than the 90% level, at which you would pass into what is called the anaerobic zone. The fact is that doing weights is a form of low level aerobic exercise, just as aerobics is really a low level kind of resistance exercise akin to using light weights at a greater frequency with much longer repetitions. If you're running, for example, your body weight is the resistance.

When you do weights, your heart rate is something you don't tend to pay much attention to. But when it comes to aerobics, it can be your best measure of whether you are pushing yourself too hard or too little (along with the talking test – if you can talk aloud but with a little difficulty, you are probably working out at the right level for you).

I think that whether you are doing weights or aerobics, you should not concentrate too much on your breathing, so long as you are sure that you don't tend to hold your breath, something that sometimes happen when lifting weights. I know instructors like to make a big thing about breathing, but I take the view that breathing should take care of itself and if you have to concentrate on too many things, the fun will be less and you will be more likely to drop out altogether. After all, no one would claim that hard exercise is really a load of laughs. Most of us would rather be doing something else, but work out for the benefits it brings, not the pleasure it gives us at the time. The feeling of an endorphin surge in the brain afterwards, though, is worth working for.

If you are fit, you should be able to work out aerobically for 30 minutes at 70% of heart rate maximum, or 70% of your lungs' maximum oxygen consumption (vO2 max). Heart rate maximum and vO2 max are not the same thing, but they are roughly equivalent. A healthy heart should have healthy lungs to support it and vice versa. A medical or sports physiology testing unit can measure your vO2 level at different rates of exertion, but at home and at the gym, heart rate is a better measure. Many aerobic machines come with metal grips that give a heart rate readout, but a chest strap and wrist monitor will give a more accurate reading. Note that some machines also give a count of calories burnt. Be wary of these. Some are calibrated to flatter. It's sobering to know that it might take half an hour of hard workout to burn the calories contained in a single Mars bar.

The old rule is that your heart rate maximum is 220 minus your age, so if you are 60, for example, your max will be 160. The trouble with this is that it's based on chronological age and averages, and individually, you may vary from this by up to 10% above or below, sometimes more. And generally the fitter you are, the lower your biological age, in which case the higher your heart rate maximum. Thus a very fit 60-year-old might have the biological age of a 45-year-old and a heart rate max, all else being equal, of 175. For this man, 70% of this max would be 122 and not the 112 that the one-size-fits-all formula would suggest.

If you are reasonably fit and working out aerobically for thirty minutes, I would suggest keeping your heart rate in the range 65–70% of maximum. If you are less fit, you could drop to the 60–65% range. Don't go any lower, though, or you could end up doing what a lot of people do, which is work out at such a low rate that it's not doing their heart and lungs a lot of good. That's still better than no exercise, of course, but you need to feel the 'burn' a bit for it to be working for you. Don't think that means it has to be painful. If it leaves you gasping for breath rather than breathing heavily, you are overdoing it.

What does 'anaerobic' mean? Without getting technical, it means that which is not aerobic. It may seem illogical, but not only is below about 60% of max classified as anaerobic, but so is above 90%. The latter point is known as the anaerobic threshold. This is a level of heart rate and oxygen uptake so high that even a very fit individual will not be able to maintain it for more than a minute or two.

One of the problems with getting your vO2 max or a stress cardiogram done for a medical check-up is that lab insurance and health and safety requirements prevent those testing you from pushing you to your maximum level for fear of precipitating a coronary event – a heart attack or angina, or perhaps even a stroke. So they stop you on the exercise bike or whatever you are on at about 65% of heart rate max, this 65% being based on the 220-minus-your-age rule. This can give a false result unless you happen to be Mr Joe Average.

Take the example above of a man with a biological age of 45. His maximum heart rate is 175. He knows this because he has pushed himself to the limit – beyond the anaerobic threshold of 90% – for 90 seconds on his rowing machine at home. He's got a heart rate of 175 by the end of those 90 seconds, and is gasping for breath. If he takes 65% of 175, he gets 114. But the lab, taking no chances, and unwilling to accept the man's protestations about his 175 max, follows the rule book and decrees that as he is 60 years old, his maximum heart rate must be deemed to be 160. The nurse running the test will only be allowed to take him to 65% of 160 in case of a coronary event. This is a heart rate of 104.

The poor guy is only just warming up at a heart rate of 104 – he isn't even sweating and he has no problem carrying on a conversation – when the nurse stops the test. Matched against the tables, the man's fitness is average, when in reality it is excellent. Because he could not be taken to heart rate max, the nurse never knows that he is fitter than average for his age, and so the test result is relatively meaningless. I should know as it happened to me when I hit 60 with a heart rate max of 180, which I was familiar with from pushing myself to the limit occasionally on my rowing machine while wearing a heart rate monitor.

While we're on the subject of types of exercise and problems with medical checkups, the other big problem is BMI – Body Mass Index. I went for a medical for life insurance a few years ago, and got into an argument with the doctor. I had rarely been fitter. 'You'll have to be careful', the doctor said. 'You have a BMI of 25.23, which puts you in the overweight category – just – up to 25 is normal'. I was 13 stone 6 lbs (85.45 kilos) and 6' 0.5" (1 metre 84 cms). In those days, easy ways to measure body fat weren't around, but I knew that I carried a lot of muscle relative to fat. I had been a surfer for many years and few sports are as aerobic as surfing. The rating known as BMI, then as now, was based on weight in kilos divided by the square of your height in metres. That would be fine if all men had the same build and the same fat to muscle proportion. But how do you explain the fact that Brad Pitt, who is 6' tall, has a BMI of 26. That means that Brad Pitt is overweight. Brad Pitt overweight? Did you see him in Troy? It turns out that by the same measure George Clooney and Tom Cruise are overweight, and Mike Tyson is actually obese.

I remember watching a TV programme a few years ago – the World's Strongest Man competition. One man had a body like most men only dream of – it looked perfect in every way, well proportioned with rippling muscles in all the right places, yet without making him look like one of those grossly overdeveloped bodybuilders. The man was 6' 1" and weighed 18 stone. In other words, the BMI boys classified him as seriously obese. In fact I doubt whether his body fat was over 10% of his total weight.

The BMI, now much touted, is the crudest of tools and does no justice at all to those who are fit. If you have a lot of muscle and very little body fat, you are likely to show up as overweight or obese on the BMI scale. Which is why body fat percentage is usually a better objective measure of fitness, provided that the measurement is accurate.

To be fair to the medical check-up organisations, they are beginning to acknowledge some of the above problems and so are not uniformly condemning those who are deemed overweight or obese by the crude BMI.

That said, it is better to be fat and fit than slim and unfit. Studies have shown that while fit and slim is best, there are many fat people who are reasonably fit and have a reasonable life expectancy. Fitness is the key.

You could measure body fat using a well-known brand of bathroom scales that offers a sophisticated model purporting to tell you your body fat percentage. The trouble is, it does not take fitness and muscle into account. It treats you as Mr Joe Average for height and weight, and even for your age in the top-of-the-range model. So the fit person using the scales comes away with the message that he is not so fit after all. The top-of-the-range scales in question do try to overcome this in a crude way by offering an alternative for individuals who would have to be almost superathletes to meet its criteria – there's no scale in between. You're either doing ten hours of aerobics a week or you are Mr Joe Average. The result is that when I step on the scales as Mr Joe Average, my body fat is deemed to be 24%, but when I enter myself as Mr Joe Superathlete, I have body fat at the 15% level and I am told that I have the body of a 22-year-old. (I am 64). That's a warning about how crude these scales still are.

To be fair to the manufacturer, they now offer an expensive model that involves holding an electrode in each hand. This gives a better body fat reading when combined with the reading through the foot electrodes. The older and cheaper machines usually get it wrong by measuring electrical impedance through the skin of the lower body only.

Your body fat reading on any body fat scales can vary quite a bit according to your level of hydration. Water accounts for more than half of our body weight, usually about 50–55% in men. The higher your level of hydration, the lower your body fat percentage will be, using the electrical impedance method incorporated in weighing scales. If you're very dehydrated when you measure your body fat, your percentage will go up. Dehydration is not a good thing and if you are trying to get your score down, denying yourself liquid is not the healthy way to go about it.

It's obvious that the average Olympic marathon runner has a different physique from the average Olympic weight lifter, and that swimmers and gymnasts have physiques somewhere in between. What all three groups have in common is low body fat – probably in the 10–15% range. Where they differ is in their muscle mass. The weightlifters do lots of resistance exercise and build up muscle bulk. The marathon runners don't carry much muscle mass. They do mainly if not entirely aerobic training and develop superb lung function along with muscles adapted to long distance running – muscles that are good for endurance without being bulky. The swimmers and gymnasts have the kind of bodies some of us aspire to. The swimmers have aerobic fitness and some degree of bulk from the fact that swimming is also a resistance sport, the resistance being provided by the water. The gymnasts have less aerobic fitness than the swimmers, and superb all-over musculature from the predominantly resistance nature of their sport, but gymnastics is aerobic too, so their muscle bulk never reaches the proportions of the weightlifter's.

If you look at sprinters, they look quite different from distance runners. Most decathletes tend to be strong on sprinting, and face the 1,500 m with trepidation. They have muscle bulk for the sprints and throwing events and have fast twitch muscle fibres designed for strength, whereas distance runners are born with slow twitch muscle fibres designed for endurance. Fast twitch muscles use little oxygen and tire quickly.

This is an interesting point and one that may affect your own choice of exercise. It shows that your fitness may be determined to some extent, possibly a lot, by the body composition you were born with. You are more likely to become a sprinter or a weight lifter if you were born with fast twitch muscle fibres. But there's a continuum. You don't simply have fast twitch or slow twitch. You're somewhere along the scale. So it's my guess that swimmers and gymnasts will be nearer the middle of the scale with muscle fibres that are 'medium' twitch. It follows that if you tend to do what comes naturally, you will gravitate towards resistance exercise the more you are a fast twitch man, and towards aerobics, the more you are a slow twitch man. The former may become a weight lifter, the latter a marathon runner. Cyclists and rowers will generally be in the middle of the spectrum.

But here is one of the traps when it comes to exercise. The weightlifter may not be looking after his aerobics requirement and the marathon runner may be passing up the chance to lift a few weights. It seems that to be really fit, we should be doing both forms of exercise, even if one or the other comes more naturally. If the weight lifter fails to look after his need for more aerobic exercise, he will probably not live as long as the marathon runner who does a little pumping iron. Of aerobics and resistance exercise, aerobics is more important for a long and healthy life. Resistance exercise may be less important, but it's still important.

We need a lot of willpower to keep on exercising for a lifetime, not just for a month following a New Year's resolution. And if either resistance or aerobic exercise doesn't feel comfortable or natural, because we're not at the fast or slow end of the muscle twitch continuum, we have to grit our teeth and get on with whichever type of exercise is hard for us, unless of course we want to give up and live a shorter less healthy life.

The commonest form of exercise for most people is walking, followed by swimming, then going to the gym. Then, in order of popularity, come recreational cycling, football, running (or jogging), golf, badminton, tennis and aerobics. Some 20% of the population (eight million males and females) go in for recreational walking, compared with 1.5% for aerobics. The percentage going to the gym regularly is 11.6%, so clearly most are not going for the aerobics sessions. Other interesting findings from the same study are that 23.7% of adult males are regular exercisers – defined as taking at least 30 minutes of continuous exercise at least three times a week. However, the figures fall with age.

Males and females combined come in at 24.7% in the 35-44 age group, falling to 16.0% in the 55–64 age group and only 6% in the 75–84 age group. In other words, there is not much interest in exercise as people age, even though that is when they may need it most. As you would expect, the study that produced this figure found considerable variation in different parts of the country, with the Scilly Isles at the top with 32% taking regular exercise, while at the bottom end was Boston in Lincolnshire with only 14.3%.

There are reports in the press from time to time that suggest that athletes and sportsmen die young or become prematurely aged with a variety of illnesses, above all, osteoarthritis. While I do believe that overexercising can be bad for your health – as can focussing too much on one sport and one part of your body at the expense of overall fitness – I am sure that for every former athlete who dies suddenly of a heart attack at fifty, there are several who will live beyond the national average lifespan for men, currently standing at 77 years. Some may have damaged their hearts in their youth (see Sudden Death Syndrome in chapter 41 on the heart), overdeveloping the muscular wall of the heart, but the most common reason I think some athletes may show signs of premature ageing and death is that they have not maintained a lifelong commitment to keeping fit. It only takes a couple of weeks for the benefits of exercise to start wearing off, and a few months after that, the former athlete who has given up is little different from the rest of the population.

Therein lies the challenge. It's no good working out for a month and then giving up for the rest of your life. Fitness requires lifelong commitment. That's an even tougher challenge than eating right all your life, and since your fitness level is even more important than your diet in the battle to keep healthy, it's a battle that will only be won by a few. The rest will not have the necessary willpower, especially in a society tempted on all sides by lazy lifestyle alternatives.

I haven't said much about stretching. It's something I don't do enough of. As you get older it's not just muscles that become vulnerable to tears. Ligaments and tendons become increasingly fragile, as I know from experience. Those who exercise a lot as they get older are inclined to find this out the hard way. You'll be more prone also to bursitis and synovitis around the joints. Your weakest points will usually be feet, knees, hips, elbows, lower back and shoulders – in other words the lower back plus all the main joints, with feet and knees most vulnerable, especially the knees.

With regular exercise you strengthen muscles, ligaments and tendons and thereby reduce the chances of injury. Be careful, though. Exercise itself, including stretching, can cause soft tissue injury. This is one good reason why it's important to listen to your body and not push yourself beyond your limits. If in doubt, err on the side of caution. All injuries heal more slowly the older you get, though a high degree of fitness will improve healing time. Muscles heal more quickly than tendons and ligaments, which can take months to get better.

I'm all in favour of the various types of yoga, and exercise programmes like Pilates. All properly tutored stretching is good for you, though men, it seems, have a problem with spending time doing stretching exercises year in and year out. There is no doubt that men tend to gravitate towards pumping iron more than women, while women tend to favour yoga and other forms of stretching. There is no good reason why this should be so, yet I'm as guilty as the next man of not stretching enough. As we get older, regular stretching exercises should form part of our weekly routine. Taking glucosamine sulphate supplements for joint health (I say this from experience despite a recent report to the contrary) probably does work, but even this is no substitute for regular stretching of the soft tissues. I wish I had the will power to do more in this area. I'm working on it.

By the time you reach 60, your body will be telling you that you need to do some stretches, because whenever you get up and run to answer the phone, you will probably feel stiff for the first few seconds. Your muscles are not ready to leap into action at the first ring. They now take longer to warm up. Do Hatha Yoga of Pilates for a year and you will notice the difference when the phone rings. Of course, if you work out aerobically, the stiffness will be less. Do proper stretch exercises and you will slow down joint and muscle stiffness by several years, to a degree that no amount of aerobics can achieve.

You could try two 15-minute sessions of yoga or Pilates once a week instead of two of those 15-minute weights sessions I suggested above, in addition to the routine stretches you should be doing before and after an aerobic or weights workout. However, I believe your body needs a holiday periodically – a period with no exercise at all, provided it is no longer than a couple of weeks at a time. Even Olympic athletes are known to 'vegge out' at the end of the season, and a couple of weeks without training is not long enough for your body to get far out of condition if you are in good shape to start with.

Don't exercise when you have a virus. Your immune system will be weakened. Moderate exercise strengthens the immune system, raising the level of white blood cells known as B lymphocytes, but only if it is unimpaired by a cold or other attack on its integrity. When you exercise you strengthen your immune system to the extent that you cut your chances of catching a virus by 50%, according to one report. It's well known that elite athletes at the peak of their form are more prone to pick up respiratory infections, which would suggest that they are suffering from what is now called over-training syndrome, the main feature of which is a compromised immune system. I know what it feels like as I exercised too hard a few years ago. My body started to tell me I had overdone it, and just to back the feeling up, I came down with a virus. It isn't just elite athletes who are vulnerable. The syndrome can apply to anyone who over-exercises. But it may only be by personal trial and error that you will find out where you personal limit lies.

There is a more serious risk if you dare to exercise heavily while suffering from a virus. Myocarditis, which is an inflammation of the heart muscle, may occur. Other factors besides a virus and over-exercising are likely to be involved.

Exercise should be taken in moderate temperatures, though this applies more to the old than the middle-aged. Exercising in extreme heat can be dangerous, especially if the humidity is high. There is a risk of heat stroke as well as dehydration. In fact anyone working out should make sure to drink plenty of liquid while exercising and not just afterwards. The danger is just as extreme when the temperature is very low, especially if an icy wind is blowing, reducing the temperature through wind chill factor. The risk is heightened if you are tired, dehydrated, stressed or have drunk too much alcohol.

Exercise raises blood levels of cortisol, lactic acid and free radicals. All are negative for health. You get rid of lactic acid, which causes the characteristic stiffness that sometimes follows exercise, by warm-down stretching after exercise, and stretching before exercise will have the same effect to a lesser extent. Cortisol is taken care of by rest and sleep. Free radicals are best handled with a healthy diet. When you exercise moderately, you lower your level of fibrinogen, a clotting factor in the blood, but if you exercise to exhaustion, your fibrinogen level goes the other way – it goes up. Fibrinogen is associated with blood platelets and an unduly high level is undesirable, especially in anyone at risk of a cardiovascular problem or stroke. About 20% of the population inherits a raised fibrinogen level, increasing their risk of clotting. This group will show a markedly raised level of the factor following exhausting exercise, and all those who exercise at extremely cold temperatures will show a raised level.

Other factors also rise with exercise: the hormones adrenaline and noradrenaline, and the feel-good neurotransmitters dopamine and serotonin. Also the endorphins, accompanied by the cannabinoid anandamide, that produce the sleepy, relaxed and slightly euphoric state of the runner's high. Endorphins are tranquillisers and painkillers rolled into one, which helps to explain why exercise is the most effective safe anti-depressant there is. You don't have to walk or run or lift weights to get the feel-good benefits of exercise. A few hours gardening will equally do the trick if you are gardening hard enough – what I call aerobic gardening.

Posture improves with exercise, especially if you work at a desk job. It's well known that most people lose height with age as their spinal vertebrae become compressed. It doesn't have to be that way. A healthy individual can help preserve height and posture with lifelong exercise. There is a caveat to this, however. One study, using an admittedly small sample, has suggested that slouching with a curved spine when seated may be better for the back and overall posture than the traditionally accepted doctrine that we should keep a straight back when seated. The suggestion is that slouching takes pressure off key points in the lumbar spine that are the most susceptible to lower back pain.

Regular moderate exercise improves the brain as well as the body, and thus slows normal age-related memory loss. This occurs because exercise increases blood flow to and within the brain. This in turn increases the number of nerve-growth factors in the brain, improving synapse pathways between the neurons. It could even be that exercise slows or may halt age-related loss of brain cells. Those who will benefit most are men who have stayed fit all their lives, rather than men who may have indulged in yo-yo exercise on and off. Even so, yo-yo exercise is better than none at all.

Exercise improves reaction times, an important measure of biological age. And exercise has been demonstrated to cut the risk of colorectal and lung cancer. In fact the physiological benefits of exercise fill books, with specific exercise regimes aimed at specific illnesses, as well as overall health. If exercise has one particular benefit that I can generalize about, it's the maintenance of a healthy vascular system – keeping all your blood vessels clear, including those in the brain.

Exercise should only be undertaken if your body is up to it as well as up for it. Many exercise-related problems from minor sprains right through to fatal heart attacks take place because exercisers have pushed themselves too far too fast, or exercise has uncovered a weakness they didn't know was there. Always start slowly and increase levels gradually if you are new to exercise, and if you are fit, or think you are, listen to your body and err on the side of caution at all times. Accident and Emergency units in our hospitals are constantly servicing the ill-prepared, often weekend warriors who pushed themselves too far out of sheer machismo. The overweight, in particular, should be careful not to over-stress their joints, especially the knees.

Non-impact exercise such as swimming and cycling is often a good introduction to aerobic exercise as it puts little stress on the joints, especially swimming. If cycling on a real bike or an exercise bike is too much for you to begin with, consider a recumbent bicycle. This allows you to peddle while lying back and is much more forgiving than an upright exercise bike, though being easier, it will take longer to burn the same number of calories. Contact sports are notorious for fractures, ligament and tendon problems, and dislocations.

You mayl help to strengthen and lubricate your joints for exercise by eating lots of oily fish for its Omega 3 content, and by taking a daily dose of the supplement glucosamine sulphate. At the same time, a supplement of the Omega 6 oil gamma linoleic acid (GLA) will help to ward off joint inflammation. GLA is found in evening primrose oil, borage oil and blackcurrant oil, but you will need to take it in supplement form to get enough.

Research in the UK shows that 50% of those joining a gym have stopped going there within six months, and that this figure rises to 80% after 12 months. This suggests that 20% renew their subscriptions, but in fact the figure is 60%, which means that 40% are paying in their second year for a service which they are not using.

The joint most likely to be involved in a sports injury is the knee and the commonest form of knee injury is an anterior cruciate ligamant (ACL) tear, in which the ligament becomes detached from the femur. Some sports are notorious for producing such tears – football, rugby, volleyball, squash, badminton and basketball. ACL tears are associated with contact sports and sports involving twisting and jumping movements rather than straight line movements. ACL tears are almost twice as likely if a near relative has suffered this injury or has had osteoarthritis of the knee.

The biggest source of absenteeism in the UK is lower back pain. Some 5 million people suffer from it annually to the point of seeking medical advice from their doctor, and half the entire population will suffer from back pain for at least 24 hours in any one year. There are many types of back pain and many causes, of which exercise may be one. I have had twinges in my lower back from time to time following workouts on my rowing machine. I put this down to not rowing with a straight enough back. It may be good for you to slouch when seated, but this appears not to be the case when it comes to rowing, where proper technique is crucial.

More intriguing is the fact that a link has been established between back pain and the size of the thalamus, a critical thinking part of the brain. Where people are older and have chronic back pain, as many do, their thalamus is found to be smaller than that of comparable subjects without back pain. The thalamus plays a key role in healthy everyday cognition. No one knows yet whether the thalamus causes the back pain or the pain causes the thalamus to shrink. What this shows is that back pain, which is often associated with exercise, can be more than just a physical problem. One of the commonest forms of pain in the lumbar spine is a prolapsed disc, more commonly if incorrectly referred to as a slipped disc. A disc between vertebrae is compressed and bulges or ruptures, causing pressure on a nerve, producing pain. A treatment called nucleoplasty has been developed for dealing with bulging or partially ruptured discs. Using radio frequency energy, tissue inside the disc is vaporized to decompress the nerve. The procedure is quick and expensive.

Even young people can get osteoarthritis if they over-exercise a joint. This is a degenerative disease in which the cartilage of joint surfaces wears away slowly. The scraping of bone on bone causes the pain that is typical of osteoarthritis. In the early stages of the disease, movement triggers pain, but as it gets progressively worse, pain starts to be felt even when there is no movement. For many men the problem can be traced back to overuse, either through an exercise programme or a sport. Hormone and biochemical imbalances which some men are born with can make matters worse. The people most at risk are dancers and elite athletes who train intensively, but gym fanatics now represent a growing percentage of those with the disease. Two words sum up the cause: overload and over-repetition. Injury too can play a part. Joint injuries do not necessarily lead to osteoarthritis – they are more probable if the joint has not been allowed to heal fully before being subjected to further stress. In one study of 300 former professional footballers, it was found that almost half had osteoarthritis, mainly of their knee joints. There is no cure for the disease, which afflicts around 1 million people in the UK. Heredity plays a part in most forms of the disease.

Possibly the most neglected area of the body when it comes to exercise is the abdomen. Thanks to the six-pack vogue of recent years, this is less true than it was. If you look at photos of muscle men of the Fifties like Charles Atlas, you will see that they never had rippling six packs. The importance of core strengthening around the middle is now increasingly emphasized thanks to the discovery of the link between intra-muscular abdominal fat in men and propensity to cardiovascular problems. Fat in this region, like any other, cannot be spot-removed by localized exercise, but exercises focussed on the midriff will challenge most men to lose fat there while losing fat all over at the same time. The exercises for the abdomen are crunches, sit-ups, front planks, side planks and back exercises that will benefit the lumbar spine.

Have you thought about aerobic gardening? At even a low level of exertion – say 60% of heart rate maximum – eight hours of gardening can burn a lot of calories in a day. Do a forty-hour week like this for a month and you could end up in pretty good shape at the end of it. I've tried it and it works, gardening at a level that leaves you floating on beta-endorphins at the end of each day. Remember to drink plenty of fluid as you go, to avoid dehydration.

You can probably stand from a sitting position with your arms folded, but do you normally put your hands on your knees when you stand up? If you do, you are showing one of the early signs of ageing – muscular decline in the quadriceps muscles of the upper leg. If you want to stay fit as you get older, you should be taking stairs two at a time, even going up escalators. This strengthens the quadriceps muscles in your legs. If you cannot manage two steps at a time, do quad strengthening exercises on a stepper and lunges with small weights.

Good footwear is important. As you get older, your feet become more prone to various aches and pains, as you'll know if you walk a lot. The best shoes for walking are running shoes, which is why you will frequently see older men walking in running shoes, even when the rest of their clothes are not running clothes. Nothing beats a good pair of running shoes for comfortable walking. If you suffer from pronation problems (meaning that your feet lean in at each heel), get fitted out with anti-pronation shoes, which are readily available at shops selling running shoes. In the unlikely event that your heels lean outwards, get running shoes built up on the outside at each heel. Note that I have not suggested getting walking shoes – not for street walking anyway. There are plenty of walking boots available for off-road walking, but when it comes to street shoes for walking, the range is surprisingly limited, which is why running shoes tend to be the answer, though these can look a bit odd when worn with a suit. Ignore what they look like and wear what is comfortable. Even off-road, if conditions are dry, I would advise wearing running shoes to walk in.

It's generally though that calcium intake is important in warding off osteoporosis, which is a man's disease too, not just something that women have to contend with in their menopausal years. In case you think that osteoporosis is just some vague thinning of the bones, think again. It's actually a disease that leaves the bones looking like a honey-comb inside – more holes than bone. In extreme cases large bones can be snapped like twigs, which is why, as people get older and more frail, they dread having a 'fall'. When they do fall and break a bone, it's the neck of the femur as often as not. That can lead not just to a hip opera-tion, but also a considerable chance of dying from a pulmonary embolism.

While enough dietary calcium is important, exercise is far more important – not exercise when you already have legs that look like hon-eycombs, but lifelong exercise so that if you fall over at the age of eighty you won't break anything but the furniture. And when it comes to cal-cium in your diet to build up your bones, remember that calcium sup-plements make little difference. It's the calcium in the food you eat that counts, so think dairy foods, especially if they have been fortified with added calcium. Taking calcium supplements in a multi-mineral capsule won't do any harm, but it won't ward off osteoporosis either.

Exercise is the key here and by that I mean load-bearing exercise. That means running, cycling, rowing and some resistance training with weights as well. Strong heavy bones are essential to a healthy old age where you don't have to be afraid of falling over every time you get up. One out of every twelve men in the UK over the age of 50 is affected by osteoporosis.

There is one treatment for osteoporosis that is showing promise. There is a group of drugs called bisphosphonates that may block the cells responsible for the destruction of bone tissue. The drug derived from bisphosphonates is called zoledronic acid. It's injected once a year. However, a better bet may be parathyroid hormone, also injected. Apparently it has the ability to regenerate bone.

....

More Tips and Traps

Free weights are useful and make for the cheapest and easiest form of home gym. However, a multigym at home is better, and muscle-specific machinery better still.

It is now known that those higher up the socio-economic scale are more likely to keep fit and persevere with exercise throughout their lives.

Exercise can induce asthma in men who are susceptible.

Men with the symptoms of the metabolic syndrome (see chapter on diabetes), but are still in reasonable shape should do more exercise, albeit of limited intensity, than the recommended average, and an hour a day of brisk walking is a good idea.

Never exercise to the point of exhaustion. Be aware of how tired you are while you are exercising and stop if you feel faint, nauseous, extremely tired or you feel a headache coming on. You should also stop immediately if you feel a tightness or pain in your chest.

CHAPTER NINETEEN
SIGHT FOR SORE EYES

Of all our senses, eyesight has to be the most precious, ahead, even, of hearing. To lose one's sight completely is like a partial death.

So it's surprising that eyesight is taken so much for granted, even though it is guaranteed to decline to some extent with age, and some of this decline can be slowed or halted, and perhaps even reversed.

When I started to develop long sight in my early forties, I was so ignorant about eyesight that I didn't even realize what was happening. I started to have difficulty reading small print and put this down to the fact that I was working long hours writing a book at the time. I believed then that you could damage your eyes by overusing them. It was only when I visited an ophthalmologist to see if the damage could be reversed that I learned that what was happening to me was normal and average for my age. I was duly prescribed reading glasses and have worn them ever since, with changes in the strength of the lenses every few years since then. The trend to long-sightedness seems to have stopped now, but with glasses that give about 2.5 times magnification. This process has taken about twenty years – again fairly average and normal. The process whereby the curve of the front part of the eye (the cornea) becomes more rounded, making the short-sighted less short-sighted and those with normal vision long-sighted usually starts in the early forties and lasts about twenty years. However, it can begin at any age and in my eldest son it began in his twenties. There is a strong genetic component to all this, so if one or both parents needed reading glasses, the chances are that you will need them too. It happens to almost everyone eventually, but for some it may not occur until they are in their sixties or even seventies. If you are short-sighted when younger, it is possible that as you undergo these corneal changes, you find one day that you can do without your glasses or contact lenses for distance vision.

Reading glasses have been with us for centuries, and when contact lenses came on the scene it was thought for a time that these would take over completely from glasses. Yet even though contact lenses have gone through several evolutions to the point of becoming disposable, spectacles have survived and even made a comeback in recent years. Men are now more likely to make passes at girls who wear glasses than they were fifty years ago, and the rise and rise of the geek, in the mould of Bill Gates, has made wearing glasses respectable, and almost sexy, since they still are thought to (and often do) betoken intelligence and therefore high earning power.

Over the age of forty or so, it makes sense to get your eyes tested about every two to three years, though your local optician will try and encourage you to have an annual test. If you have no problems with your eyesight apart from needing glasses, I would suggest that annual check-ups are probably a bit over the top. An optometrist's tests are fairly standard and will include testing your central and peripheral vision, whether you are long- or short-sighted or neither, whether your eyesight is different in each eye, whether you have a raised fluid pressure within the eyeball, indicating glaucoma. A more thorough test will look for (or ask for) signs of age-related macular degeneration (AMD), floaters in the field of vision, cataracts and, if you have diabetes, signs of diabetic retinopathy. If you have signs of any of these disorders, you are advised to see a good ophthalmologist, and a good optometrist should say as much. The cost of an eye test is covered by the NHS for those who are eligible.

Good vision is often described as 20/20 or 6/6 vision, but the very best vision of all is 6/5 vision, sometimes known as fighter pilot's vision for obvious reasons.

Laser treatment for short-sightedness has been around for a long time, though it has never been very popular, given the fact that even a small risk of failure in an eye operation is likely to make most of us think twice about going ahead with it. Not for nothing do eye surgeons usually operate on only one eye at a time. The procedure for short-sightedness involves a reduction of the curvature of the cornea, thereby reducing its focusing power. The average age of those undergoing this operation is 38. Long-sightedness affects about 25% of people over 45 and 50% of those over 60. Over 80% of people with sight loss are over the age of 60.

Lasers for eye surgery are constantly being improved. One of the newest systems is called Zyoptix. In a trial on a number of short-sighted patients, most had their eyesight restored to near perfect – 20/20, 6/6 or even 6/5 – within a month of treatment. Old laser procedures were unable to treat patients with a variety of idiosyncratic variations, but with Zyoptix, it is claimed, there are very few short-sighted people who cannot be treated. The technique uses the latest in iris recognition software, much like the system developed for security purposes. The result is a system that is fine-tuned to individual variation. Lens tissue can be removed, the natural shape of the cornea is preserved and night vision problems are eliminated.

In the UK over 100,000 laser eye surgery procedures are performed annually.

Recently a procedure that involves neither lasers not cutting has been developed for improving long-sightedness. It is called conductive keratoplasty (CK) and involves the reshaping of the cornea (the front part of the eye) using radio waves. The result is the opposite of the technique used to counter short-sightedness. The curvature of the cornea is increased. The procedure is quick and lasts about ten years, at which point it can be repeated. The average age of those opting for the operation is 55. Results with CK are not guaranteed and what happens to the eyesight of the minority for whom the procedure is not a success is far from clear. It is claimed that success is defined as normal or near normal vision a few weeks after the procedure, although some improvement is said to be immediate. The operation is claimed to be successful for 92% of those with low to moderate levels of long-sightedness.

Age-Related Macular Degeneration (AMD)

The part of the eye at the back is called the retina and the sensitive centre of the retina, made up of photoreceptor cells which process light, is called the macula. The photoreceptor cells are called retinal pigment epithelial (RPE) cells. They can be damaged over the years by blue rays from the sun, leading to their progressive failure known as age-related macular degeneration, which can result eventually in blindness if left untreated. Age-related blindness from macular degeneration is the commonest form of sight loss. The macula is the part of the eye responsible for precise vision.

Oxidative damage from free radicals increases the damage. Yellow pigments found in food called lutein and zeaxanthin (the isomer of lutein) have the ability to absorb blue light and combat the damage. So what foods contain lutein? Spinach and spring greens are primary sources, though spring greens, like kale, another source, are not very tasty or popular on the menu. Other sources of lutein, though not quite as rich in the pigment, are watercress, red peppers and broccoli. Foods rich in lutein also have the advantage of combatting cataracts.

Lutein can be bought as a supplement in capsule form and one study showed that a supplement of 5 mg per day increased macular pigmentation by 36% in a year. It isn't known whether degeneration can be reversed with lutein, but it seems clear that supplements can at least slow the process.

AMD normally starts after the age of fifty, though this doesn't mean that everyone over fifty will suffer. It usually starts in the commoner form known as dry AMD. The first sign is that objects no longer appear sharply defined. If the disease progresses to the so-called wet form, the central area of vision becomes misty and is eventually blanked out. The figures for the prevalence of AMD in the UK vary considerably according to whom you consult – from three million sufferers down to 150,000, though I suspect the variation is partly attributable to how you define degeneration. Of those who suffer from AMD, about 10–15% have the wet form. Women suffer more frequently than men from AMD as they are less able to absorb lutein. People with blue eyes have a higher risk, as do those with a parent or parents who suffered from AMD. About one quarter of all people over the age of sixty show some signs of AMD and current projections suggest that by 2070 as many as one-third of the UK's (ageing) population will be affected, most by the less serious dry form, for which there is no treatment at present, whereas drugs are starting to appear that will alleviate the wet form and are safe and effective. AMD is the leading cause of sight loss in the elderly.

With age, the eyes become more sensitive to glare, which is why, as car drivers get older, they often try to drive less at night to avoid the glare from oncoming headlights. This is because, with age, the eyes become less sensitive to green and blue light. Here too lutein and zeaxanthin may help. All the same, it is not advisable to drive at night if you find that glare is a serious problem for you. One-third of drivers in the UK over the age of 60 do not have a regular eye test and could be putting themselves and others at risk.

One of the most promising potential cures for AMD is a form of stem cell therapy currently undergoing trials, though, assuming it passes muster, it will be some years before it is generally available. If it works, it will deal with both dry and wet AMD. The wet form progresses more quickly and is by far the more serious form. It is called 'wet' because abnormal blood vessels develop behind the macula and leak blood and fluid, causing damage to the sensitive cells of the macula. As many as 90% of cases of blindness from AMD stem from the wet form of the disease.

There have been intense efforts in recent years to find a drug that will halt or reverse wet AMD. One drug, Visudyne clearly slows the development of the disease, but two others, both expensive to the point of being unavailable on the NHS except in extreme cases where sight has already been lost in one eye, are now available and are more effective. These are Macugen and Lucentis, though it is the latter, costing £28,000 for a 14-month course, which is said to be the more effective of the two. These drugs are known as anti-VEGF treatments. A US study showed that Lucentis could prevent vision loss from AMD and even improve sight in 90% of cases, and did so without any serious side effects.

If tests on mice translate to success in humans, there may be another interesting treatment for AMD using a drug which activates a blood protein called Robo4. The protein appears to prevent the development of the abnormal blood vessels that are the main problem in AMD. It doesn't get rid of abnormal vessels which have already developed, but it appears to stop them from growing any further, as well as preventing the leakage that normally accompanies them. Robo4 stabilises blood vessels which would otherwise leak. Interestingly, it's also thought that it might be used to successfully treat diabetic retinopathy, the leading cause of sight loss in men and women of working age.

Another approach to preventing the growth of abnormal blood vessels in cases of wet AMD and also diabetic retinopathy comes in the shape of a drug which synthesizes VEGF165b, a vascular endothelial growth factor (VEGF) which blocks the formation of new blood vessels. Trials are still ongoing in association with the charity Fight for Sight and the drug company PhiloGene.

Cataracts

Cataracts are caused by damaging ultraviolet rays from the sun. Proteins in the lens of the eye are damaged and the lens appears cloudy. Vision becomes progressively blurred and blindness can occur if the condition isn't treated. Almost 40% of cases of vision loss in people over the age of 75 are due to cataracts, which are uncommon in those under 50 years old, and common in the over 70s. Cataracts are easily detected and treated. Around 40% of those over 75 develop a cataract in one or both eyes.

The current standard treatment involves the implanting of a multifocal lens through an incision in the iris. A new technique, however, involves implanting a different lens in each eye, one with a fixed focal length for long distance vision and another with a fixed focal length lens for short distance vision. The brain, in theory, then adjusts to give the effect of a single unified seeing ability that can range from focussing on close-up to far away. These so-called monovision lenses may, however, produce strong glare as well as, reputedly, excellent vision.

It seems that eating a healthy diet protects against cataracts, especially if you eat enough DHA, one of the Omega 3 oils found in oily fish. Omega 3 oils are also helpful in combatting the problem of dry and gritty eyes, though this is more a women's than a men's problem.

Also helpful against cataracts is an adequate intake of lycopene, the red pigment found in tomatoes, watermelon and ruby grapefruit, for example.

Glaucoma

Glaucoma is common in men over the age of 50, especially if they have diabetes. Symptoms include pain in the eye, blurred vision and tenderness in the skin around the eye. It's caused by a build-up of fluid in the eye causing a rise in intraocular pressure. If left untreated, this can damage the optic nerve and cause a blind area in the field of vision. Anyone over the age of 50 should be checked for glaucoma and the test for this is readily available at most opticians. Unfortunately, though, it is no longer on the BUPA menu of tests as it used to be. Glaucoma detected early can be treated successfully with eye drops and drugs.

Diabetic Retinopathy

This eye disease is a complication of diabetes. Small blood vessels in the eye leak, depriving the retina of sufficient blood. Diabetics should have their eyes tested for this problem, the earlier the better.

Floaters

These are the drifting spots that many of us will have seen in our field of vision at one time or another. They are actually shadows cast on the retina by small innocuous pieces of tissue in the vitreous humour. This is the jelly-like tissue at the back of the eye. No one knows why floaters happen, but they are common and usually disappear after a while. However, the sudden appearance of large floaters should be treated as an emergency as they can signal retinal detachment or bleeding into the eye.

Retinal Detachment

If the retina at the back of the eye becomes partly or, worse, completely detached, usually as the result of trauma, immediate treatment is necessary so that the retina can be re-attached by an ophthalmologist. If there is a delay, it may be too late and impaired eyesight or blindness in the affected eye may result. The most common sign of retinal detachment is an impression of a dark curtain moving across the field of vision from one side to the other, or of a dark patch in the centre of the field of vision.

A part of the retina absorbs ultraviolet light and allegedly is strengthened by eating spinach.

Posterior Vitreous Detachment
This is fairly common and unlike retinal detachment it is not a serious problem. It is age-related and is caused by the normal shrinking of the eyeball that occurs with age, usually after the age of fifty. It usually heals itself after a while, much as floaters do. Often there are no symptoms, but when there are, they usually take the shape of tiny lightning flashes at either the side of the field of vision. These are more apparent at night or in dark surroundings, and may appear in one eye only or in both.

Night Vision
Folklore has it that eating carrots helps us to see in the dark, and there is some truth in this piece of ancient wisdom. The beta carotene in carrots, and for that matter in foods like mangoes, apricots and sweet potatoes, is said help the eyes to adapt more quickly to the dark, though this has been disputed by some experts.

Eye Examinations by your GP
A doctor giving you a check-up will often shine a light into your eyes and take a good look at your eyeballs. He can assess quite a lot from this. He can see how healthy your arteries are and whether you might have high blood pressure. He can see whether you have a high blood fat level. He may be able to detect signs of diabetes and other ailments. Diabetics should have an annual eye test.

However, for a thorough examination of your eyesight it's best to go to a good ophthalmologist. Most of us don't look after our eyes as well as we should. Regular testing is important and I would suggest that unless you are absolutely confident about your eye health, you should see an ophthalmologist every three years after you have passed the age of sixty. In the meantime, eating a good balanced diet is essential, and for your eyes, that means a diet rich in lutein, lycopene and beta carotene, although there is growing evidence that you should be careful not to consume too much beta carotene. Like that other well-known anti-oxidant, vitamin E, you could do yourself harm by taking too much.

CHAPTER TWENTY
SEXUAL PERFORMANCE

On the eve of my 62nd birthday I became a father again – for the third time. I now have a daughter aged 29 and two sons, one aged 33 and one aged 2. And no, they do not all have the same mother.

And yes, it is very different second time around. If you have more time to spend with your child when you are over sixty, you will get tired more quickly than when you were younger, but you will be more perceptive and therefore be able to offer more as a father, even if that 'more' tends to be as a teacher rather than as an athlete competing with a smaller athlete at running and climbing. If you are like me, however, you will still get bored sometimes and find yourself wishing for a bit more intellectual challenge.

While Picasso and Charlie Chaplin are held up as examples of famous men who had children in old age, it has to be said that it is risky. While mothers are unlikely to be over 50 and are advised to have their children before the age of 35, it's certainly true that men can go on being fertile much longer, and fathering a child in your 60s should not be a problem for many, provided the woman in question is young enough. Some younger women prefer older men, but they are the exception, so unless you are famous and rich as well as sexually fully functional, your chances of having a fecund and nubile woman willing to take on procreation with you might be quite slim in your sixties.

Men do become less fertile as they age and we'll discuss the male menopause, better known as the andropause, in a moment. The sperm production of older men reduces in volume, and the sperm which are produced are likely to be more fragmented and less mobile than when the man was younger. This increases the chances of a less than fully functioning foetus, and if the woman is over say 35, the chances of a congenital defect in the child, particularly Down's syndrome and autism spectrum disorders (ASDs), increase with every year over and above that threshold, the more so the older the father. Thus a woman of say 45 and a man of say 65 run a considerable chance of having a child with one or more birth defects in the event of a pregnancy. And the chances of miscarriage rise correspondingly. One study found that when the father was over 40, the chances of autism were six times greater than when the father was under 30. The mother's age, however, does not seem to affect the risk of autism. These facts are significant because men, like women, are tending to become parents at an older age and DNA fragmentation and genetic mutations in sperm are known to increase with the father's age.

But again we are talking about averages, always a dangerous thing. A man of 65 might have the biological age of a 50-year-old and his 45-year-old partner might have the biological age of a 35-year-old, in which case the odds of a problem decrease significantly.

To make a success of being an older father, you need more than biology on your side, though. It helps to be quite rich and to have time on your hands. On balance, and I speak from experience, it is a very rewarding if expensive thing to do. If it is unplanned, it can still be rewarding. If planned, so much the better, provided that the child is healthy and whole. If not, a child that is flawed can and should still be loved just as much, though given the choice, we would all prefer a child that turned out physically and mentally complete.

Viagra and Cialis do not improve fertility, only erectile function. I have never tried either, but despite the claim that they produce few side effects, I would be as willing to try them as most other drugs – that is, not at all if I can help it. I have little doubt that the side effects of drugs are downplayed by drug companies as a whole, and with the billions of dollars that go into drug research and development and the millions that go into the PR effort to convince doctors to prescribe them and the public to take them, it is little wonder if the public end up underestimating the damage that can be done by pharmaceutical drugs. I am not saying no to all drugs ever. I am advocating that they be taken with extreme circumspection. Viagra is not taken to save lives but for recreational purposes and perhaps even to save marriages. Men who use this drug or similar drugs such as Cialis or Levitra should be careful if they suffer from sleep apnoea, as airway congestion can become worse and occasionally life-threatening.

There are many prescription drugs that are known to affect sperm quality. These include a number of antipsychotic drugs. Some of the benzodiazepines are able to produce chromosomal abnormalities in sperm. Some of the most widely used antibiotics also have a damaging effect, as does chloroquine, a commonly used antimalarial agent. In fact, many drugs reduce sperm quality in a variety of ways, and may also alter hormone balance generally. The anabolic steroids have this effect, as does nitrofurantroin, an anti-microbial drug. Fortunately most damage from this drug appears to be temporary and sperm quality will usually return to normal once use of the drug comes to an end.

Chlamydia is usually thought of as a woman's STI (sexually transmitted infection), so it may come as a surprise to learn that it's also common in men and that those who are carriers may have such a high level of damaged sperm that their partners cannot conceive. In those who have contracted Chlamydia in the past, the level of healthy sperm is typically only one-third of that found in those who are unaffected. This may be enough to make them infertile. And though Chlamydia is more often caught in youth than in middle life, the genetic damage it can do can last in the form of permanently fragmented DNA in sperm. In fact more male fertility problems may be attributable to Chlamydia infection than any other cause. Often it is only when in vitro fertilisation (IVF) is considered that sperm damage is discovered. Since Chlamydia in males is usually symptom-free, a man may have lived for years not knowing that he is infertile or sub-fertile.

Where there is a problem achieving a conception and the problem is down to the male, the frequency of intercourse and/or ejaculation may be a factor. It used to be thought that to optimize the chance of conception, ejaculation should take place about every three days, thereby giving sperm production time to recover optimally. The latest research shows, however, that daily ejaculation gives the best results. Longer intervals may increase sperm volume, but of poorer sperm quality. A daily interval gives enough volume and maximises quality, sperm being fresher when newly produced.

It should be noted, however, that following a successful conception, the quality of the child produced will be defined by the quality of the ovum and the fertilizing sperm. Not all sperm from the same batch are equal and the chances of successful offspring are enhanced when the strongest sperm wins, which is of course one argument against IVF with its somewhat more random sperm selection.

Can a healthy lifestyle improve and prolong libido and fertility? I would say almost certainly yes, but I cannot point to any researched proof of this. It just seems obvious that if you are above-average healthy for your age, you will also be more potent.

An ageing body is not the only enemy of male potency. Illness, fatigue and depression, which often share the same symptoms, can also undermine libido. While erectile function and fertility are not the same thing, it is true to say that they are connected. A rampant libido is probably a better sign of strong healthy sperm than a permanent brewer's droop. So a lifestyle that is healthy may contribute to sexual libido and fertility at the same time.

Some of the more plausible supplements on the market that are said to promote erectile function by promoting better blood circulation are arginine (an amino acid), cordyceps (a Chinese mushroom), ginseng and ginkgo biloba. To these might be added Peruvian maca powder, derived from a root, and said to work as an aphrodisiac and improve fertility. Experiments with rats have shown that it does have this effect, though similar experiments with humans are still awaited. Garlic is said to improve erections by dint of increasing blood circulation, in which case we are back to the idea that anything that improves circulation is good for you – the brain, the heart – even the penis.

I believe that the best route to good erectile function and healthy fertility levels is good nutrition and moderate exercise, combined with an absence of tiredness, illness and depression. For avoidance of the latter, a happy sexual relationship is almost certainly a prerequisite as few things kill off a marriage or other relationship more thoroughly than an absence of sex, unless both partners are happy with such a situation. Taking supplements may help a bit, but these are no substitute for general overall health.

To achieve that, a healthy level of exercise goes without saying. This is probably a good place to raise the spectre of anabolic steroids (see chapter 29 on performance-enhancing drugs). A lot of misconceptions surround this group of synthetic hormonal drugs. Anabolic, in case you are wondering, simply means muscle mass-enhancing. The opposite is catabolic. There may occasionally be good grounds for hormone supplementation (of which more later), but anabolic steroid drugs are bad news and it is not for nothing that in most countries their sale is illegal. The trouble with these drugs is that even in moderate doses they flood the body with synthesized testosterone which inactivates the body's own testosterone production and thereby reduces fertility. Many drugs can be classed as anabolic steroids, but the body simply does not need them unless you want to look superhumanly muscular and shorten your life.

Testosterone-enhancing substances which are less well known and are not classed as anabolic steroids include DHEA (dehydroepiandrosterone), Gamma-oryzanol, androstenedione and Tribulus Terrestris. Many such substances are banned in the UK but not in the US. The reason for this is that they share many of the negative outcomes of anabolic steroids and are therefore dangerous. Ironically, perhaps, most of the anabolic steroids actually end up not only reducing male potency and fertility, but producing feminising characteristics such as male breasts. They may also produce heart arrhythmias.

The androgen (male sex hormone) DHEA is worth particular comment as it went through a huge vogue in the US a few years ago. There it is sold legally as a supplement, while in the UK it is a banned substance. The adrenal gland produces DHEA naturally. In young men it is by far the most prevalent steroid hormone circulating in the blood. However, between the ages of 35 and 70, the blood serum concentration falls to only 20% of its peak level. Just to make things confusing, in about 15% of men, DHEA level actually increases naturally with age. We know little about DHEA's function, but it may serve as a precursor to testosterone and oestradiol. Low levels of DHEA are linked to increased risk of cardiovascular disease in men over the age of 50.

There have been several well controlled tests on DHEA. These showed that this sex hormone raises the level of androstenediol, another male hormone, in men. It also produces a rise of about 10% in the blood concentration of insulin-like growth factor. The tests showed no increase in libido, but there was a marked improvement in quality of sleep, energy level and ability to handle stress. Doses of 100 mg per day appeared to increase lean body weight and muscle strength. However, the better view is that there is not enough research to show that replacement therapy with DHEA does not result in negative side effects. The big drug companies have not invested money in further research as DHEA is a molecule and therefore cannot be patented. One thing is clear, and that is that those with a high prostate specific antigen (PSA) reading (see chapter 43 on the prostate) should not risk taking DHEA. Perhaps its use is best restricted to those with abnormally low levels of DHEA, and only under medical supervision.

BPH (Benign Prostatic Hyperplasia) which involves progressive enlargement of the prostate gland and affects most men in some measure after the age of 50 is not thought to have a negative effect on erectile function or to increase your chances of prostate cancer more than slightly (see chapter 43 on the prostate). However, should you be unfortunate enough to get prostate cancer and have a prostatectomy, impotence will follow. The good news is that you can be impotent and still be fertile. As I've said, the two do not necessarily go together, but there is some association, so it's unlikely that if you are over 60, have had your prostate removed and are impotent, you will be fathering children in large numbers.

Men, like women, have a biological clock. It's just that in men it all happens more slowly and is less noticeable as a result. In fact the male biological clock starts ticking at age 25 on average. Currently about a quarter of all children are born to fathers over the age of 35, but men this age are twice as likely to be infertile as men under 25. Many men of all ages are infertile or sub-fertile. It's far from being only a female problem.

The term andropause has been invented to match the term menopause applied to women when they reach the end of their fertile life. The male hormones (androgens), especially testosterone, go into decline with age. The male biological clock is measured by sperm count and quality, erectile function, free testosterone level and by semen volume. If you are trying for a pregnancy with your partner and fail, don't assume that it's all her fault, or that the only solution is IVF. The problem could be an infection in the male, blocked ejaculatory ducts, or even a varicosity of the testicular blood vessels (varicoceles), all of which are treatable conditions. A low sperm count could be caused by a number of other factors such as undescended testicles and testicular cancer.

Let's list the alleged symptoms of the andropause, which reads like a list of the main features of old age itself:

Depression and nervousness
Diminished libido
Fatigue
Disturbed sleep
Poor concentration
Poor memory
Erectile dysfunction
Lack of libido
Flushes and sweats
Anger and irritability
Sadness
Unsociable behaviour
Lack of energy
General malaise
Mood disturbances
Reduced muscle mass and strength
Increased central and upper body fat
Decline in human growth hormone
Decline in insulin-like growth factor
Decline in DHEA
Decline in free testosterone
Osteoporosis
Vasomotor disturbance
Reduced cognitive functioning
Reduced visuo-spatial skills

The blood tests that should be carried out to identify andropause are those that measure: gonadotrophin, prolactin, sex hormone-binding globulin (SHBG), and early morning free testosterone. DHEA, insulin like growth factor and human growth hormone levels are useful extra tests that could be carried out at the same time.

Many men are not aware that sperm and semen are not the same thing. Sperm are produced in the testes, while semen is produced in the prostate gland. What should your sperm count be? In your mid-twenties it ought to be around 60–80 million sperm per millilitre of ejaculate. You're marginal if your count is between 20 and 40 million, and under 20 million your chances of achieving conception may depend on luck or laboratory IVF techniques such as intra-cytoplasmic sperm injection (ICSI), where the success rate is fairly poor.

Sperm and testosterone production are stimulated by follicle stimulating hormone (FSH) and luteinizing hormone (LH).

Several factors other than age can affect sperm production and quality, including heat and illness. Hot baths and tight pants are best avoided if a healthy sperm count is required. The shock that can come with bereavement, job loss or divorce, when associated with depression and sudden weight loss, can have a marked if temporary impact on sperm production. Certain diseases can cause genetic faults in sperm, namely Marfan syndrome, polycystic kidney disease, haemophilia A and neurofibromatosis, and these diseases are more likely to occur or get worse with age.

Let's look at testosterone in more detail. The important measure of testosterone is the amount of FAT (free active testosterone), which is the free bio-available testosterone in the blood. FAT level should be at least 5% of total testosterone level. In the US, the normal male range for the hormone is expressed as 300–1,100 nanograms per decilitre of blood. Men below the 300 threshold tend to have little interest in sex, are non-confrontational and are usually physically weak and socially inhibited. Men with high levels of testosterone tend the other way, to aggressiveness and competitiveness. One study found that women lawyers, male actors and football players had above average testosterone levels, while clergymen had below average levels. High levels of testosterone in those with low intelligence frequently result in criminal behaviour. More intelligent men with high testosterone levels are likely to be ambitious, energetic and successful, even driven. They attempt to influence and control others, express their opinions forcefully and freely, give vent to anger openly and tend to dominate social interactions.

An interesting finding is that testosterone levels can go up and down, not just with age, but with social status. There is a two-way interplay. Testosterone breeds success, at least in the intelligent, and success breeds testosterone. The loss of self-esteem associated with traumatic loss, such as when a man loses his job, can have a direct and immediate impact on sperm production. Conversely, on finding another job, testosterone level may rise again.

In the UK, doctors measure testosterone in nanomoles per litre. The basic minimum requirement used to be 9.8 but routinely laboratories give the normal range as 10 to 35. The average 60-year-old should have a free testosterone level of about 19 nanomoles per litre and in the view of one doctor, a level in the 11–16 range should be considered inadequate, though clearly age should be taken into account. It is important when measuring free testosterone that the sample should be taken very soon after the subject wakes up. The norms for testosterone are based on samples taken early. Samples taken later in the day will give lower readings and will not be meaningful.

An abnormally low testosterone level may be the result of testicular dysfunction or hypothalamic-pituitary dysfunction, and may be inherited or acquired. It may also be the result of a sample not being taken at the right time of day – early in the morning. In one study over an 18-year period, it was found that men with a below average testosterone level were 33% more likely to die, after other possible factors had been taken into account. When testosterone is low, a man's oestrogen (female hormone) proportion is usually higher and therefore closer to the male/female hormone balance in a woman. This may lead to a more rounded shape, an increase in abdominal fat and development of male breasts (gynaecomastia). These are signs, among others, of the metabolic syndrome, and a warning of the possibility of diabetes, heart failure, hypertension, raised cholesterol and cardiovascular disease.

There is much still to explore where testosterone is concerned, and we should bear in mind that it may be the testosterone derivative dihydrotestosterone which is ultimately more important. Given that prostate cancer is a major cause of death among men and may be linked to a higher than average testosterone level, caution is needed before too much good or bad is attributed to testosterone. Testosterone supplements are still an area of considerable argument.

Some researchers have found that testosterone level is not critical to sexual functioning in younger men, provided that it is within the normal range. However, the potent metabolite dihydrotestosterone does seem to have a significant effect and may therefore be a more important marker in older men (see chapter 43 on the prostate). We know that it is this testosterone derivative that is implicated in male pattern hair loss and that men who lose their hair are generally regarded as having a high sex drive. This correlates with the theory that clergymen are not noted for their sex drive, have been shown to be low in testosterone (and presumably dihydrotestosterone) and generally have a thick head of hair well into old age. Even more interesting therefore is the theory that low testosterone correlates with a longer than average lifespan, and that baldness correlates with cardiovascular disease. We might postulate from this that those with a thick head of hair and a low sex drive will live longer. However, it would be wise to bear in mind the research maxim that correlation does not imply causation.

On average, free testosterone level drops about 1% each year from age 30, which means that the average male will see his testosterone level halve by the time he dies. By then his serum total testosterone (bio-available plus non-bio-available testosterone) will have dropped by perhaps as much as 80%. This is the process that most marks the andropause. The surface signs of falling testosterone usually become more marked after the age of about 55. Falling testosterone levels in the normal ageing process result from a combination of changes in pituitary gonadotrophin secretion and testicular failure and are undoubtedly influenced by heredity.

A testosterone test is readily available from most medical testing labs. Free testosterone rather than total testosterone should be tested, and for good measure, you should get your SHBG score. This is the level of a protein called sex hormone binding globulin that circulates in your blood. The level rises with age, and the lower your score the better. SHBG takes free testosterone out of the blood and binds it to tissue, thereby reducing its availability to the body's testosterone receptors that control libido. Paradoxically, obesity reduces SHBG, but also reduces free testosterone. There are other proteins that bind testosterone, but SHBG is the most important.

Another lab test that is useful is the Free Androgen Index, which takes into account your sex hormone levels generally, not just testosterone. Test results will generally show your score against a normal range.

Should you take testosterone supplements in one form or another (orally, in skin patches or by injection) if you have a low testosterone level and are worried about it, or are trying to get your partner pregnant? Testosterone replacement therapy (TRT) for men is an area for expert advice, and testosterone replacement supplements are only available on prescription in the UK. It seems to me that if it were good to take testosterone supplements, we would all be doing it by now as one way to stay younger for longer. There has to be a downside, however, to tampering with nature in this way. My best advice, if you are seriously interested in taking testosterone replacements, is to see your doctor and get a referral to an endocrinologist specializing in this area. Otherwise, you should find that a healthy diet, clean air, not smoking and exercise, particularly resistance exercise should help slow the rate at which your testosterone level declines, so long as you manage to avoid fatigue, illness and depression.

On the other hand, while it used to be thought that testosterone supplementation would cause cardiovascular problems, the opposite is now thought to be true. Significantly, clinical practitioners in the complex field of TRT have found that the rate of testosterone decline with age is more important than the actual testosterone level itself. However, to measure the rate of decline would require testing over a number of years and from a younger age, and this is impractical as few younger men with no testosterone worries are likely to think of getting a reading for the sake of a periodic measurement of their rate of decline in later life.

It was thought for some years that TRT for men might result in an increased risk of prostate cancer as this cancer is associated with higher than normal levels of testosterone. For this reason, testosterone therapy involves careful clinical analysis and follow-up that includes monitoring any change in PSA level. To date no noticeable rise in prostate cancer has been associated with TRT.

TRT has been found to improve lean body weight by reducing fat around the middle and by increasing muscle tissue in the upper body. But does TRT do a lot for a failing sex life? Some 50% of men between the ages of 50 and 70 complain of impotence. However, as many as 80% of cases of erectile dysfunction are now believed to have a medical cause such as diabetes, hypothyroidism, cardiovascular disease and multiple sclerosis. There is no clear evidence, however, that in those cases which do not have a medical cause, TRT brings your sex life back to how it used to be.

When it comes to potency, the key factor is the capacity of the muscles in the walls of the artery providing blood to the penis to relax sufficiently for engorgement to occur. This process may be facilitated by Viagra (sildenafil citrate). The more cautious view is that unless there is cardiovascular disease present and the risk of a drug interaction with nitrites, Viagra is a safer remedy for impotence than TRT. There is still too little known about the possible side effects of supplementation with testosterone.

Men who are heavy users of mobile phones have been found to suffer a reduction in sperm volume and quality, a finding attributed to the electromagnetic fields generated by mobile phones. It is known for a fact that electromagnetic fields can damage the Leydig cells in the testes. These control the secretion of luteinising hormone, which is responsible for testosterone production. Mobile phones, it has been established, can heat body tissue and therefore might well damage sperm, which are known to be susceptible to heat. However, to date, absolute proof of a link between mobile phone electromagnetic fields and sperm quality is still lacking and stress and obesity have been suggested as alternative explanations, as well as sedentary occupations that involve long hours behind the wheel of a vehicle, as this is likely to raise temperature around the testes and damage sperm. If phones are risky, they may do more damage in the trouser pocket than held to the head.

The mobile phone theory gains some plausibility in light of the recent finding that some forms of cancer are more common in people living close to mobile phone relay masts.

Erectile problems and fertility problems, while different, go hand in hand. Sort out one and you should sort out the other. Above all keep your weight down and your body fat at the right level. Research shows that high body fat levels are the enemy of high testosterone, as fat can be converted into oestrogen-like compounds that reduce testosterone production. Blood fat can also clog the small arteries that carry blood to the penis.

It's also worth knowing that extreme exercise may lower cholesterol beyond a healthy level. We hear a lot about high cholesterol, but little about those who have too little of this waxy substance that actually helps to produce testosterone. So while moderate exercise will raise your appetite for sex and aid potency, too much exercise will have the opposite effect. Very thin men who over-exercise will tend to have a poor libido. Moderate regular exercise should be the rule, which is why marathon running on a regular basis is unlikely to do your sex life a lot of good.

Avoid use of recreational drugs. Marijuana has been shown to reduce sperm count and quality. Little research has been done on the effects of pharmaceutical drugs on fertility, but it seems likely that many will have a negative impact. The selective serotonin re-uptake inhibitors (SSRIs) such as Seroxat and Prozac, used to treat depression, have been found to definitely reduce sperm count. Other side effects of the drugs are delayed ejaculation and impotence, and it is thought that SSRIs may prevent sperm from getting into the semen required for successful ejaculation.

Some measure of erectile dysfunction is found in at least 40% of all males by the age of 60, and this rises to 60% by the age of 70. However, libido and serious erections go together, so there is no point in having an erection if the desire isn't there, or the desire if the erection isn't there.

Which brings me to the subject of male attractiveness to the opposite sex. It used to be thought that women were attracted to money and men to nubile good looks. The latter is still true, but with the advent of better incomes for women who work, women now tend to put looks up there with money. That's a tough call for men, especially as they get older, and it partly explains the trend for older women to prefer younger men as never before. In other words, a man had better be attractive and sexy to get and keep his mate, right down to exuding the right pheromones in sufficient quantities. As he ages, he will give out fewer of these female-attracting substances which come from glands alongside the sweat glands. It's no surprise that pheromone levels go hand in hand with testosterone levels, and that if one is low, the pulling power of the other will be equally lacking. We should not underestimate the importance of pheromones wafting invisibly through the air. At a subliminal level, they signal to a woman that the corresponding testosterone is there – or not.

Falling testosterone will not only show up in reduced drive and lower pheromone levels. It may be accompanied by reducing muscle mass, an expanding waistline, male breasts (now known as man boobs, moobs or moobies) and a saggy backside. To make matters worse, falling testosterone levels may be accompanied by anaemia, a disposition to Type 2 diabetes and the cardiovascular problems that this can cause.

Did you know that testosterone affects the length of your ring finger (the one next to your little finger) in the womb, and that this in turn, in adulthood, may indicate the strength of your libido, your drive and your sporting ability? In a man the ring finger should be longer than the index finger (the one next to the thumb), and the greater the difference on your right hand, the higher your fertility and testosterone levels in your peak years (your mid-twenties). Of course, as you get older and your testosterone level falls, the length of your ring finger relative to your index finger will remain the same. Research in this area has suggested that the average male has a ratio of 0.98, while elite athletes and those with a high sex drive may have a ratio as low as 0.90.

If you are trying to get your partner pregnant, artificial lubricants are not a good idea as they slow sperm motility. On the other hand you could argue that they provide a hurdle to sort out the men from the boys among sperm and thus be sure of the very strongest if conception occurs. I would not risk it though, as damage to the embryo might be more likely. The sperm might be deformed but still be a strong swimmer.

Testosterone indirectly helps to burn fat, which is one reason why, as men age and testosterone falls, it becomes harder and harder to keep your weight down. Testosterone injections might keep weight down in older men, but the downside outweighs the benefit of any anabolic steroid injections or supplements. This applies equally to dehydroepiandrosterone (DHEA) and androstenedione, which allegedly boost sex drive. The former is a testosterone-like steroidal hormone and the latter can be converted into testosterone. The body produces both naturally and both decline with age.

....

More Tips and Traps

As men age, testosterone level drops, but oestrogen level rises slightly, making men less macho (and less likely to commit crimes). This is normal.

When trying to achieve conception, you should avoid all drugs, including antibiotics, as all drugs affect fertility to some degree.

If you have children after the age of 60, expect lots of viruses to which you will have little immunity. Most infections that your child picks up at play school will, unfortunately, come your way.

Be aware that if you have had a vasectomy and get it reversed, there is a chance that your fertility may be impaired.

Dutasteride, the drug most commonly used to treat benign prostatic hyperplasia (BPH) (see chapter 43 on the prostate) tends, even after you have stopped using it, to reduce ejaculate volume, but not, allegedly, sperm count or quality.

Sexually transmitted infections (STIs) should be got rid of before conception is attempted.

A sufficient intake of zinc and selenium are important for maintaining fertility and erectile function in the older male. They help to maintain testosterone levels and to support the immune system. Zinc supplements should be taken with plenty of vitamin C.

Caffeine and alcohol should be avoided if conception is the objective. This applies to the man's partner equally.

Supplements of the Omega oils, the essential fatty acids are thought to boost fertility but there is no proof of this.

Impotence is thought to be a marker, sometimes, for cardiovascular disease.

CHAPTER TWENTY-ONE
FOOD TOXINS

I am guilty of eating fruit without washing it first. This should not be too much of a problem if government Health and Safety regulations are widely adhered to, but I still don't like the thought of whatever it is I'm eating not being natural. I try to just eat organic, but again I am guilty, since I only succeed about half the time. So I do ingest a lot of stuff that is sprayed on fruit and vegetables to make them last on the shelf for days on end without wilting, even though inside they are losing some of their food value with every hour that passes; especially if they are exposed to sunlight and street pollution, as foods on market stalls usually are.

The trouble with not washing things properly is that even if you do, you are still left with whatever is inside the fruit or vegetable that has come from the fertilizers and insecticides sprayed on them in the field and orchard. You don't know what this is. The labels don't tell you. If it's anything like what is fed to non-organic farmed salmon, you have reason to be worried and more reason to go organic. But organic food often looks so limp and old in the health food shops and even in some of the supermarkets. Where there is a lower sales volume, produce will tend to hang around longer and you cannot put a sell-by date on a loose piece of fruit. The non-organic produce may look more tempting. This could be because it is truly fresher, or it could be because it has been sprayed. The long-life ingredient may even be some chemical that was fed into the soil in which it grew.

Information is woefully lacking, despite the improvements in labelling over recent years and requirements of a sell-by date clearly marked on some types of product. Heath and Safety will tell you that the additives that they allow are kept within strict safety limits. But this has not prevented major scandals and the sudden withdrawal of certain foods, usually processed foods, every so often.

If we eat food from supermarkets – and most of us do – we may be ingesting a variety of chemicals and man-made pollutants. When tests were carried out on 27 basic foods, including bread and eggs, every one was found to be contaminated with something that should not have been there. A survey of blood samples from 352 people over a five-year period showed signs of toxic chemicals. The levels found were low, well within legal safety limits, but who is to say what the long-term effects of such pollutants will be? Safety levels are set for toxins one at a time and no one knows what effect two or more of these might have in combination. Eight man-made contaminants all found in food at legal levels have been linked at higher levels to cancer, asthma, heart disease, diabetes, obesity, endocrine problems and foetal damage. These chemicals are: phthalates, organotins, alkylphenols, artificial musks, perfluorinated chemicals, brominated flame retardants, polychlorinated biphenyls (banned) and organochlorine pesticides (banned). You have to wonder what flame retardants were doing in food. It seems that some of these chemicals may have leached into food from the packaging.

When it comes to genetically modified (GM) foods, the light is still red in the UK, unlike the US, where GM produce has been on the market for years, especially in the production of soybeans, which find their way on to the UK market in a number of products. The EU has relaxed the rules on what is GM, though, and now up to 0.9% of food labelled GM-free can contain genetically modified organisms (GMOs) instead of the previous maximum of 0.1%. In a similar vein , organic food has only to be 95% organic to be labelled organic. The combination of the two changes alters the rules of the game for organic farmers. They still cannot knowingly allow GM elements in their produce, but the new rules mean that any accidental slippage on this front will be permitted up to the new limits. Thus in theory a food could be 5% non-organic and 'accidentally' be made up 0.9% from GMOs and still be legally labelled organic. The invitation to cheat and allege accidental contamination if challenged is all too obvious. As organic food sales continue to soar compared with non-organic, it is important that supermarkets in particular declare their organic policy and whether they will choose to adhere to the old GM gold standard of 0.1% or the new 0.9%. The UK organic food market is now worth in the region of £2 billion per annum, so much is at stake. The 0.1% level is still maintained by the Soil Association in certifying organic produce, and many organic producers would be reluctant to risk losing that seal of approval.

Farmed salmon has been the target of much criticism from organisations hostile to intensive fish farming that is not organic, and now the Soil Association and the Organic Food Federation certify salmon that is organically farmed. The same strict rules are being applied increasingly to meat, where the greatest fear of many consumers is that production has been boosted by the use of hormones in animal feed or directly through injection.

Health claims made in advertising for a number of foods have come under attack from the Advertising Standards Authority as well as falling foul of new European Union directives. Claims that cannot be substantiated have always been outlawed, but now the game has got tougher for the manufacturers in terms of how much research they must produce to back their claims. Manufacturers of tea products, probiotic drinks, HDL cholesterol- raising margarine and products with added Omega 3 have all been challenged. A British Medical Journal article has suggested there is no clear evidence for the benefits of Omega 3. I would not stop taking it yet though.

The Soil Association has threatened to withdraw organic certification for produce from thousands of poor organic farmers in Kenya, not because their produce is not organic, but because flying it to the UK market creates a carbon footprint in so-called 'food miles'. That may be so, but I don't think that is a matter for the Soil Association. It shows the extent to which influential organisations can be hijacked by political agendas. The matter of carbon footprints and the air-freighting of produce should be left to others and not become part of any definition of what constitutes organic.

CHAPTER TWENTY-TWO
HAIR TODAY –
GONE TOMORROW

By the age of 50, more than half of all men are showing some visible sign of hair loss, and many more are losing hair, albeit the signs are not yet visible.

So is hair loss a marker for ageing? It seems that the link between ageing and hair loss that is male pattern baldness is weak. The loss is the result of the effect of the enzyme 5-alpha-reductase on testosterone, the result of which process is dihydrotestosterone. It is this stronger version of testosterone that acts on the hair follicles. Dihydrotestosterone is therefore a derivative of testosterone, the prime male hormone, and is implicated not only in hair loss but also in prostate problems, perhaps not surprisingly, given the prostate's close link with the testes where sperm and most of the body's testosterone are generated. For this reason, it is often said that men who lose their hair early have an above-average sex drive and by and large this is true. The same men are likely to have hairy chests, and even hairy backs in extreme cases, and as they get older, they will be the first to have hairy nostrils and ears as well. Decline in testosterone usually begins about age twenty-five in males.

But how does this fit with the theory that says that as man evolves away from his ancestors among the great apes, he is becoming more hairless on top? A hairy chest would seem to suggest the opposite. Modern science simply doesn't know how to explain this apparent contradiction. Meanwhile those of us who are challenged in the follicle department can console ourselves that a good many women find receding hairlines and even baldness attractive (not least as a sign of higher intelligence, which translates into money in many women's minds). Which is just as well if you are driven more than most by testosterone and the sex drive that goes with the territory. I remember when, a few years ago, the then French prime minister, Laurent Fabius, who was totally bald, was voted the sexiest man in France.

That is some consolation, but there are few of us thinning on top who would not opt for a thick head of hair instead if we had the choice. The problem is that we don't have too many serious choices, even though there are millions waiting to be made by the first scientist who comes up with a way to make plentiful hair sprout from unproductive follicles.

In my view, Minoxidil solutions (whether 2% or 4%), which have been on the market for about twenty years as a rub-on answer to the problem are little better than a psychological crutch. I should know as I tried Regaine, the brand name of the product, for about ten years. It certainly did not grow any new hair. Whether it helped slow the rate of loss is doubtful, but of course that cannot be measured as there is no way of knowing what the effect would have been without the application of that messy liquid every evening.

Then there is Finasteride, a drug widely used to treat the enlarged prostate (see chapter 43 on the prostate). As an oral supplement for hair loss, Finasteride, under the trade name Propecia, has been around for about ten years. I have not tried it personally, as I avoid any regular use of drugs if at all possible, but I have taken Nourkrin tablets for the last eight years as an all-natural alternative. This is a Scandinavian product made principally from fish cartilage. It is said to reduce dihydrotestosterone production (as is Finasteride) and therefore hair loss. I cannot say that it has been effective any more than Minoxidil. I am more challenged on top than eight years ago, but maybe things would have been worse without it. The good news is that the substance is natural, unlike Finasteride, and it does seem to have a positive side effect. It makes your skin freer from blemishes of the seborrhoeic variety, and so is sold also for this benefit. Whether it actually restores hair, though, is doubtful.

Hair transplants have been around for about 40 years. How well they work depends a lot on the individual. The younger you are when they take place, the better the results. However, this is only hair redistribution and there is a limit to how much hair can be taken from the tonsure area to be replanted higher up. Until not long ago, plugs of follicles removed for transplantation were usually about 4 mm in diameter. About 40% of the follicles 'took' in the average patient and these would typically last about 30 years before themselves falling prey to hair loss. Today the micrograft is more common. Plugs are much smaller, the 'take' is better, and they give less of a tufted appearance. However, their lifespan is likely to be no longer than that of the 4 mm plugs. Work has been going on for years to find a way of cloning unlimited numbers of an individual's hair follicles in a laboratory, to be transplanted using the micrograft technique. The fortune to be made by the first successful lab to succeed is incalculable. In the meantime, transplants (assuming you are not daft enough to go for a hairpiece) are the best, albeit inadequate, solution. The better alternative, though, is probably to make a virtue of baldness and make the most of all that testosterone that comes with it. Fortunately, perhaps, shaven and bald heads (you can't always tell the difference) seem to be fashionable these days.

Do not, in desperation, fall for quack hair loss products. There is an abundance of charlatans out there happy to fleece you in exchange for their snake oil, or to convince you that the likes of Minoxidil and Nourkrin will grow your hair back. Well they won't, despite all the alleged scientific proof you will be offered, especially on the Internet. With luck they might slow the rate of loss, but you will never know for sure. If in doubt, do as I did and try Nourkrin. At least it will do your facial skin some good and being natural, it has no negative side effects.

Or get a urologist to prescribe Finasteride if you are also having serious prostate problems and going to the loo to pee three or more times each night. Then you may at least help your prostate and with luck your hair. The version of Finasteride available for treating prostate problems (Proscar) is much more potent than the over-the-counter version sold to deal with hair loss (Propecia), so if you have a prostate problem and are losing your hair, you could end up killing two birds with one stone. Don't expect your hair to grow back, but Proscar could slow hair loss.

If a piece of research in the last few years is to be believed, those who are bald on top, especially around the crown, are more prone to cardio-vascular problems than those with a full head of hair. From this it may be concluded that those with plenty of hair stand a better chance of living longer. The explanation, if the findings are correct, lies in the role that testosterone and dihydrotestosterone play in the genesis and evolution of heart disease – and stroke as well. The reasons are still poorly understood.

Maybe it's nature's way of making use of the most prolific for procreation purposes and then getting rid of them when their job is done. It's true that when you look at photographs of men over 90 and even over 100 years old, they seem to still have a surprisingly large amount of hair for their age. If these findings are correct, the worried well man who is also worried about his hair loss faces an extra challenge if he wants to live to a ripe old age. That challenge is to try even harder to eat well, exercise appropriately and be contented with his lot. He may be obliged by nature (for which read his genes) to pay a heavy price for his higher than average testosterone level.

Greying hair can happen any time after the age of about twenty and may well have been occurring for a few years before it is even noticed. It starts with the sideburns and beard area and from there moves to the rest of the head and the chest. The rest of the body comes later and the pubic area last of all. This latter fact suggests that the proximity of the testes has something to do with it and that greying of hair may be connected with the sex hormones in a way similar to hair loss. This is pure hypothesis, though, as it is very often those with a thick head of hair who go grey first, or at least as early as those thinning on top. In other words there may be no connection between greying hair and hair loss despite the fact that pubic hair seems to be the last to go grey.

Hair goes grey as the melanocytes which make pigment gradually cease to do so. Grey and white hair is simply hair with less or no pigmentation.

There is no known cure for greying hair and in many cases it can make a man look more distinguished as well as older, something that can have advantages when it comes to job promotion. The only thing you can do about greying hair is to dye it, or otherwise change its colour more naturally with a product like Grecian 2000. Most dyed hair can be spotted while hair treated with Grecian 2000 is less likely to show telltale signs of having been tampered with.

If men with early hair loss are more prone to cardiovascular problems, it would be easy to conclude that by getting castrated, men could extend their lifespan, since castration stops hair loss dead in its tracks. Castration will not restore hair lost, but will prevent further loss, or any loss at all if castration takes place before puberty, as used to happen when boys were castrated as singers.

What does the future promise? It looks as though a combination of stem cell manipulation and gene therapy may enable the body to generate healthy new hair follicles in much the same way that there is currently hope that one day it will be possible to grow entirely new organs. There is promising research in this area based on experiments with mice, but it is likely to be many years before anything usable appears on the market.

loss at all if castration takes place before puberty as used to happen when boys were castrated as singers.

What does the future promise? It looks as though a combination of stem cell manipulation and gene therapy may enable the body to generate healthy new hair follicles in much the same way that there is currently hope that one day it will be possible to grow entirely new organs. There is promising research in this area based on experiments with mice, but it is likely to be many years before anything usable appears on the market.

CHAPTER TWENTY-THREE
I HEAR WHAT YOU SAY

It may be fortunate that you are not a teenager today. Research has identified that nine out of ten young people who have been to a club, a rock concert or a pop festival will have impaired hearing afterwards and in many cases the damage will be permanent. Hearing may not be as precious as eyesight, but most of us would not like to lose it, or even have to wear a hearing aid. Rock music can produce dullness of hearing and may also induce tinnitus, a ringing in the ears which can be difficult to endure. Both are signs of irreversible hearing damage and it may be that there are going to be a lot more people around in a few years who are hard of hearing. The government is considering imposing legal sound limits for music in public places.

My father had what he called cocktail party deafness, where it is increasingly difficult, as you get older, to make out high range sounds against background noise. Having a conversation in a noisy place gets more and more difficult until the only solution may be to leave. I have inherited the problem from my father, so I know what he meant. I find one solution is to sit down somewhere and get the person you wish to talk to to sit down as well. The noise level seems to be less at a lower level and it's also more comfortable that way, assuming you can find some-where to sit.

Annual check-ups normally include a hearing test that measures hearing in each ear at a variety of different sound levels. You will find out that way if your hearing is normal for your age. If it is below par, you may feel you could live with a hearing aid, though there is still some stigma attached in some people's mind to wearing one, no matter how concealed they are and how skin-coloured. The stigma seems to be associated with the idea that if you are deaf you must be old, and nowa-days nobody wants to look old if they can help it. One answer to the problem comes in the form of a pair of glasses which have a hearing aid concealed in the arms of the frame. There's nothing to fit inside the ear itself, and although the arms tend not to be of the thin invisible variety, there is no stigma to wearing glasses.

Thanks to research into hearing problems, it looks as though we are not too far off the day when hearing aids can be thrown away and surgery of the inner ear will take care of most hearing loss problems. Already some people who were born deaf have had a modicum of hearing restored. One day in the not too distant future, the gift of hearing through surgery should be routine. In the meantime, hearing aids and their batteries are getting smaller and ever less noticeable.

Don't SCUBA dive if you have a virus that prevents you from equalizing as you go down. The same applies to flying in a plane where the pressure on your eardrums may be difficult to control. If you have an inner ear infection, it can be very painful. Painkillers with ibuprofen may help, and if there is a bacterial infection, antibiotics will need to be used. For stronger painkillers, see below. If you have an inflammation of the outer ear canal, as often happens after a swim, especially in the tropics where minute particles of coral may have entered the canal and irritated its sensitive lining, use eardrops and make sure that they contain hydrocortisone. This is an absolute must if you want the drops to work and there is any degree of bacterial infection.

If the pain is unbearable and you are away on holiday with no option but to self-medicate, you should also be carrying in your first aid kit a strong painkiller and a strong anti-inflammatory drug. I take dihydrocodeine for extreme pain relief and Ponstan forte to reduce inflammation. These drugs usually work for any part of the body, not just the ears. For that matter, any nerve pain in your teeth, which might be excruciating, and any inner ear pain involving a nerve will benefit from this mix of painkiller and anti-inflammatory. For lesser pain, a painkiller with ibuprofen to take care of the inflammation will usually do.

If old earwax is pressing on an eardrum, it may cause headaches. There are many reasons for headaches and it's surprising how often this common cause is overlooked. Get your doctor to check your ears from time to time and syringe out any wax if that seems to be a problem.

Follow up at home with over-the-counter eardrops designed to soften ear wax. This should then get washed out next time you have a shower.

If you swim regularly in freshwater pools and find that the chlorine irritates your outer ear canal, making it itchy to the point where you constantly want to scratch it, get a prescription for one of the antibiotic ointments that will deal with the problem. A tiny drop rubbed into each ear around the canal opening will usually clear up the problem in a few hours. I use Tri-adcortyc otic ointment and it always does the trick.

CHAPTER TWENTY-FOUR
KILL GERMS DEAD

Cleanliness was once rumoured to be next to godliness. The problem with cleanliness is that you can have too much of it, especially as a child. There are claims that the recent considerable rise in child asthma is due not just to air pollution, but to too much hygiene in a child's world, compared with the good old days when children's were meant to get down and dirty. This is attributed to homes being too clean, but the fact is that children today are less likely to spend time out of doors getting covered in mud, now that society has become so protective and the out-side world is seen as dangerous for children. Dirt contains bacteria and bacteria help to build the immune system. Without sufficient exposure in their early years, children will grow into adults with inadequate immunity against a wide range of hostile invaders. They will also be weaker internally as the good bacteria we all host will have a tougher time maintaining a balance in the eternal war against the bad bacteria we also host. Result: weakened immunity in children and adults against a variety of diseases, of which asthma is one. At least so the theory goes, but the picture is still far from clear.

Hygiene has been a medical mantra for over a century. Older readers will remember the threat of typhoid (one of the salmonella group of bacteria), scarlet fever and diphtheria. Infected ice cream was often rightly considered a source of the problem, but those infections are largely gone thanks to rigorous Health and Safety controls. Today there is much less domestic hand washing than there once was. But infections can be picked up in any number of ways. The ice cream vendor may not have washed his hands. You may sit on the grass and pick up germs from unseen dog faeces. I'm often dismayed at the way today's sandwich makers will happily handle food in front of you while wiping their nose with the back of their hand, or sneezing all over the food. Hepatitis is caught from infected food and water and although it is more often passed on in Third World countries, you might pick it up in a restaurant where someone who is infected and handling food has not been too careful after going to the loo.

Just as there can be too much hygiene, there can be too little, as the publicity given to the rise and rise of the MRSA and Clostridium diffi- cile bugs in UK hospitals demonstrates. You would not want a surgeon to open you up without having scrubbed up beforehand. Even those vis- iting a patient in hospital should wash their hands thoroughly on arrival. You would be ill-advised to use a public lavatory without being careful about where you put your hands. You will not be welcome any- where with a virus if you are not careful about how you sneeze.

Only one person in three in the UK washes their hands before eating, after sneezing or after patting an animal. Doctors and nurses regularly touch patients with diseases, but many omit the cardinal requirement to wash their hands after each examination. Many of us, doctors included, may leave germs on doorknobs for others to pick up, especially door knobs in public places like lavatories. You only need to shake hands with someone or kiss them on the cheek to get a bacterial or virus transmis- sion. Touch your nose with a hand which has been in contact with a virus and before long you may be coughing and spluttering.

It may come as a surprise to know that the kitchen and not the bath- room is the most germ-infested room in most houses. Many houses will have spotless bathrooms, yet the kitchen will be a breeding ground for bacteria. The fridge may be overcrowded or not cold enough in warm weather. Food may be reheated that was not sufficiently chilled in between. Food that is not properly cooked, especially poultry, may carry disease that can be passed on, especially salmonella. Chopping boards are a favourite haunt of bugs. Cooked food and raw food and the implements that touch them should be kept well apart, inside the fridge and out.

But bacteria are getting smarter and developing resistance to antibi- otics, so that scientists are having to move ever faster in developing new antibiotic drugs. Tuberculosis, which can still be fatal, is making a comeback with a superbug strain that is resistant to most antibiotics.

The answer may lie in smart drugs and the latest technique being explored to tackle resistance is to confuse bacteria by challenging them on two fronts simultaneously. This is done using two enzymes which bacteria may exploit to copy their genes to reproduce. This presentation of two options confuses the bacteria and slows them down in their effort to develop resistance, thereby giving the antibacterial drug time to be effective.

Another approach in development is using parts of live viruses which produce an enzyme that will devour bacterial cells while ignoring human cells. So far there is some experimental success against pneumococcus, streptococcus and anthrax. If tests pan out, the plan is to tackle infection with a once-weekly shot from a nasal spray.

The message about hygiene seems to be a mixed one. More hygiene to avoid disease or less hygiene to build up the immune system? I think that for children, there is probably too much hygiene these days, while for adults who presumably have undergone most of the development of their immune system which comes through infection, there is probably too little attention being paid to hygiene. Hand washing should be more frequent, last longer and be more thorough, preferably with a disinfectant. You don't have to be obsessive about touching doorknobs, shaking hands, and eating out or lunching on sandwiches. But care and attention will often pay off, if only in helping you to avoid a nasty cold, or worse, a bout of flu, bronchitis or a serious gastric infection.

It may be that you cannot avoid picking up *Helicobacter pylori*. This is spread through close contact with someone, usually a family member, and about half the population are thought to be infected with the bacterium. Most people don't know they have it, yet it is thought to trigger about 85% of cases of peptic ulcer. Generations suffered with ulcers. My father has several feet of his gastric tract removed surgically, his ulcers were so bad. That was not good for his digestion, even if most of the ulcerated lining was removed. I have had the bug too, probably passed on many years ago by my father. I have had ulcers which have come and gone naturally without much discomfort. (I claim to have a cast iron stomach, which is probably the explanation for so little pain). I now have signs of ulcer scarring spotted by endoscope. But I have no more *Helicobacter pylori* bacteria. They were got rid of in two weeks with a cocktail of three antibiotics. A breath test afterwards confirmed that they had gone. Nowadays it's that easy. So whatever caveats I may have about drugs, I fully support them in some circumstances.

I would not like to see a return of the common childhood diseases of a hundred years ago. Typhoid fever weakened the mitral valve of my maternal grandfather's heart and he died at the age of 32 when there was no cure for such damage. Today it's a simple operation. I had chicken pox, mumps, measles and German measles as a child. So did everyone else I went to school with. I developed useful immunity and don't think I would necessarily have been better off without these diseases, which are usually quite mild in children, but not in adults. I have had shingles as an adult, a return of my childhood chicken pox after decades lying dormant. I have had numerous jabs. I have travelled widely in the Third World and never had anything worse than a couple of bad bouts of Delhi belly, one of them actually caught in Delhi from food I unwisely bought from a street vendor's stall. The other occasion was when, as an untutored youth, I drank communal well water in Morocco.

My advice is to be careful about your own hygiene, but if you have small children or grandchildren, let them play in the woods and get mucky from time to time.

CHAPTER TWENTY-FIVE

LOOK GOOD – FEEL GOOD

How we look – to ourselves – has a lot to do with how good or bad we feel and this strongly influences how happy we are. If happiness is important – and to most of us it is – looking the way we want to look matters a lot.

I'm reminded of the story of the supermodel who had a figure and face that most women would die for, but who had terribly low self-esteem because she hated her body. To her it was less than perfect because she had thighs that she (alone) thought were fat. Not surprisingly she was in therapy working on the fact that she had such a terrible body image. The story goes to show that it's not how you look that matters, but how you see yourself, and how you think others will see you, even if this view is distorted, as it obviously was in the case of the supermodel.

I used to think that attractive-looking people must have high self-esteem and ugly people none at all. As I learnt more about psychology, I found out that very often this was not the case. There were undeniably fat and ugly people who were happy with themselves the way they were, and there were beautiful people who hated the way they looked. Of course, all else being equal, it helped to be better-looking, in much the same way that money doesn't bring happiness but is sure helps.

The explanation for levels of self-esteem lies in many factors of which the way we look and our ability to make a reality check on ourselves is only one. Deeper influences are at work, foundations of self image that have their roots in infancy and childhood and the way in which we saw ourselves through our parents' eyes. Not surprisingly a loving parent of either sex is a good starting point for self-esteem, and a lack of this combination lies at the root of many of society's problems today in dealing with its own so-called underclass, though the problem can go right through all classes if one parent is absent as a role model. A child needs a caring parent of either sex because we each have a masculine and a feminine side to our personality, no matter which sex we are. To round out each of these sides, the child needs the corresponding parent of either sex. This is the most fundamental reason why even the best single parenting can rarely be enough.

Having said that looks are not all that they are cracked up to be, I have to admit that we live in a looks- and youth-obsessed society. Those of us who are middle-aged like to point to the fact that our fathers were already old by the time they were forty or fifty. That is how we remember them. We may be living longer now, but just because we wear jeans at fifty doesn't really make us any younger. To our kids we are probably just as old-looking as our fathers looked to us. It's just that we act younger and dress younger and then try to fool ourselves that therefore we are younger and can push back the barriers of age. We say we are not middle-aged until we are fifty, not forty, and not old-aged until we are seventy-five, not sixty-five. But medical science is less forgiving and is driven by the facts of ageing rather than the media and what they tell us about ourselves. We should not forget that if our average life expectancy is now seventy-seven, for every man who dies at the age of ninety-seven there will be one who dies at the age of fifty-seven. Heredity still plays the biggest part in how long we will live, and I don't have my genes on my side. The average age at which my four grandparents died was fifty-five.

Looking good matters, but you have to make the most of what you have got, as no amount of money will buy you the appearance of a super-model. There have been a number of TV programmes extolling the virtues of a makeover for women. These have concentrated on diet, exercise, hairstyle, clothes and make-up. The candidates for change have tended to be fat and frumpy, with an obvious potential for improvement. With professional help, these women have been made to look somewhat better, but the important point is that without exception they like their new look and their self-esteem rises. The message the viewer is left with is that it's important to look good in your own eyes and if others think you look better, that's a bonus. You don't have to look like Scarlett Johansson or Brad Pitt to like yourself.

The same applies to men. If you like yourself the way you are, that's great. If you don't, try to do something about it. But I suspect that in most cases if it matters that much to you, you may be better off using a good counsellor or psychotherapist to raise your self-esteem. It all depends on you. For some it will make a difference and for those who are more troubled, improving your appearance probably won't – or not very much.

Let's assume that you are not deeply troubled about your appearance, but like most men you would like to look better if you can, without going to too much trouble. Virtually everyone would change a handful of things about their appearance if they could, no matter how high their self-esteem. It's well recognized that being taller is attractive to women and also helps at job interviews. But there isn't much you can do about your height, or Tom Cruise, at 5' 7" and with several hundred million dollars at his disposal, would have done something about it by now. Lifts in your shoes and high heels for men are not a good idea. Like wigs, they are seen as phoney. The same goes for padded shoulders in jackets.

So what can you do? Before I elaborate, let's get one thing clear. Your personality, your intelligence, your sense of humour will all play an important part in how others see you, especially women. The evidence is incontrovertible that women are not like men in what attracts them to the opposite sex. The views of feminists notwithstanding, men prefer young pretty nubile women and their brains are far less important. Women prefer men who are intelligent (for which read 'high-earning'), amusing and, only in that order, tall and good looking. Interestingly it has been noted that this pattern is changing and as women become more self-supporting in the workplace and therefore less in need of a man to support them, they have also become more like men in what attracts them. Women are now placing more importance on a man's looks than they used to.

This being so, men will need increasingly to look good to attract a mate. So should a man think about how he looks, for himself, or for his ability to attract a mate (or several)? Here is where we see a connection with the idea that self-esteem is important, because if you like yourself enough, all of yourself and not just how you look, high self-esteem will be perceived as confidence and confidence will hugely attract the oppo-site sex. This way the confident man who is short or ugly can score more highly than he would without confidence. We see this too in the way that the rich, who are often successful, have the confidence to overcome problems of height and looks and attract women in a way that makes other men envious. You only have to think of Aristotle Onassis and Jackie Kennedy, or Serge Gainsbourg and Jane Birkin. Fame and money can clearly go far in compensating for the negatives. Henry Kissinger, like Tom Cruise famously married a woman much taller than himself.

Mind you, the above marriages were no shining examples of wedded bliss. They mostly ended in divorce, or premature death in the case of Serge Gainsbourg, who was an alcoholic.

Women like men who dress smartly, I'm sure, but they place even more importance on cleanliness in a way that most men don't. That doesn't mean starched shirts, not does it mean jackets and ties. It means regular changes of shirts, socks and underwear, and frequent showers and baths, especially in hot weather. Unless you are cultivating a beard or (no longer fashionable) designer stubble, being clean shaven helps too. For those who are challenged up top, it's fortunate that the hair-styles of recent decades have given way to much shorter hair. But given the choice, it probably isn't a good bet to shave your head to the point of looking like a club bouncer. Too many tattooed men with shaven heads featuring on TV in football riots have given the shaven head a bit of a bad image.

I suggest that you don't try to dress too young for your (biological) age. Jeans may be fine, but if you look fifty, you will look stupid dressed in thongs and baggy shorts that come to below your knees, while wear-ing a singlet up top. On the other hand, if this is how you like to dress, you are unlikely to be reading this book in the first place, so this may be pointless advice.

Keep your skin in good condition. By that I don't mean get yourself a deep suntan of the kind that goes well with gold chains round your neck, unless you are trying to make a deal with someone in Marbella. Better to have no tan at all these days, or a very light one. Avoid tanning appara-tus at all costs.

I'm against the use of aftershaves and colognes for men. I can't say what they do to your skin – probably nothing that is good for it – but, like deodorants, they mask the natural odours of the body, in particular pheromones, those agents of smell which seek out receptors in women as part of the unconscious mating game. Far better to let nature do its stuff than to mask yourself off, thereby reducing your chances of exhibiting your attractiveness to others. If you stay clean and have a shower once or twice a day (women don't like the smell of stale sweat), you will be doing yourself a favour.

The best treatment for your skin is good nutrition. By that I don't mean particular foods that are meant to be good for your skin, the way that many health food shops market products specifically for one purpose or another, often based on little evidence. I mean good nutrition generally will affect your overall well-being, inside and out, of which your skin is a part.

The same can be said for exercise. You can feel as though you are glowing after a good workout and you probably are. The glow may be sweat, but the look of your skin will be healthier if exercise is regular and accompanied by healthy eating and drinking habits.

Glasses or contact lenses? I don't think it matters from a looks point of view. Educated men and women are still more likely to need glasses than those less educated. Some women will be attracted by nerdy-look-ing glasses, but the best bet is probably rimless glasses that are all but invisible from a distance. That way you can wear glasses without mak-ing it too obvious. I may be wrong, but I get the impression that after years of people moving to contact lenses, glasses have made a strong comeback, and maybe contact lenses are in long term decline. I wear glasses for reading and have never worn contact lenses. To me they seemed like a lot of hassle and they probably are.

The problem with getting older and wearing glasses is that you start forgetting where you put things, and if it's your glasses you have mis-placed, you may need them to find them. That can be a small problem. They may be in their case after all. You may even be wearing them. It's been known to happen.

Should you change anything in your appearance more dramatically? If you can afford it and it will make you feel better, the answer is probably yes, if you really, really want to. I'm referring to cosmetic surgery and the like. Face lifts, tummy tucks and hair grafts will all make you look better, provided that you get the best that money can buy. If you have the highest self-esteem in the world, of course, you will be happy with the way you are and won't need to make any changes. There are many clinics out there which will lighten your wallet by a few thousand pounds to make you feel better. The worst candidates for cosmetic surgery are those who are delusional about their bodies, those suffering, for example, from body dysmorphic disorder, who have a distorted and negative view of how they look. Many surgeons will not treat such men and women, knowing that their view of themselves afterwards will usually remain negative. Most candidates for cosmetic surgery have a realistic view of their appearance and usually get the improvement they are looking for.

Where no surgery is involved, cosmetic treatments are an unregulated industry, which is why you will see so many advertisements for 'non-surgical' cosmetic treatments, many of which are borderline 'surgical'. Others depend on drugs that may not do what they purport to do, or might even be dangerous. There are a few charlatans and many who are just not very good at what they do.

When it comes to surgical treatments it will cost more to get the best, but where your appearance is concerned and there is a risk of a botched job, I suggest you go for the best, not just the best you can afford. Otherwise don't do it. Finding the best is not easy, just as it isn't easy to find the best medical consultant in a given field. Research long and hard, using all possible resources, especially the web, and you may come away with a short list of cosmetic surgeons who appear to be rated, not just by their clients but by other surgeons. Search the medical journals online and see if those on the shortlist have written papers or pioneered new techniques. If they have, that is usually a good sign. Avoid any clinic that advertises, and if you can, go to a surgeon who has a sole practice and is not part of a larger stable of surgeons doing guest appearances at a for-profit clinic run as a company. Needless to say, the surgeon should have FRCS after his name or at least the equivalent.

Treatments considered to be possibly dangerous, as well as being unregulated, include: volumisers, mesotherapy, Isolagen, celution, flab jabs and contour lifts. Buyer beware. However, there are some treatments that are reliable and safe. I have covered dental whitening in the chapter on teeth. Red thread veins on the face, especially the nose and cheeks, are ruptured capillaries that come from high blood pressure, alcohol abuse and too much sun. They can be removed by laser in a process known as photothermolysis, which, in plain English, is laser cauterisation. After-signs fade quickly, though may show up slightly if over-exposed to the sun. A few thread veins may still make an appearance, but these can be treated with another visit to a clinic. The same laser treatment can be used to remove acne scars.

Laser treatment isn't always safe, and because a lot of laser treatments – hair and wrinkle removal, for example – are not considered to be 'surgical', they are unregulated.

A good facial leaves most men with a feeling of wellbeing at any age. It will exfoliate dead skin and blemishes like blackheads. With luck this pampering experience can be extended to include taking care of the nostril and ear hairs that grow exponentially after the age of 50, along with maybe a trim of the eyebrows, which grow in strange ways as you get older.

Looking good makes most people feel good, and looking better makes them feel better, but if they have narcissistic tendencies, the pursuit of a good appearance may simply be a manifestation of this personality trait. My advice to anyone more than normally dissatisfied with the way they look is to explore these feelings in therapy. The answer in the end may not be an eyelid lift or a nose job, but the insight that it's OK in life not to be perfect. On the other hand you might also come out of therapy realizing that a few surgical changes to the way you look would give you the boost that you need, in which case going ahead with surgery might be worth the time and cost. Avoid Botox injections, though. It may get rid of deep lines temporarily, but it's a poisonous substance.

Women still account for about 90% of all cosmetic surgery, but the rate at which men are opting for surgery is growing from year to year.

What are the treatments that men turn to most frequently? Nose jobs take first place, followed by tummy tucks and liposuction to reduce 'love handles' and male breasts (see chapter on performance-enhancing drugs). Increasingly men are turning to facelifts and eyelid surgery, as well as botox injections. If you are over fifty and keep in good shape, you are likely to notice that while your muscles are firm, your skin above them may be showing signs of sag, especially if it has been exposed to too much sun over the years. This is not something you can do much about. Skin loses some of the underlying collagen as you get older, and while good nutrition, exercise and staying out of the sun all help, the fact is that you cannot do as much to stop your skin sagging as you can to prevent your muscles from atrophying (sarcopenia). The result is that you may be fitter for your age than you look. You may even have a good sixpack without it being visible.

CHAPTER TWENTY-SIX
WHAT IS METABOLISM?

The word metabolism is often bandied about without much real comprehension of what it means. Metabolism is a complex process defined briefly as the collective chemical processes of the body.

The control centre in the brain called the hypothalamus is in command of the pituitary gland, which controls other glands. One of the glands under the control of the pituitary is the thyroid gland, which produces the thyroid hormones. Some of these control metabolic rate, the speed at which metabolic processes take place. One of the functions of the thyroid is control of energy use. The thyroid produces thyroxine (T4) and its more active form T3, two hormones which play a principal part in regulation of metabolism.

A measure of health is Basic Metabolic Rate (BMR) and this measure is increasingly used as an indicator of physical fitness. It can also to some extent be used as an indicator of biological age, which is often referred to as metabolic age. BMR is defined as the amount of energy needed to maintain basic body functions such as breathing, heart rate and temperature. About 70% of normal calorie expenditure is for the maintenance of such functions, which may come as a surprise. Much of this expenditure takes place while we are asleep. The other 30% is mainly accounted for by muscular activity as we go about our daily lives. This latter 30% does not form part of the BMR calculation.

BMR declines with age, as does the need for calorie intake in the form of food and liquid. Exercise and overall healthy living can slow this process of decline. There is a good deal of truth in the popular view that we become less active as we get older and that this is the reason why people find it increasingly difficult to control their weight. Appetite declines with age in most people, but since exercise is important in keeping weight down, the process of putting on weight with age probably has more to do with declining exercise and calorie burn than it has to do with how much is eaten. We could eat large quantities of all kinds of food and not get fat if we exercised enough, but unfortunately, with age and falling BMR, fatigue sets in more and more quickly and recovery times become longer, so the seemingly simple solution of more exercise to keep BMR high is not as easy as it sounds. Healthy living habits can slow the ageing process, but nothing so far discovered by science will reverse it. You may slow the rate at which BMR declines, but it will decline nonetheless from about the age of 10. Illness temporarily raises BMR as the body fights to cope with the extra demands placed on it.

BMR is normally measured at rest in kilojoules (around 4 kilojoules = 1 calorie or kilocalorie) used per square metre of body surface per hour. Men who can eat almost anything in any quantity as they get older without putting on weight, apart from being much envied, are usually examples of naturally high BMR, usually well above the average. These men will probably have a biological age below their chronological age, even if they do very little exercise. This suggests that while it's within our power to control BMR to some extent, much of it is down to our genes. Men who remain naturally slim into old age, even without a calorie-restricted diet, are known to have a longer lifespan, all else being equal

The term 'metabolic syndrome' does not refer to a specific illness but to a cluster of symptoms that are associated with a slowing down of the rate at which the body's chemical processes occur through poor internal regulation and general bodily inefficiency. The way in which this happens is complex and much still remains to be learnt. Usually those suffering from this complex of symptoms are suffering from obesity and diabetes (see chapter 15 on diabetes). They will tend to have high blood pressure and high cholesterol.

CHAPTER TWENTY-SEVEN
OSTEOARTHRITIS: WEAR AND TEAR

Osteoarthritis should be distinguished from the autoimmune disease rheumatoid arthritis. Both attack the joints, but the latter is progressive and is found three times more commonly in women, whereas the form of joint swelling and pain that is osteoarthritis has no sexual preference. It develops in response to identifiable stress or trauma to the joint, usually a combination of injury, age-related wear and tear and poor nutrition. Inappropriate exercise can actually cause the problem or make it worse, though appropriate exercise is healthy and fear of osteoarthritis should not discourage you from exercise. Osteoarthritis usually becomes noticeable in middle age.

It's often said that professional athletes are those most likely to suffer from osteoarthritis as a result of injuries they received while competing. The implication is that too much exercise is bad for you (see chapter 18 on exercise). Bones that have been broken earlier in life and may have left a joint slightly damaged can also give rise to the pain of osteoarthritis. The repeated use of the same muscles, tendons and ligaments in a particular sport can cause problems in the joints affected.

Joint pain is often interpreted as a synovitis or a bursitis, both of which involve the sheath covering a joint and adjacent soft tissue. But the commonest form of joint pain is where bone rubs against bone because the sheath and its lubrication have failed and spongy tissue between bones has shrunk or been rubbed away.

Some areas of the skeletomuscular framework are the most likely to be affected. These are the feet, the ankles, the knees, the hips, the lower spine (the lumbar vertebrae), the hands, the elbows, the shoulders and the neck (the cervical vertebrae). Painful joints in these areas are so common that there are hospitals specializing in the foot and ankle only, and within them consultants who maybe specialize in only the toes, for example, or just cases of Achilles tendinitis. Tennis players regularly suffer from wrist problems (usually tenosynovitis) and elbow problems (tennis elbow). Like skiers and footballers, they may also be prone to knee injuries caused by twisting movements.

The ligaments, tendons and bones may all be affected together and understanding how these work is complicated. Few people seem to know the difference between a tendon and a ligament. A tendon joins muscle to bone, whereas a ligament joins bone to bone.

Can osteoarthritis be reversed, or is it a case of making the most of the disease and taking drugs to get rid of the painful swelling? It seems that in its early stages osteoarthritis, can be cured with a combination of drugs, physical therapy and good nutrition. Taking supplements of glucosamine sulphate and chondroitin appear to help mild cases (see chapter 14 on supplements), but men with more advanced symptoms will need drugs to counter the pain, stiffness and swelling, which are all symptoms that are much the same as those that signal the presence of rheumatoid arthritis.

The more usual forms of treatment for osteoarthritis are rest, immo-bilisation of the limb in extreme cases, NSAIDs (non-steroidal anti-inflammatory drugs) with pain killers, and perhaps steroid injections, though I tend to think that anything with steroids should be a last resort. Many who suffer from osteoarthritis would not be without NSAIDs, yet these drugs are not without their side effects, which vary from one individual to another. If the joint is inflamed, stiff and painful, this class of drugs can do wonders. They are taken regularly by millions in the UK, not just for osteoarthritis, but also for sprains, gout and a range of inflammatory conditions. They make life bearable for a great many people, enabling them to be active and to get a good night's sleep.

Side effects of NSAIDs may include intestinal discomfort, nausea and loose bowel movements. Such problems are usually bearable, but in a few cases there may also be severe intestinal bleeding. A few people even get a perforated gut, which can be fatal. Each year an estimated 2000 people die in the UK as a result of gastrointestinal bleeding caused by NSAIDs. In sufferers from heart disease, NSAIDs have been known to set off heart failure, whereby the heart is progressively less and less able to pump blood effectively. These drugs, especially in those over 65, should not be prescribed if there is a history of kidney or liver problems, severe indigestion or recorded sensitivity to NSAIDs.

A safer treatment for both oesteoarthritis, as well as some cases of rheumatoid arthritis, is a preparation made up of the old familiar scurvy remedy rosehips and rosehip seeds. These have an anti-inflammatory effect that reduces joint inflammation. This can be seen in lowered levels of C-reactive protein in the blood. This protein, which is a marker for inflammation, is also thought to serve as an indicator of heart problems (see chapter 41 on the heart). Rosehips work on inflammation, not by virtue of their vitamin C content, useful though that is, but thanks to a fatty acid called GOPO. Rosehip preparations should be used as an addition to normal drug treatment and not as a substitute.

NSAID medication is normally accompanied by pain-killing drugs, aspirin and paracetamol being the usual choices. The most common NSAIDs are misoprostol, diclofenac, mefenamic acid, indomethacin and ibuprofen. A combination of misoprositol and diclofenac can avoid some of the intestinal problems that NSAIDs can cause.

NSAIDs are normally classed as COX-1 or COX-2 inhibitors. They are inhibitors because they inhibit the enzymes COX-1 and COX-2, which speed up the action of prostaglandins in the stomach. Of the two, COX-2 inhibitors were found to be less inclined to cause gastrointestinal bleeding, but most were withdrawn as they were deemed to promote an unacceptably high rate of cardiovascular disease. Etoricoxib (marketed as Arcoxia) was a COX-2 inhibitor which escaped the ban and has since proved its worth, being effective in cutting down pain and inflammation while not engendering any rise in heart disease. Its advantage in reducing the incidence of gastrointestinal side effects, when compared with COX-1 inhibitors, appears to be acknowledged. Overly large doses may produce a rise in blood pressure.

The largest selling NSAID in the world is currently diclofenac, marketed as Volterol. I have never taken it, but can vouch for the effectiveness of mefenamic acid (Ponstan and Ponstan forte) when taken in conjunction with a powerful painkiller. The occasion was not a bout of osteoarthritis, but three ribs broken on a rock while surfing in

Mauritania. That I have never suffered from arthritis I put down to a healthy diet and regular supplementation with glucosamine sulphate, despite the fact that I exercise a lot and therefore put quite a lot of strain on some of my joints. I do acknowledge, though, that as I get older, my tendons and ligaments get more fragile, and if they are strained unduly, recovery can take a long time, whereas torn muscles heal fairly fast.

A discussion of osteoarthritis would not be complete without a mention of the painkillers which are taken by the million every day for a hundred different complaints. The brand Anadin contains aspirin and caffeine. The latter ingredient may keep the sufferer awake, but it potentiates the analgesic effect of the aspirin. Anadin Extra has the same ingredients as Anadin with the addition of paracetamol. On the other hand Anadin Ultra contains only the NSAID ibuprofen.

Veganin is as popular as Anadin. It contains codeine phosphate, caffeine and paracetamol. The different combinations of ingredients in different painkillers are intended to work with different sources of pain and inflammation.

Aspirin has a long history. It was a surprise to many a few years ago when it was declared to be useful to people who had suffered a heart attack or who had angina. The blood thinning effects of aspirin are believed to reduce the risk of a clot forming. There are still those who maintain that an aspirin a day should be taken by all men over 40 as a way of warding off heart attack. I'm not inclined to share this view. Aspirin is certainly a decoagulant, but it also has its side effects, and no one knows what the effect might be of taking it for years on end. It is well known that it should not be given to children under the age of 16. It can exacerbate and cause ulcers in the vulnerable. It can cause indigestion. Alcoholics with cirrhosis of the liver have been known to die after taking aspirin. In such cases it turns out that there was a varicosity in the gullet. There is some evidence that the combination of ibuprofen and aspirin may be detrimental to those suffering from cardiovascular disease, the ibuprofen negating the cardioprotective effects of the aspirin.

What is appropriate exercise and what is excessive exercise when it comes to osteoarthritis? From experience and the fact that I have reached my sixties without the slightest sign of osteoarthritis despite a lifetime of regular exercise, I would say that each individual is different. Good nutrition is important. So is a variety of exercises that spread the risk among all the main joints in the body without putting too much stress on any one in particular. Professional sportsmen may not have so much choice, which is why they are prone to get osteoarthritis in particular joints in middle age. I am inclined to think that many professional sportsmen, when they stop playing, let themselves go. Apart from the fact that they may start to eat unhealthily, many will give up regular exercise, whereas the key to exercise is to make it a lifelong activity. The positive effects of exercise can be lost very quickly, and being healthy in youth does not guarantee a healthy middle age, let alone old age.

CHAPTER TWENTY-EIGHT
SIGNS IN YOUR SERUM

Many readers will be familiar with the kind of blood and urine tests that are carried out when you go for a BUPA or similar screening. A GP may send you off to a lab for tests if there are symptoms that need a closer look. However, most of us probably don't have a full understanding of what the test results mean. It's only in the last few years that doctors have been more forthcoming about letting their patients know what was going on inside them. Before that, the medical world liked to lay claim to an arcane bank of knowledge that the rest of us were not meant to understand. Test results went to your doctor, normally, and only to you with your doctor's permission. Now that has changed and with or without your doctor's consent, your screening clinic will usually give you a copy of the results, while another copy goes to your doctor. If you want more information in layman's terms, there are websites aimed at the patient, though even now a little learning can be a dangerous thing, and the growth in patient websites has led to a lot of misinformed self-diagnosis, often by the worried well.

It is frequently suggested, not least by members of the medical profession, that expensive private screening centres which will take on clients without a doctor's referral are a risky thing. The centres argue that even if your chances of finding something are minimal, you will be thankful if you are one of the small percentage who discover an aneurysm or a tumour, and most of these clinics still insist on sending a copy of their report to your GP. It's the ultra-expensive screenings which have received the most criticism. Most of these are so expensive because they now include a magnetic resonance imaging (MRI) or electron beam computed tomography (EBCT) scan (usually shortened to CT scan), either a whole body or a partial scan. Either way, it can be very expensive. Most critics will point out that it's better not to know in advance that you have such and such an illness if there is no known cure for it. Fair point, but before the screening, you do not know if anything found will be curable or not, and if it is, you will be thankful and think the money well spent.

Clinics offering scans claim that serious ailments are found in 2–3% of clients, though these figures don't say how many were untreatable. The risk of getting cancer from the radiation dose of a CT scan is said to be between 1 in 1,200 and 1 in 2,000, so it's something you would not want to do on an annual basis. If you did, your risk of cancer would rise to 1 in 50 after 30 years of an annual scan. However, it's good to get an idea of the risk by comparing with other ways in which we are exposed to radiation.

Radiation is measured in millisieverts (mSv). A year of normal living exposes us to about 2.5 mSv a year. A chest X-ray gives us only 4% of this amount. And a dental X-ray just a fraction less. On the other hand a barium X-ray to look at the colon gives three and a half times as much radiation (8.7 mSv). An angiogram gives around the same dosage.

The clinics like to do a whole body scan as this is more profitable than just looking at parts of your body. However, this doesn't mean using CT for the whole procedure. CT is best for the colon, the heart and the lungs (for example, for measuring calcium deposits in the coronary arteries – see chapter 41 on cardiovascular disease), but an MRI scan, which produces almost no radiation, is preferable for most of the rest of the body, particularly the abdomen, the brain, the cerebral arteries and the pelvis, including the prostate. A CT scan of the heart and lungs will produce about 1–1.5 mSv, whereas a whole body CT scan would expose you to about 10 mSv. CT scans represent 40% of the medical radiation exposure in the UK, but only 6% of the number of X-rays performed.

For-profit MRI and CT scanning is controversial, not only because it's expensive, but also because such scans can pander, for profit, to the fears of the wealthy worried well and lead to further sometimes unnecessary testing. Private clinics offering CT and MRI scans are still largely unregulated. My view is that they have a useful role to play if you can afford them, and the risk of cancer from a CT scan is low enough to make it worth taking.

If you go the whole way with some of the diagnostic menus now on offer, you could spend up to £3,000, and a lot more at some of the residential clinics in the US. And even then you would not get some of the tests that we cover below.

Health screening clinics should not be confused with biomedical (also known as biochemistry or pathology) labs which carry out analysis of blood, urine, saliva, sweat and even hair in the search for hundreds of different diseases, some of which we will take a look at in this chapter. The big screening clinics may have their own analytical labs, but most of those in the major city centres will use outside labs for some or all of the tests. In London in the private sector, the London Clinic and the Doctor's Laboratory are two of those most widely used. Anyone can go direct to the latter if armed with a doctor's referral and doing so can be less expensive than going through a third party, which will have marked up the cost of any test. That said, this kind of screening is not cheap. But what price health?

Blood and urine screens tell the doctors a good deal about your state of health. However, these screens are basic and may suggest you should have further tests, along with other types of screening. BUPA include a faecal test looking for occult (hidden) blood in their repertoire in case you have diverticular disease or perhaps polyps in your colon which could lead to cancer. However, there are many tests for which you could be referred, the most common being old fashioned X-rays, and now, more frequently, MRI and CT scans, lung function tests (spirometry), further blood tests, endoscopy of the oesophagus, stomach and bowel ('top and tail' in the trade), and a whole battery of tests for cardiovascular problems.

An annual check-up with BUPA, BMI (British Medical Insurance) Healthcare, one of the Nuffield Hospitals clinics or a similar screening centre will usually include an electrocardiogram. If this throws up any suspicious heart rhythms, there are other tests that you may have to have. These include stress cardiograms where your heart is monitored while you work out on an exercise machine, usually a bike or a treadmill, at increasingly testing levels. Beyond that is the stress echo cardiogram, which stresses your heart via an adrenaline drip while measuring the response. This test can be very useful in diagnosing heart failure and is not used as much as it should be.

Then there's the thallium scan, which uses the nuclear isotope thallium (in very small quantities, for safety) to give a picture of your heart. It shows whether the blood supply to the heart is sufficient and whether supply to the coronary arteries in particular may be threatened in the future. Another tool for giving an informative picture of the heart's health, one that allegedly shows more clearly than ever before what the risks are for the patient, is the CT scan (see above), which detects calcium in the heart and surrounding blood vessels, calcification being critical in the process we call hardening of the arteries. From this can be inferred the degree of atheroma (fatty plaque) present. The CT scan, it has been concluded by the American Heart Association, is most worthwhile as a predictive tool in those who are at medium risk for a coronary event. The calcium score has now become an established further weapon in the cardiologist's armoury of test procedures, though there are cardiologists who are sceptical about its value.

Diagnostic screening is routine in the NHS. However, given the cost, screening is only applied according to strict guidelines. There is no CT or MRI scanning for diseases for which there is no known cure, and the disease being sought must have an early stage, that is, a stage at which it can be tackled with a reasonable chance of a cure.

Even doctors can be confused about which kind of scan is best for which (likely) disease. When it comes to the joints, the spine and the brain, MRI scans are generally best, while CT scans are usually the first choice for looking at the coronary arteries, the lungs and the digestive tract. Dentists prefer CT scans to X-rays. An MRI scan is better when it comes to detecting a brain tumour, but after a stroke, the CT scan is the better option as it can quickly spot the difference between a stroke caused by a burst artery and the more frequent stroke that comes form a clot. The latest type of MRI scanner is the Philips Tesla Open High Field MRI scanner, which is particularly good at looking at joints and does not require the patient to disappear inside a tube.

Many scans will throw up question marks rather than answers, leading to further tests, the majority of which will show there is actually no problem, even if there is an abnormality. Just as everyone has a different body on the outside, all our internal organs differentiate us from each other as well, and this is one of the problems that radiologists have to face. For the private clinics, though, it can work to their financial advantage, especially if a positive result has to be checked out through further procedures by the clinic, whether the positive turns out be false or not. If there is an invasive procedure (for example, a prostate biopsy), the costs and the discomfort mount considerably, and the result may turn out to be negative.

However, a positive result (positive in the medical sense that you do have a problem) might seem to make it all worthwhile. It's a hard call to make sometimes. More often than not, though, what looked dodgy turns out to be a benign tumour, a scar or a cyst, for example. I've got a so-called 'cascade' stomach, an omega-shaped epiglottis, a small cyst at the base of one of my vocal chords and another cyst on my left kidney. These are personal idiosyncracies. They haven't been discovered by an MRI or CT scan, but they do illustrate how each of us will have odd bits and pieces, usually, as in my case, nothing to worry about. However, I wouldn't have discovered them if I hadn't had a barium X-ray, endoscopy of my pharynx, larynx and nasal passages, and an ultrasound scan of my abdomen.

A screening measures blood pressure and whether or not this represents a risk. Blood pressure rises, it is said, with age. This is not an inevitable process, but a function of declining physical fitness that generally comes with age. There is no reason why, by staying fit, you should not maintain the same blood pressure you had at the age of twenty. If your blood pressure turns out to be on the high side (hypertension), you may have to wear a 24-hour monitor to check whether you really do have elevated blood pressure. I went through this and found that the only reason I had moderately high blood pressure when I went for a BUPA screen was not white coat syndrome (nervousness around doctors), but the increasingly awful traffic conditions I had to drive through to get to the BUPA centre each year, not to mention finding somewhere to park. Epidemiological studies have shown that men who live longest generally have a blood pressure level that is slightly below normal.

Similar to the 24-hour blood pressure monitor is the 24-hour heart monitor, which is likewise an encumbrance that you have to wear round the clock to check on any suspicious rhythms which may have shown up in a screening. These monitors may be uncomfortable to wear and do not make for a good night's sleep, but are worth the discomfort for what they tell you.

A test that is not unfortunately included in a BUPA screening but should be is an ultrasound scan for an abdominal aortic aneurysm (AAA). The aorta is a vital artery that feeds blood from the heart to the organs in the abdomen. It can develop an aneurysm in men over fifty, a bulge which, if it bursts or leaks, which it usually does in the end, is fatal in about 85% of cases, even if medical help is to hand. Aneurysms tend to run in families and as my father had one (spotted in time, luckily), I have had a check-up too. Result: negative. Aneurysms under 5 cm in diameter rarely burst, whereas an aneurysm more than 6 cm across is at serious risk of bursting. It is generally thought that if you are checked and do not have signs of the telltale bulge at age 65, you are unlikely to die of a burst aneurysm.

Men who smoke are at increased risk since smoking encourages the build-up of atherosclerotic plaque, the cause of the aneurysm. Men who are obese or hypertensive (often the two go together) are also at increased risk. All men over 50 should be screened for an AAA, since it's the third largest killer of men over 65. Screening is relatively cheap and is radiation-free as it involves an ultrasound only. One out of every ten men screened for an AAA between 65 and 79 is found to have one, waiting to burst and probably kill him. Screening all those in the risk group could save 3,000 lives a year.

Aneurysms in the brain (cerebral aneurysms) are, like aortic aneurysms, more likely to occur in men where there is a family history. Here's food for thought, though. For a healthy man with no family history of brain aneurysm, the chances of getting one are 0.6%. However, when a range of people are brain-scanned as part of a general check-up, a cerebral aneurysm is found in 2% of cases. However, cerebral aneurysm is notoriously difficult to treat successfully, unlike aortic aneurysm, and in many cases an aneurysm in the brain, if found, is better left alone. Many operations on cerebral aneurysms result in death or permanent disability. With this kind of record, scanning the brain for aneurysm may not be such a good thing.

If you have the test for an aortic aneurysm, (and you should get it done every five years from age 50 on), ask the radiologist to check your kidneys at the same time. About one in twelve of all men over the age of sixty will have a cyst growing on a kidney. This is harmless, but if what looks like a cyst shows up, have another ultrasound scan three to four months later to see if it has grown much, if at all. If it has, it could be a tumour rather than a cyst – unlikely but possible.

Every headache isn't a sign of a brain tumour that should send you rushing for a scan, but if unusual headaches persist, it might be worthwhile having a scan to find out more, bearing in mind what I have said above about cerebral aneurysms. One argument for a scan, though, is if you are a smoker and are over 40 years old. Then a CT scan is a very good idea, notwithstanding the dose of radiation.

There will probably come a point where you wonder about the cost of a whole battery of medical tests if mostly the results turn out to be negative, and the cost is something to be reckoned with. BUPA medical insurance and like insurances will only cover test costs according to strict guidelines. BUPA insurance will not cover the cost of their own BUPA screenings, which cost several hundred pounds. They will not cover the cost of a private GP consultation, and they will only pay for the cost of a specialist consultation if you have been referred by a GP with symptoms that require further investigation. In other words, if your visit to a screening centre is speculative to see what it might pick up, the cost is down to you. Even so, in my view, health insurance and regular screenings are usually worth their cost if you value your health above the other things that you might do with the same amount of money. It just helps to be well informed about what tests might make a difference and which probably are not worth their cost and the time and trouble they involve.

The worried well (sometimes known cynically as the 'worried wealthy') might want to get tests done on a speculative basis to find out how healthy they are – or not. We have not yet entered the age of the gene screen, but that's not far off, possibly driven by the insurance industry and its actuarial need to find out what the chances are that you have an inherited disposition to, say, obesity or a major coronary event. When that does happen, it will be expensive at first, but possibly subsidized by the insurers themselves. However, the psychological impact of knowing from your genetic profile what your percentage chance is of dying from such and such a disease may be something that most of us could live without, even if it might help us focus more on certain aspects of our lifestyle. Already it's possible to use DNA analysis to determine propensity to obesity, coronary artery disease, Alzheimer's disease and manic depression (bipolar disorder).

There are, however, many tests that can be carried out that can be quite useful, but are not a part of the usual menu. To give an example, about one person in eight has a blood factor which makes them prone to deep vein thrombosis (DVT), which is a particular danger to those who fly a lot over long distances or spend hours at a time behind the wheel of a car (see chapter 2 on air travel). Some members of my extended family are prone to DVT and three have died of a pulmonary embolism as a consequence, including my mother. DVT problems tend to run in families. However, a blood test that looks at Factor 5 Leiden identifies whether you are one of those at increased risk. I've had the test done and I'm not in the high risk group.

In the chapter on fertility I touched on the subject of the so-called male menopause, the long slow decline in fertility and erectile function which men go through as they age. There are a number of male hormones (androgens) and their level can be measured from a blood sample. The most important of these is testosterone, some of which is so-called 'free' testosterone, circulating in the blood, while some is tissue testosterone, which is 'bound' by sex hormone binding globulin (SHBG). This blood factor increases with age as testosterone declines, making testosterone less available in the blood and therefore less available as the driving force behind the male reproductive drive. The male hormones collectively are measured under what is called the Free Androgen Index, the normal range for which is 410-1080 nmol/l.

It is well known that testosterone level declines with age, and the sex drive that goes with it. Free testosterone in the over-50s should be in the reference range 5.6–19.0 pg/ml, and this is usually taken as the measure of a healthy libido – that is, healthy for your age. However, there is some doubt that free testosterone is what really matters and a growing body of endocrinologists is persuaded that dihydrotestosterone (the testosterone derivative responsible for male pattern hair loss and benign prostatic hyperplasia) may be the best guide to enduring virility – or lack of it. The normal range for dihydrotestosterone is 1.40–5.20 nmol/l. It is discouraging for those challenged in the rug and prostate departments to learn that hair loss is associated, according to one study, with a higher incidence of cardiovascular disease.

One of the advantages of regular screenings, preferably annually after the age of 50, is that trends can be observed for the various factors scored. This can be useful. For example, a prostate specific antigen (PSA) score that is still on the low side but rising sharply nonetheless after years of stability may need further investigation.

One of the wonders of modern medicine is the endoscope in its many forms. It may be embarrassing to have it shoved up your rear end (colonoscopy), but the pictures of your own colon, which you can watch in full Technicolor on a screen, make it almost bearable, and if a pre-cancerous polyp is found, going through the ordeal becomes justified, especially as the equipment allows the surgeon to remove the polyp there and then for later examination for signs of cancer. However, endoscopy from the top end is more uncomfortable, even though you will usually be sedated. The surgeon will be looking for signs of a diverticulum (pouch) or even signs of cancer or Barrett's oesophagus in the wall of your throat, gastritis in your stomach and perhaps a sliding hiatus hernia where your oesophagus and stomach meet. In your stomach he will also look for signs of ulcers and any indication of stomach cancer. You are only likely to undergo colonoscopy if there has been cause for referral for further tests, for example blood found in a routine stool test such as that carried out by BUPA. Colonoscopy may be indicated if there is a family history of bowel cancer, rectal bleeding, chronic heartburn or a prolonged change of bowel habit.

What do all those results mean when you undergo a medical health screen? Is your cholesterol dangerously high, is your immune system compromised, does your blood clot too quickly or too slowly? We'll look at what the most common tests mean and then take a look at some others that you may consider useful, but which you won't find on the BUPA menu.

Here's what you will get on a typical basic health screen menu, using BUPA as an example:

A medical history and lifestyle questionnaire will be completed, and also possibly a dietary questionnaire

Resting 12-lead electrocardiogram

Lung function test

Vision test (distance, mid-distance, near sight, with and without glasses; horizontal, vertical and lateral fields; colour blindness)

Hearing test of each ear from 500 Hz (low frequency) to 8,000 Hz (high frequency)

Height and weight measurement

Body Mass Index (BMI) calculation

Body fat percentage test

Waist to height ratio measurement

Blood profile (see below)

Blood pressure and pulse rate measurement

Urine analysis (see below)

Bowel cancer test (stool test looking for occult blood) (for men over the age of 45)

Chest X-ray (only if deemed necessary – more likely if you smoke, are over 65 or travel a lot)

Thyroid hormone blood test ('later life' screen includes this, otherwise it's an extra)

Rubella antibodies blood test (optional)

PSA (prostate specific antigen) test for men over 50

Cardio-respiratory test on an exercise cycle to measure the state of heart, lungs, circulation and metabolism under exertion from aerobic exercise (optional)

Report and health action plan. This will show your chances (as a percentage) of having a heart attack within the next ten years (cardiovascular risk score).

There is also an interview with a doctor to discuss the results of the tests, and it's possible to have extra blood samples taken for tests not on the standard menu, though this can be more expensive than going direct to, say, the Doctor's Laboratory armed with a letter from your doctor.

The following are only some of the hundreds of tests that can be done. However, I have appended comments where these are useful. Let's start with the haematology tests that come from a small blood sample taken as part of all general screenings.

Blood Cells

Haemoglobin (HGB) (red blood cells)
Low levels may suggest anaemia, which should be investigated. Among other things, anaemia can indicate cancer of the gastro-intestinal tract.

Haematocrit (HCT)
Blood percentage composed of red cells

Mean cell volume
Shows size of the red blood cells

Mean cell haemoglobin (MCH) concentration
Quantity of haemoglobin in the red blood cells

White blood cells
These cells combat infection and repair damage. A low B lymphocyte count indicates a compromised immune system

Platelets
Cells responsible for clotting

Erythrocyte sedimentation rate (ESR) (the rate at which red blood cells clump together – the more inflammation, the higher the rate).
Rate rises with age and with anaemia. This non-specific blood test may signal infective, malignant or inflammatory disease, may expose rare types of anaemia, or may indicate the presence of lymphoma, leukaemia or myeloma. Bacterial and viral infections and autoimmune diseases will raise the ESR rate. Lowered levels may also indicate pathology.

Kidneys

Urea
Raised blood levels could indicate kidney disease.

Creatinine
Raised levels in blood and low levels in urine could indicate kidney disease.

Estimated glomerular filtration rate (eGFR) (not part of standard BUPA screen)
Using creatinine score and taking sex, race and age into account, the eGFR is a more accurate measure of chronic kidney disease (CKD) than creatinine alone. There are five scoring bands and the lowest, a score of under 15, suggests that dialysis or kidney transplant may be the only solution. A healthy score is a score above 100.

Heart

C-reactive protein (CRP) and hs-CRP (high-sensitive CRP)
A marker for inflammation, CRP is also recognized as one indicator of possible cardiovascular disease. Inflammatory proteins cause certain red blood cells (erythrocytes) to clump together. By measuring this process, the presence of inflammatory proteins can be detected. A rate which does not fall following treatment for angina or a heart attack may signal a failure of recovery. As well as heart problems, CRP can suggest arthritis, bowel disease, tumours, peripheral arterial disease and potential stroke. A healthy score, indicating low risk, is below 1 mg/l. A score above 3 mg/l indicates a need for investigation.

Plasma homocysteine
(The lower the score the better. Elevated levels may indicate cardiovascular disease).

Creatine kinase (CK)
Raised levels require further investigation, particularly for heart disease. One type of CK rises significantly in the 72 hours following a heart attack.

BNP
A peptide that may indicate predisposition to cardiovascular disease.

Lipoprotein (a)
Ranked alongside the tests for homocysteine and C-reactive protein as a guide to risk of cardiovascular disease.

Muscles

Calcium
Important for muscle contraction and nerve arousal. High and low scores may both suggest a problem.

Diabetes

Glucose
Blood sugar level
A blood glucose test for diabetes is more accurate than a urine test, especially in men in middle life and beyond. However, glucose in the urine may indicate diabetes, as glucose in urine is not normal.

Insulin (not part of standard BUPA screen)
May indicate risk of diabetes or presence of diabetes according to the level

Glycosylated haemoglobin (not part of standard BUPA screen)
Also shows blood sugar level

Insulin-like growth factor (IGF-1) (not part of standard BUPA screen)
An amino acid metabolite

Gout

Uric acid
Level rises with exercise. Consistently raised levels increase risk of gout.

Liver

Gamma GTP, alkaline phosphatase, aspartate transferase and bilirubin
These factors indicate whether liver function is normal. Higher scores may signal problems such as hepatitis, cirrhosis, bile duct blockage, pancreatic disease, cancer of the liver and excessive alcohol consumption.

Albumin
A lowered level may signal cirrhosis among other conditions.

Gamma glutamyl transferase (not part of standard BUPA screen)
An enzyme measured in assessing alcohol damage to the liver.

Lipids (blood fats)

Total cholesterol (HDL, LDL and VLDL (very low density lipoprotein)
LDL cholesterol
Triglycerides (blood fats predictive of cardiovascular problems)
HDL cholesterol
HDL as percentage of total cholesterol. The percentage should ideally be 20% or over in men.

Refer to chapter 10 on cholesterol. Note that readings of VLDL and LDL Pattern'A' and LDL Pattern 'B' are not normally included in general screenings unless specifically requested (and paid for) as an extra. Likewise lipoprotein lipase (LPL), which may indicate a tendency to obesity.

Urine analysis

Blood
N indicates that blood is normal. (A trace of blood in the urine could be indicative of cancer of the bladder or untreated prostatitis (infection of the prostate).

Protein
N indicates that protein level is normal

Glucose
N indicates that glucose level is normal. This factor is important for identifying a tendency to diabetes, but blood glucose level is usually more significant than urine glucose level.

The tests that follow might be useful one day:

Haematology
Serum ceruloplasmin
Serum copper
Red cell GSH – PX
Red cell copper
Red cell fragility (H2O2)
Neutrophil fragility (H2O2)
Neutrophils
Lymphocytes
Monocytes
Eosinophils
Basophils
Cytokines

Immunology

Rheumatoid factor (Latex) for propensity to rheumatism
Rheumatoid factor (RAPA) for propensity to rheumatism
Helicobacter pylori (from breath test)
This measures the difference between the pre-urea and the post-urea values. HP thrives in the stomach and duodenum and is responsible for up to 85% of ulcers, some of which may lead to stomach cancer.
Serum immunoglobulin
Serum immunoglobulin G2
Immune globulin (IgG, IgG2 and IgM). IgG2 deficiency is associated with chronic upper and lower respiratory tract infection.
A high level of Immune globulin suggests a yeast overgrowth: candida albicans, possibly caused by antibiotics
Immunoglobulin A (taken from saliva)
Natural killer (NK) cells
T cells

Endocrinology

Free testosterone
Bound testosterone
Corticotrophin (adrenocorticotropic hormone – ACTH) – a precursor of testosterone
Sex hormone-binding globulin (SHBG)
Dihydrotestosterone
Free androgen index
Gonadotrophin
Dehydroepiandrosterone (DHEA)
Dehydroepiandrosterone sulphate (DHEAS)
Growth hormone (GH)
Growth factor (GF)
This may rise with regular but not excessive exercise, or rate of GF decline may be slowed. The higher the score, the better.

Luteinizing hormone (stimulates sperm and testosterone production)
Follicle stimulating hormone (FSH) (stimulates sperm and testosterone production)
Melatonin
Thyrotropin releasing hormone (TRH)
Cortisol

Bladder Cancer

Detected with the Bard test, which detects microscopic traces of blood in the urine. However, this test gives an unfortunate number of false positives.

Amino Acids

Free tryptophan
Tyrosine
Leucine
Glutamine
Isoleucine
Valine

The latter four amino acids are collectively known as the BCAA group

Blood Clotting Risk

Fibrinogen
Platelet aggregation 1 Im ADP
Platelet aggregation 2 Im ADP
Platelet aggregation 5 Im ADP

Mineral Levels including Toxic Metals

Zinc
Copper
Nickel
Chromium
Manganese
Sodium
Magnesium
Ferritin (iron maintains serum zinc levels)
Transferrin saturation (storage iron)
Lead
Cadmium
Aluminium
Mercury (using the Kelmer test)

The latter group of four is made up of toxic minerals that may accumulate in body tissue over your lifetime, causing cellular damage, especially nerve damage (lead may accumulate in the brain, for example). The first group (zinc etc.), at the right levels, are positive for health.

Electrolytes (dissolved salts) (to measure kidney damage)

Sodium
Potassium (important for correct rhythm)
Chloride
Bicarbonate

WBC Motility and Metals Sensitivity Screen

The former checks white blood cell motility, while the latter checks the degree to which neutrophils (white blood cells) and lymphocytes are attracted to a range of metals such as mercury, nickel, lead, cadmium, silver and gold, indicating sensitivity to these metals.

Osteoporosis Screen

Blood and urine tests to identify deficiency of nutrients important for healthy bone growth. Bone density can also be measured using an ultrasound bone densitometer.

Vitamin Deficiencies

Vitamins are normally measured from a blood sample, but B12 and folate from urine.

Essential Fatty Acids

Omega-3
Omga-6
Omega-9

Biogenic Amines

Serotonin (5-HT), a biogenic amine involved in mood, sleep, sensory perception, temperature regulation and appetite.
A high level of serotonin is a good indicator of an absence of depression. Popular anti-depressant drugs such as Prozac, a selective serotonin re-uptake inhibitor (SSRI), raise serotonin levels.
Norepinephrine (a catecholamine and adrenal hormone partly responsible for mood regulation).
Epinephrine (another catecholamine and adrenal hormone which serves as a neurotransmitter).
Dopamine (a neurotransmitter involved in emotional response and some aspects of movement).

Toxic Effects Screen

Test to detect liver damage caused by drugs and other chemicals

Pesticides Screen

Measures levels of a range of pesticides, chlorinated compounds, PCB's, and recent exposure to organophosphorous compounds.

Chronic Fatigue Syndrome/ME from a blood sample Thyroid problems

Human herpes virus-6
Epstein–Barr Virus antibody profile
Lymphocyte subsets (CD3/CD4/CD8 ratio)
Thyroxine (T4)
Thyroid-stimulating hormone (TSH) from the pituitary gland stimulates the thyroid gland to produce thyroxine

Rheumatoid Arthritis

Prostaglandins (a type of fatty acid released in the blood in response to inflammation)

Deep Vein Thrombosis Risk from a blood sample

General haematology profile (see above)
Anticardiolipin antibodies
Factor V Leiden
Factor 11 mutation

Viral Antibodies 2 from a blood sample

Influenza A and B antibodies
Parainfluenza 1,2,3 antibodies
Adenovirus antibodies
Respiratory syncytial virus (RSV) antibodies

Specific allergens capable of causing chronic and seasonal rhinitis (such as dust mite allergy and hay fever)

Various tests for as many as 240 allergens

Lymphocyte Sensitivity Tests for environmental chemicals

Petrol exhaust fumes
Diesel exhaust fumes
Various other pollutants

Thyroid function

Free thyroxine (FT4)
Free triiodothyronine (FT3)
Thyroid stimulating hormone (TSH)

It isn't easy to give advice on screening, as so much will depend on your financial position, your age, the state of your health and the amount of time you are prepared to put in. Then there's location. You might not live near a major city centre, in which case you might have to travel to get tests carried out. And there's the thorny question of NHS versus going private. Some of the best consultants are to be found in the NHS, and many of these will also take on private clients. I have had lung function tests carried out on the NHS and I was impressed with how thorough these were. A bonus, surprisingly, was that I did not have to wait long for an appointment. I have also had stress cardiography done privately in an NHS hospital. This too was impressive, though admittedly I might have had to wait longer for an appointment if I had gone through the NHS.

I've had long experience of private treatment (on medical insurance). I've visited a good few Harley Street consultants over the years. Some were impressive and some weren't. None was cheap. Many of these consultants also work in the NHS and if I can generalize, I would say that those who worked in both sectors were more impressive all round than those who worked solely in private practice. Of course this is a sweeping statement and should perhaps be taken with a pinch of salt. One thing I am sure of is that if you are well informed, you will get a lot more out of either sector. The private practitioner will generally take more time to listen to you and may for that reason make better diagnoses. But there are plenty of doctors in Harley Street and its environs who will not give you any more time than would an NHS doctor, or treat you in the way all patients deserve to be treated. Needless to say, I don't tend to go back to such doctors if I can help it.

Screening is important and if you are really serious about having a healthy life, I hope you will consider the advantages of some of the tests outlined above and perhaps follow some of the implied guidelines. Do not, however, go for the whole list of tests unless you really are a hypochondriac.

CHAPTER TWENTY-NINE

PERFORMANCE-ENHANCING DRUGS

Performance-enhancing drugs are not just used by bodybuilders. They seem to have appeared in every branch of professional sport, and detection techniques are constantly having to be updated to stay one step ahead of the cheats. While it may be unfair to obtain advantage over fellow competitors by taking anabolic steroids and other drugs to build muscle tissue and get ahead, athletes and others who do so may pay a price and a heavy one at that. The word anabolic refers to the building up and repairing of the protein molecules (amino acids) that are the building blocks of our muscles. The opposite is catabolic, that which breaks down protein molecules to release energy.

Steroids are sex hormones (called androgens when they are male sex hormones), in particular testosterone, an important ingredient in building up muscles. Various anabolic steroids are widely available under the counter and on the Internet, and since they do not present the same degree of threat to society that comes from recreational drugs, hard and soft, their production and sale are less of a target for government intervention. Steroid drugs are widely used on a prescription basis for treating a variety of diseases, so it's not surprising that obtaining them without a prescription is relatively easy.

The proper name for anabolic steroids is anabolic-androgenic steroids. Apart from building muscle mass, these drugs enhance male sexual characteristics. There are over 100 different anabolic steroids on the market, and officially they are only available on prescription. Usually they are used to treat adolescents showing inadequate sexual development. Sometimes they are used to treat impotence or muscles wasted by diseases like HIV.

The supplements dehydroepiandrosterone (DHEA) and androstenedione (see chapter 14 on supplements) are available over the counter in the

US as they are not classed as anabolic steroids there, but as food products, even though they are not a food. These supplements are best classed as steroidal supplements. Whether they have anabolic effects is unclear, though they do increase testosterone production. Taken in large doses, they are likely to produce the same side effects as anabolic steroids.

Anabolic steroid use, although illegal, is widespread, especially in the USA. The motivation for taking these drugs tends to be either muscle gain or fat reduction. Some users suffer from body dysmorphic disorder, believing themselves to look smaller or fatter than they actually are. The drugs taken by users tend to be many times more powerful than their prescription equivalents.

What are the risks of steroid abuse? Some are relatively minor such as acne. But there is increased risk of depression, heart attack and stroke, and cancer of the kidneys and liver. In some cases, height may be stunted. The thyroid gland may be damaged permanently. Lifespan is probably shortened. Sperm production may drop and sperm may be damaged as the testicles may atrophy, though these changes will reverse if use of the drugs is halted in time. Some of the damage is permanent, some reversible if the drugs are discontinued. One irreversible effect is accelerated male pattern baldness. The drugs also raise the blood level of LDL 'bad' cholesterol (see chapter 10 on cholesterol), and raise the incidence of blood clots, which is why there is an increased risk of heart attacks and stroke. The left ventricle of the heart may also grow in size.

Other reported effects of steroid abuse include: increased energy, sexual arousal, nervousness, irritability, mood swings, distractability, confusion, forgetfulness and euphoria. In heavy users of steroids, there is a tendency to addiction.

There is little doubt that anabolic steroids disrupt normal hormone production.

However, many of the men who take them (it is usually men as most women have no wish to grow a beard) have little idea of how much damage they may be doing to themselves. Taking doses of anabolic steroids is not natural and only to be recommended under strict supervision where there may be a genuine medical requirement. Otherwise, paradoxically, the end result of regular dosing with such drugs is the opposite of the initial effect. True, as some athletes have discovered, you really can build bigger, stronger muscles and record better performances with these drugs.

The first other noticeable effect is increased aggressiveness. Men on steroids have been known to attack others and even commit murder or suicide. For this reason there is an expression 'roid rage' to describe steroid-induced anger. (Medically it is known as hyperexcitability). This may be accompanied by mania and delusions. Research concludes that high usage of anabolic steroids results in apoptosis or programmed cell death in the brain. This is a natural process to get rid of damaged cells, and testosterone injections have been used successfully to kill off certain types of cancerous cell. Apoptosis induced by steroid drugs is not the aim of the bodybuilder, weightlifter, sprinter or competitive cyclist, however. There is a fair chance, from what is now known, that he will be speeding up the onset of Alzheimer's and Huntington's disease.

Other side effects from steroid supplementation come later in the form of feminising characteristics. That is the paradox. The very thing that the drugs were intended for in one sense – increased masculinity – ends up the other way round. Though the reasons are poorly understood, the body eventually reacts by producing less and less testosterone of its own, and this leads to signs of feminization such as breast development, not to be confused with genuinely muscular pectorals. Breasts in this condition may even, in extreme cases, lactate. That is just the tip of the iceberg where side effects are concerned. The message is a clear one – taking anabolic steroids does not pay. To make things worse, steroid use can seriously interfere with the performance of prescription and over-the-counter medications that you really should be taking.

The body image pressures of today's world have led to a huge rise in the number of males, mostly young men, taking anabolic steroids bought illegally, often at the gym. It is believed that there could be as many as 100,000 users in the UK, the same number as the estimate for heroin users.

CHAPTER THIRTY

PHARMACEUTICAL DRUGS

The drugs we get on prescription are, as everyone knows, a multi-billion pound industry that has become very political in the last few years as governments have to decide whether, if they have a taxpayer-funded health service, they can afford some of the newer drugs developed by the pharmaceutical giants. A course of treatment with some of these drugs can cost many thousands of pounds a year. For the rich this may not be a problem, but for most people, many of these drugs are unaffordable. It seems likely that in the future governments may take more aggressive steps than in the past to cap the price of some drugs. The manufacturers argue, of course, that they are responsible to shareholders and that without the investment they have made in research and development, these drugs would not exist. Both sides have a fair point.

Drugs get ever more targeted as they get more sophisticated, so that the term 'smart drug' is often heard. This implies a drug that will pinpoint its target, rather like a laser-guided missile, and do its job without affecting anything else. That's what the big drug companies would like you to believe, though the reality is usually a drug that is far less smart than the PR handout claims. That is why the law now demands that the leaflet that comes with prescription dugs and some over-the-counter remedies list known side effects. I say known side effects because over the years more will often be discovered in addition to those that were found during the trial period before the drug was certified for release. Many of these side effects will be found on the blogs and websites of disgruntled users who, rightly or wrongly, have come up with ways in which they believe they have been harmed by such and such a drug.

A few years ago I took mefloquine (trade name Lariam) as an anti-malarial before travelling to Sao Tome and Principe in the Gulf of Guinea. True, I didn't catch malaria, but I was dismayed at the way my brain felt weird for days after taking the drug, as though a few billion brain cells had been wiped out at a stroke. I checked on the web and found hundreds of others had had a similar experience and some were even trying to mount a class legal action against the manufacturers. What this experience illustrates is that it pays to treat the manufacturers' lists of side effects as an understatement. Many of the real problems with drugs may not surface for years – the thalidomide scandal comes to mind – and if you are going to take drugs at all, you should do so only after you have considered the alternatives, if there are any.

Not for nothing is alternative medicine so called. A lot of it is untested and a lot of it doesn't work. Some herbal remedies have unwanted side effects and some are downright poisonous. But most herbal remedies, even if they do not work, don't have any noticeable side effects. The problem with pharmaceutical drugs is that they do have side effects, usually a whole load of them. If your doctor or consultant is doing their job properly, they will draw your attention to these and discuss them with you. However, in reality most won't bother or will dismiss the issue in a couple of sentences. Don't be fobbed off. Everyone is different and everyone will react slightly differently to a drug. You need to arm yourself with information – use the Internet again – and go through a list of relevant questions. There might be a clash with another drug you are taking, or with a herbal remedy or supplement. You might be allergic to the drug. Many people are allergic to penicillin, for example.

Self-medication with drugs bought from a website, or in a country with lax regulation governing the sale of drugs, can be fraught with risk. Viagra is the best-known drug bought on the web, but there are many others readily available this way. The lesser danger is that you will get something that is diluted or possibly is not what it purports to be at all – and you won't even realize. The greater risk is that you could be taking something toxic. It makes sense not to take any prescription drugs unless they have been prescribed by your doctor or consultant. Online or telephone consultations with doctors who can prescribe drugs should be avoided for any problem that is potentially serious, as there is likely to be a financial motive behind such services, and the chances of misdiagnosis in this way are considerable. Your health is not worth the risk.

Some people point out that self-administration of supplements is self-treatment with drugs, and that all supplements are drugs in a sense. This applies particularly to herbal remedies and is the reason why there has recently been a tightening of the rules governing the sale of herbal remedies over the counter. Some of those that have been readily available for years may be toxic in very large doses and lack sufficient evidence of their safety and effectiveness to convince the regulatory authorities. It's a tough call. Many of those herbal remedies that have long been favourites could be doing some good, and if they were seriously toxic, we'd have heard about it long ago.

Most patients are happy to leave the doctor's surgery with little awareness of the downside of what that prescription holds in store for them. As likely as not, if it isn't for statins to treat high LDL cholesterol, or for an anti-depressant, it will be for an antibiotic to treat a virus that may or may not have a bacterial infection as a secondary. Most doctors admit to being too free with prescriptions. The patient may have developed a resistance to the antibiotic in question. Often, there will be no bacterial infection, despite the colour of the mucus. Patients like to go away with a prescription, but common viruses do not respond to drugs, so doctors feel under pressure to diagnose a secondary infection, a bacterial one that will respond. The over-prescribing of antibiotics means that many bacteria are now resistant to a wide range if antibiotics.

The drugs themselves deplete good bacteria in the digestive tract, yet few patients are advised of this and counselled to take a course of probiotic supplements to replenish their store of good bacteria in the gut, without which bad bacteria such as *Helicobacter Pylori*, which causes up to 85% of ulcers, will flourish. The billions of good bacteria found in probiotics are widely available from supermarkets in the form of a pleasant drink, but you will get more for your money if you simply buy a course in sachet or capsule form from your nearest health food store. I would suggest a 4–5 week course rather than the two-week course generally recommended. If you are on a course of antibiotics, it is imperative that you finish the course, even if symptoms have already cleared up. You would be surprised how many people fail to follow this advice.

Any discussion of pharmaceutical drugs would not be complete without mention of the placebo effect, or what I call the psychosomatic cure. Most doctors are familiar with what is called the sugar pill and many prescribe them in cases where they feel that symptoms are conversion symptoms, that is, they are induced in the body by the power of the mind. A sugar pill, as the name suggests, does not contain any drugs, but the patient is not told that. The patient believes he or she is taking a drug when they are not, and lo and behold, a cure often results. The mind brought on the symptom and the mind took it away again. The placebo is the basis for treating patients who may show signs of hypochondriasis – imaginary illness.

However, many bodily symptoms induced by the power of the mind over the body are all too real. They normally take the form of elusive pains, headaches and rashes. Getting rid of them may not even require a sugar pill. Sometimes a trip to the doctor is enough on its own to get rid of the symptom. And since there is no underlying illness, hopefully, the whole problem may have gone. Most doctors are savvy enough, though, to realize that something must have induced the symptom in the first place, and while there may be no underlying lesion or cancer, for example, the symptom may be a distress signal that indicates the common twin complaints of anxiety and depression, triggered by any number of things of which acute stress is probably the most likely. In such cases, treating the symptoms with a sugar pill will not always be enough.

Work on the placebo effect has identified that it is linked to the release of endorphins, one of our natural painkillers, in the brain. The expectation of relief triggers the release of endorphins and that is how the sugar pills work. The effect is also seen with real drugs. There is evidence that a large part of the healing effect of anti-depressants can be put down to placebo and an expectation that the drugs will bring relief. It's thought that the placebo effect takes place in a part of the brain called the rostral anterior cingulated cortex (rACC). This part of the brain is associated with perception of pain. It's rich in opiate receptors and becomes noticeably activated when patients are given a placebo or an opiate drug such as morphine or codeine. This demonstrates the power of the mind to direct the body, but it also shows to what extent we carry our own pharmacopoeia around inside ourselves, including powerful painkillers.

We should not have to live with drugs, yet we cannot live without them. Some people would rather die than touch them and you cannot help being sympathetic to that position. Drugs without side effects would be ideal, but unfortunately that is a hopeless dream. The task of the manufacturers is to produce drugs that do their job while minimising the side effects. It's a balancing act. They know that if the side effects are too horrendous, officialdom will not grant approval. But they also know that if the side effects are minimal, that usually means a drug that won't be effective enough to sell and pay for its development costs while making a profit.

There is a constant stream of press releases from drug companies as they try to grab headlines for the latest wonder drug. Often, for reasons of publicity, headline claims are exaggerated. Cure is the miracle word – cure for cancer, cure for baldness, cure for diabetes, cure for Alzheimer's. The list of breakthroughs with a mix of hype and truth is a long one. But we do need pharmaceutical drugs. They save and extend lives. Herbal remedies have a role to play, but because they tend to be safer, they also tend to be less effective, and many are not effective at all, except on a placebo basis.

It's worth remembering that many diseases will clear up eventually on their own without the help of drugs, such is the power of the body's own defence system. In fact, when drugs appear to have brought about a cure, it may be the body and not the drugs that are responsible.

CHAPTER THIRTY-ONE
POLLUTION: A DIRTY WORD

I have a newspaper headline in front of me: 'London Air Dirtier than Bombay's'. Anyone who cares about their health and looks at the facts of air pollution in London or most other major British cities will be shocked. We may be careful to exercise properly and eat all the right things, but to a large extent the air that we breathe remains outside our control unless we move to live somewhere else.

London has one of the highest levels of nitrogen dioxide in the world, whether in the home, the workplace or the street. In one survey of 13 cities, only Seoul in South Korea rated worse for outdoor levels of this gas. Nitrogen dioxide is produced mainly by power stations, gas appliances in the home, cigarette smoking and, not surprisingly, traffic, which accounts for about half of all nitrogen dioxide pollution. As we'll see, traffic emissions are responsible for just about every nasty pollutant out there in the atmosphere. Nitrogen dioxide irritates the lining of the bronchial tubes, making the lungs susceptible to some other pollutants that are described in this chapter. Those most at risk are the elderly, children and those with lung problems already, especially asthmatics. Nitrogen dioxide is a major component of smog.

Exhaust fumes, according to one study, account for as many as 6,000 UK deaths each year from heart attack. In other words, air pollution affects more than just the lungs. When pollution surges for climatic reasons, hospital admissions for heart attack rise.

Black smoke air pollution has also been linked to angina, and nitrogen dioxide has been linked to heart rhythm problems. Black smoke comes mainly from diesel vehicles and consists of fine particles resulting from incomplete combustion. It contributes to winter smog. Black smoke particles are not the same thing as diesel particulates, but the two are commonly found together. Stricter regulations in recent years have reduced the amount of black smoke in the atmosphere.

Carbon monoxide is an odourless but poisonous gas that acts as an impediment to the healthy circulation of oxygen in the body and can kill when inhaled in sufficient quantity. Air polluted with carbon monoxide makes breathing more difficult for many people when they exert themselves. A power lawnmower may emit carbon monoxide at the same time as it is being pushed. The combination of exertion and the pollutant may be dangerous for some people. Oxygen transportation to the vital organs, including the heart and brain is reduced, and those with cardiovascular problems are at increased risk. Car drivers may be exposed to as much as 12 times the outside street level of carbon monoxide, so being insulated inside your vehicle does not protect you. Quite the opposite. Carbon monoxide comes from the incomplete combustion of carbon-containing materials like coal, oil and wood. Avoid cigarette smoke and unflued heating and cooking appliances. However, avoiding vehicle exhaust fumes altogether is more difficult, especially if you live in a city.

I like to walk to work and back each day at a healthy four miles an hour. Like those who cycle in the city for the sake of exercise, I have an increased risk of lung contamination from the many air pollutants I breathe, especially as I am breathing deeply to keep up an aerobic level of exercise. If I were breathing more shallowly, the damage might be less. Unfortunately years of walking to work are already taking their toll in the form of frequent if still not serious lung ailments, mostly bronchial. This shows the unfortunate risk of taking outdoor exercise in a city environment. Arguably it might be healthier to take a taxi or the tube to work, but for the fact that the air inside the taxi may be worse than the air outside, and the air in the Underground, as most London commuters know, can be extremely dirty. If you live in Central London, your risk of dying as a result of air pollution is 2.8% higher than if you live in Inverness.

All new cars have for many years been fitted with three-way catalytic converters to limit carbon monoxide, nitrogen oxide, sulphur dioxide and other pollutants. Unfortunately these devices are now known to increase the atmospheric levels of two very nasty sulphur pollutants:

hydrogen sulphide and carbon disulphide (a carcinogen and neuro-toxin), compounds which replace what was sulphur dioxide. The gas hydrogen sulphide can compromise critical bodily functions and may be implicated in a range of lung diseases including cancer. It may alter antibodies in the lungs, weaken the immune system and enhance the chances of a lung infection. That is how lung cancer often begins. In the last 500 years, the amount in the atmosphere in London is estimated to have grown a hundredfold. The gas is also thought to be implicated in the recent rise in asthma cases in UK cities, especially among children. It does this by altering the way the lungs regulate the breathing cycle. The problem could be reduced were car manufacturers to switch to lean burning engines and do away with catalytic converters. However, given the cost involved and the power of the car manufacturing lobby, this is unlikely to happen.

Coal fires may have been banned in UK cities and choking winter smog banished as a result, but the main constituent of smog – sulphur dioxide – is still out there, catalytic converters or not. This colourless acidic gas, together with nitrogen dioxide used to cause acid rain (sulphuric acid and nitric acid) and damage trees, plants and stonework as well as lungs. In simple terms, sulphur dioxide is produced from the burning of sulphur compounds found naturally in coal and oil. Sulphur dioxide is most likely to be felt by asthmatics. A tightness in the chest and coughing are characteristic.

In fact much air pollution could be reduced or prevented were the government to get tougher in its aim of counteracting the effects of global warming and climate change. But in this battle, the effects of air pollution tend to get played down or lost against the publicity showered on the issue of carbon dioxide and the effects of its footprint on climate. The suspicion has to be that governments make so much money out of motorists and the taxes they pay that covertly they do not wish to reduce vehicle pollution at all if it will cut revenues. Or at least they would like to see pollution reduced but not revenues, and the only way to do this is to make the cost of traffic ever more expensive to drivers and companies. Unfortunately having fewer drivers on the road paying more does not win votes.

Government hypocrisy is similarly evident when it comes to smoking and alcohol, but at least here we can make personal choices. Vehicle emissions are not so easy to avoid and in the end, unless we move home, we are limited in the extent to which we can reduce the 'passive smoking' of vehicle pollutants. Not driving a vehicle ourselves will not help unless we all do it or drive a non-polluting car.

Carbon dioxide is seen as the big bad wolf when it comes to vehicle pollution because of the emphasis on its alleged role in global warming. Car manufacturers have responded with electric, biofuel, gas-driven and hybrid (electric and petrol) vehicles in an attempt to lower their carbon footprint and meet ever tougher government regulations as well as public expectations. Petrol engines produce more CO_2 emissions than diesel engines – from about 10% more to 25% more. Nowadays the drop in diesel performance compared with petrol is relatively limited, and diesel is increasingly popular as it gives more miles per gallon, even if it does cost slightly more per litre. But petrol and diesel both produce CO_2 and these emissions will remain a major contributor to global warming for years to come. By 2011, more diesel than petrol-driven cars will be sold in the UK. While this may be good news on the CO_2 front, it's bad news when it comes to diesel particulate pollution (see below).

Ozone forms one of the worst pollutants not directly attributable to vehicles. It's a secondary pollutant formed in the air by the action of sunlight on hydrocarbons, volatile organic compounds (VOCs) and oxides of nitrogen. Ozone is a constituent of photochemical smog and impacts healthy lung function by reducing the lungs' resistance to disease. It may also cause chest pain, coughing and general lung irritation. It's particularly a risk factor for asthma, and may sting the eyes and nose as well as the throat. Unlike most other air pollutants, ozone is not generated in the same place that it does its damage. It is likely to be found in wide-open country places and equally likely to come from a country thousands of miles away. So local action to limit ozone may have little effect. A solution here has to be a global one. Susceptible people, as many as a third of the population, should not exercise outdoors when reported ozone levels are high.

There is an interesting paradox where ozone is concerned. In urban areas nitric acid from vehicle emissions interacts with ozone in the atmosphere to form nitrogen dioxide, with the result that ozone levels in the vicinity are reduced. In other words, if car engines produce less nitrogen dioxide as a result of anti-pollution manufacturing controls, less ozone in the atmosphere will be eliminated, an undesirable side effect of reducing one pollutant. Ozone levels are highest in summer and higher the greater the temperature, therefore average levels will rise as a result of global warming.

Benzene is a hydrocarbon which comes from petrol fumes and exhaust fumes. Motor vehicles account for more than two-thirds of this noxious and carcinogenic bi-product of crude oil when it is upgraded to fuel oil. It is not found in diesel, but may be found in cigarette smoke and some glues and cleaning products. It's what we smell when we fill the car with petrol. Benzene is particularly linked to increased risk of leukaemia. It may also cause anaemia in those with high exposure.

1,3-Butadiene is another petrol derivative and is likewise carcinogenic. Links have been shown to leukaemia, lymphomas and bone marrow cancers. Road vehicles account for over two-thirds of this pollutant.

Formaldehyde is a colourless gas which comes from chipboard, foam insulation, plywood, bonfires, cigarettes, some fabrics and – no surprise – vehicle exhausts. However, building materials and synthetic materials in the house present a greater risk from formaldehyde than cars when it comes to indoor and workplace pollution. Formaldehyde may cause eye, throat and lung irritation, but for most people the risk of lung disease is small.

Polycyclic aromatic hydrocarbons (PAHs), of which there are many types, come from the production of coke, coal burning and, yes, motor vehicles and cigarette smoke. Some PAHs are carcinogenic, but with the fall in cigarette smoking and the use of coal domestically, the risk has subsided. Our greatest risk from PAHs comes from levels found in some of the food we eat, illustrating how easy it is for soil contaminants to find their way into our diet.

Dioxins are a bi-product of combustion involving chlorine and organic material including fossil fuels. They are extremely carcinogenic and are a product of industrialisation. They rose and rose in our soil and atmosphere in the period from around 1800, and only began to fall about twenty years ago as the result of strict government curbs. Levels in cities remain twice as high as levels in the countryside. Dioxins accumulate in the body's fat cells and are found in soil and air. They have devastated flora and fauna in the British countryside over many decades and only now are there some signs of recovery. A lesser relative of the dioxins are the furans, which are also carcinogenic, but are much less toxic than the various dioxins. Dioxins have been found in farmed fish, especially salmon, and in fish from the sea, particularly mackerel and herring. Airborne dioxins get into the ocean food chain when they reach the surface of the sea and are absorbed by plankton. Tiny quantities of dioxins may still be found in some meat, eggs and dairy products, but this is rarer since strict emission laws were enacted in the last decade.

Polychlorinated biphenyls (PCBs) are found in various varieties in the air and soil, and like the dioxins which they resemble, they are carcinogenic. Air and soil levels, thanks to tighter controls, have fallen in the last twenty years, but soil levels and consequent food levels are still too high.

Microscopic particles in the air and generated mainly (over 25% nationally but over 75% in urban areas) by diesel exhaust fumes may be the most dangerous pollutant of them all. The best known is Particulate Matter Ten (PM10). These particles are so-called because they measure 10 microns or less. They are made up of solids or liquids in the atmosphere. Being so small, there is no face mask available that will prevent these particles from being inhaled. The current limit for PM10 recommended by the World Health Organisation is 50 micrograms per cubic metre, a level normally exceeded in many parts of London. Non-diesel sources of PM10 are fine wood and coal ash, land dust, coal smoke, pollen, sulphates and various types of industrial processing. PM10 has been linked to lung and heart disease

However, even smaller particles, especially PM2.5 and PM1 are now believed to be more dangerous. It's unfortunate that in recent years governments have done so little to discourage diesel vehicles. By 2012, more than half of all cars in the UK will be diesel-powered. Admittedly the government is aware of the problem, but the fact that reducing levels of carbon dioxide emissions in the war against global warming has been given more importance than lowering other forms of air pollution means that targets in areas like diesel particulates have been fairly lax. The power of the car manufacturing lobbies has only made things worse.

Public transport has been routinely encouraged to reduce private car usage, yet most buses and taxis are diesel-powered. There are signs that this may change in the future as hybrid vehicles and electric buses and taxis become more commonplace, but the transition is likely to be slow. In the meantime, city dwellers are at considerable risk from diesel fumes, probably more than from petrol fumes. Likewise those who burn solid fuel for heating are likely to be at risk.

The problem with particulate matter is that it is so fine that the body is not equipped to filter it out, for example through the hairs in the nose which can normally stop larger particles. Those under 10 microns present a problem as they can penetrate deep into the lungs and damage the air sacs (alveoli). The fine particulates can cause asthma, chronic bronchitis, emphysema and other lung conditions. Ultimately they can be carcinogenic, as well as contributing to heart disease in older people.

Volatile organic compounds (VOCs) are carbon-containing substances which can evaporate easily. They come from vehicle fumes, cigarette smoke, household chemicals and synthetic materials. They are implicated in the formation of ground-level ozone.

Asbestos is a natural product which, when crushed, produces fibres of varying lengths. In recent years awareness of the risks of asbestos pollution have grown and it is now banned as a building material. Asbestos fibres inhaled and lodged in the lungs do not go away. Eventually, often decades later, they may cause lung cancer. Sometimes it only takes a few fibres, which is why, while those who have worked with asbestos are most at risk, anyone in contact with asbestos could succumb to asbestosis and lung cancer. The form of cancer linked to asbestos is called mesothelioma. It affects the lining of the lung or abdominal cavity. Brown asbestos is particularly dangerous.

Lead is no longer used for water pipes, but many older houses still have their water supply fed through old lead pipes. It is a heavy metal pollutant which is not expelled from the body. Eventually it may lodge in the brain, and it used to be thought that adults in the UK may on average have as much as half an ounce of lead lodged in their brain by the time they die. This figure should be dropping over time as more and more of us live in lead-free buildings. Lead is the most common of the heavy metal pollutants and also used to be found in paint until it was banned. It was also a common air pollutant until lead-free petrol became universal. Needless to say, even small quantities of lead in the brain can damage intellectual functioning and the nervous system. Children are more vulnerable to exposure than adults.

Mercury is another metal pollutant, and one (in the form methylmercury) that has overtaken lead in the consciousness of the worried well through its association with oily fish and the dilemma this presents for those of us trying to get our two or three portions a week of such fish for the sake, as much as anything, of their Omega 3 content. We could turn to farmed salmon as a way of avoiding mercury in wild salmon and other oily fish, but frankly I would rather take my chances with wild salmon than eat farmed salmon. In fact, it has been claimed that farmed salmon contain just as much mercury as wild salmon. More likely to contain mercury are the larger predators: shark, marlin, swordfish, barracuda and the bigger tuna, particularly bluefin tuna. Safer, therefore, in theory at least, are oily fish such as herring, mackerel, sardines, pilchards and the smaller tuna, though you are unlikely to be able to find out at the supermarket which type of tuna you are buying. Anchovies are an oily fish frequently found to be contaminated with mercury. It's more likely that mercury will be found in the flesh of oily fish. It's not that so-called non-oily fish don't ingest mercury too – it's just that they store their oil in their liver rather than their flesh, and we don't tend to eat fish liver.

Why might you ingest mercury by eating some of the bigger predator fishes? The theory is that those fish nearer the top of the food chain may contain mercury from the smaller fish they have eaten, and the mercury will have worked its way up the chain from algae on the seabed or reef. In fact salmon eat algae directly. I am unconvinced that you should go easy on wild salmon and tuna, and while barracuda from the Caribbean may be genuinely risky, you are unlikely to find any in your local Tesco.

There may be more of a case where shark and swordfish are concerned. Until there is more information available I am going to carry on eating wild salmon and tuna with some frequency.

The effects of mercury poisoning are similar to those of lead poisoning: nerve and brain damage. Again children are more at risk, which is why fish is not advised as a food for children before the age of about two.

Fish may also be contaminated with PCBs and dioxins (see above).

I have covered the advantages of Omega 3 oils in another chapter (see chapter 14 on supplements), but feel that the subject needs to be covered here from another angle. Manufacturers of fish oil capsules now compete on the purity of their Omega 3, and on their ratio of EPA to DHA. The purity debate is interesting. Pharmaceutical Omega 3 is molecularly distilled to remove from fish oil the man-made and natural pollutants that the fish has ingested. Regular cod liver oil, it is argued, is not molecularly distilled and contains contaminants. Another argument in the war of the Omega 3s is that not all oil capsules contain fresh unoxidised oil, and there are suggestions that this lack of freshness is masked by some manufacturers with chemical additives.

It seems strange that on the one hand we are advised to eat fish for health, and on the other, we are told to limit fish to twice a week in case of poisoning from contaminants such as mercury, PCBs (see above), and organochlorine (OC) pesticides. That's rather like saying that you should eat poison for the sake of the goodies that come with it, but don't take too much. It gets worse. When it comes to salmon, do you eat wild salmon (if available), organic farmed salmon or non-organic farmed salmon? The latter has come in for much criticism, much of it deserved, but it is still the salmon most widely eaten in the UK. Farmed and wild salmon are said to have equal concentrations of mercury. Farmed salmon, even organic farmed salmon, have higher levels of fat than wild salmon, and if they are non-organic, they are also likely to contain unacceptable levels of PCBs (see above).

The problem is not limited to oily fish or salmon. Wild cold water fish may have high levels of toxins such as organochlorine pesticides, mercury and PCBs. As fish get older, their PCB levels rise. Levels of PCBs in fish vary by species, and sole, interestingly, is a fish with a low level, while mackerel (an oily fish) and cod have high levels. Squid and mussels come somewhere in between.

None of which resolves the problem of what fish to eat, if any. As I've said, I'm not prepared to give up fish altogether. In fact, I will eat wild salmon (which I prefer as it's leaner) three times a week, given the chance. But when it comes to Omega 3 supplements, I can only suggest you find a brand that you feel you can trust, in which the oil is molecularly distilled and is pharmaceutical grade. Now that some researchers are doubting the proclaimed health benefits of the essential fatty acids, the picture may be a very different one a few years from now, especially if fish from the wild become a thing of the past.

Radiation damage is a hard one to pin down. The debate about the effects of mobile phones and relay masts will no doubt carry on for some years before being resolved. You'll recall the debate about microwave ovens twenty years ago. That now seems to have been settled and they are deemed safe to use. But should you really be using a mobile phone while their safety is still unclear? Most reports so far give mobile phones a clean bill of health with the caveat that the long-term position may be different. We simply don't know yet. I don't use one except in emergencies, not so much for fear of being contaminated by radiation – it's just that life is so much more pleasant without one. Radiation, though, is all around us and most of it is natural, coming from the sun, the earth, and even the food we eat. Radioactivity itself is not an air pollutant, but radioactive gases or particles can be breathed in and may cause cancer. Serious effects of radiation pollution are burns, cataracts, sterility and even death, as after a nuclear attack. Exposure may even cause DNA damage which, in turn, may affect the unborn.

It's not just old people and children who are most at risk from air pollutants. Among the rest of us, about one in five is thought to be at risk of contracting a lung disease, asthma being the most prevalent.

It's clear that vehicle exhaust emissions are a major culprit. Diesel vehicles are a worse polluter than petrol vehicles, but power stations that burn coal to generate electricity are also a major source.

A few years ago, face masks aimed at reducing the amount of pollutants breathed in were common among cyclists. Now they are rarely seen.

The reason seems to be that they are not very effective, especially against the most dangerous air pollutants, the fine particulates under 10 microns. And pollutants such as ozone, which is a gas, cannot be stopped by a mask.

Some people still swear by masks, though, especially to prevent asthma attacks and allergic reactions. They are even claimed by some to reduce the risks of catching bacterial and viral diseases. There is a small chance that this might be true with a very fine mask, but except in the event of an ebola or bird flu pandemic, I think this is pushing things a bit far. For those who do want to use a face mask, there are many brands available, some more effective (and expensive) than others.

EU directives and UK government action have gone some way to limiting the worst pollutants from vehicle emissions, but much more should have been done by now, and could have been done at relatively little cost.

Against progress we also have the weight of the government's tax take, the fact that almost everyone now drives and drivers are voters. The carbon footprint in the atmosphere is important, but the government should be as concerned about public health as it is about climate change. There should be a rapid move away from diesel vehicles altogether. The fine particulate matter that diesel vehicles produce is a long- term health threat to all those who live in cities. Congestion charging, pollution charging, toll roads and charging per mile are only partial solutions in a country wedded to the car at any price. The better quicker solution has to be more restrictive regulations governing engine exhaust emissions. Without such controls, thousands will suffer and even die from otherwise avoidable diseases.

On a sobering note, a major study in the US (the so-called Six Cities Study) was undertaken a few years ago to see whether particulates from power stations and diesel exhaust fumes had an impact on life expectancy. Particulate Matter 2.5 was the chosen particulate that was examined. The findings of the study matched those of another study by the American Cancer Society and were corroborated by a third study by the Health Effects Institute in the US. The finding, after all other factors had been accounted for, was that PM2.5 led to a 26% greater chance of a shorter life in the most polluted of the six cities than in the least polluted.

Local authorities have a legal obligation to monitor air pollution and meet certain targets for clean air. You should be able to find out about pollution levels in your area by calling your local council.

Street pollution in towns is heaviest directly beside busy roads, and pollution levels fall rapidly the further you are from traffic. However, streets and buildings trap pollution. If you have a choice, live as far away from traffic as you possibly can.

Cars are far from being pollution-free inside. Pollutants from your own car engine and from the air over the road outside get into your car, raising levels of benzene, carbon monoxide and nitrogen dioxide in particular. A pedestrian on a busy street will have less exposure to pollutants than those inside the nearby cars, but will be more exposed than pedestrians away from the traffic. Pollution tends to be especially high in carparks, tunnels and petrol stations.

Maps are published by the National Environmental Technology Centre showing levels of different kinds of pollution in different parts of the country. This can be useful if you are concerned about where to live and have a choice. With the possible exception of ozone, you should be able to avoid much air pollution by living in the country well away from traffic, especially if you do not drive. However, you would be better off at altitude in a windy location than tucked away in a valley. Pollution is normally worse in still hot weather in the summer and in still foggy weather in the winter. Remote coastal areas are another part of the country likely to be relatively free of pollution.

Asthma is on the increase, along with other diseases related to pollution such as seasonal and perennial allergic rhinitis, and vehicle pollution in particular, especially particulate pollution, which has grown with the expansion in vehicle numbers, appears to be the major factor involved.

CHAPTER THIRTY-TWO
PRIVATE MEDICAL INSURANCE

Several million people in the UK are covered by private medical insurance. Is it a good thing? I think it is and I've had cover for about the last thirty years. I don't think you need to belong to the ranks of the worried well to have private cover. It usually means better care in the event that you are hospitalised for a long-term illness. Emergencies aside, the chance to choose your consultant and pick the best may be critical to outcome. I think this is more important than whether you are in a public ward or a private room with TV and a menu from which to choose your meals, however welcome that might be. The important thing is the fact that you can be treated almost immediately. This can be life-saving in some cases, despite the fact that the NHS will generally try to prioritise more urgent treatments and operations, which only makes it harder for you to get to see a consultant of your choosing if you are a patient in the NHS.

Why would anyone not have private medical insurance? Perhaps they are so healthy that they think it isn't worth the cost, and cost does seem to be a factor, with annual premiums running at about £1,000 a year for men around the age of sixty, for example, and possibly a bit more if they live in London. And that's if they are part of a group or company scheme. If not, it can cost quite a lot more. That might seem like a lot of money, but where health is concerned, I would say that this isn't the time to be niggardly. The argument that health insurance is only for the rich doesn't hold water. That may be true for a small number of the population, but what do we find when we look at the lifestyles of those said to be below the poverty line? We find that many can afford to smoke and drink, to buy lottery tickets, to have a mobile phone, to have a DVD player and possibly more than one TV in the home, as well as at least one computer and the latest PlayStation. Cut all those out except perhaps the TV and the saving would more than pay the private medical insurance premium for all the family. Ultimately it's a matter of priorities. Some people put their health first and some don't.

That would be alright except that it affects others when people don't take care of themselves and their consequent illnesses have to be paid for by taxpayers who do look after themselves, whether or not the taxpayers have private cover. It's an interesting debating point and explains why some doctors have questioned whether smokers with lung cancer should not go to the back of the queue. The same could be said about obese people with diabetes, though the reply might be that the problem is not their fault but the result of the genes they inherited.

Private medical cover in the UK won't save you the cost of a private visit to a GP, so that is an extra cost to think about. Nor will it cover dental work, cosmetic surgery or treatments in general which are a matter of lifestyle choice rather than medical necessity. In the US, GP visits and dental work can be covered by insurance at a cost.

In the UK it isn't possible to get an NHS doctor to refer you to a consultant privately if you are insured. At least that is the theory. However, if your GP works in both the NHS and private practice, as some do, especially in London, it may be possible to get round this hurdle if the GP knows you well, in which case you could see the GP on the NHS and the consultant under your insurance. Very few GPs, even in London, work entirely in private practice these days. The same is true of consultants, and even among Harley Street consultants, many will often spend part of the week elsewhere working for the NHS. Many of them could get more than enough work purely in private practice, but work in the state sector too out of a sense of duty, even though this may mean that their income is less.

Most people with private cover such as that offered by BUPA get it at a preferential rate through a company scheme to which they belong, and most well-run companies will offer private cover. It is surprising, therefore, how few people take up the offer when the company is not itself paying the premium on the employee's behalf. In the US, company cover is much commoner than in the UK, and there it is generally paid by the company. If the company pays in the UK, this is a taxable benefit in kind at a tax rate of up to 40%. I believe it is time the government encouraged private medical cover for the workforce by making premiums tax-deductible. More people would sign up, thereby saving costs on the NHS budget, and while the tax loss on the one hand might be wiped out by the tax gain on the other, I think there would be a long-term gain to the Exchequer as more people acquired the habit of looking after themselves better which comes more naturally with private cover.

CHAPTER THIRTY-THREE
PRIVATE MEDICAL CONSULTANTS

A dilemma that faces anyone looking for a consultant in the private sector, given that you have a choice, is how to find the best one for you. They cannot all be equally good, but presumably they all have enough work to do. The government has published league tables grading hospitals in various ways, but has baulked at doing the same for consultants. Understandably the medical profession itself is hostile to the idea. Some doctors become so famous that they get a reputation in the media, usually for pioneering work in some life-saving area of medicine. But more often than not the best consultants are known only by reputation among doctors, not among the public, and your GP may have his own reasons for recommending a particular consultant that might have little to do with how good they are. They might even be friends or play golf together.

There have been attempts to publish the names of consultants by specialism in newspapers and even in a couple of books that I am aware of, though these listings would need to be updated regularly to be really meaningful and this has not happened. The basis for such publications has usually been research into who other doctors rate as good or even as the best, but doctors have generally been reluctant to cooperate. We are talking here about the private sector. In the public sector you have even less chance of finding out who are the best, just as you have little opportunity of choosing your consultant.

However, there is one trick that I have learnt. You can become knowledgeable about your medical problem by using the web. It's well known that this can lead to all kinds of self- diagnoses that turn out to be wrong, but assuming that you do know for a fact what your complaint is, websites like www.bmj.com can be extremely helpful because the chances are that if you can find major articles there about your illness, and you probably can, the writers are probably fairly expert in that field, especially if their name comes up repeatedly as the author or co-author of a number of articles. Look for recent articles as some may be quite old. By looking for a consultant this way you also get to learn more about your disease, and in my experience, the better informed you are, the higher your chances of successful treatment, especially if you manage to find the best consultant or one of the best.

Here's another tip. A lot of the best consultants teach other consultants in the teaching hospitals, so you may find that those with the most *British Medical Journal* articles to their name also have Professor in front of it. You may not find a UK consultant in two other publications I recommend, and you may have to pay to view anything more than a summary of the articles, but I suggest that if you are researching a medical subject, you look in the *Journal of the American Medical Association* (www.jama.com) and the *New England Journal of Medicine* (www.nejm.com). There are many specialist medical journals which you can also refer to, but as a starting point at least, I recommend these. The NHS websites will also provide some information, but often at a basic level. So if you are at all well informed already, you could skip these and go straight to the sites I have suggested. I have listed a number of useful websites at the back of this book, but one in particular is, in my opinion, the best of all: www.hon.ch. If you want serious medical research reports as well as simple user-friendly descriptions of diseases, try this site first.

Here's another tip I have found handy when seeing a consultant. Even in the private sector, where you are not as rushed as in the NHS, consultants will still mostly give the impression that they are in a hurry and their time is important. They vary a lot, but a surprising number still seem to forget that if you or your insurer are paying them about £200 an hour, they owe it to you to be careful listeners. You are not going to change them, and getting them to listen to every word of your saga is only one step easier than getting it all off your chest in the few seconds you will be spared by an NHS doctor. My suggestion is that you write down what you want to say to the doctor, symptoms, past treatment, the lot. Keep to the point and try to limit it to one side of printed A4 paper.

Insist that the consultant read it in front of you at the start of the consultation. They will find it hard to refuse and you will save a lot of time. The consultant will get a more coherent picture of your problem than they would probably get from listening to you for the first ten minutes. That way you have more time (you are usually allotted thirty minutes for a consultation) for examination and discussion of options.

If your summary contains references to things you have found in say the BMJ, especially if there are references to articles by the consultant sitting in front of you, you may get more and better attention. Many consultants are known for their big egos, especially cardiologists. If you are in a position, through age, occupation or education, to establish a rapport with the consultant as equal to equal in the eyes of the world, this may work to your benefit too. Don't count on it, but empathy between you can often go a long way in getting the best out of the consultant. A fawning attitude will not help, on the other hand. The consultant will often treat it as an invitation to talk down to you in words of one syllable.

CHAPTER THIRTY-FOUR
RECREATIONAL DRUGS

On the assumption that most readers will be over the age of 40, this might not seem a very appropriate subject. Taking illegal drugs is mainly a youthful activity, and it's unlikely that anyone in the ranks of the worried well, having reached, supposedly, the age of wisdom, would be crazy enough to take recreational drugs. So let's not even mention heroin, crack cocaine, crystal meth, LSD, ecstasy and amal nitrate. If you are still tempted by the drug of choice in your student days, marijuana, it helps to know that this drug, for all its relaxing qualities and the fact that it is medically helpful to people with multiple sclerosis (MS), is worse for you than cigarettes, especially if, unlike Bill Clinton, you do inhale. The more dangerous form of pot known as skunk contains a higher concentration of tetrahydrocannabinol. Among hardcore drug users there is an increasing incidence of hepatitis B and C. The consequences of crystal meth and heroin use are so serious that they often result in death, while even limited use of most drugs may cause sperm deformity with consequent reproductive problems, including foetal abnormalities.

Regular users of marijuana are 40% more likely, according to one report, to suffer from a psychotic illness such as schizophrenia. They are more likely than cigarette smokers to contract lung cancer and emphysema and one joint is said to cause as much lung damage as five cigarettes. Marijuana also increases your chances of depression, anxiety and suicide. Long-term users may find that it reduces testosterone and increases the risk of feminising characteristics such as male boobs (see chapter 38 on smoking, which lists the harmful effects of smoking cigarettes. Smokers of marijuana are prone to all the listed diseases too, generally to a greater degree than cigarette smokers). Regular use of cocaine and heroin damages sperm.

Cocaine is the drug most likely to be offered to the over 40s these days, particularly at fashion and media parties. It may be fun at the time, but the list of damaging side effects continues to grow, quite apart from the damage to your nose that comes from regular use.

There is an area of crossover between recreational drugs and medical research into diseases such as Alzheimer's, where there is an ongoing hunt for drugs which will slow, halt or reverse memory loss, including normal age-related memory loss. A drug called Modafinil, developed for the treatment of narcolepsy, a sleeping disorder, is arousing interest for its ability to boost short term memory, sharpen mental acuity and ward off fatigue, a bonus for those sitting exams or who need to stay awake and alert for long periods without resorting to more traditional stimulants such as caffeine and guarana. It also seems to reduce impulsiveness. The popularity of drugs like Modafinil is spreading from the US to the UK, despite the fact that it is only available on prescription. As with so many drugs, Viagra and Cialis in particular, it is available without prescription on the internet. But no one yet knows what the side effects of this so-called 'smart drug' are, apart from some degree of headache. However, it doesn't seem to be addictive.

A drug straight out of the Alzheimer's research lab, Donepezil, appears to have much the same effect as Modafinil, slowing the loss of cognitive ability that is typical of Alzheimer's disease. Cognitive skills are enhanced and short-term memory improves. Another drug, propanolol (a beta-blocker) removes negative emotions and has been used to treat post-traumatic stress disorder (PTSD), while ritalin, mainly used in treating attention deficit hyperactivity disorder (ADHD) in children, is said to enable adults to think and plan more clearly, while boosting spatial working memory without loss of concentration. Amphetamines, which have been around for a long time, have been found to promote neuroplasticity, another word for connectivity in the brain. This has turned out to be of benefit to stroke patients. However, such use of smart drugs and traditionally heavily controlled drugs like amphetamines begs the ethical question of whether their use should be restricted to those with an illness such as Alzheimer's, or whether healthy people should also have access to them simply to improve their performance.

The competition among drug manufacturers to come up with drugs to treat Alzheimer's disease and other forms of dementia is intensifying each year as more and more people succumb as a result of growing longevity. A group of drugs called ampakines is showing progress in this area for their ability to improve memory, as is another group called Mem compounds, being developed in three separate forms in the US.

The side effects with such drugs are even more of an issue. The unwell will generally tolerate a certain level of side effects in return for the plus side of the drugs they take. Whether this would be wise for the healthy is another matter, especially as the long- term side effects are unknown. I remember the days when it was said that marijuana had no side effects. By the early Seventies this view, always naïve, had been thoroughly contradicted.

Smart drugs may not be as damaging as heroin and crystal meth, but they are still restricted to prescription-only, and it would be an unwise doctor who prescribed them for non-medical reasons.

CHAPTER THIRTY-FIVE
SPARRING PARTNERS: RELATIONSHIPS

There's a mountain of self-help books on relationships. I have read many of them – maybe as many as a hundred. I have been divorced and remarried. I have trained as a counsellor with the aim – never fulfilled – of becoming a relationships counsellor. Am I any the wiser? Yes, a bit. But the deeper you get into this field, the more you realize how much there is that you do not know. Here I can only write down a few of the things that seem to be true of most relationships today.

You probably know the statistic that around 40% of marriages in the UK end in divorce. You may not be aware that more children are now born outside marriage than inside. Or that about 60% of cohabiting couples with children split up before the eldest child is five years old. It used to be commonplace to talk of marriage as though it were the only form of relationship into which children were born. Now it is more appropriate to talk of marriages and cohabitations, and of husbands and wives in the first instance, and of partners in the second. I will leave the subject of gay partnerships out of the equation as that's a subject for a book in itself.

If you are getting married, you may think it a good idea to have a prenuptial agreement. If you are already married, a mid-nuptial agreement so-called is a good idea, though still a rare thing. And now that the law has changed to give cohabiting partners property-sharing rights if they split, it is a good idea to have a separate property agreement drawn up before the cohabitation starts or soon thereafter. If your assets are or are likely to become unequal (and the man is usually the richer partner), a formal agreement is a very good thing. Such agreements are not currently binding in English law, as they are in say France and the US, but I believe they soon will be, and in the meantime they do have some weight in a court of law provided that there has been what the law calls 'full disclosure of assets' and the parties have each been advised by a solicitor and signed the agreement without coercion in front of a lawyer.

If children are involved or are likely to be, the law defends their interests and is very strict. Thus any agreement entered into cannot override the statutory rights of children. A sensible well drawn up agreement should cover the entitlements of children in case separation or divorce occurs.

One of the problems with agreements of this kind is that where there is inequality of assets, one or the other party, usually the poorer, may be less inclined to enter into the agreement unless it is a generous one in their favour. Otherwise they might prefer to take their chances in the divorce court should it come to that, especially given the generosity of the English courts, which have made the UK the divorce capital of Europe, though I suspect the pendulum will eventually swing back to a more equitable position in due course. In the meantime, the rich are increasingly disinclined to get married at all.

If you are asking yourself what a chapter on relationships has to do with a book of health advice for the worried well, we should remind ourselves that few things in life are as negatively stressful and therefore dangerous to health as divorce, not to mention the months and years of unhappiness before divorce proceedings begin. The health risks of non-productive stress can easily lead to depression on the one hand and cardiovascular problems on the other. And that's just for starters. The immune system can be severely compromised, sperm count can plummet, weight loss can happen suddenly, and we're talking muscle loss, not fat. The list goes on and on and could, if we knew how to gauge it, be responsible for shortening our lives if the divorce were stressful enough.

I have said elsewhere in this book that married men live longer (on average, of course). Conversely single women live longer. Again, correlation is not causation, but the link does appear to be strong. Men do not like being single very much and when they get divorced or separated, will tend to seek out another marriage or cohabiting relationship as soon as possible. Women, arguably wiser after a break-up, are more likely to take their time or never get hitched again.

Over many years, if the twelve year itch has been survived (apparently the twelve year itch is real, not the seven year itch), relationships that last for decades may bring a couple so close emotionally that the death of one can lead to the death of the other partner soon after. It happened to my 93-year-old great uncle. He has been married since his twenties. When he died, his wife died within a few days. By the time you are that age, your immune system cannot easily stand major emotional shocks.

There are many reasons why marriages founder more easily nowadays. One reason is that we expect too much of our partners. We expect them to be confidant, lover, friend, companion. If we expect too much of marriage as the solution to our natural need for emotional intimacy, we are likely to be disappointed. Until fairly recently, less was expected of marriage and of partners because we had friends, family, church and community to give us emotional support. But for the last sixty years at least we have come to expect our wives and partners to fulfil all our emotional needs and this is especially true of men, which is why we feel so bereft if we split. Men don't have the same emotional networks to rely on in times of trouble, so we urgently seek new relationships to get the support which women will find in women friends and family members. Women though, in a working world, are moving in the direction of men and have less by way of support systems than they used to.

When we are stressed by a failing marriage, if we have friends and family to turn to, we are less likely to see our blood pressure rise and hear the baying of the black dog of depression. Our cognitive performance is also strengthened by having a confidant in troubled times. And when we are happily married, apparently, this measure of health is better than when marriage is unhappy.

Marriage is now a minority option. Only 45% of households contain a married couple and the figure is expected to go on dropping, adding to the housing shortage. It has to be wondered why life expectancy is increasing when you consider this fact and throw in upward trends in problems like obesity and Type 2 diabetes. The best explanation might be that better nutrition in the last sixty years and the successes in the fight against disease have outweighed the downside of other factors. Maybe we would be living even longer if there were not an epidemic of obesity with 40% of the UK population now officially overweight or obese.

It should come as no surprise that all else being equal, men (and women) with religion, strong family and community ties, and a happy marriage tend to live longer. Men who have men friends in whom they can confide – and this is rare – also have an advantage. Women have best friends for this purpose. Men rarely have a best friend nowadays – at least not someone with whom they can share their deepest feelings and secrets. There was a time 20 years ago when 'new man' was a popular concept. New man was popular with women – but only as a friend. New man has not stood the test of time. The problem was that he just wasn't sexy enough and wearing your heart on your sleeve didn't turn out to be a turn-on. Men are therefore stuck, if I can generalize, with relying on their partners for intimate emotional expression. If the relationship heads for a split, the one person they might have relied on to share their feelings is not available to them. It's little wonder men suffer more when a relationship fails and seek another relationship as fast as they can.

A strong and happy marriage generally demands that the partners make space for each to enjoy their interests separately. After the honeymoon period is over (about six to twenty-four months usually), most partners become themselves again and try to live with reality rather than the fantasy they made their loved one into. People who are married are, according to research, slightly happier than people who are not. The divorced are unhappiest of all. One conclusion from this is that it is better to never be married than to be divorced. Putting that another way, it is better to stay single than marry the wrong person, but of course we don't know the person is wrong when we marry them or we would never take the plunge in the first place. Second marriages, it is well known, are generally shorter than the first, and third marriages are even shorter.

If happy marriages last longer, does that mean that marriages can make you happy if you weren't happy to begin with? Sadly not. It seems that happy people have happy marriages and unhappy people have unhappy marriages. Needless to say, happy people are more likely to stay married. And their partner is more likely to be their best friend and a strong emotional support. Those who expect the most from marriage ('she will solve all my problems and make me happy') are most likely to be disappointed. A happy marriage is first and foremost about what each can give to it, rather than what each can get out of it.

Making your partner your best friend and confidant should be a big factor in a happy marriage, but equally important is not cutting out family and friendships in the process. Keep these strong as well, and the marriage grows in strength and happiness. It has been well established that marrieds see less of their family members than do siblings who are unmarried. Marrieds need to make the effort to keep in close touch with family members, despite the added demand on time.

Marrieds tend to associate with other marrieds. Marrieds with children associate with marrieds with children. There is a risk in this narrowing process. If you get divorced, you may find that you no longer get invited round by the marrieds, but with the unmarrieds you have burnt your bridges.

It's often said that the main causes of divorce are sex and money. These can be powerful contributors and underlie many a marital row. But in fact there is evidence that the biggest reason is children. I have had children in two marriages and I can see how this happens. It's not just the added expense of children, though this is very real. It's the time and energy that children take up, year in and year out. When both parents are working, especially, fatigue can be very real. Children take up time, getting in the way of friendships and family relationships. They can leave parents drained of physical and emotional energy, even if there is household help. Tired parents have little time or inclination for sex. From there, depression is often just round the corner. In fact the slippery path to separation can occur almost without either partner knowing why it is really happening. Fights that seem to be the cause may only be symptoms of something deeper and unrecognised, which is why a good counsellor or therapist can be worth their weight in gold. They have saved many a marriage simply by identifying the real cause of the problem and leading their client to the insight that may produce a workable solution. Being aware that children strain a marriage may be half the battle in saving the marriage, and perhaps a missing sex life too.

After all, it's rumoured that couples are so busy nowadays and so tired that they have little inclination to get sexual. It's easy to see this as falling out of love, which it may be, but the reality is often simply that when you are exhausted from too much office work, childcare and housework, sexual feelings fly out the window. One solution is for the couple to lower their material expectations and, if both work, for one to give up work or only work part-time. An alternative is to have a marriage without children, an option that would have been unthinkable a few decades ago, but which can work very well in relationships based mainly on friendship and companionship – someone to share in the experience of doing things. Such relationships can work particularly well as second marriages when children have flown the nest.

Happy experiences cause dopamine, a neurotransmitter, to be released in the brain, along with oxytocin. Chocolate, orgasm, even cocaine and amphetamines have this effect. Exercise causes endorphins to circulate in the brain and the effect is similar. Thus happiness in the crudest sense comes down to chemicals, including also serotonin, which, as we have seen, is another neurotransmitter which signals happiness. When serotonin goes down far enough, depression results.

High self-esteem is another factor in happiness in general and marriage in particular. Just as happy people make more successful marriages, those with high self-esteem tend to be more happily married. At its most basic level, self-esteem comes down to personal attributes, a loving upbringing and inherited genes. Whether we have high or low self-esteem is often down to factors outside our control. Being happy and marrying happily may therefore depend on serendipity as much as our personal efforts and understanding. With insight we can go a long way towards making the most of what nature and nurture gave us, and good counselling and therapy can help a great deal on the road through life. Ultimately, though, the way our relationships turn out and their effect on our health may be as much in our stars as in our hands.

You're never too old to fall in love. When you're in love, your brain produces dopamine, serotonin, testosterone and various neurotransmitters. Romantic love is a form of addiction and addiction is associated with raised dopamine levels. Beware of romantic addiction which becomes an obsession. Not for nothing has romantic love sometimes been called a form of madness.

....

More Tips and Traps

We are unconsciously drawn to partners whose immune system is quite unlike our own. This way offspring will have a wider range of immunity.

Oxytocin is a hormone produced when we feel we are in love. It contributes to bonding and therefore has sometimes been called the trust hormone.

Chocolate can produce a feeling of well-being similar to being in love. It contains phenylethylamine (PEA), a form of the amino acid phenylalanine. Production of PEA is stimulated by orgasm and exercise.

CHAPTER THIRTY-SIX
SKIN: BURNING AMBITION

The UK now has more cases of the most serious kind of skin cancer (melanoma) each year than Australia – about 9,000 in fact, of whom about a fifth will die. Admittedly we have three times the population. When we look for the reasons behind the steadily rising trend, they aren't hard to find. We get more sun at home thanks to an increasingly hotter climate, and more of us take more holidays abroad than ever before. Over 50% of skin cancers in the UK are now linked to British rather than foreign sun exposure. However, Australians produce 3.4 times as much vitamin D from sunlight as UK residents.

For centuries a suntan was a sign of poverty, indicating that you worked in the fields, as likely as not. A pale skin, especially in a woman, was seen as a sign of beauty. The second half of the twentieth century saw an explosion in travel and the fashion fad of the suntan. Millions today are paying the price for overexposure to the sun's UVA rays, and while most will not suffer from one of the forms of skin cancer, many will become prematurely wrinkled and sun-marked, evidence of the damage done years before to the dermis and epidermis by penetrating solar rays and insufficient protection. It's often the bad case of sunburn in youth, especially, that underlies the skin cancer or just plain old sag and poor skin of later years.

You would think we would have learnt the lesson by now. Some exposure to sunlight is important and normal. Without it we would not get enough vitamin D and would suffer from rickets, a disease widespread in the nineteenth century. Inadequate exposure to sunlight can also make you more vulnerable to tuberculosis (TB), which is currently showing signs of a comeback. Vitamin D is protective of the immune system by supporting the level of macrophages, T and B lymphocytes, and the formation of monocytes. Allegedly it's protective against some forms of cancer, including colon and prostate cancer, and, paradoxically, even possibly melanoma itself. We get vitamin D from eating oily fish and we synthesize some vitamin D in our skin, but not enough, so getting some from sunlight is essential to health. It's mainly the sun's UVA rays that produce tanning and potentially skin cancer, while the UVB rays are what triggers vitamin D production. Even UVB radiation should not be overdone, however. The lesson to be learned is that you should get enough sunlight for vitamin D synthesis, but not enough to tan the skin more than very lightly.

Vitamin D is fundamental to the absorption and retention of calcium, which is why a deficiency is conducive to osteoporosis. It's important to the secretion of insulin and the thyroid and parathyroid hormones. We store vitamin D in summer to see us through the winter, when sunlight is insufficient. About twenty minutes exposure to sunlight daily in the summer is enough for most people. But whereas a little sunlight does you good, you can have too much of a good thing. A suntan is after all a sign that the skin has reacted to the threat of being burnt by producing a protective pigmentation called melanin. The only good things you can say about a tan are that it may protect you from further damage and may make you look good.

However, there's an interesting sociological phenomenon afoot when it come to tanning. First to be into the tanning craze in the last fifty years were the more affluent, especially as this slice of society could afford the trips that others could only dream of. Now that worldwide travel is affordable by all but the poorest, we have a situation where the less educated but now relatively affluent go on holiday and return proudly displaying their (often lobster) tans, while those better educated and informed, and probably more affluent still, are gradually returning to the Victorian ideal of a pale skin. The former still incline to holidays spent lying on the beach or a lounger, baking under the sun, while the latter are more likely to be covered by a hat and enjoying a more cultural or active holiday experience. Thus it ever was that the different social classes had different ways, with the habits of the less educated imitating those of the better educated some years behind. Nowhere has this phenomenon been more visible in the last thirty years than in the sphere of travel, to the point where the traditional overseas package holiday, once the birthright of the working classes, is being rapidly replaced by independent holidays abroad.

Most people know that too much sun is bad for you, but many are still tempted by the lure of a suntan to show off proudly as a fashion statement back home, where, given the kind of summers that the UK now gets, the tan can readily be topped up by a bit of local sunshine.

I used to get a tan on surfing trips abroad, and was not too worried about skin damage, even when I got nasty sunburns on two or three occasions. I would describe myself as darkish fair – my only freckles are moles which the sun has put on my skin over the years. Have I had too much sun? Definitely. Does it show? Yes, but it could be worse. You cannot spend half your life sitting for hours on a surfboard under a tropical sun and not absorb too much of its rays. Modern sunscreens are a relatively recent thing. They didn't used to have factors and were never water-resistant. That has all happened in the last twenty years. Now we have SPFs (Sun Protection Factors) that go up to 50. However, there's a difference between 'water resistant' sun screens which will wash off after half an hour in the surf, and the few on the market that will actually stay on for several hours and may legally be described as 'waterproof'. The latter will, unsurprisingly, tend to have a high SPF (20 or above), and it is these long- lasting high factor creams, if you can find them (and it isn't easy) that I would recommend using if you go in the water a lot. The one I currently use really seems to work and to last for hours. It's claimed that it will penetrate through to the epidermis where it binds with the keratin. I wish sunscreens like this had been round when I was surfing off tropical islands long ago. I don't surf or snorkel today without slapping on plenty, and when I'm out of the water, I wear a hat out of doors.

But the damage was done years ago and I have paid a certain price. I have had a BCC (basal cell carcinoma) on one eyelid, and several solar keratoses (also known as actinic keratoses) on my scalp and forehead. I have had a benign lentigo on my back and a malignant one on my scalp. The small scaly keratoses have been removed by cryotherapy (application of a freezing foam) and the rest by surgery under local anaesthetic. Keratoses which prove more resistant may be cauterized or even surgically removed. Other ways of removing a keratosis are by curettage (scraping), with or without electro-surgery, though this form of treatment runs the risk of scarring or leaving white patches on the skin. Dermabrasion and chemical peels may also be used, but are not a good idea if you plan to go into the sun again within a few months of the treatment as this may also cause changes in pigmentation. Another approach, sometimes painful, is to apply a cream to the keratosis to sensitize it, and then to apply a photodynamic light. A gel which combines diclofenac and hyaluronic acid, and which burns keratoses off, a bit like a wart remover, may also be used and is handy as it can be self-administered following a careful consultation with a dermatologist. It is only available on prescription and is marketed in the UK under the trade name Solarase.

The good news is that none of this makes me much more likely to get a malignant melanoma (MM), the dangerous form of skin cancer that is steadily on the increase. There is still much to learn about malignant melanoma. For one thing, it sometimes appears on areas of the body not much exposed to the sun, and even sometimes on people not much exposed to the sun, yet a link with sun exposure appears to be there in most cases. It is risky too in that, in men, it more usually appears on the back where it may not be noticed until it has reached an advanced stage, at which point it may have metastasized and spread to other parts of the body. As we get older, there is also a greater chance that if we get an MM, it will be on the face. If you feel you are at risk, get your partner or a member of your family to check your back and scalp from time to time.

It goes without saying that you should avoid sunbeds and sunlamps. Going to a tanning clinic before going on holiday may seem like a wise precaution, but you would be better off staying out of the sun or using an adequate sunscreen – or both. Many if not most tanning centres now use equipment considered dangerous other than in small doses. Not for nothing has the rate of malignant melanoma doubled in the past twenty years. Sunbeds and tanning centres have played a part in this trend. Reflected UVA and to a lesser extent UVB rays from snow, sand and water are stronger and more dangerous, in that order. Up to 80% of UV rays penetrate mist and light clouds, which is why the new generation of solar panels can generate electricity quite effectively in winter. UV radiation gets stronger closer to midday, closer to the summer solstice and closer to the equator. What is less well known is that it gets stronger with altitude, snow or no snow.

An SPF of say 20 theoretically extends 20-fold your UV protection compared with using no sunscreen at all. It has been said that above the level of 15 or 20 – thereabouts – extra factors do not make any difference.

Too much sun may lead to prickly heat, heat exhaustion and even sunstroke, which can be fatal in extreme cases if left untreated (by re-hydration and cooling the body's core temperature down).

A malignant melanoma will usually have several of the following characteristics: it is raised, it has an irregular shape, it is dark brown or black, often a mixture of the two, it is growing in size and is larger than the blunt end of a pencil, it is becoming itchy and painful, it is inflamed with a reddish edge, it is bleeding, oozing or crusting. If you are fair or have more than 50 moles, you may be at increased risk of MM, especially if any of your moles are unusually large, multi-coloured or irregularly shaped. A family history of MM increases the risk.

Now I am ultra careful about exposure to the sun. I still get scaly bits on my scalp and I make a point of getting a good dermatologist to give me a check-up every other year. I still surf and that means going into the water covered in a high factor sunscreen that will stay on for several hours. I still get tanned after a few days of surfing somewhere hot and sunny, but because I get enough protection from the cream I use, I don't get badly burnt. Even the best creams won't protect you completely. But it's either a steadily built-up tan – not ideal but it could be worse – or I give up surfing, and as surfing is my passion in life, I take the risk – carefully.

Basal cell carcinomas, also known as rodent skin ulcers, are common, and solar keratoses, the least dangerous form of sun-induced skin lesion, are even commoner, but equally, are pretty harmless. They tend to occur more frequently the older you get, especially from the age of 50 or so onwards, and especially if you are challenged on top in the rug department.

Even BCCs are not threatening unless left untreated for a long time. I had my eyelid BCC for two years before I realized it was more than a stye. A rarer form of skin cancer is squamous cell carcinoma, and this too only becomes threatening if left untreated.

About 100,000 people are treated each year in the UK for the lesser forms of skin cancer, but it's malignant melanoma (malignant moles) that's the killer. Sunburn makes melanoma twice as likely, especially if you are fair-skinned or freckly and were badly sunburnt as a child or young man. If you were (and I mean a sunburn bad enough to cause blistering and peeling skin), you have all the more reason to avoid getting burnt again in later years. About 85% of all skin cancers are thought to be attributable to sun exposure, with sunburn (rather than simply steady tanning over the years from say an outdoor job) being the real culprit.

Now cancer researchers have identified a gene that is implicated in between 15% and 20% of melanomas. The gene known as RAS is susceptible to sun damage and when this occurs, a malignant melanoma is more likely to occur.

Mole mapping has become popular in recent years in the private sector. You get your moles looked at and photographed and then compare them a year late to see if they have changed for the worse. This approach seems to me to be a bit over the top and just another money-spinner for the private clinics, unless of course you have the time and money as well as sufficient inclination. Usually, if you think you are at risk, a good once-over visually by an experienced dermatologist is a good idea, including a look at your scalp, unless your hair is particularly thick. What matters is not just how moles look, but whether they are changing and if so, how fast.

There may be big advantage to having a lot of moles, even if it means a slightly increased risk of skin cancer. A recent discovery is that people with more moles age more slowly and are less likely to develop heart disease and osteoporosis.

I've suggested that sun tanning and skin cancers are moving down the social scale. True, the signs are not there yet in the lowest 20% of the population by income. In fact many dermatologists still see the problem as a middle class one, but it has been suggested recently that this may only be because middle class people are more likely to seek medical help when they have a suspicious skin lesion. In other words, the theory that the problem is moving downmarket but is masked by the reluctance of the working classes to seek medical help, despite their growing love of overseas holidays and a tan to bring home as a souvenir, would appear to have credibility. As I have suggested, at the top end of the market, the problem is declining as the better educated increasingly avoid getting burnt in the first place.

However, there's also the time lag factor. Rich kids fifty years ago may well have got sunburnt then and thought nothing of it. If they are rich adults today, they may be paying the price in skin damage. However, the chances are that they are now better informed than they were in the Fifties and Sixties, and if they do get a suspicious- looking mole, perhaps one that darkens and changes shape and shade fairly rapidly, they will probably know what to do about it. I had a mole on my chest a few years ago and it was looking a bit suspicious. I went to see a dermatologist about something else. He spotted the mole and removed it under local anaesthetic on the spot, just in case. The mole was duly examined by the pathology lab and turned out not to be malignant. Better safe than sorry.

Sunscreens, it turns out, mainly protect from UVB rays (up to 80% of rays are filtered out), but it's the UVA rays, which are more dangerous, which sunscreens are less effective at blocking, and which cause most skin damage. UVA rays compromise the effectiveness of the immune system as well. Ultraviolet light hitting the skin gives rise to free radicals which damage the skin and contribute to the ageing process. The best known antidote to free radical damage is anti-oxidants. So now we have on the market sunscreens which contain various anti-oxidants derived from the likes of green tea, cranberries and grapeseed, as well as vitamins A, C and E, the so-called anti-oxidant vitamins. It seems clear that anti-oxidants can help to repair skin damage – when eaten. What has yet to be demonstrated is whether anti-oxidants added to a sunscreen penetrate the skin sufficiently to be of any use. Without further evidence, it seems wise to consider this a sales tactic, and to treat with scepticism the claims made for the many new sunscreens on the market, including those containing ferulic acid (but see my comments below on nanoparticle research and dermal absorption).

When it comes to repairing wrinkly and sun-damaged skin, you will hear the word retinol again and again. Retinol is a form of vitamin A and is widely touted in skin creams in concentrations up to 0.4%. It's a form of vitamin A and has been claimed to reduce normal age-related wrinkles in old people, but properly controlled tests to show reversal of skin damage caused by the sun are still lacking. Retinol is not without its side effects. These include irritation, and the skin may thin and become sensitised to sunlight. Body chemistry converts retinol to tretinoin (retinoic acid), which is an active form of vitamin A. Retinol and tretinoin creams can produce skin benefits, but if they contain more than token amounts, they are only available on prescription owing to their side effects.

Retinol 0.25% cream, available only on prescription, does have some positive effect on ageing skin generally, as well as sun-damaged skin (see below) in particular. It tends to cause a slight reddishness in the skin when first applied and this may take several months to disappear if you continue to use the cream. I have tried it to reduce age spots on my face, those darker pigmentation marks that are left as suntans fade and you get older. I can report that after about six months of applying the cream lightly twice a day, the marks fade somewhat, but do not disappear. I get the impression that even indefinite use of the cream would not get rid of them once and for all. If you do feel like trying it, get a prescription from your doctor. Retinol works by speeding up the process of skin renewal and allegedly improves skin elasticity by stimulating collagen and elastin production. It also controls keratin production. But do not waste money on expensive retinoid face creams, most of which are marketed for women and tend to be expensive. Other natural products that are said to repair sun damage to the skin are vitamin B3 (niacin), vitamin B5 (pantothenic acid), vitamin E and the dipeptide carnosine.

Can food and supplements help ward off sun damage to the skin and heal the damage that may already have occurred? Allegedly they can. Foods rich in anti-oxidants combat free radical damage and sun exposure is said to trigger the release of free radicals. Essential fatty acids help, and these can be derived from oily fish, which also provide vitamin D. Dark green leafy vegetables, carrots and sweet potatoes provide carotenoids, which help with sun protection, as does the lycopene found in tomatoes.

Liver spots, age spots, sun spots – there are several terms that refer to the patches of brown skin that many of us develop on the backs of our hands and on our faces if we have been exposed to a lot of strong sunlight in our lives. Women are more likely than men to be treated for this kind of skin damage, but there is no reason why the same kind of treatment should not be applied to men. A number of clinics now offer a combination of laser treatment and intense pulsated light (IPL) therapy. This deals with broken capillaries as well. Brown liver spots become darker after treatment and this skin patch falls off after about a week. Usually at least two treatments are needed and prices vary considerably from clinic to clinic.

Researchers in Italy claim to have discovered that lutein can help protect us against harmful UV radiation. Lutein is an anti-oxidant found in plants and vegetables. It protects plant chlorophyll from ultraviolet damage. The research claims that lutein – in this case lutein derived from marigold flowers and known as FloraGLO – can protect human skin from oxidative damage caused by free radicals in the same way that it protects plants. It hydrates the skin when taken orally as a supplement, but may also, allegedly, be absorbed through the skin to give increased protection. This suggests that there may be something to the claims of the manufacturers promoting their expensive anti-oxidant sunscreens, but if so, lutein may have an advantage in being more than just an anti-oxidant – it's also nature's answer to attacks on chlorophyll by ultraviolet. But we should remember that human beings are not plants and our skin is not filled with chlorophyll and photo-protective lutein. In any event, eating plenty of spinach, watercress, red peppers, romaine lettuce and kale will provide plenty of lutein and do you a world of good, whether it really gives you added sun protection or not. The effect will be negated, though, by alcohol consumption.

Recently came news that US scientists are developing a skin cream that can cause the skin to tan without exposure to UV rays and therefore without the risk of skin damage. The cream is said to turn on chemically the skin's natural tanning function. The research was based on work with genetically modified (GM) mice. The cream simulates the fair skin of red-haired people. Previously it had been accepted dogma that the oxidative impact of UV rays caused DNA damage in skin cells, melanin (from melanocytes, the melanin-producing cells) and the consequent tanning effect being the body's natural protective response. The research discovered that in red-haired fair-skinned people, who cannot tan, there is a receptor called MCIR on the surface of their melanocytes which is different from the MCIR receptor of others.

MCIR reacts in response to a hormone, MSH, generated by the sun's rays, and this process leads to production of a chemical called cAMP. High levels of cAMP induce more melanin production, giving a deeper tan. The 'abnormal' MCIR receptor in fair-skinned people prevents this production of melanin. This discovery led to tests on the GM mice to see whether the tanning response of the melanocytes could be induced without exposure to UV rays. The mice were duly treated with a substance called forskolin. The mice turned a nice tan colour and this was found to protect them against skin cancer. Further research should show whether forskolin will penetrate the human skin sufficiently to produce the same effect and allow men to get a tan without putting themselves at risk of skin cancer – assuming that they still want a tan in the first place. However, it's my bet that this kind of a tan, if it ever becomes available, will carry its own risks, as yet unknown. Still, that could be preferable to the skin damage caused by too much exposure to sunlight.

There's another way in which sunlight damages your skin. UV rays go through the epidermis to the dermis, where they alter the texture of a substance called hyaluronic acid. This normally has the consistency of a plump egg white. Attacked by UV rays, this acid will shrivel over time, leaving your skin looking old and dried out.

Let's get back to the problem of the solar keratosis, since this is the commonest form of sun-induced lesion found on men's skin. I've said that a solar keratosis is generally harmless and that is true, provided that you deal with it or it goes away naturally, as sometimes happens.

However, some keratoses turn into squamous cell carcinoma which, although uncommon, can be fatal in cases where it is allowed to get to the point of no return. This transformation is thought to be exacerbated when the human papilloma or wart virus (HPV) is present. One should be aware therefore that malignant melanoma is not the only potentially fatal form of skin cancer. Your risk of skin cancer is not insubstantial when you are younger, but grows as you get older, and it is over the age of fifty, especially if you have overexposed your body to the sun, that you will start to notice all kinds of scaly bits on your skin. I notice them especially on my legs, but these are harmless small patches that tell me that my skin is not able to renew itself as well or as quickly as it once could.

Solar keratoses affect some 60% of men over 40 in the sunnier parts of the USA, and some 68% of older men in Australia. Figures in the UK are lower but rising, the figure for Liverpool, for example, being 15% of older men. The figure for southern England is thought to be higher.

Much debate in the worlds of dermatology, sunscreens and anti-ageing face creams centres around the vexed question of how much or how little of a given substance can genuinely be said to be absorbed through the skin to a level where it is effective. Into this debate has come nanotechnology and what are called nanosomes, particles about 80,000 times thinner than a human hair. No one knows yet how safe these are, but nanoparticles of pro-retinol A have already appeared in creams on the cosmetics market. US research claims that these particles are safe when applied to the skin, and the evidence suggests that they really do penetrate the epidermis through to the dermis. But whether they are effective there as a skin restorative remains to be seen. If they do work effectively, sunscreens with nanoparticles of anti-oxidants will probably not be far behind.

On a positive note, moderate exposure to sunlight is not just a good thing to give us plenty of vitamin D and prevent us from getting rickets. Vitamin D can also help in the prevention of lung and colon cancer, depression, pain, cardiovascular disease, hypertension, psoriasis, multiple sclerosis, TB and rheumatoid arthritis. It can also boost fertility and reduce the symptoms of diabetes.

CHAPTER THIRTY-SEVEN
SLEEP PERCHANCE
TO DREAM

When you think about it, isn't it surprising how much some of us will pay for a car compared with the amount we are prepared to spend on a bed? Yet we spend much more of our lives in bed than we do in a car.

Sleep is still something of a mystery. Go without it for several days – a common form of torture – and you will die. There are two distinct kinds of sleep – deep sleep (non-REM sleep) which is dreamless and rapid eye movement (REM) sleep which is lighter and in which we dream. The first seems to be mainly about recharging our batteries and repairing brain cells, with systems shut down or running in low gear. Non-REM sleep usually takes place in the first hours of sleep. Muscles are relaxed or paralysed, reflexes go into automatic mode, metabolism slows down and the body rids itself of chemical toxins. Higher brain activity ceases.

The second type of sleep, in which we dream, is still a great puzzle. It could be that it serves a number of functions, chief among these being the need to file away thoughts and events and perhaps, unconsciously, make sense of these in a symbolic way. REM sleep occurs more in the latter part of the night, up to the time when we wake up.

Most of us do not get enough sleep – or enough quality sleep. About 5% of the population is not just sleepy but excessively sleepy. In the UK the average adult sleeps for only about seven hours each night. Research suggests that most of us need between eight and nine hours of good sleep. Yet the pressures of life mean that many of us get less sleep than our bodies are telling us they need. For the worried well that clearly presents a dilemma. If we want to live longer, we'd rather be awake when we do so. My advice is to find your natural sleep pattern and go with it. What time you may spend unconscious will be more than made up in extra years and quality of life. We talk about exercise and nutrition in the same breath when really we should be talking about exercise, nutrition and sleep – all equally important for the worried well. Sleep is rest and one of the most important aspects of exercise and activity is rest because it is recovery time.

Don't be a cheapskate when it comes to beds. Most people will sleep best on a mattress that's not too soft and not too hard. The idea that a very firm mattress is good for you, especially if you suffer from lower back pain, has now been discredited. Get a mattress that's big enough to stretch out on, and if you are tall this may mean getting a mattress and bed specially made. I like a bed 7' by 7', preferably all to myself for a better night's rest, but I have to share my bed with my wife, so here's a useful tip. Unless you like cuddling up and playing spoons as some young couples do, get a bed with a slatted base for the mattress and actually have two mattresses side by side instead of one. Then you can have separate duvets, and in a bed 7' wide, you have effectively got two single beds. Yet you can always snuggle up with your partner at a moment's notice if you want to. Chances are that you will end up with different TOG ratings for your individual duvets. This way you get the best of both worlds.

What gets in the way of a good night's sleep? Alarm clocks, for a start. We all know from experience that the trouble with alarm clocks is that our inner alarm usually beats us to it and we wake up just before the external alarm goes off. Don't set the external alarm, though, and chances are you will sleep in. I tend to use an alarm clock only if I really have to get up at an early hour – perhaps to catch a plane. Otherwise I recommend waking up naturally. I appreciate that that's a luxury that isn't available to everyone, but it really is the best way if you can manage it. That way you sleep as much as you need to.

Windows open or windows shut? Curtains open or curtains drawn? That is one of the battlegrounds on which my marriage is played out. My wife likes the windows open and curtains open all year round. We both agree on windows being open in the summer, but I believe that cold damp air is bad for the lungs. The solution is to have the central heating on in winter at a level that is sufficient to warm the cold air coming in a slightly open window. The problem is that the warming of the air may also dry it out too much. The lungs are at their best when provided with warm and slightly damp air, the kind of air that comes in during the summer, provided that you don't suffer from hay fever. Really cold damp air can cause bronchial congestion in the vulnerable.

And the curtains? We're still battling over that one. I like them closed in order not to be woken by daylight, so that I can wake up in my own good time. My wife is an early riser and likes to be woken by the light, even at 5 am in the summer. So far, we have compromised a bit, and the curtains (which have blackout linings) are left closed barring a thin sliver to let in the glow from street lighting and the dawn.

Dust mites can be a problem, or worse still, bed mites (see chapter on allergies). Both can be treated with sprays that are moderately effective and this is a lot cheaper than replacing mattresses and pillows. To those who are vulnerable, allergies are a real plague, and often they are worst in bed at night. If you live in a city, it's possible that you will acquire a respiratory impairment of some sort from vehicle fumes – mainly carbon monoxide as well as particulate matter from diesel fumes. It's worse if you are one of the growing number suffering from asthma, which is frequently caused by in-home air pollution. Sleeping with the windows closed may lessen the risks of respiratory problems, while at the same time depriving us of 'fresh' air. It was common in the first half of the twentieth century for the rich to visit sanatoriums high in the Swiss Alps if they suffered from tuberculosis or other maladies affecting the lungs. While such visits are no longer fashionable, they had their merits, as anyone will know from experience who has trekked high in the Himalayas or skied at one of the particularly high resorts in France or Switzerland. Once you're acclimatised to the altitude, it's amazing how quickly breathing can become free and easy so far from allergens and traffic pollution.

The ideal bedroom situation for a couple is one in which the bed is big and is split into two beds within the bed frame. The curtains are pulled closed, the windows are almost closed in winter and are open in summer. There is no alarm clock and you wake slowly at your own pace after sleeping between eight and nine hours. The mattress is neither too hard nor too soft, and you sleep under a down duvet that is varied in TOG rating according to the season of the year and the room temperature.

There is central heating, but it is turned down to a modest level so that the room is never hot and stuffy. In fact it should be slightly chilly in the room in the middle of the night. And unless you are allergic to down, your head lies on a good down pillow. If you are allergic, the pillow and duvet, like your mattress, can be covered with zipped hypoallergenic covers. From time to time your mattress is turned over and reversed end to end – a bit like rotating car tyres periodically. It's also sprayed against dust mites, though I don't think this is something that can ever be conquered completely.

I write this as a worried well person who does suffer from nasal congestion caused by allergic reaction to all sorts of things in the room and coming through the window. The result is that I snore slightly from time to time. That isn't a problem for me, but it is for my wife. Snoring can be a real problem in some marriages and has been known to lead to separate bedrooms and even divorce. In the UK, 15 million people, mainly men, are estimated to be snorers. The worst kind of snoring is associated with sleep apnoea, which affects about half a million people in the UK. This is a malady which results in the sufferer snoring in a rising crescendo before ceasing to breathe for periods of up to fifteen or twenty seconds at a time, before starting to breathe again, often with a roar. More seriously, these people may be inclined to heart attack, although the reasons for this are not understood. Between one and two percent of adult males in the UK are thought to suffer from sleep apnoea. It's also associated with high blood pressure, increased risk of heart attack and stroke, and if you are a sufferer, your chances of falling asleep while driving increase sixfold as you are likely to be tired from waking up again and again in the night. Sleep apnoea sufferers tend to have poor concentration and feel tired most of the time.

Men suffering from serious sleep apnoea may benefit from continuous positive airway pressure (CPAP). This counters the central problem, the periodic closure of the airway. A mask is worn during sleep and air is forced into the airway to keep it open. The treatment is available on the NHS for moderate and severe cases.

It's important that any treatment for snoring is based on an accurate diagnosis, especially if surgery is going to be involved. Often it may not be possible to prevent snoring. Those who suffer from sleep apnoea should consult an ENT specialist, however, as the problem can be life-threatening.

An Ear, Nose and Throat (ENT) consultant will usually inspect your nasal passages using a flexible endoscope to take a look at the back of your throat, your larynx, your nasal cavity, your sinuses and your nasopharynx (the passage from the nasal cavity to the back of the throat). He'll be looking for nasal polyps, signs of sinusitis, or blockages that may be caused by enlarged turbinates or a deviated septum – or, assuming you haven't got a virus or bacterial infection, signs of swollen membranes caused by an allergy. You could have an enlarged uvula, tonsillitis, asthma, or pre- or post-nasal drip. Allergic rhinitis may be chronic or seasonal. The consultant may take a sample of tissue or mucus for analysis if they suspect a serious infection. If surgery is undertaken, it may be done under local or general anaesthetic.

Most people snore a bit when they have a cold – women too, though it's true that it's more often a male problem. Some people only snore when they are sleeping on their back. Despite the advertisements you will see for cures for snoring, most of these will not work or will only work partially. Some may even do damage if done by unqualified practitioners. With so many possible causes of snoring, it isn't surprising that there is no simple cure, which is why consultants will often advise living with the problem if it's chronic. Surgery should not be undertaken lightly.

A snorer's partner can suffer from loss of sleep. One third of bed partners are woken nightly, and one half occasionally by the snoring of their bedmate. The resulting loss of sleep can make them drowsy and anxious the following day.

Shakespeare was undoubtedly right when he pronounced sleep a blessed thing. For those who are tired, it can come as a great relief. For those who are driving while tired, it can be a life-saver, provided that it doesn't occur while actually driving. A great many road accidents are caused by drivers falling asleep at the wheel, and the older you are, the more likely this is. If you feel drowsy while driving, pull over somewhere safe and have a nap in the car. Some cars are now being built with an alarm device that will sound if your car starts to wander off your side of the road. This may be mandatory in a few years. Between 10% and 20% of fatal road accidents are attributed to a driver falling asleep at the wheel.

Our energy levels tend to have two peaks in the day, the first soon after we wake up and the second around mid to late afternoon. It has been found that having a short sleep in the middle of the day can leave you refreshed and ready for whatever the remaining waking hours can throw at you. It used to be called a siesta and is now more likely to be called power napping. You don't have to be Spanish and it doesn't have to be for two hours after a heavy lunch. A couple of thirty minute naps at your desk may do the trick, though a nearby sofa to stretch out on is a better bet. According to one study, that is all you need to cut your risk of cardiovascular disease by 64% if you are a working man. If you do not work, the improvement is still a worthwhile 36%. These findings seem to suggest that working men, who are probably more stressed, have more to gain by taking a nap in the middle of the day. It may even explain the French paradox (see chapter 3 on alcohol) – Frenchmen and others living a Mediterranean lifestyle may suffer fewer heart attacks, not because they drink red wine, but because they get adequate amounts of sleep thanks to their long lunch and siesta routine.

Seemingly, even such short breaks can have a significant effect on our level of restedness and wakefulness afterwards. As we get older, we may find ourselves nodding off anyway, especially after a meal, so why not turn this into a virtue and lie down properly for a short while. If you sleep for longer than twenty minutes, your body is probably telling you that you need more sleep. Listen to it (assuming you won't lose your job over this) and sleep for half an hour. I say this with one reservation, though. I've sometimes found that if I sleep in the daytime I find my regular sleep pattern disrupted and it may be difficult to get to sleep at night. It's thought that more than thirty minutes in the middle of the day will produce this effect later on.

Sleep is induced in various ways. It helps to be tired and it helps to have a routine and go to bed at the same time each night. A warm bath in the evening also helps, as does not eating anything in the two to three hours before going to sleep. Switch off your mobile phone. A nightcap such as a milky hot chocolate will help according to a recent study. Milk contains the amino acid tryptophan, which is a precursor of melatonin and serotonin, both of which can help you relax – unless of course you suffer from benign prostatic hyperplasia (BPH) (see chapter on the prostate), in which case you would be better off not drinking anything for at least three hours before going to sleep. Otherwise you are only adding to the number of trips to take a pee in the middle of the night. I find that reading puts me to sleep pretty easily, and a good novel is probably the best bet.

A lot of people watch TV in bed before going to sleep and I admit to being one of them. I'm not sure that this is conducive to sleep. Perhaps it depends on what you watch. I like to watch the news at ten o'clock, and given the fact that most news is bad news, I'm inclined to think I would sleep better and have more pleasant dreams if I did not watch anything, or watched something more restful. A fevered imagination is not a good recipe for a good night's sleep. A good tip is to take the TV out of the bedroom altogether.

It's a well researched fact that people who are depressed or anxious, and people who have depleted self-esteem (the three often go together) sleep poorly. Insomnia is thought to affect between 15% and 20% of the population at any time, and this is not surprising, given the high incidence of depression.

An alcoholic drink at bedtime is definitely not good for your health as alcohol interferes with sleep, including the benefits of filing away our thoughts and memories in our dreams. Added to which, alcohol is a depressant, which is the last thing a depressed person needs. So a healthy nightcap is a hot chocolate, not an eggnog with a shot or two of whisky. Coffee is a big no-no, of course, being a stimulant. The caffeine triggers the release of the stress hormone cortisol and keeps you awake. Coffee should be avoided within six hours of going to sleep. If you exercise before going to bed, this will also prevent you from falling asleep easily, and exercise also produces cortisol.

Should you take drugs to help you sleep? The answer is 'no' unless you are desperate. It is now established that while sleeping pills may get you off to sleep, they will not ensure restful sleep and you are likely to wake up feeling tired, quite apart from a long list of nasty side effects.

Melatonin is a powerful hormone produced by the pineal gland (the mystic 'third eye' of Hindu tradition). We produce melatonin naturally when we are ready to go to sleep. Some people advise taking it as a supplement to reset your body clock on long distance flights across several time zones (see chapter 2 on air travel). My advice is don't touch the artificial version. For a start I don't believe that it does reset your body clock. It's not for nothing that it's banned in the UK as an over-the-counter supplement. Like all hormone supplements, it carries risks and should be avoided. I've tried it once and once was enough. It left me feeling as though I had something seriously wrong with me – a mixture of psychologically and physically wrong, yet hard to describe. It wasn't quite a depressed feeling, but almost.

What does sleep actually do to our bodies? If we don't get enough of it, we produce more of the stress hormone cortisol (which is bad), and less growth hormone (GH), when more is better. Too little sleep reduces production of adenosine triphosphate (ATP), the energy molecules in our muscles, with the result that we feel tired. If we live in a city, melatonin production comes into play roughly between 9 pm and 8 am. Our nights are artificially lit by electricity, but once our circadian (body clock) rhythms were dictated by natural light and dark, and this varied with the seasons. When we do go to bed, it is best if there are no intrusive lights, not even street lights brightening the bedroom through the curtains or blinds. The darker the better. It seems that a little light while we sleep may even increase the risk of some cancers, which is why blind people have a reduced cancer risk

Lifelong lack of sufficient sleep leads to cardiovascular problems, faster ageing (and a shorter life), and a weakened immune system. It may also lead to damage to brain cells, loss of memory, impaired learning ability, lowered energy levels and reduced creativity. Fail to sleep enough and you will eat more than your body needs – the surplus will be stored as fat. Blood pressure may rise, together with the risk of obesity and diabetes. In fact the current epidemic of obesity may be partly linked to the trend towards shorter sleeping hours.

It might seem paradoxical at first glance – that by sleeping more we might lose weight. Aren't fat people supposed to be lazy and spend more time in bed? What research shows is that although we may burn more calories while awake, we are also giving ourselves more time to snack and eat too much. A study of narcolepsy, in which sufferers fall asleep suddenly for no apparent reason, has shown that sleep and appetite are controlled by a type of brain chemical called orexins. People with narcolepsy are short of orexins and fall asleep easily. This led to the discovery that insufficient sleep causes changes in the hormones regulating appetite. When people have low levels of the hormone leptin and high levels of the hormone ghrelin, they feel hungry. The role of leptin in appetite control was already well known – what was new was the discovery that these people also have inadequate sleep, typically less than eight hours and sometimes as little as five hours per night. They also tend to crave carbohydrates.

The story did not stop there. It seems that the EP3 receptor, a protein switch which responds to the hormone Prostaglandin E2 (PGE2) may be lacking or inadequate in people with a tendency to overeat, and these people may be getting less sleep than they need. Further research is needed, but this angle on the obesity dilemma is interesting. Ten years ago, no one would have linked obesity with inadequate sleep. The pressures of our hyper western lifestyle seem to account for the trend towards fewer hours of sleep. But evolution takes place slowly and we are still programmed to a seasonal life without the alleged benefits of artificial light. Were we still living in caves, it is thought we would be sleeping at least nine hours per night on average and possibly up to ten hours – more in the winter and less in the summer.

Should you sleep longer at the weekend, perhaps to make up for lack of sleep during the week? Catching up is better than nothing, but your body should ideally have the same hours of sleep each night, including weekends. If you have an extra hour on Saturday and Sunday mornings, your body clock will be thrown out on Monday and Tuesday when you revert to shorter hours. You will then feel sleepy at the beginning of the week and your immune system will be less resilient.

The main cause of insomnia is anxiety in all its forms.

Many people swear by valerian, a herbal remedy, as a good soporific, something that will help you to get to sleep if you're anxious. Nutrients in valerian raise levels of the neurotransmitter GABA, which helps induce sleep and also relaxes the muscles in the bowel, helping those who suffer from irritable bowel syndrome (IBS). It's best taken as a tincture half an hour before sleep, perhaps in camomile tea mixed with a little honey as a sweetener.

The body's energy level goes up and down around the clock. From around 6 pm to 8 pm is a high energy period for most people, while low periods tend to be after lunch (siesta time) and from 2 am to 6 am.

Here are some interesting facts from a recent survey:
   86% of couples sleep in the same bed
   66% of partners agree on when to go to sleep and when to get up
   32% of men claim that they never snore
   37% of men say that they are never woken at night by their partner
   60% of people never talk in their sleep
   67% of people never sleep through the alarm clock going off
   53% of people never use the snooze function on the alarm clock
   78% of men rarely or never pray before going to sleep
   Most people go to sleep between 10 pm and midnight during the week and an hour later at weekends
   Most people wake up between 6 am and 7 am during the week, and an hour later at weekends
   3% of men admit to taking a cuddly toy to bed
   36% of men sleep in the nude – this peaks in the 45–64 age group, then falls sharply
   62% of men sometimes or rarely remember their dreams
   36% of people have a preference for the right side of the bed
   57% of men fall asleep on their left or right side, 12% on their front and 10% on their back. The rest vary or don't know.
   59% of men sleep 6–8 hours per night during the week, and 17% sleep 8–10 hours. This changes to 47% and 35% respectively at weekends
   60% of people think they get about the right amount of sleep, but 36% claim not to get enough

CHAPTER THIRTY-EIGHT
THE FAG END OF LIFE

I have just read that a woman has quit smoking at the age of 107 – not to avoid lung cancer or to live longer, but because she could no longer be bothered to go to the trouble of lighting up. So it's possible to give up at any age.

There is not much to say about smoking cigarettes that has not been said many times before. The worried well are unlikely to be smokers, though some may be former smokers who succeeded in giving up. The overall number of smokers in the UK has declined in recent years, but this trend masks the fact that more teenagers than ever before are smoking and the big increase has been among girls. The heaviest smokers are to be found in the 20–24 age group. At the other end of the spectrum, older males and females have quit in their tens of thousands in the last thirty years, especially at the upper end of the socio-economic scale, where smokers are now almost non-existent. This suggests that those who are better informed about the risks are more likely to quit.

However, if you correlate this finding with levels of obesity, you find that smoking and obesity are equally problems at the lower end of the socio-economic scale. If those higher up the ladder are better educated and better informed about the risk, this is only a partial explanation of the difference. Even the poorest member of society would be hard-pressed not to be aware of the dangers associated with smoking. At risk of not being politically correct, I suggest that there is a failure of will, not knowledge, the further down the scale you go. A psychologist might define this as lack of impulse control, an inability to say 'no' when it comes to cigarettes, or food that may taste good but may not be very healthy. It should come as no surprise that smoking rates are highest among the unemployed.

The damage that smoking tobacco can do was suspected as far back as the early seventeenth century when King James 1 wrote and published a book about this dirty new habit from the New World. In those days, smoking was all pipe smoking. Cigarettes were a Spanish invention in the nineteenth century. Over the centuries, cadavers were cut up by generations of medical students, and lungs were examined, many exhibiting the damaging signs of nicotine and other chemical compounds found in tobacco. The link to lung cancer was assumed long ago. It was only in the last sixty years that those fighting the financial muscle and influence of the big tobacco companies were able to prove the link In the UK about 35,000 people die each year from lung cancer and about 90% of these cases are caused by smoking. The disease tends to be diagnosed late, in which case the prognosis is poor. In 1950 no less than 82% of men in the UK were smokers. From 1950 cigarettes became publicly synonymous with lung cancer, but in recent years a growing list of the terrible things that smoking can do to your body has appeared, and each year something new is added.

The list makes for sobering reading. Smoking can cause or exacerbate the following:

Lung cancer
Heart disease
Emphysema
Bronchitis
Immune system damage
Stroke
Sleep apnoea
Pharyngitis
Tonsilitis
Laryngitis
Cancer of the nasopharynx
Cancer of the larynx
Cancer of the mouth (which accounts for one sixth of all cancers in the UK)
Cancer of the oesophagus
Cancer of the bladder
Cancer of the cervix

Diabetes
Asthma
Sinusitis
Chronic rhinitis
Male pattern baldness
Penile vasoconstriction resulting in erectile dysfunction
Peptic ulcers
Damage to foetus
Lowered fertility
Acceleration of skin damage associated with ageing
Snoring
Irritation of the soft palate
Impaired memory
Impaired mental function, especially in the right hemisphere
Reduced blood glucose level
Raised level of the stress hormone cortisol
Gum disease (six times more common than in non-smokers)
Reduction in iron
Reduction in B vitamins

With a list like this, it's perhaps surprising that anyone still smokes, unless they have a death wish. Many do give up smoking and among adults in the UK, it's thought that only about 30% now smoke. Many people have quit and some have never started. It is said that a heavy smoker loses a day of their life for every packet they smoke. Another dictum I have heard is that it will take as many years not smoking as you smoked to clear your body of the damage done. Smoke for twenty years and it will take another twenty to get rid of the signs. While these are broad and unproven generalisations, it seems probable that the damage done by every cigarette can never be completely undone, and even those who quit will always pay some price for their addictive habit. Another saying about smokers is that they die ten years younger than the average age for the population.

For years lung cancer got all the publicity, but as you can see from the list above, there's a lot more to the damage that smoking can do. Serious smokers develop 'sticky' blood. Platelets increasingly clump together, making thrombosis more likely. At the same time, carbon monoxide from cigarette smoke removes oxygen from the blood, leaving the heart undersupplied with oxygen.

One of the battles fought against cigarettes has been the campaign to stop 'environmental tobacco smoke' – so-called passive smoking. The lobby for a ban on smoking in public places has made big progress in recent years, but hard evidence that passive smoking is damaging to non-smokers has proved hard to come by. There is little doubt that passive smoking cannot be good for you and probably causes some impairment. The problem has been in identifying cause and effect. The official figure for UK deaths per annum as a result of passive smoking is around the 600 mark, but that is deaths. It says nothing of the damage that passive smoking might cause without a fatal result.

Smokers are easily addicted, it is said. But can smoking have any positive side effects apart from the feeling of relaxation and wellbeing that comes from smoking? This enhancement of mood results from the release of beta-endorphins in the brain. Research has established that smokers are less likely to get Parkinson's disease, a neurological disorder affecting movement. Nerve cells in the part of the brain which controls movement called dopaminergic neurons are lost in Parkinson's disease. The disorder is usually treated with dopamine, which calms the shaky movements of the sufferer. Smoking triggers the release of dopamine, so that there is less need for dopamine supplementation. Not everyone who smokes benefits equally, suggesting there may be a genetic factor at work.

Scientists have identified a cluster of genes that are linked to a propensity to get lung cancer. Those who inherit one copy of the cluster have an increased risk of lung cancer, and this risk rises further if two copies are inherited. However, the overall increased risk is limited if the person is a non-smoker. The picture is different if they smoke and the chances of a smoker getting lung cancer if they have inherited two copies of the gene (one from either parent) are considerable. The gene cluster in question is found on chromosome 15, and interestingly, there appears to be a link not just with lung cancer but also with the circulatory problem classified as peripheral arterial disease (PAD), which matches the fact that smokers are not just at risk of lung cancer but also of serious cardio-vascular problems.

What this discovery shows clearly is that a disease like lung cancer has a strong genetic component, in addition to the obvious environmental factor. When you consider the degree to which factors, genetic or environmental, may increase the chances of lung cancer or any other disease, it's important to get a sense of perspective. If your chances of getting say cancer double from 1 in 10,000 to 1 in 5,000, the odds are still strongly in your favour. However, if they change to 1 in 4, that's a different matter. Improvements in the odds with most diseases as a result of one therapy or another are more likely to be like the first of these examples, but in some cases such as lung cancer for smokers with two copies of the gene cluster I have described, the second example is a better picture of the odds you start with. In fact the exact odds are calculated at 23 in 100. Knowing you have the gene cluster may in the future encourage more people to abandon smoking or never start.

Smokers, like the obese, cost the NHS less than healthy non-smokers over their lifetime. That sounds paradoxical at first, but the reason is that those who are really unhealthy die so much younger than the healthy that their care ultimately costs less. The healthy are likely to live a long time and then get cancer or Alzheimer's, both of which are expensive to treat.

....

More Tips and Traps

Smokers are at increased risk of a cerebral or aortic aneurysm – either of which may be fatal if it bursts.

Beta carotene increases the risk of lung cancer in heavy smokers.

Many smokers drink heavily and the combination of the two is known to have a serious multiplier effect on health. Thus those who smoke and drink are thirty times more likely to get mouth cancer.

Heavy smokers tend not only to have bad breath, but also stained teeth and gum disease.

Cigarettes are toxic to the human body. I'm sure that the worried well don't need to be told that, but if you do smoke, it's your funeral.

CHAPTER THIRTY-NINE
SAD: STRESS, ANXIETY AND DEPRESSION

Stress is often associated with what is called the Type A personality: driven, ambitious, multi-tasking, articulate, perfectionistic. But stress isn't always damaging to health, as used to be thought. The key is whether or not you have much control over your own destiny and whether your self-esteem is high or not. If you are all ambition but no autonomy, you are more at risk from stress and the damage it can inflict. That is why men further down the social and employment hierarchy are generally more prone to cardiovascular and other problems than those with more status and higher paid jobs. However, the saying that money doesn't bring happiness is probably true, and often it can be a part of the problem, however much of the stuff you have or don't have.

It does seem true that driven personalities who are successful may still be prone to stress, anxiety and depression if they are never satisfied with their success and are always trying to achieve more, even if others would be more than happy to have achieved so much. Such types probably had a parent, usually a controlling mother, who lived through them and urged them on, yet never gave sufficient praise or any praise at all, always urging the child on to more. For such children, coming second was never going to be enough, and so a sense of failure was perhaps instilled for a lifetime, no matter what was achieved. The lesson is clear and it is an insight that may need the help of a therapist – settle for second place or any place that the world would count a success and provided that you have considerable autonomy, you will be a far happier person.

A few years ago, a writer invented the term Marketing Man to describe the Type A personality. As well as showing many of the features I have described above, Marketing Man exhibits traits of ruthlessness and a tendency to adapt chameleon-like to his surroundings. Often the parents are divorced. These types are manipulative, they tend to treat others as commodities and use them to meet their own ends. They can be distrustful and over-anxious to analyse others' motives. Their relationships often lack depth and commitment. In short, they exhibit narcissistic and psychopathic personality traits. While this may sound sinister, it's a picture that fits a high proportion of today's business leaders and politicians.

Are such men depressed? Some are and some aren't, depending on whether they have come to terms with their limitations, or whether they will always remain driven, forever seeking another million or that elusive knighthood. Coming to terms with one's own human limitations can often best be achieved with a good therapist as guide. The objective will be self-acceptance, the foundation of self-esteem. The outcome, if successful, is likely to mean that you put family and friends before money, celebrity and physical appearances. You give up climbing the social ladder in favour of deepening the relationships you already have or creating new relationships based on a higher set of values. It's easy to see why so many celebrities, having reached the top, cannot handle the slide down the other side of the hill. The result may be not just anxiety and depression, but also substance abuse and deeper mental illness that may become life-threatening.

The signs of stress are anger and frustration, anxiety and depression. Our genetic inheritance plays a part too. Like father like son – or mother – or grandfather for that matter. Men low in serotonin, nitric oxide and MAO-A (an enzyme which breaks down adrenaline) are more prone to anger. Stress raises the hormone cortisol and steers corticosteroids to the hippocampus in the brain, where they can accumulate, impairing memory and sense of self, increasing the anger impulse. Enhanced levels of testosterone and noradrenaline also raise anger levels, as the drunken fights between teenagers on our city streets late at night demonstrate. You won't find many eighty-year-olds out there fighting for no particular reason.

Stress raises levels of prolactin and may reduce levels of testosterone and DHEA sulphates.

Today we can look at stress and analyse it with brain scans and biochemical tests. The outward signs are obvious. The anger may give way to what we commonly call burnout, in which energy, enthusiasm and confidence all fly out the window. Anger quickly elevates adrenaline and slowly elevates cortisol levels. It's cortisol release that wakes us up in the morning. The level peaks a few hours later and then falls, but in people who are depressed or sleep-deprived it remains elevated

A sustained high cortisol level over months and years is now known to weaken the immune system and accelerate ageing. The structures called telomeres, which wrap around chromosome clusters are shorter in people chronically stressed. In fact a consistently high cortisol level can take years off your life, adding to the anger, frustration and misery that raised the level in the first place. Almost always self-esteem is low in such cases.

An interesting recent finding is that people with reduced self-esteem have a smaller than normal hippocampus in their brain. This is thought to make a positive response to stress more difficult. However, the reduction of cortisol to lower than optimum levels in people with burnout suggests that in that particular syndrome the brain acts to save itself from too much damaging cortisol by going to the opposite extreme. So some people produce too much cortisol year in and year out, while others don't produce enough, with the result that they suffer from apathy and lethargy. Apathy may be indicative of depression, but this is not always the case.

Before resorting to pills or therapy or a combination of both, are there simple ways to relieve stress? Here are some suggestions: a holiday really can unwind you and also improve your reaction times, provided you leave the phone and laptop at home and are not unduly harassed by the airport process, which may now cause enough stress to counteract all the good the holiday might do you. As communities are no longer the support structures they once were and as our lives have generally become too hurried in the pursuit of material things, we tend to have fewer friends and see those we have less often. This is a pity as social isolation is one of the biggest stressors, and friends and family are the best answer.

What are some other ways of reducing stress? Exercise needs little further mention at this point. While it raises cortisol levels for a while, and this helps speed up metabolic rate, the cortisol subsides before long and the benefits of the exercise, unless it was excessive, will outweigh any damage. Exercise helps in the battle against depression by improving circulation. Poor circulation is now known to lead to depression. Make sure to get enough sleep and have a regular sleep pattern and this will help to protect your heart. Join a club, take up a hobby, go to church every Sunday, help a cause or a charity on a voluntary basis. You may be surprised at how good you will feel helping others instead of yourself. And look at your sense of humour. If you ever look at the 'Lonely Hearts' columns in the papers, you will see that GSOH (Good Sense of Humour) comes up again and again. Women rate humour close behind intelligence and up there with looks when it comes to looking for a partner.

If you want to find out if your cortisol level is too high, or possibly worse, it is chronically low (what researchers call 'blunted'), get a saliva test done to check the level and then check it again a year later. Once the level is blunted for too long it may be impossible to reverse.

One response to stress is to resort to comfort foods. This can increase the quantity of inflammatory proteins in your body and in turn this can impair your body's response to stress.

'Burnout' is closely linked with chronic fatigue syndrome, better known as ME, and with post-traumatic stress disorder (PTSD) and fibromyalgia.

What does a doctor look for if he suspects that you are suffering from anxiety and depression, (and you will rarely find one without the other)? He – or more commonly 'she' these days – will ask about your sleeping habits. If you're depressed you will sleep poorly and may tend to wake in the early hours of morning. You may lose weight, and this may occur rapidly in cases where there is acute distress, as in a bereavement. The appetite dies from one moment to the next. Speech may slow down and there may be constant rumination, especially if depression is associated with feelings of guilt. (Could I have prevented his/her death?). The depressed man feels tired and his reaction times slow down. His anxiety may make him taciturn, irritable, obsessive and agitated. The doctor will have no lack of questions to ask even without calling on biochemical and neurochemical tests. Psychosomatic symptoms of anxiety may include dizziness, light-headedness, swollen lymph nodes, chest pain, a raised heart rate, sweating and breathing difficulties. Feelings of panic may induce hyperventilation, numbness or tingling in hands and feet and occasionally spasm in the fingers and toes.

The doctor may want to gauge the patient's hedonic tone. This is the term used in measuring the capacity to feel pleasure. Loss of pleasure is known as anhedonia. It's obviously related to hedonism, a word most of us are more familiar with. The person suffering anhedonia will find that he has lost the ability to enjoy things that used to give him pleasure. The pleasure response is no longer operating. Psychiatrists and hospitals have a written test aimed at measuring levels of anxiety and depression called the Hospital Anxiety and Depression (HAD) scale. A variant known as the SHAPS scale is designed to identify those who would best respond to anti-depressant drugs.

You may notice that I haven't used the word 'sadness' at all. This is because sadness is a difficult term in any discussion of depression. Not unreasonably, some counsellors and therapists argue that sadness is a normal part of daily living and should be clearly distinguished from the state that is true depression. But establishing a distinction is about as easy as trying to separate endogenous (home-grown) depression from exogenous (externally triggered) depression. If you lose a loved one, is the feeling one of sadness or depression? And if you decide it is depression and your counsellor agrees and tells you it is exogenous depression, is it still exogenous two years later if you are still depressed, or has it now become endogenous chronic depression because you should be over bereavement from six months to two years after the event, according to the text books? There is no easy answer. I don't believe in the 'stiff upper lip' approach to all of life's knocks, but equally there is something to be said for not reaching for a counsellor every time something goes wrong. Bad things happen. Fact. It may be true, though, that the stronger your immune system, the better you will cope when things go wrong.

There are natural remedies you can take to combat depression, of which the best known is St John's wort from the Hypericum shrub. It's widely used in Germany, but having tried it, I don't think it works. Recently it has been suggested that it may even serve as a mild poison.

Then there is tryptophan, a protein that we get from our diet – salmon and turkey are good sources – and which is found in chocolate. The brain uses tryptophan to make the neurotransmitter serotonin, which lifts mood, lowers anxiety level and helps you to sleep better. As a supplement it's banned in the UK except in the form L-5-hydroxytryptophan, but it's available over the counter in the US. I've tried it and found it to have unpleasant side effects: nausea, light-headedness and headache. I suggest you avoid taking it as a supplement.

Which brings me to prescription drugs for anxiety and depression. Each decade there seems to be a new fashion in pills you can pop (and now even patches that you just stick on your skin), and one by one they all get taken off many doctors' menu as more and more side effects are discovered. We've been through diazepam for mild anxiety and depression, and for serious depression the tricyclic drugs and the monoamine oxidase inhibitors (MAOs). For the last few years, starting with Prozac, we've had a growing number of serotonin selective re-uptake inhibitors (SSRIs) (also known as 5HT re-uptake inhibitors). Now these too are beginning to come in for the inevitable flak as the list of side effects grows. Some research even suggests that they don't work, except for a possible placebo effect. I'm not saying they should not be taken. They may have saved many people from suicide and allegedly driven a few to it. But they are hard to withdraw from, they may need to be taken for several years, they slow cognitive processes and speech, and in about 15% of cases, the depression may return after complete withdrawal.

I suggest that if depression has not become too deep or prolonged, the best cure is a combination of time, counselling or therapy, a healthy diet and plenty of aerobic exercise sufficient to induce the production of endorphins, giving a light sense of euphoria. However, for serious and genuine cases of depression I would agree that resorting to SSRIs for a time, unless the side effects are unbearable, is the way to go, provided that you have a good doctor or psychiatrist to keep an eye on things and a good counsellor or therapist to listen to you empathically. This assumes that they really do work, of course, and I expect we'll find out the answer to that in the next few years. The ability of the big drug companies to convince the market and doctors alike that their drugs work should not be underestimated. Thirty million prescriptions for anti-depressant drugs are written in the UK each year.

Shingles is a recurrence, in adulthood, of a herpes virus, the chickenpox virus that most of us had as children. The varicella–zoster virus can lie latent for decades and re-appear as shingles when the right trigger comes along and immunity is low. This can be the result of age, stress or taking immunosuppressant drugs. I'm including it in this chapter as I've had it and I would guess that the cause was stress, though I cannot be sure.

Shingles is fairly common in middle-aged men and it can be a serious illness if not caught quickly. It tends to appear as a blistering red rash, often painful, that develops rapidly close to the nerve ganglia that has harboured the virus all those years. Treatment is with an antiviral agent, either famciclovir or valocyclovir, taken orally for a week or more. At the same time a cream is applied to the affected area. If treatment is not rapid enough, scarring may result. There is now an anti-chicken pox vaccine available for adults who had chicken pox as children, and this appears to prevent shingles. Just as stress is one of the causes of shingles, depression is one of the after-effects. This is exogenous depression and should pass, though anti-depressants, counselling or therapy may be needed.

Stress is caused by many factors, and loneliness is one of the most significant for most of us as we get older. Already more than half of the UK population lives alone. Stress, particularly the stress of loneliness leads to anxiety and anxiety to depression, which is why they are so often inseparable. Loneliness is a major problem in a society which puts so much emphasis on youth and where communities and the extended family have gone into terminal decline. Loneliness begins in middle age and gets worse in old age. Men suffer more than women as men tend to have few if any close friends with whom to share their problems. The best counter to moderate depression is the message of this book: exercise and a healthy diet. For example, it is said that eating unrefined carbohydrates in the form of whole grain cereals will raise the level of the neurotransmitter serotonin in the brain, making you feel good. The endorphins released by aerobic exercise have the same effect, though they can be dangerous as they leave you feeling mildly stoned, in a sleepy kind of way, and this can be risky if you drive a car in this condition.

The feel-good factor can be engineered a number of ways. The young and the old are, on average, happier than the middle aged, though you would not want to wait for old age to find happiness. If research in the US is to be believed, attending regular monthly meetings, gardening, voluntary work and entertaining all make us happier in ways that money does not. Watching TV, however, has the opposite effect. Laughter is therapeutic, and if you cannot share a drink and a laugh with friends, the next best thing may be buying a few comedy films on DVD and watching them with someone else, as laughter is contagious in company. People who have religious conviction and attend church regularly tend to be happier and live longer, though failing a conversion on the road to Damascus, this option is not open to most of us. True, we can go to church, but real faith cannot be bought or based on reason. In many ways true believers are to be envied.

An overview of depression would not be complete without a look at seasonal affect disorder (SAD). This is unlike other forms of depression, though it may overlap with them. It is said that SAD is a response to a biochemical brain imbalance brought about by reduced daylight hours and sunshine. It's a circadian rhythm disorder, which means that our body clock is affected. Darkness induces melatonin, the sleep hormone, in what is probably a sign of a primitive urge to hibernate and conserve energy during the winter months. SAD normally occurs in autumn and winter, but may also occur in times of unusually dull and rainy spring and summer weather. Reduced serotonin levels make things worse. The cure for SAD for some years was (and for some still is) a powerful light, exposure to which in the days of winter gloom can effectively lift mood by suppressing melatonin production with a light level of as much as 2500 lux. The problem is not only the high cost of the special boxes that emit the right light, but also the time required sitting in front of or very near the machines, usually as much as two hours a day. Now there is a machine that does the same job in thirty minutes and you can get on with other things as long as you are near the light.

For 85% of sufferers, light boxes do seem to work, though a psycho-somatic cure may be partly involved in many cases. In the UK, 90% of the population is said to suffer from some degree of SAD, and I can vouch for my own personal feelings of gloom in winter. It might partly explain why, as we get older, we tend, especially if we are empty nesters, to take our main annual holiday far away in the winter sun and stay in the UK in the summer. Some SAD sufferers will react to the depressed mood induced by nothing more than winter gloom by staying in bed longer, or by comfort eating, thereby putting on extra weight in the winter which they will try to get rid of when spring comes around.

Some of us are said to suffer from a lesser form of SAD, the sub-syn-dromal variety. The sufferer is listless, irritable, hungry and lethargic. In other words they are not truly depressed, just suffering a bit from the winter blues. I'm sure many readers will recognize the feeling. This lesser variety of SAD is five times as common as full-blown SAD. Both forms will respond to normal anti-depressant treatment.

It's said that depression affects all social classes, both sexes and mar-rieds just as much as singles. Depression in men peaks around the age of 50. By the time men reach 70, it's said that they are as happy as they were in their twenties, provided that they are mentally and physically fit.

Amongst doctors, including psychiatrists, there is now a growing reaction to the tendency to medicalise normal sadness by calling it depression and over-prescribing anti-depressant drugs as a result, despite the enormous lobbying power of the drug manufacturers to make us believe that depression is more widespread than it is.

Sadness and true depression share many symptoms, the commonest of which are: insomnia, hypersomnia (oversleeping), fatigue, apathy, loss of weight and change in appetite, depressed mood, lack of interest in other people and activities, physical slowdown, feelings of guilt, feelings of worthlessness, indecisiveness, lack of concentration and thoughts of death or suicide. The more symptoms one has and the longer they last, the more likely it is that there is true depression, especially if there is no obvious cause. The distinction is not clear, however, and it is quite possible for sadness to develop into depression over time.

People with a variant of the gene called 5HTT are more likely to suffer from depression., but only if it is triggered by a stressful life event such as bereavement or job loss, so the theory goes. Others suffering from such life events are likely to be affected by sadness rather than depression.

One of the natural opioids and therefore an anti-depressant that the body makes for itself is oxytocin. It is found in great abundance in lactating women and is less plentiful in men. It is also one of several goodies in chocolate that are known to enhance mood and relieve feelings of depression, leaving you feeling contented. Oxytocin applied experimentally to men via a nasal spray has been found to boost their trust in others and enhance their ability to read facial signals, skills more commonly associated with women.

CHAPTER FORTY
MAKING THE MOST OF YOUR MOUTH

We British have some of the worst teeth in the world thanks to poor dental hygiene and a diet overly rich in sugar. Over fifty percent of Brits admit to having bad teeth and 47% of the population suffer from gingivitis, the periodontal disease which affects the gums. Seventy-two percent of the population have visible plaque on their teeth. Twenty-four percent of people in the UK are said to have halitosis. Only one third of us think we have good teeth. Nineteen out of twenty of us will be affected by gum disease at some time in our lives. And thanks to poor gum health, a large percentage of the population suffers from bad breath.

If you are over forty, chances are that you have more fillings than your children, since painting children's teeth with fluoride was not around when you were growing up. And chances are that your worst fillings have eventually been replaced by crowns. Hopefully, however, you have managed to avoid dentures, implants and bridges. The latter, although now made of porcelain, involve sacrificing the integrity of at least two adjacent teeth.

There are various nasties that can invade your mouth. First of all there is dental caries, the kind of tooth rot that comes from not brushing and flossing enough and leads to cavities which require fillings. A healthy diet, low in sugar, will help support the many good bacteria to be found naturally in saliva. Bad bacteria, however, also colonise your saliva, and it is these which convert sugar into the acid which we know as plaque.

Is eating a lot of fruit good for you, therefore, considering the sugar content is in the form of fructose? As far as I know, fruit sugar, with its low Glycaemic Index (GI) factor compared with sucrose (such as common table sugar) is less conducive to bacteria that cause caries. However, if you have ever seen Third World populations addicted to chewing sugarcane from childhood onwards, with stumps for front teeth, you will realize that even fructose should not be taken to extreme or be regarded as an excuse not to floss or brush. On the other hand, a fruit like cranberries contains the anti-oxidants known as procyanidins (also found in grapeseeds), which are alleged to be helpful in combating gum disease.

A recent researcher came to the conclusion that teeth should be brushed three times a day, after meals, for a minimum of two minutes and only after thorough flossing. I'm guilty of only brushing twice a day and only flossing once a day (in the evening), so I still have some way to go. If you tend to only brush your front teeth or to brush for only a few brief seconds, think again, and perhaps buy an egg timer. Most egg timers are based on a three minute cycle and three minutes rather than two is unlikely to do any harm.

Make sure you don't use anyone else's toothbrush. It's bad enough having your own bad bacteria in your mouth without adding anyone else's. And ideally you should change your toothbrush about every three months. Try to make sure your brush has bristles that are round tipped and made from nylon.

Soft, medium or firm bristles? Dentists mostly recommend medium bristles. Too soft and they may not be effective: too hard and they may be over-abrasive and damage the tooth enamel. But what about the vexed question of electric versus manual tooth brushing? Oral hygienists seem to prefer electric and I have read that electric toothbrushes, according to one study, remove 17% more plaque. I've tried both and I admit that recharging electric toothbrushes or getting more batteries can be a hassle. In the end I have gone back to manual. Electric toothbrushes have always seemed to me a bit like electric shavers in that there is always one more gizmo out there to blind you with science – 40,000 pulsations per minute, built-in timer, tongue freshener, interdental cleaner – but when it comes down to it, does it really make any noticeable difference in the end? I'm still happy with the foil shaver I bought twenty years ago.

If your teeth are tightly packed, waxed floss works much better than non-waxed and it takes care of the 40% of your tooth surface that is not reached with a brush. Regular flossing reduces the presence of inflammatory agents capable of damaging the health of the body's blood vessels. In other words, floss for a healthy vascular system.

When you go to the oral hygienist they will spend most of their time getting rid of the plaque (the film, sticky initially and later hard) on the enamel surface of your teeth, and the tartar which is the deposit around the gum margins. Plaque is an acid coating formed by bad bacteria in the mouth. It forms quickly after a meal as bacteria multiply, coating the teeth in a layer that not only makes the teeth look more yellow eventually, but encourages the caries that is dental decay – through the enamel and in the dentine layer below. It takes about forty minutes after a meal, but longer after a sugary meal, for your saliva to return to the right balance and in that forty minutes the damage to your teeth can be done by an explosion in bad bacteria. It makes sense, therefore, to floss and brush as soon as possible after a meal or even a snack.

Plaque is normally at its worst on the back of the lower incisors, since this is where saliva and food debris is most inclined to gather. Any staining is therefore likely to be worst here, a point worth remembering when you brush your teeth. It's all very well concentrating on the outside of your incisors for a better smile, but remember to focus too on the inside of your teeth and the lower incisors in particular.

It's often said that as we get older we get 'long in the tooth'. This is true for most people, but it's still being debated whether this is inevitable and whether the process can be reversed. That it can be slowed is in no doubt. Of course, our teeth don't get longer, it's simply that the gum margin shrinks and recedes. The process is speeded up if gingivitis is present. This is a disease that results from tartar deposits. It invades the gums just below the edge, causing them to bleed, most noticeably when you brush your teeth. It's another form of bacterial disease. Between them, plaque, tartar, caries and gingivitis can play havoc with your mouth. Since your gums help to hold your teeth in place, gum recession will inevitably weaken your teeth and eventually may lead to the loss of some teeth altogether. If the teeth are not artificially replaced, the result in old age can be an unwanted 'gurn', where the face appears to collapse in on itself, aided by bone resorbtion as the jawbone recedes without the healthy pressure that it normally gets from teeth bearing down on it from the opposite jaw.

Good dental hygiene is important in the battle against gingivitis, but so are healthy eating habits, which will protect your teeth not least by encouraging healthy bacteria in your saliva. It has been noted from time to time that skulls of primitive peoples dug up from the past often exhibit healthy dentition, even in adults of advanced years. The assumption is that these people did not have toothbrushes or tooth-paste, but ate a healthy diet which encouraged sufficient good bacteria in the mouth to protect their teeth and gums from disease.

The health of the saliva in your mouth is vital. Unhealthy saliva leads to a tongue coated with bad bacteria which generate a sulphurous bi-product, causing bad breath. This is the cause of bad breath in 90% of cases (see below). The best way to have a healthy mouth is to have a healthy diet, rich in anti-oxidants. The diet factor most important for oral health is co-enzyme Q10 (ubiquinone or CoQ10), which is pro-duced naturally in the body but declines with age, as well as with intense exercise and illness. It's an essential co-factor of enzymes involved in converting sugars and fat into energy (as ATP) within the mitochon-dria, the minuscule powerhouses within the muscles.

CoQ10 is a fat-soluble anti-oxidant which protects the lipid (fat) environment of cell membranes from oxidative damage induced by free radicals. It's involved in correct cardiovascular functioning, and through its role in the process of energy production, it supports the immune system, which has a high-energy requirement. It's the main source of energy for the good bacteria that keep the mouth healthy, whereas bad bacteria rely mainly on vitamin K. There is a strong argu-ment that supplementation with CoQ10 helps in the battle against bad oral bacteria, especially in the fight against plaque and tartar. There are no known side effects from taking CoQ10 supplements except occa-sional stomach upsets, though that isn't something I have experienced and I have been taking CoQ10 as a daily supplement on and off for some years. I do not favour supplementation for a wide array of micronutri-ents which are made naturally by the body, but CoQ10 is one that seems worth a shot. Studies on people with gum disease have shown a shortfall in CoQ10 in many, as well as a reduction in blood leukocytes, essential at sufficient levels for a healthy immune system.

We produce around three pints of saliva each day. This essential process requires fluid intake and as we age, the brain becomes less efficient at telling us to drink enough. The result can be dehydration without us even realizing it, especially if we are trying to drink less in order to pee less if we are suffering from benign prostatic hyperplasia (see chapter 43 on the prostate). So inadequate fluid intake may affect saliva levels and therefore oral health. To make matters worse, our salivary glands become less efficient with age. The thing to look out for, therefore, is a dry mouth. Medications can make this worse, especially the tricyclic anti-depressants, antihistamines, beta blockers, anti-diarrhoeals, drugs to treat urinary incontinence and some of those used against Parkinson's disease.

The easy solution might seem to be to drink more liquid. The further solution, if possible, would be to find a way of avoiding the drugs in the first place. There are drugs which will stimulate saliva production, but this seems to me to be replacing one dilemma with another. There are mouth sprays available which are designed to solve the problem without resorting to drugs. Some of these, like many toothpastes, also contain ingredients aimed at reducing plaque and tartar.

While it isn't a complete solution, my answer to the problem of a dry mouth is to drink more of the right liquids and maintain a healthy diet – plus take a supplement of CoQ10 daily. Sugary foods are definitely bad for your teeth as they cause acid which leads to plaque and caries. Even fruit, fresh or dried, and real fruit juices can be bad for your teeth if they are not brushed within half an hour of eating and drinking. One food that is good for your teeth, however, is hard cheese, which helps to promote plaque-fighting saliva.

I read a report some years ago which suggested that toothpaste was unnecessary and that if you brushed your teeth with just a little water for lubrication, the result would be he same. Toothpastes come with a new miracle ingredient all the time, but if you think about it, if you rinse thoroughly after brushing, is there anything left in your mouth to perform miracles? I suspect that a good many ingredients are invented by marketing rather than research and development departments. However, it does seem to be true that brushing with a fluoride toothpaste improves oral hygiene. Whether the many alleged whiteners in toothpaste actually work is another matter. None of them contains the strong bleaching agent hydrogen peroxide that is the main staple of bleaching treatments available from dentists.

Less than 10% of UK mains water is fluoridated, compared with 70% in the US, Ireland and Australia. The argument over fluoridation of tap water has been going on for over fifty years. Fluoride is a natural mineral found to strengthen tooth enamel, helping fight decay. It also cuts the amount of acid which bacteria can produce on the teeth. However, there are those who say that the individual should be able to choose, instead of having fluoride treatment thrust upon them by government in the shape of universal fluoridation of the water supply. Some water is naturally fluoridated. For all its dental benefits, fluoride comes with a downside called fluorosis, a discolouration of the teeth. It's also believed that fluoride consumption over many years may exacerbate osteoporosis and some forms of cancer, particularly bladder cancer.

There is one toothpaste that does seem to have a lot of extra ingredients which may make it worth its higher cost. This is Janina, a toothpaste with no less than 16 ingredients designed to whiten teeth gradually and battle plaque and tartar. You get over the problem of rinsing it all away by swallowing your saliva, complete with residual toothpaste, after brushing, thus leaving a coating of the toothpaste on your teeth. No rinse cycle.

The marketing of toothpaste and toothbrushes has always been about whiter brighter teeth. If you have such teeth naturally, that's great. In the US, every parent who can afford it signs up with an orthodontist to look after their children's teeth. That's why Americans always seem to have film star smiles. In the UK we are slowly catching up, but we still lag years behind the US, except in the upper realms of the well-to-do. No one doubts that naturally white and straight teeth look better. Teeth can be straightened at any age, though adolescence is still the best time and few adults in the UK are to be seen wearing braces.

But it just may be that more children, adolescents and adults are now wearing braces than you realize. The new generation of braces are clear and cover only a few teeth (or a single tooth) at a time. They are now called brackets or aligners or retainers. They are generally removable by the patient, and are held from behind the tooth, making them even less visible. The dentist moves the process along every couple of weeks or so and at the end of say 12 months you have a mouth full of re-aligned teeth. It's not cheap, but maybe for some it's worth it. The new clinics focusing on cosmetic dentistry emphasize how important a good smile is for getting a job or winning hearts. I'm sure that to some extent they are right. They have even invented the term smile lift to go with facelift, emphasizing that no surgery is involved in getting your teeth looking right.

Fortunes are being made in the UK capping teeth. My argument with this is that it is usually obvious when teeth have been capped, though you tend to get what you pay for and some procedures are more natural than others. The other reason why it may be obvious that teeth are capped is that most patients go for a white that is too white. And if they don't get their whole mouth done, there may be a startling contrast with their teeth at the back. Think too of what it will look like at the age of eighty to have the teeth of a twenty-year-old film star? No one wants to draw attention to the artificiality of their teeth – the more natural the look the better. My father was a dentist and he always said that the strongest teeth in an adult were not white but faintly yellow – not the yellow that comes from plaque, but the natural colour of the dentine showing through the enamel. He used to talk of people with 'good ivories'.

Teeth were once filled with gold, or with amalgam which contained mercury. Not a good idea in today's world. Mercury has been consigned to the dustbin along with lead paint and asbestos insulation. The material used for fillings has gone through several incarnations. In the process, it has moved towards matching the colour of the surrounding tooth as accurately as possible. A problem with the tooth-coloured materials used in the past was that they did not last long enough and became less shiny. Resins that were hardened using ultra-violet light have been the preferred choice for matching fillings in recent years, but now there is a better option using nanoparticles which are thirty times smaller than the particles used in the past to form fillings. The particles are as small as 20 nanometres. These fillings last longer, keep their shine longer, don't pick up food and wine stains so easily, and are more resistant to plaque, thanks to their shiny surface.

For those who can afford it and who have lost teeth, implants are increasingly the name of the game. Good implants will look just like the real thing. However, implants are not only expensive (£2,000 and upwards per tooth), but require quite a lot of patience. The process, even for a single tooth, can take as long as six months from start to finish. The procedure only works if you have healthy jawbones and gums to start with. An anchor is implanted in the jawbone and to this is attached a post-like fixture to which the tooth itself is fitted. Titanium pegs sited under openings in the gum may also be used to reduce the time it takes for the whole process. Modern implants have been round long enough for predictions to be made that they will last at least thirty years and possibly longer, provided that the jawbone that holds them remains healthy and strong. Already research is progressing towards regenerating bone with bone morphogenic protein-2 (BMP-2). Currently under trial, BMP-2 is one of 20 proteins that instruct cells to grow different tissues. BMP-2 is responsible for new bone production. However, I suspect it will be some years before we see routine jawbone regeneration.

It costs only a few hundred pounds for a teeth whitening mouth tray fitted by a dentist or qualified practitioner to match your teeth (avoid mail order home kits – they may be cheap, but you will probably regret it). It's rather like wearing one of those metal braces you may have had to wear as a child. You wear it overnight for a couple of weeks or so. It contains a hydrogen peroxide solution freshly put in the device each evening, and does its work while you sleep, unless of course you are prepared to wear it during the day.

It may be true, according to one American report, that the first thing that 63% of people first notice about you when you meet them is your teeth. It has been suggested that you can take years off your apparent age with whiter, better-looking teeth.

As we age, the outer enamel of our teeth wears away, revealing more of the yellowish dentine below. That's not to contradict what I have said about whiter teeth being less strong than teeth that are more 'ivory-coloured'. I think a distinction has to be made between teeth that are, thanks to our genes, more yellow than others', and teeth that are becoming yellower with age as the enamel wears down and the dentine shows up. True it may not be possible to distinguish one source of yellowing from the other and the two may both be present. If your teeth are yellowing with age, whiteners of any kind will not help. Capping with veneers may be a solution, but you may feel that this would be inappropriate at your age.

What do whitening treatments actually do? It seems to be true that if you have teeth stained by so-called chromogenic foods and drinks such as coffee, tea, tomato sauce, blackcurrant juice or red wine, these are better removed with a whitening treatment than with a whitening toothpaste, which may do little if anything to solve the problem. A technique carried out at the surgery rather than at home, usually over three visits, applies a hydrogen peroxide gel activated with an ultra-violet light to oxidise the stain, meaning that it dissolves it, so to speak. Dentists use a scale to describe degrees of tooth whiteness and this technique is said to lighten teeth by between three and ten degrees. Apparently some tooth and gum sensitivity may result from the process, but no structural tooth damage. However, you may be left with a contrast between your newly white teeth and any veneers and white fillings, which will remain close to their original colour.

All whitening techniques involve bleaching the teeth. The process is only usually good for about 18 months, by which time your teeth will probably have reverted to their original shade. More depressing, however, is the fact that whitening treatments have recently been found to have a number of negative side effects that result from swallowing tiny portions of the compound used. The limit allowed by Health and Safety is 0.1% hydrogen peroxide, yet the typical amount of hydrogen peroxide in tooth whitening gels is 3.6%. Swallowing even a small amount of hydrogen peroxide can cause stomach upsets and if any of this powerful bleaching agent finds its way into a deep crevice in a tooth, it can sometimes damage dental nerves and blood vessels. Some whiteners are so acidic and abrasive that they actually damage the tooth enamel. Home kits are therefore risky and even in-surgery treatments may have a variety of risks. That whitening toothpaste will at least be safer, even if not very effective. The chances are that it will contain abrasives, detergents, enzymes to form a protective layer, and anti-bacterial agents, but at least it will not contain hydrogen peroxide.

Capping teeth with veneers has been popular in America for a very long time. In the last decade veneers have got a lot better and most are currently made from wafer-thin porcelain. Many ageing American celebrities would not be seen dead without them. The veneers are bonded to the tooth permanently, so there's not much point in changing your mind if you don't like the results. But at least the underlying tooth is no longer filed down as used to happen years ago. If you don't like the idea of laminated porcelain being stuck to your teeth, and no expense is spared, an alternative comes in the shape of veneers that are made by building up layer on layer of resin sculpted to each individual tooth.

It would be unusual to get all your teeth veneered, and I suspect this is because the molars, apart from being less on show, would be too difficult a shape for veneers. However, the contrast between veneered and unveneered teeth can be evident to anyone looking closely at your mouth, and even the best veneers will usually be detectable as such if you look at the area where the veneer abuts the gum margin.

No discussion of oral hygiene is complete without saying something about bad breath (see chapter 8 on bad breath). If poor oral hygiene is the main cause of bad breath, it ought to be largely curable, at least for non-smokers. Bad bacteria on the tongue are largely the problem. They produce a sulphurous odour. There are short-term solutions to bad breath best performed after the teeth have been properly cleaned by an oral hygienist and any caries or gingivitis has been dealt with. These involve rinsing the tongue with a number of alcohol-free solutions. There are even tongue manicure services.

But such treatments are only palliatives aimed at the symptoms and not the underlying causes. More important, as ever, are good eating and general health habits and possibly supplementation with Co-enzyme

Q10, as outlined above. However, even then, the problem may not be helped if there are other problems such as allergic rhinitis leading to nasal congestion and sometimes post-nasal drip. Saliva then becomes mixed with bacteria-filled mucus and the combination may be more than the good bacteria in the saliva can handle. In this case, good eating habits should be supplemented with a daily intake of sugar-free live yoghurt and perhaps a probiotic supplement rich in good bacteria. Cranberry juice, though it contains a little sugar, is said to reduce the stickiness of bacteria in your mouth, making it harder for the acid made by bad bacteria to stick to the enamel surface of the tooth. Chewing sugar-free gum after meals is said to encourage saliva flow. That sounds sensible.

Tongue scrapers are available to clean your tongue, and could, like flossing be part of a regular daily routine. However, a scraper is only treating the symptoms, not getting rid of the problem. The same can be said of anti-bacterial mouthwashes. I have read of conflicting verdicts on their effectiveness, no matter what ingredients, after the fashion of toothpastes, they may contain. My view is that they probably only work briefly and do little for the underlying problem, which is to ensure a minimum of bad bacteria and a maximum of good bacteria in your saliva and around your mouth, including your tongue. The long term solution needs to be one of good diet, exercise, tooth brushing, flossing and regular visits to the dentist and the oral hygienist. If you look after your mouth and teeth well, you may be able to get away with only visiting the dentist every two or three years, and maybe the oral hygienist only once a year. If you have problems, though, even just bad breath, more frequent visits would be wise.

Oral cancer accounts for one sixth of all cancers in the United Kingdom. Yet it is largely underestimated when it comes to oral hygiene. Fifteen million people in the UK suffer from mouth ulcers at some time in their lives. The ones to watch for are those which do not heal within three weeks. You should look out, too, for any lumps in the mouth, and any red or white patches. The highest risk group is smokers, who are six times more likely to get oral cancer than non-smokers. Alcohol doesn't help. For smokers who drink, the risk of oral cancer is increased thirty-fold. Unsurprisingly, a healthy diet helps protect against mouth cancer.

Cancer isn't the only serious problem linked to poor dental hygiene. People with gum disease are more likely to suffer from atherosclerosis according to one report, though again, we should remember that correlation is not causation. Self-neglect in one area is likely to be accompanied by self-neglect in others.

CHAPTER FORTY-ONE
TAKING CARE OF YOUR HEART AND LUNGS

The heart beats three billion times in the life of a man of eighty. There are 300,000 heart attacks in the UK annually. Each year 130,000 men die from cardiovascular disease (CVD) and a further 70,000 from a stroke, which is the most frequent cause of disability. Respectively they are the first and third biggest killers of men, cancer taking second place. We are living longer on average and the rate of death from cardiovascular disease is falling. But how much longer can it go on falling before it rises again, as the long term effects of the obesity epidemic take hold, replacing cigarette smoking as the primary target for change in lifestyle on a national scale? People are exercising more – in some cases – and eating better – in some cases – but at the other end of the scale growing numbers are eating less well and exercising less. The lack of adequate exercise appears to be the greater of the two problems.

Research has highlighted the fact that those who are fit despite being overweight or obese are less likely to suffer from a coronary event than those who are the correct weight but are not fit. Those who are underweight and not fit are at even greater risk, though this might seem to fly in the face of alternative research that suggests that those who live longest are below average weight. And it begs the question, if you accept the first of these propositions: is being underweight a cause of illness and death, or is illness the reason for being underweight?

A harbinger of a heart attack is often but not invariably angina. The symptoms for both are similar. With angina, there is generally a feeling of pain and tightness across the chest, especially during physical exertion. The pain usually radiates to the neck, the jaw, the face and the arms, particularly the left arm, and sometimes also to the back and the stomach area. There may be sweating and breathlessness, even at rest. Attacks can last up to half an hour or more. Most angina is what is called unstable angina, also known as crescendo angina or pre-infarct syndrome. Angina may be the first sign of an impending heart attack, or there may be no tell-tale signs such as those that sometimes show up in a stress cardiogram or blood tests looking for markers. An angiogram, an X-ray of the arteries may give the all- clear even though a heart attack is pending, since degenerative changes to the endothelial wall of an artery that presage a clot may not yet be discernible. Unstable angina is usually initiated by an atheromatous plaque rupturing without fully blocking an artery. A coronary thrombosis is usually preceded by angina in about 65% of cases. If you have an attack of unstable angina, your risk of a heart attack in the following three months is about 35%. All angina attacks should be regarded as an emergency and treated immediately.

Unfortunately many men who are having a heart attack think that it's indigestion. It may be indigestion, but it's better to be safe than sorry and get emergency help fast, even if the pain is only a mild one. Most people having a heart attack wait an average of ninety minutes before calling for help. As a result, many die unnecessarily. The average heart attack victim is not treated until two hours and 40 minutes after the attack starts. One third of heart attacks are fatal before the victim reaches hospital. The message is clear. If in doubt, assume the worst and call for an ambulance. This isn't the time for a stiff upper lip, even if it turns out that it was only indigestion after all.

The main difference between angina and a heart attack is that angina usually (but not always) subsides with rest, while the pain from a heart attack is not affected by rest.

The main emergency treatments for a heart attack once the victim reaches hospital are clot-busting drugs together with procedures to open up arteries that are blocked.

There is a marker that is linked to imminent danger of a coronary event or stroke. This is a protein for a hormone called NT-proBNP which is produced under extreme stress. Anyone showing an increase in this hormone will already have self-evident signs of cardiovascular problems. So it is not the kind of marker that you would be tested for as part of a routine check-up. It is therefore only of real use in monitoring those with a known condition and at serious risk.

It is important to understand that about half of all coronary events are not explained by 'normal' risk factors such as age, heredity, high blood pressure, high cholesterol, weight, diabetes and smoking. This explains the fact that often a heart attack comes out of the blue and strikes those who, on the face of it, were in perfectly good health. If you were below normal weight at birth, you stand an increased risk of a cardiovascular problem, stroke or diabetes in adult life, all else being equal.

Medical science is finding many answers to the age-old issues of heart attack and stroke, and some new issues are being raised as a result, such as whether strenuous exercise is bad for your heart.

One report answers this question by announcing that superathletes of the kind who participate in iron man and similar endurance events, as well as a number of athletes competing at the elite level of other sports are prone to heart rhythm problems and even sudden death syndrome (SDS). They are prone to ventricular arrhythmia (VA) in which the heart adopts an irregular rate and rhythm. Of athletes with VA, 82% have been found to have a dysfunctional right ventricle, the heart chamber from which blood is pumped to the lungs. All the athletes in the study had enlarged right ventricles, reflecting their level of exercise, but 82% were not emptying the chamber effectively and had a 20% blood residue in the right ventricle at the end of a heart beat. Athletes with a family history of heart problems may be more at risk. They should look out for signs of fainting, light-headedness or palpitations.

Sudden violent exercise should be avoided by those who are not fit enough for exertion which they are not accustomed to. Men who leap to play squash when they are not in shape are a classic example of a heart attack waiting to happen. Men who suffer from chronic hypothyroidism (an underactive thyroid) are at risk for angina and may need angioplasty and stents if a heart attack is to be avoided next time they exert themselves too much. Hypothyroidism is often a problem which runs in families.

Every disease now seems to come complete with a growing list of genes which suggest a predisposition, and heart attack is no exception. Inheriting a gene called apoE-4 raises LDL cholesterol, so-called 'bad' cholesterol (see chapter 10 on cholesterol). Those with the gene are up to 50% more likely to have a coronary event than those without it. Another gene carried by between 20% and 25% of the white population raises the risk of heart attack by 60% in men of all ages. These are identified via a DNA 'spelling mistake' known as a single nucleotide polymorphism (SNP). We inherit two genes (one from each parent) on chromosome 9 called CDKN2A and CDKN2B. If we inherit an SNP variant of one of these genes, our chances of heart disease go up, and if we inherit two SNP variants, the risk is higher still. The increase in risk with two variants is between 30% and 60% depending on which study you follow. The risk of heart attack in men under 50 is said to double with two variants.

Researchers are looking at ways of enhancing HDL cholesterol level (see chapter 10 on cholesterol) genetically on the grounds that HDL, the so-called 'good' cholesterol appears to scavenge 'bad' LDL cholesterol from the arteries. For these researchers, the way forward lies in finding a way of stimulating a natural genetic mutation of HDL by editing the protein's genetic structure.

There is another gene which serves as a marker for increased risk of sudden unexpected death from a heart attack. It is a rare (one in 500) inherited disorder called thickened heart muscle hypertrophy. Not everyone carrying the gene will suddenly drop dead. The gene may never express itself. But the worrying thought is that many who carry this gene show no obvious signs of a problem. As genetic science develops, we can expect to find further genes and gene clusters that will predict susceptibility to cardiovascular disease, though whether that will be a blessing, except to the insurance industry, remains to be seen.

In the chapters on smoking and diabetes, I have covered two areas closely related to cardiovascular problems. It is a fact that although those who are overweight die sooner, to the extent that it makes you fat, eating fat makes you happier, according to one survey. Arguably smoking makes you happier too, at least until you get lung cancer. All of which, in my opinion, is not a good reason either to get fat or to smoke. Having said that, I have to admit that one report shows that obese people who have had a heart attack or angina, if treated correctly, live longer than those who are not obese and have had similar attacks. Another study suggested that those who were overweight – not obese or underweight – were likely to live the longest. This runs contrary to the findings of another report claiming that those who live to a very old age are slightly thinner than average. It seems that fitness is more important than fatness, as men who are normal for Body Mass Index (BMI), but unfit are twice as likely to die as men who are obese but fit. (Yes, it is possible – look at champion Sumo wrestlers, for example). In fact, such men are more likely to live longer than unfit men of any body weight. However, not surprisingly, I think that those who live longest are men who are fit and are not obese or overweight.

The fact that overweight men who have had a heart attack are likely to live longer than men of normal weight who have experienced a similar cardiac event comes as a surprise to researchers. Various theories have been suggested. The hypothesis is that fat people have higher levels of cannabinoids in the brain. These are the mood-enhancing neurotransmitters akin to the active ingredient in cannabis. Relaxation makes people live longer and fat people are generally happier than thin people. They also score lower for platelets, meaning their blood is less likely to clot, though the fact remains that despite their positive outlook after a cardiac event, fat people are more at risk than beforehand. It has been suggested that the triglycerides (blood fats), which are higher in fat people, may become cardioprotective after a heart attack.

The standard treatment for men over 50 with persistent angina is a combination of drugs and angioplasty. The partially blocked artery is opened up with a catheter and held open with a stent. This solution will not last forever and further treatment may be needed in the future, which is why it is important for those who have had a minor surgical treatment like this to adopt a healthy lifestyle on a permanent basis. It used to be that bypass grafts to circumvent the arterial blockage were the norm. Unlike angioplasty, this involves major invasive surgery, and unsurprisingly, angioplasty has proved a lot more popular in the last few years, though it is said by some that bypass surgery will make a comeback soon on the basis that it is more enduring and more effective.

There are also critics who say that both angioplasty and bypass surgery should be only a last resort, and that they have limited benefit.

In fact one study has reported that you are better off without either angioplasty or bypass surgery, though the counter argument to this is that those who had neither may have been making plenty of effort with their diet and exercise regime instead, while those who had angioplasty or bypass surgery took the lazy route and did not exercise or eat healthily. In other words the best outcome might be an angioplasty or bypass plus better nutrition and more exercise. Those with angina should do more to change their lifestyle, though it is doubtful how much a change can achieve when an artery is already badly clogged. The hunt is still on for drugs that will immediately get rid of atherosclerotic plaque with minimal side effects.

So let's assume that you want to live to a healthy old age. My father used to say that he dreaded the thought of dying of cancer, as his mother had done. His wish was granted and he died suddenly from a heart attack (myocardial infarction) at the age of 70. Had he lived to be 80 or 90, he might well have died of cancer. The longer you live, the greater your chances of dying of cancer, rather than a heart attack or a stroke.

Most of us, though, would rather die at 90 from cancer than from a heart attack at 70, given the choice. And to some extent we do have a choice. If we look after our heart and our blood vessels, we really will live longer. And looking after the cardiovascular system, assuming that you don't smoke, means three things: exercise, healthy eating and adequate rest and sleep. By protecting your body against cardiovascular problems and stroke, you will also help to ward off cancer, or at least postpone it. It's surprising how many people, even educated people, still believe that getting cancer is a matter of chance. Like the genes you were born with, chance does play a part, but cancer depends very much on what you eat, what you breathe and how fit you keep. So by looking after your heart through good nutrition and the right amount of the right type of exercise, you are also keeping cancer at bay.

It's said that by looking after your health you can add two to three years – healthy years – to your lifespan. I reckon that if you look after your health all your life and not just in short bursts, that could be ten years or more.

Blood Pressure

One third of the UK population has a blood pressure (BP) level higher than it should be. This figure rises to two-thirds in the over 65s. One-third of those with high blood pressure are unaware of the fact. They are an accident waiting to happen. One third of those who know they have high blood pressure are not being treated for it. Of those who are being treated, one half are not being treated appropriately.

High blood pressure is caused by arterial constriction (hardening of the arteries) and by a corresponding constriction of lesser blood vessels. The nine or so pints of blood going round our system gradually have less and less space to move in.

The now standard drug treatment for high blood pressure for those under 55 is an ACE inhibitor or an angiotensin receptor blocker to start with. For those over 55, they should start with a calcium channel blocker (a so-called calcium antagonist) or a diuretic. If these fail to work adequately in either group, they should change to an ACE inhibitor or angiotensin receptor blocker plus a calcium channel blocker, or to an ACE inhibitor or angiotensin receptor blocker plus a diuretic. If that fails to do the trick, the next combination is an ACE inhibitor plus an angiotensin receptor blocker plus a calcium channel blocker plus a diuretic. If even that fails, the last resort is to boost the dose of diuretics or to prescribe an alpha- or beta-blocker. Most men prescribed drugs for high blood pressure will also have a high cholesterol level and will be prescribed a statin at the same time as their anti-hypertensive drugs. The reduction in cardiovascular events from taking the current generation of drugs to treat high blood pressure is considerable, justifying their side effects in the majority of cases. Stroke and diabetes rates have also been shown to improve dramatically.

Many men with high blood pressure are already on beta blockers. The new regime that turns to beta blockers only as a last resort does not mean that those already on these drugs should abandon them without careful discussion with their advisor. Beta-blockers will still be included in most treatments for heart failure or angina, or for those who have already had a heart attack.

High blood pressure (hypertension) is one of the signs of possible diabetes (see chapter 15 on diabetes) and is commoner in those who have diabetes or a pre-diabetic condition. It is often called the silent killer because it has no symptoms except for the occasional headache. Nobody knows exactly what causes it. The best way to determine your blood pressure is to buy a blood pressure wrist monitor at the chemists and take readings at home when you are relaxed. Your blood pressure will rise during and after exercise and also when you are stressed or have been eating or drinking. If you have a relaxed and easy-going personality (Type B personality), your lower reading is likely to be in the late afternoon, whereas if you are more inclined to stress (Type A personality), take your reading soon after waking in the morning, before the events of the day have stressed you out. Readings should be taken when you are relaxed. Take the best of three, taking each a few minutes apart on the same arm, lying down comfortably with the monitor raised on a pillow so that it is level with your heart. You will probably find that if you take your reading on either arm, you will get an average on each that is different from the other. That is normal to some extent, but if you find that the variance is over 10%, see a cardiologist, as it can sometimes be a sign of a serious problem.

Low blood pressure – say 100/60 – can be a sign of a problem and should be investigated. A pressure of say 110/65 is marginal for further investigation, unless you are a marathon runner, in which case it might be considered normal.

Your blood pressure is divided into systolic pressure (when the heart squeezes, to put it simply) and diastolic pressure (when it relaxes). Each is equally important. In a healthy person blood pressure should not rise with age. Doctors tend to suggest that it is alright for a reading to be a bit higher, the older you are. They are simply being indulgent because the older you are, the less healthy you are likely to be. You are doing very well if you have a reading of say 115/75. You are doing well with 120/80. You are just within acceptable norms at 135/85 and you are marginal for high blood pressure at 140/90. At 160/100 you have hypertension and it should be investigated further, though if this is the reading you are getting at the doctor's, you could be the victim of white coat syndrome –

an elevated reading due to nervousness. This is why taking readings at home when you are relaxed is so important.

Though periodic rises in blood pressure caused by stress are not a serious long-term problem, they can become one if they occur too frequently over an extended period of time. Chronic stress should therefore be avoided, unless it is what I call positive stress (see chapter 39 on stress).

What are the diseases that chronic high blood pressure produces? The big players are cardiovascular disease, including heart failure (cardiomyopathy), stroke, Type 2 diabetes and kidney disease.

About one in ten adults suffers from some degree of restless leg syndrome (RLS). This involves a tingling feeling in the skin and an urge to move the legs. People with RLS tend to have higher blood pressure caused by the leg movements and therefore to run a higher risk of cardiovascular disease.

Since high blood pressure, like a high cholesterol count, is indicative of increased CVD risk, it's important to know what can be done to keep blood pressure down. A recent study showed without a shadow of doubt that salt (sodium chloride) intake should be low –no more than 6 mg a day. That means not adding salt when cooking, not adding salt to food at the table, and not eating processed foods with salt added, except in small amounts. The salt you get otherwise in your food and drinks should be enough.

A company has now come up with an artificial salt that might ease the problem of those who love plenty of salt in their diet no matter what it might be doing to their blood pressure. About 40% of salt is made up of sodium, which is the problem, not the chloride. Sodium chloride should not be confused with potassium chloride, which is a necessity in a healthy diet, provided that you are under 60 and don't have too much in your diet. Too much potassium can be bad for the elderly. Potassium salt is plentiful in most fruit and vegetables and is a useful aid to keeping blood pressure down.

Cocoa, rich in anti-oxidants, has been found to be an effective way to lower blood pressure, improve circulation and reduce the risk of heart attack. If you can manage your blood pressure down this way rather than by taking drugs, so much the better. This might seem like a good excuse to indulge the chocoholic that is in most of us, except that chocolate, despite a high cocoa content in some brands, also contains sugar and saturated fat, and is dense in calories. Too much sugar in the diet can lead to weight problems and weight problems go hand in hand with high blood pressure and Type 2 diabetes. Sugar is also thought to play a part in the development of atherosclerosis and it's a fact that whereas 40% of deaths in the general population are attributable to a heart attack or stroke, among diabetics the figure is over 75%. Diabetics often do not discover they have diabetes until they have had a heart attack.

In other words, chocolate is not a no-no, but it should be eaten sparingly as an occasional treat, and only in a high cocoa variety. The cocoa is rich in polyphenols and oxytocin, the ingredient that causes that relaxed feeling in the brain. A better way to take cocoa is as a drink, preferably as a nightcap, unless you suffer from benign prostatic hyperplasia (BPH) (see chapter 43 on the prostate). The best way of all to get the benefit of cocoa's anti-oxidants is to buy cocoa nibs in bulk from a health food retailer and add these to your morning muesli.

Tea, especially green tea, is considered by some to have the same effect as cocoa on blood pressure, but research has not borne this out, though green tea is undoubtedly a rich source of anti-oxidants.

Too much alcohol damages the heart muscle, increases blood pressure and can make you fat.

The best way to get blood pressure down or keep it down is to get plenty of the right kind of exercise and diet. The heart is a muscle and it needs exercise. On the diet front, the message is that too much saturated fat, and worse, trans (partially hydrogenated) fat will do your blood pressure no good at all.

Heart Rate
Don't think that because you have a slow heart rate you are necessarily fit. It's generally true that as you get fitter your heart beats more slowly, since a healthy heart can pump enough blood with fewer beats. The trap is this. As you get older, your heart rate tends to slow down and your

blood pressure tends to rise. My resting heart rate is usually round the 62 beats per minute mark, but it can sometimes be as high as 72 and as low as 54. If you exercise a lot and your heart rate falls as a result, that is probably a good thing, but be aware that ageing could also be slowing it down, or a combination of both. The lowest resting heart rate recorded was allegedly 29 beats per minute in a champion Nordic skier. Few of us could hope to attain anything like that level, though I have seen my wife's rate as low as 39, and she is always very fit.

Don't take your resting heart rate just before you embark on an aerobic workout. It is known that if you are fit and used to exercising regularly, the heart will anticipate your need for more oxygen before you start and your heart rate will increase accordingly. If your resting heart rate is say 72, this may jump to 90 just before you start, and of course it will rise from there as you exercise, gradually more slowly after the initial rise, though it will take some time to reach a level where it stays where it is. More commonly you will find, after the initial jump and a further rapid jump after you start, that your heart rate keeps going up a beat every minute or so until the session is over. To give you an example: If I plan to work out for 20 minutes at around 70% of my maximum heart rate (maximum about 180), my heart rate will jump to 90 just before I start, then climb to about 120 in the first five minutes, then climb to about 130 over the next 15 minutes. After I stop, my heart rate will fall back to about 100 after one minute. The rate at which your heart rate drops after a workout is an important guide to cardio fitness. My average heart rate in the session will have been around 126, which is 70% of my maximum.

Do not be misled by guidelines that say that your maximum heart rate is 220 minus your age. I'm 64 and on that basis my maximum would be about 156. But as I've just said, my maximum is around the 180 mark. How do I know? Because with all-out effort I have managed, not long ago, to raise my heart rate to that level, albeit for only a few seconds. It is not possible to sustain exercise at the maximum heart rate for very long and even at 90% of maximum, you will be unlikely to keep going for more than a couple of minutes. The 90% level is what is known as the anaerobic threshold and at this level your lungs already feel like they are

going to burst and you are starting to gasp. At this stage you are producing a lot of lactic acid. Talking is out of the question, whereas at say 65%
of maximum, you should be able to carry on a conversation, if somewhat
breathily. It's often said that you should work out somewhere between
60% and 70% of maximum heart rate. Being able to talk while exercising really is a good guide if you are not wearing a heart rate monitor.

However, how do you know what your maximum heart rate is? The
220 minus your age rule is flawed to the extent that it can be out as much
as 10% and sometimes more either way. Exercise bikes and the like that
you may be put on for your annual check-up with BUPA, for example,
will always be calibrated according to the 220 minus your age rule and
therefore treat you like Mr Average. The alternative would be to get
you to work out to your maximum. You can do this at home (though I do
not advise it unless you know your body very well and you are very fit),
whereas doctors and nurses cannot take the risk of you having a heart
attack under their testing regime. If you have a weak heart or say an
aneurysm waiting to burst in your abdomen or your brain, you could
kill yourself, so their position is sensible, albeit you run the risk of not
being tested accurately for your personal level of fitness.

Heart Arrhythmias

An irregular heartbeat is an arrhythmia, but not all arrhythmias involve
irregular heartbeats. This is because an irregular heartbeat is only one
of many types of cardiac arrhythmia. The two forms of irregular beat
most often encountered are atrial fibrillation, and extra systoles, the latter normally being a benign occurrence, usually caused by caffeine,
stress or lack of sleep. Atrial fibrillation, on the other hand, is a very real
and worrying condition for about 1% of the population. About one-
third of all stroke victims have atrial fibrillation.

A fast but regular beat in the 160–200 beats per minute range is
known as a paroxysmal tachycardia. I used to get this occasionally for no
apparent reason. Attacks lasted a few minutes. It first started when I was
thirteen and has not recurred since I was in my forties. However, there
are more serious arrhythmias such as those occasioned by exercise and
these need to be investigated. I have one of these, possibly caused by too

much exercise: Wenckebach block. This is what is described by cardiologists as First Degree Block or Mobitz type 1 block. It comes in two varieties, one of which is considered dangerous and eventually requires a pacemaker, and another which is benign. I appear to have the benign variety. It began in my mid-fifties and shows up each year in the electrocardiogram (ECG) that comes as part of my annual BUPA check-up.

Any form of arrhythmia needs careful consideration, especially in those exercising heavily, to rule out the possibility of sudden death syndrome (SDS), which is usually found in young sportsmen and is associated with hypertrophic cardiomyopathy, characterized by a thickened heart wall or irregular heartbeat. Cardiomyopathy is the general term for heart failure, a disease which results in the heart progressively pumping blood less and less efficiently.

Men at serious risk of fainting as a result of a sudden drop in their heart rate and blood pressure are usually fitted with a pacemaker, which detects the early signs of fainting and stimulates the heart to increase the rate at which it is beating. However, some men faint without any prior drop in heart rate and blood pressure. Now a new kind of pacemaker is available which handles this by detecting a reduction in the size of the right ventricle of the heart, a warning sign of an impending fainting episode. The pacemaker reacts by slightly increasing the heart rate, thereby improving blood flow to the brain, thus preventing fainting.

It has been found that men who were breast fed are less likely, on average, to suffer from high blood pressure, cardiovascular disease, diabetes, obesity and heart attacks, when compared with men who were bottle-fed as babies. They are more likely to have above average levels of HDL 'good' cholesterol (see chapter 10 on cholesterol). They are also likely to have a stronger immune system.

Heart Attack
When you have a heart attack, fatty deposits block a coronary artery or break away and travel to a point where they block oxygen supply to the heart muscle and upset ventricular rhythm, often fatally, making the heart unable to pump blood as it should. This causes the event doctors refer to as a myocardial infarction. The deposits are made up of fatty

yellow cholesterol, blood platelets and fibrous plaque which has developed within and may later burst away from the endothelial wall of an artery. The wall of the artery, once smooth, will probably have become hardened over time with the deposition of minute amounts of calcium (detectable with a CT scan). Cholesterol travelling in 'bad' low density lipoprotein (see chapter 10 on cholesterol) will have become attached to the artery wall, forming the fatty deposits called atheroma in a process known as atherosclerosis. It is now believed that it is when this plaque is soft that it is most likely to burst and form a clot that may travel to the heart and cause a heart attack. Contrary to former belief, older harder plaque is now thought to be more stable and less likely to break away. The risk from calcification of the artery comes from the fact that as the artery hardens it is less able to transport blood as effectively as a healthy artery. At the same time, it is more likely to become the site of plaque. Thus the attack on the heart is threefold, from hardened (calcified) arteries, from plaque and consequent narrowing (stenosis) of the coronary arteries, and from clots.

One approach to the problem of hardening of the arteries is to look for ways of preventing it. A promising approach appears to lie in a substance called matrix gla protein (MGP), which, in combination with vitamin K, appears to reduce the calcification process. Leafy green vegetables are rich in vitamin K.

The build-up of plaque is progressive over the years and begins in most males before the age of twenty. There can be few men over the age of fifty who do not have some evidence of atherosclerosis, though most will be unaware of the problem without thorough diagnostic testing. Lifestyle factors and heredity play an equal part in the equation. Often it is only when a man has had a heart attack that he realizes it is time to give up smoking, reduce the stress in his life, eat less fat and salt, exercise more and consume a healthier diet. Even then, he may be unaware that he is not getting enough rest and sleep.

Some doctors advise taking a low-dose aspirin each day to ward off the risk of heart attack, or to prevent a recurrence if you have already had one. Unless you really are at risk, I would tend to say no to a daily aspirin, even if you were one of those who do not experience stomach burn from the key ingredient, salicylic acid, which works by thinning the blood, thus reducing the risk of a clot. There are food products that, according to some, have the same anti-clotting effect as aspirin. One is curry powder, which contains turmeric, the key ingredient in which is curcumin. Hawthorn extract is said to lower blood pressure, though what sound medical evidence there is for this claim I have yet to find. Omega 3, the much-touted essential fatty acid, is said to be cardiopro-tective before and after a coronary event, though a recent report has questioned the benefits of Omega 3. Others point out that Omega 3 lowers the heart's irritability level, thereby enhancing its ability to maintain rhythm.

However, there is a time when aspirin should definitely be taken, and that is if you are having or have just had a heart attack. It's claimed that this can be life-saving. Two full-strength doses are recommended, and anyone on glyceryl trinitrate tablets for angina should take these instead. Aspirin should not be taken without first taking medical advice. It can cause bleeding in the stomach and this may be fatal in those with high blood pressure. For the same reason it should not be taken by any-one prone to gastro-intestinal bleeding.

Folic acid (folate) has its supporters and detractors as a supplement to support the fitness of the heart and the brain. The balance of the evi-dence suggests that folic acid is more useful against stroke than against heart attack. Allegedly it operates by lowering the level of homocys-teine, a metabolite of the amino acid methionine, but it is probably only effective in some people, and in others it has been suggested that it may even increase the risk of cardiovascular disease. There is limited evi-dence that folic acid may help reduce the risk of some cancers and Alzheimer's disease. Folic acid is found in green leafy vegetables and whether supplements are a good idea is, as with many supplements, debatable if you are getting a healthy diet. If you do take it, you should take the vitamins B6 and B12 at the same time.

An annual flu vaccine arguably cuts the incidence of flu and reduces death rate from flu in the elderly. However, it turns out that the annual flu jab may also reduce the incidence of heart attacks and death from chronic ischaemic heart disease (IHD) caused by previous heart attacks.

One-third of those at known risk from heart disease do not receive an annual flu jab, presumably because they have not made the connection between flu and cardiovascular disease. The link is theoretical rather than proven and is based on the hypothesis that inflammation caused by flu destabilises atherosclerotic arterial plaque.

The symptoms of a heart attack are well known. As with angina, there may be pain and tightness across the chest, radiating out to the neck, jaw, face and arms, and perhaps the back and the stomach area. If pain continues even when the victim lies down, this is another sign. The victim may feel sweaty and nauseous and be short of breath. Less typically, there may only be a feeling of being unwell, with an ache or heavy feeling in the chest, or even just a slight discomfort under the breastbone. There may be light-headedness and dizziness. The feeling may be confused with indigestion, but you should never assume this is the case unless you know for sure. Other symptoms include a feeling of fatigue, swollen ankles and legs, and palpitations.

What should you do in the event of someone having a heart attack? They should sit with their back to a wall, their knees drawn up. Their clothing should be loosened and they should, if they are able, chew two full strength aspirins (unless there is a reason why aspirin should not be given – for example, a history of gastrointestinal bleeding) or take a large dose of their glyceryl trinitrate tablets (or spray) if they are on these for angina. Try to get the victim to cough as described in the next paragraph. An ambulance should be called immediately.

If the heart if fibrillating (fluttering rapidly rather than beating) and you have a home defibrillator, this should be applied. The newest versions have a built-in ECG monitor and a computer that gives instructions according to the ECG trace.

If you are on your own and think you may be having a heart attack, you can help yourself after calling for an ambulance and before you lose consciousness, as often happens. If you have aspirin handy, take two as described above. Sit on the floor with your back to the wall and your knees drawn up, take a deep breath and cough long and hard as though trying to cough up sputum from your lungs. Repeat every two seconds and continue until help arrives. If there is someone there to help you, they should support your knees and monitor your condition until help arrives. They should not attempt cardio-pulmonary resuscitation (CPR) unless you are unconscious and have stopped breathing.

Some personality types are more prone to cardiovascular disease than others. One study suggests that men who are more in touch with their feminine side – who are right brain dominant and possibly have a higher oestrogen level relative to their testosterone level – are less likely to suffer a cardiac or similar event. The men in question are found to be fairly sensitive and in touch with their feelings, along the lines of what used to be called 'New Man'. One research group discovered that 17% of boys were born with a 'female brain', which meant that they had low exposure to testosterone in the womb. Conversely, 14% of women had a 'masculine brain' from high exposure to testosterone.

Another study looked at the personality types commonly ranked as A, B, C and D. Type A is driven, ambitious, bossy, short-tempered and perfectionistic. Type B is relaxed and easy-going. Type C is conformist, introverted and self-controlled. Type D is shy, insecure, gloomy and likely to avoid contact with others. Type A is prone to heart disease. Type B has the best outlook of the four types and is the least prone to illness. Type C tends to be a candidate for cancer. Type D has a high risk of repeated heart attacks. Men of Type D are most likely to be single and have few friends, which possibly explains the fact, often repeated, that single men do not live as long as married men. Of the four groups, Type D has the worst prognosis for cardiovascular problems. It is theorized that men in this group are the most stressed of the four types. Type A has the next worst outlook. Those who are extraverts are less likely to suffer a heart attack than those who are introverts. Here, again, Type B comes out on top.

Another study focussed on which weather conditions were likely to induce heart attacks. Not surprisingly, extremes of heat and cold were found to make a difference, but an interesting finding was that even more significant was humidity level, more particularly, high levels of humidity, especially in hot climates, which should serve as a warning to anyone vulnerable, especially if elderly, planning a holiday overseas.

Fibrinogen, a clotting factor in the blood, can be measured. Too high a level may indicate cardiovascular problems ahead, though it is now considered a poorer signal than calcium deposits in the coronary arterial system, though this too is now thought by some cardiologists to be a poor indicator. A raised level of calcium identified by a scan has been found to correlate with 'central obesity' in men with evidence of a pot belly. Exercise may lower fibrinogen level and help get rid of deep abdominal fat, but it is a fact that the kind of fat in this area, which produces dangerous hormones, is extremely easy to put on and extremely hard to get rid of. Many men show signs of abdominal fat as early as the age of 20. Prevention is better than cure and keeping fat down through diet and exercise should be a lifelong task, however difficult this is. If fat is kept down around the middle, fibrinogen levels should stay low and likewise calcium levels in the coronary arterial system.

Those most at risk of a heart attack are elderly, living alone, poorly educated, with a limited income. Men over 50 living alone are twice as likely to develop heart disease. Men living alone are more likely to smoke, be obese, have high cholesterol and make few visits to the doctor.

It is sobering to know that when the only solution to survival is a heart transplant, as many as 50% of those on the waiting list die before a suitable donor heart can be found. Of those who receive a new heart, 20% do not survive the operation. Of those who do, a number will die over the following five years, generally of complications connected with the transplant.

Stroke

In the UK there are 70,000 deaths each year from stroke, the third killer after cardiovascular disease and cancer. There are three main kinds of stroke. An ischaemic stroke is caused by a blood clot and is the commonest type. Less common is a haemorrhagic stroke caused by a burst blood vessel in the brain. And some strokes are caused by an embolism, a blood clot that reaches the brain's arteries from another part of the body. A series of very small repeated strokes (transient ischaemic strokes) is another less frequent type. If you have had a cardiac event such as a heart attack, you are at increased risk of stroke. Aspirin for those who have had a stroke or are at risk is recommended except for those who have had a haemorrhagic stroke (since aspirin makes the blood less likely to clot), inflammation of the digestive tract or high blood pressure. Obviously those who are allergic to aspirin should not take it under any circumstances. Allergy mainly occurs in women.

The main cause of ischaemic stroke is a clot resulting from the furring (atherosclerosis) of the cerebral or the carotid artery, especially the latter. Preventive measures are largely the same as for coronary heart disease.

The effects of stroke can vary from a tingling sensation or weakness in the arms, to widespread paralysis, coma and death.

Research has shown that strokes which occur in the evening and at the weekend are more likely to be fatal, especially haemorrhagic strokes, with an increase in fatalities of around 25%. The probable reason for this is that hospitals are more likely to be better staffed during normal business hours.

Peripheral Arterial Disease
Those at risk of a coronary event are equally at risk for peripheral arterial disease. About 12% of men are affected by blockages in the iliac arteries from the heart to the legs, the femoral arteries in the thighs and the smaller arteries in the lower legs. Symptoms range from mild to severe. At the mild end of the spectrum will be a feeling of general lassitude. Towards the other end is severe intermittent claudication, a pain in the calves, especially on walking uphill in cold weather. Rest relieves the pain. The symptoms of extreme peripheral arterial disease include poor circulation in the legs and cold blue feet. If drug treatment fails, angioplasty sometimes resolves the problem, or a bypass graft, or even, in extreme cases, amputation. The latest approach, still experimental, is to inject genes that will stimulate neo-angiogenesis, the growth of new blood vessels that will bypass blocked vessels.

Pulmonary Embolism
A clot called a thrombus may form in a distant part of the body and move to the heart, the lungs or the brain, causing a heart attack, a pulmonary embolism or a cerebral embolism, all of which can be fatal. A deep vein thrombosis (DVT) most commonly forms in the blood vessels of the legs, the groin or the pelvis, and is especially common following surgery,

particularly hip replacement surgery. It is the DVT beloved of critics of air travel, who have called it Economy Class Syndrome, though evidence has shown that it is no more related to air travel than it is to long distance travel by train or car. The dangerous element is sitting still for long periods, rather than the lower air pressure and restricted oxygen of modern air travel (see chapter 2 on air travel). A clot on the lungs, if large enough, can cut oxygen supply to the heart and kill its victim within minutes. Any breathlessness and pain in the chest should be investigated. It could be a heart or lung problem.

Treatment is with careful administration of clot-busting drugs which block the ability of the protein thrombin to form life-threatening clots – careful because there is a risk of the drugs dislodging further emboli. Warfarin and heparin have been the drugs usually used to thin the blood and reduce the risk of clot formation. However, warfarin may trigger intestinal bleeding, while heparin requires a lengthy course of injections. Now a drug is available that seems to offer a better solution, not just in the hospital but for home use after surgery. The drug is called Pradaxa, and fast on its heels is another drug likely to be as effective or even better: Xarelto.

Increasingly DVT is referred to as venous thrombo-embolism (VTE). It's responsible for one out of every ten deaths in UK hospitals, which is 20 times as many as are killed by the MRSA superbug. Twenty-five thousand people die from a VTE in the UK each year. Those at risk should move about as much as possible as lying in bed can lead to clot formation.

Screening

Two blood tests to get done from time to time (they're not part of the BUPA menu) are C-reactive protein (CRP) and homocysteine. They can cost anywhere from about £20 to £100 each to have done and both in their separate ways are thought to be indicative of heart and artery health. C-reactive protein (CRP) (more strictly high-sensitive CRP) is a protein that is increasingly used as a marker for inflammation, and is therefore a guide to problems in a number of areas, and not just artery inflammation signalling vascular disease. It is alleged to be a useful marker of trouble ahead with bowel disease, some cancers and arthritis. The lower the rate the better. A high rate may indicate that the patient has already had or may be inclining towards a stroke, heart attack, angina or peripheral arterial disease. A low level of CRP is under 1 mg/l, and a high level with high risk is over 3 mg/l. There is now hope that a group of statins primarily designed to lower cholesterol levels will also reduce coronary artery inflammation. Lipoprotein (a) is another measurable marker for cardiovascular problems.

There have been arguments for and against CT scans to identify calcium deposits in the lining of the heart's arteries. Apart from the radiation dose that comes from a CT scan, some cardiologists doubted whether calcium levels were indicative of cardiovascular risk. Now the highly respected *New England Journal of Medicine* has published research showing definitively that scans for calcium deposits correlate clearly with predictions of coronary risk, including angina. A score between 101 and 300 indicates a risk eight times as great as that of those without any detectable coronary calcium, rising to ten times as great with a score over 300. Private screening clinics are the easiest if not the cheapest way to get a calcium scan done (see chapter 28 on screening).

Screens for risk of stroke rely on X-ray angiograms to detect larger clots in susceptible arteries. But smaller clots need more sophistication, which is where PET (position emission tomography) and CT scanning (see chapter 28 on screening) come into play. Small inflamed plaques that might be at risk of breaking away are identifiable and can be treated by drugs, or failing that, by surgical removal.

CHAPTER FORTY-TWO
THE IMMUNE SYSTEM

You will often read that such-and-such a food or exercise will 'boost the immune system'. While this may be true, in many cases it may be wishful thinking, since not a lot is known about what specific foods can do for the immune system. Do anti-oxidants boost the immune system by tackling free radicals? Yes, but just about everything you eat that is good for you will help your immune system. Exercise, on the other hand, initially weakens the immune system, before strengthening it, which is why top-flight athletes are known to be prone to catching colds.

The immune system protects us against foreign substances, particularly parasites, and against diseases carried by microbes as bacteria or viruses. This type of immune protection is innate. It is mainly characterized by the destruction of pathogenic agents by white blood cells (phagocytosis), or by localized swelling which calls white cells to battle. Immunity can also be acquired as a result of contact with a hostile agent or an agent that is perceived as hostile. This results in an 'immunological memory', which will give further protection in the future from similar attacking forces.

Antigens are the substances, usually proteins, which evoke an immunological response, and this response takes the form of antibodies. When the response is not to a foreign body, but to one which the immune system fails to recognize as part of ourselves, the result is an autoimmune disease, for example, rheumatoid arthritis and multiple sclerosis (MS). Autoimmune reactions are commonly treated with either replacement of deficient hormones, immunosuppressant drugs, corticosteroids or non-steroidal anti-inflammatory drugs (NSAIDs). Autoimmune problems are not normally curable. They may last a lifetime, but are generally manageable.

A recent genetic breakthrough has given renewed hope to MS sufferers, made possible by the mapping of the human genome. Three genetic variants are now known to contribute to the likelihood of MS, and with this discovery comes hope of a cure or better management of the disease as two of the genes are linked to controlling the activity of T lymphocytes, the white blood cells which sometimes 'get it wrong' and lead to the body attacking itself. What causes MS is largely a mystery, but this breakthrough will partly answer the question, as well as provide a new tool in identifying susceptibility to inheriting the disease.

Most activity by the immune system is not an autoimmune response, but is directed against pathogenic organisms from outside or the toxic products which the invaders produce.

Immunity may derive from having a disease, or artificially by vaccination, which involves deliberate exposure to a disease using a diminished form of a pathogenic microbe. This confers active immunity. But if a serum already containing the antibody is injected, this confers what is called passive immunity.

Disordered immune response may not only take the form of an autoimmune disease, but also an allergy (see chapter 4 on allergies). The challenge for the immune system is to distinguish cells that are foreign and hostile from those that are part of ourselves or are foreign but benign. Given that the body contains millions of foreign cells at any time and takes in many more continuously, it's not surprising that the human body can sometimes be seen as a battlefield.

The main defence forces are the lymphocytes, a specialised type of white blood cell with two sub-types. T lymphocytes (T cells) produce what is called a cell-mediated immune response and derive from the thymus. T cells become sensitised to attack specific antigens. They operate on a delayed basis, as in the case of rejected transplant organs. T lymphocytes divide into killer T cells and memory T cells. T cells are mainly active against parasites, fungi, viruses and some cancer cells.

Red bone marrow produces a different type of antibody, the B lymphocyte. When activated by recognized antigens, B lymphocytes differentiate into plasma cells which create specific immunoglobulins, proteins that have the capacity to serve as antibodies and are able to circulate in blood plasma, from which position they can quickly attack and incapacitate particular types of antigenic bacteria. Antibodies of this type can be transferred by blood serum injection from a donor and produce an immune response in the recipient. This is passive immunity. As different individuals will have one of several blood groups, matching blood group between donor and recipient is fundamental.

Saliva forms a part of the immune system. It regulates oral hygiene (see chapter 40 on teeth), is formed by glands in the mouth and is composed of mucus and enzymes.

Weakness in the immune system can be acquired as the result of a virus. The best known example is the human immunodeficiency virus (HIV) giving rise to acquired immunodeficiency syndrome (AIDS). Those who are HIV-positive have a compromised immune system that is vulnerable to a variety of diseases, some of which most of us would not find seriously threatening nowadays, but which can be life-threatening to someone with weakened immunity. Pneumonia is a typical example. While some viruses can weaken the immune system, so can some drugs, both illegal and pharmaceutical.

There is still a lot to learn about the immune system, especially now that the medical world increasingly recognizes the interdependence of mind and body. Some interesting research a while back wanted to test whether a positive mental attitude to cancer could improve outcome. The research concluded that it could not, but others have contested this and the absolute answer is still unknown.

Every individual is as different as their DNA, so it may not be surprising to learn that some people who smoke will succumb quickly to lung cancer while others who smoke all their lives may live to a grand old age and never get the disease. Some people can be carriers of a disease, for example tuberculosis, without developing TB.

What does strengthen the immune system and what weakens it? Let's take shingles as an example. The varicella–zoster virus (VZV) is a virus that was once chicken pox in the child, has lain dormant in nerve ganglia for years and returns in adulthood, usually in middle life, as a painful outbreak of skin lesions. It is thought to be triggered by stress which has led to a weakened immune system. In bad cases, scarring can occur and even damage to eyesight in severe cases affecting the face. Most outbreaks are on the face or upper part of the body. Treatment is with drugs and needs to be rapid to be fully effective. The pain of post-herpetic neuralgia can be reduced, it is said, with reishi mushrooms, which are rich in anti-inflammatory polysaccharides.

We don't yet know what the long term effects are of many childhood illnesses, but shingles brings home the fact that some illnesses never go away completely and can even return to plague us later in life if we are predisposed and the immune system is compromised for any reason. Stress of one kind or another seems to be the key factor.

In fact the best way to keep your immune system strong may be to lead a happy guilt-free life. If you worry a lot and feel guilty every time you eat chocolate or a hamburger, you may be doing yourself more harm by worrying than by eating the food in question. Guilt is not something that is easily controlled. But the message here may be that you will be better off – and by implication live longer – if you can avoid stress as much as possible. I say this with a proviso. See chapter 39, where we take a look at stress and find that the important thing is to be in control of your own life, doing the things that you want to do.

Immunoglobulin A (IgA) is the most plentiful of the five types of antibody we make in response to infection. It's mostly found in the digestive tract and it can be measured in a sample of saliva. IgA fights the low levels of infection we are exposed to at all times, but when it comes to a more unusual battle, say with a bacterial attack, the measurable amount in our saliva decreases immediately after the battle is won. In other words, the aftermath of a battle to fight a particular disease is a weakened immune system which may take time to recover. The older your biological age, the longer your recovery will probably take.

IgA levels are known to fall immediately before and during academic exams, and may rise afterwards if the results are good, or even before the results are published if the candidate feels he or she has done well. Counter-intuitively, though, stress has been known to boost levels of IgA. This has been found to be the case with computer game players and air traffic controllers during working hours. Again we see that different kinds of stress can produce different effects, with some stress being positive and some negative.

Most of us who exercise do so more out of guilt than with pleasure in mind. It would be interesting to know whether those who exercise for pleasure get more immune benefits than those who exercise out of guilt or simply for the health benefits, the two often going together. I suspect that they do.

The lymphatic system is the body's drainage system, getting rid of waste products at the cellular level, and is therefore another part of the immune system. The lymphatic system is capable of getting rid of infectious organisms and cancer cells.

What happens to the immune system as we get older? The body becomes more susceptible to disease. Response to vaccines declines. The production of auto-antibodies (antibodies to the bodies own molecules) rises. T cells become less able to deal with antigens, and fewer T cells respond to infections as thymus function begins to fail. B lymphocyte response also goes into decline. This skews the balance in the perennial battle between antigens and antibodies, giving antigens an increasingly stronger hand. The result is increased susceptibility to infection. This is why it may be important that the older you are, the more important it is that you get an autumn flu jab each year as an immune system booster. Sixty is a good age to start. Note, however, that annual flu jabs have their detractors, some of whom say they are completely useless (see chapter 11 on colds and flu).

As a general rule, the best route to a strong immune system is lots of moderate exercise, loads of laughter, plenty of healthy food, perhaps a modicum of supplements to get an extra boost, and above all a positive mental attitude to life and the avoidance of negative stress. Smoking, lack of sufficient quality sleep, and alcohol, unsurprisingly, may compromise the immune system.

CHAPTER FORTY-THREE
PROSTATE PROBLEMS

This walnut-sized organ that sits just below the male bladder can grow, usually after the age of 50, into an organ the size of a small orange. It grows in size in all men. It's said that all men who live long enough eventually develop prostate cancer, though few will die of it as they will die of something else first. That does not mean that it is not a serious killer. Prostate cancer is one of the most serious cancers in men in the UK, thanks to the fact that we are tending to live a bit longer. It strikes 35,000 men a year and kills 10,000. It will affect one out of every fourteen men in their lifetime – mostly men in their seventies. If you are between 40 and 50 years old, you probably have some awareness of the problems associated with this small but troublesome gland. If you are over 50 you should be fully aware of the problems and you should have a prostate specific antigen (PSA) test annually and watch the year-over-year trend to see if the count is rising and how fast it is doing so. Men with a family history of prostate cancer should start PSA testing once they reach 40. PSA is a protein produced by the prostate cells. A small quantity can be found in a blood sample.

Your PSA score should ideally be below 4 at age 50 and below 6 at age 65. Your PSA level rises gradually as you get older. The trouble with the PSA screening test is that it can give false positives and false negatives – that is, it may suggest you have prostate cancer when you haven't and vice versa. If your score is over 10 there is a need for further investigation. It's important to note whether your score is rising each year and, if so, how fast this is occurring. If you score doubles in a year, there is a need for further investigation. Two-thirds of men with a high PSA score do not turn out to have prostate cancer.

Until recently the PSA test, though imperfect, was the best first-round diagnostic tool there was. Now a new test, the Progensa Prostate

Cancer Antigen 3 (PCA3) test, named after a gene, is looking promising in the effort to spot prostate cancer early on, and to distinguish between BPH (benign prostatic hyperplasia or enlargement of the prostate) and prostate cancer. The PCA3 test measures a genetic chemical. High scores signal prostate cancer specifically. One of the good things about this test is that it may avoid the need for biopsy where previously this was necessary in borderline cases to determine if a cancer was present. A prostatic biopsy normally involves a local anaesthetic and the removal of up to a dozen tissue samples, a procedure that can leave you in pain for days afterwards, as well as cause infection and permanent damage to the prostate. If it's found that there is no cancer, only BPH, you can be left wishing there were an easier way of giving you the all-clear. And prostatic biopsy results are not always foolproof. Now the PCA3 test is likely to change forever the way we test for prostate cancer. However, it does cost twenty times as much as a PSA test, so now that the government is planning to introduce prostate screening for all men over 50 on the NHS, it will be interesting to see whether they feel it's worthwhile to opt for PCA3 testing, taking into account the money that might be saved in cancer treatment.

Most men who have a regular check-up and are over 50 have had a digital rectal examination. It may be embarrassing to have a doctor poking his fingers up your fundament to feel the size, shape and consistency of your prostate, but when you consider that it's to see whether you might have what could be a fatal cancer, the embarrassment can seem like a small price to pay. Even an experienced doctor will discover only about 40% of tumours this way. Consider this alongside the fact that the PSA test may fail to show that you have prostate cancer when you actually have it, and the digital examination pays its way if it picks up a cancer. Plainly it has been hard until recently to detect all prostate cancers without a biopsy, though there was one further non-invasive test before the PCA3 came along. This was transrectal ultrasound, but even this was not foolproof. Now, if the PCA3 really can detect cancer from a mixed sample of prostatic fluid (semen) and urine, the days of damaging biopsies may be numbered.

I used to take Saw Palmetto to try to limit night and day visits to the lavatory for a pee. I was taking as much as 1800 mg a day. Then I heard of the study in the *New England Journal of Medicine* (see below) that concluded that Saw Palmetto, a commonly used herbal remedy for BPH, has no effect on the prostate. I had tried not taking it before and things had not seemed to get worse, though I went back to Saw Palmetto just in case I was wrong. The new study seemed to confirm my suspicions.

More than half of all men show signs of a prostate problem by the time they are 60. The problem occurs in all racial groups. As men age, a steroid-metabolizing enzyme called 5-alpha-reductase type 2 increasingly converts testosterone into the more powerful form dihydrotestosterone, which locks on to the testosterone receptors in the prostate. The result is male pattern baldness (see chapter 22 on hair loss) as dihydrotestosterone affects the hair follicles in the scalp. At the same time, dihydrotestosterone causes the prostate to grow in size. Prostate enlargement results in the urethra, the tube that carries urine from the bladder to the penis, becoming constricted.

The part of the prostate affected is the core of the prostate, the part surrounding the urethra, whereas prostate cancer largely attacks the perimeter of the gland. This was good news for a while, as it seemed that prostate enlargement had no link to prostate cancer. More recently, however, this view has been challenged with the discovery that those suffering from BPH might be slightly more susceptible to prostate cancer, which may attack the core of the prostate too in some cases. Link this with the fact that most men develop BPH eventually, and the fact that eventually all men get prostate cancer if they live long enough. My view is that if you get BPH, and you probably will eventually, it will increase slightly your chances of getting prostate cancer. However, you can get one without the other.

The symptoms of BPH are among those found under the collective term lower urinary tract symptoms (LUTS):

- Frequent trips to the loo, day and night, perhaps every couple of hours or so.
- An urgent desire to pee, especially on standing up after sitting down for a while, or when leaning against something (usually a kitchen work surface) which puts direct pressure on the bladder.

- Occasional dribbling, usually when you cannot get to the loo in time.
- Delay in starting to pee.
- A weak urine stream, often with stops and starts.
- Inability to empty the bladder, which may have reduced capacity caused by muscle build-up in the bladder walls as a result of straining to pee.

BPH should not be confused with prostatitis, which refers to an infection of the prostate which may result in pain and blood in the urine. Prostatitis should be treated urgently, usually with antibiotics.

The frequency problem comes from an inability to empty the bladder. If left untreated, BPH can lead eventually to kidney damage and other complications. The problem of BPH is usually manageable for a number of years without any serious form of treatment, and this approach has acquired the term 'watchful waiting'. Things can and usually do get progressively worse, though there may be times when the symptoms stabilize for a while. There's an international scale, based on a series of questions about symptoms, which defines how serious your case is. For example, a score of nineteen puts you at the upper limit of the moderate range, while at twenty you enter the severe bracket. At that point watchful waiting usually gives way to some form of intervention, with drugs being the next step.

Drug treatment usually involves two drugs. The first is an alpha blocker similar to those used to treat high blood pressure, the drug most commonly used in the UK being Flomaxtra XL This drug reduces the constriction on the urethra and dilates the point at which the urethra meets the bladder. The result is better flow, though frequency, urgency and emptying of the bladder are unlikely to be affected. I have tried Flomaxtra XL and was disappointed. Flow improved for a few days, but then deteriorated again, and none of the other symptoms improved. To make matters worse, there were a number of unpleasant side effects such as dizziness, drowsiness and a slight headache. I quickly gave up Flomaxtra XL.

The second part of the usual chemical treatment is a drug that tackles 5-alpha-reductase and is said to reduce the size of the prostate by about

30% over a period of about six months – enough to make surgery avoidable. This drug is finasteride, which now comes in a combination form called dutasteride – combination because it combines an alpha blocker with finasteride, although, interestingly, it appears that dutasteride works no better than finasteride alone. Finasteride on its own is marketed as Proscar in the UK. Avodart is the brand name for the combination drug.

Finasteride and dutasteride treatment result in impotence in 3–4% of those who take them, along with loss of libido. The manufacturers allege that they will not affect fertility, but research on this point is scant to non-existent. They will also cause an allergic reaction in some, will reduce ejaculatory volume and will leave some men with swollen pectorals (man boobs) that are tender to the touch. To put it more bluntly, the drugs will have a feminising effect, accelerating a trend that happens to most men anyway with age.

This is an important point. As men age, their free testosterone declines. At the same time, their level of oestrogen (female hormone), of which all men have a little, stays constant or rises slightly. In other words, in the testosterone/oestrogen mix, the female hormone acquires a higher proportion. For this reason it's sometimes said that the man and woman in a couple where both are over seventy start to resemble each other.

For the last decade, legions of men have used a diluted form of finasteride called Propecia in an attempt to stop hair loss (see chapter 22 on hair loss). It does not, however, seem to work, at least not in the diluted form sanctioned for sale over the counter. It may be that there are some hair benefits from the stronger prescription version used to treat BPH, though I doubt whether finasteride or dutasteride can actually restore hair. However, it may slow the rate of loss, and as the cause of male pattern baldness (which is inherited) is the same as the cause of BPH, men suffering from one will normally suffer from the other. Therefore, so the theory goes, you could kill two birds with one stone by taking finasteride or dutasteride. But would you really want to take these drugs for years? They won't work forever anyway, and eventually men with BPH may be forced to try more radical treatment.

That means one of the many invasive and less invasive treatments on the market. Look on the web and you will find that there are at least a dozen of these. The most radical is complete prostate removal (prostatectomy), though this is usually reserved for prostate cancer. The trouble with prostatectomy is that it leaves you completely impotent, though most of the other treatments, like the drugs, can have this side effect and even affect fertility.

Some approaches to treatment involve laser surgery and ultrasound. The best-known treatment short of prostatectomy is still a transurethral resection of the prostate (TURP) in which blockages of the urethra are chipped away to create an enlarged passage through which urine can pass from the bladder. Unfortunately this does not halt further enlargement of the prostate, impotence may result and there is likely to be retro-ejaculation at orgasm, with semen passing into the bladder rather than joining up with sperm. (Note that orgasm is possible even when one is impotent).

It should be plain that there is no ideal solution to a problem that millions of men face as they get older. Drugs have only a partial effect and produce side effects. Surgery has many pitfalls and the prospect of impotence is not one that many men can stomach, except as a last resort.

Which brings me to herbal remedies and supplements. The good thing about supplementation generally is that side effects are usually minimal or non-existent. The downside is that they are likely to be less effective. One reason why almost all pharmaceutical drugs produce unwanted side effects is the fact that they are strong. They may do what they are meant to do, but the price you pay often comes in the shape of a long list of side effects that might shorten your life, especially if the drugs have to be taken for years or, worse, for the rest of your life.

It's too soon, as I write this, to give you my verdict on the herbal approach I have adopted personally in my battle with BPH. I have found from years of experience that Saw Palmetto, the most widely touted herbal remedy, makes little or no difference. This finding has been confirmed by a recent scientific study, and contradicts previous studies of Saw Palmetto. However, the new study is the first to meet the tough standards required for publication in the venerable *New England*

Journal of Medicine. The results have set the cat among the pigeons for many producers of Saw Palmetto supplements, and also the manufacturers of a pharmaceutical grade version known as Permixon, available only on prescription.

My solution to the problem, one that might or might not work, was to use the web to find every non-pharmaceutical remedy that I could. The next step was to try all of these together, taking a daily half dose of each. These are remedies that their suppliers claim will work alone, without need of other remedies to back them up. I won't name the dozen or so that I'm currently taking and have been taking for the last three months, as it's too soon to say whether they really work. If they do, I would expect to see reasonably good results at the six-month mark. I doubled the dose a week ago and may increase it again at the five-month stage.

I started with a score of nineteen on the international BPH symptom test (see above) and after three months my score is down to sixteen. If this treatment with natural plant remedies works, I would expect a score of around ten at the six-month stage. I could live with that and it would mean avoiding pharmaceutical drugs or surgery, at least for some years. I don't expect my prostate to ever be the size of a walnut again. On the plus side, there are no side effects with the current dosage and I do not expect any. Add to this the fact that even if I took dutasteride instead, I could not expect an improvement of more than about 30% after six months, and I would have to take the drug for the rest of my life to keep my score down, getting all the side effects in the process.

The biochemistry of the prostate is complex and scientists are still trying to figure out how the prostate works at the molecular level so that they can devise ways to deal with BPH and prostate cancer. What follows is still largely in the realm of scientific conjecture.

It's known that the enzyme 5-alpha reductase type 2 can convert testosterone in the prostate to 5-alpha dihydrotestosterone (DHT), the powerful form of testosterone that accounts for male pattern baldness and BPH, and possibly also for an increased risk of cardiovascular disease and prostate cancer.

Phyto-remedies (plant remedies) are widely used, especially in Europe, to tackle BPH, often with some success. They are unlikely to reverse prostate enlargement completely, but may halt further hyper-plasia and partially improve symptoms. They have the advantage over drugs of producing few side effects.

Many plant oils contain phyto-oestrogens, oestrogen-like polyphenolic molecules with the ability to disrupt hormones. Oestrogens are the collective term for the female hormones. Phyto-oestrogens, while they mimic oestrogens, are oestrogen antagonists in that they block the neg-ative effects of oestrogen. (Agonists have the opposite effect). The main dietary sources of phyto-oestrogens are soybeans, chickpeas, barley, flaxseed, beans, lentils and peas. Red clover is rich in phyto-oestrogens, which take the form of sterols (for example beta-sitosterol) and differ from the more commonly eaten soy phyto-oestrogens.

The range of phyto-oestrogens from soy includes lignans, flavones and isoflavones. Lignans are also plentiful in flaxseed (linseed), though it isn't known whether they play a part in reducing symptoms of BPH. There are several types of isoflavone, but the two most involved in reducing BPH appear to be genistein and daidzein. Opinions are mixed as to which of these molecules has the more important part to play, so isoflavone supplements aimed at BPH usually contain both. (These are usually the same supplements aimed at reducing symptoms of menopause).

Daidzein is broken down by bacteria in the gut and converts to the metabolite equol, which, being an oestrogen antagonist, competes with free oestrogen circulating in the blood, reducing the volume of free oestrogen. One theory is that free oestrogen, like dihydrotestosterone, may play a part in promoting prostate enlargement, just as the phyto-oestrogens may have the opposite effect.

However the main theory on equol is that it may be effective against prostate enlargement by challenging at either of the following two stages. It may be that it prevents 5-alpha reductase type 2 from convert-ing testosterone into alpha-5 dihydrotestosterone. Some testosterone will nevertheless be converted. However equol molecules may be able to step in again and bind 5-alpha dihydrotestosterone, preventing it from locking on to the cytosolic androgenic receptor and the alpha-1 adrenoceptor, the two androgen (male hormone) receptors in the prostate. In other words, it may be able to block and even reverse prostatic enlargement at either stage.

It's reckoned that daidzein converts to equol in about 30% of those who eat it, which may be bad news for the other 70% if they suffer from BPH. In the UK, about 30% of men have equol naturally in their blood. Japanese men consume large quantities of isoflavones, thanks to a diet rich in soy foods, and suffer very little prostatic hyperplasia – or hair loss. An enlarged prostate and male pattern baldness are known to go together. Japanese men also tend to have a longer lifespan than men in other parts of the world.

The average Japanese male has a plasma concentration of genistein of 180 ng/ml compared with an average of only 10 ng/ml in males in western society. The average Japanese male consumes more than 20 times as many isoflavones as the average British male. The conclusion may be that we should be eating a lot of soy products on a lifelong basis. It may also be significant that soy consumption increases thyroid activity.

Heredity has been shown to play a large part in prostate cancer, and 18 genes have been positively linked to prostate cancer. Now a test that identifies eight of these genes (the most significant being on chromosome 3) is being offered by an Icelandic company, deCODE Genetics. Certainly testing positive for some of these genes can indicate a strong risk of cancer, but there are many critics who say that this type of screening is premature and could worry unnecessarily those who are found to have several of the genes, which is likely as some of the genes in question are extremely common. Having them may show increased risk, but it does not show with certainty that prostate cancer will be triggered in that individual, in which case ignorance may be the better option – or a PCA3 test (see above).

Since vegans are said to be 50% less likely to get prostate cancer, this might seem like a positive recommendation for a vegan diet. But whether being a vegan affects the incidence of BPH does not seem to have been researched.

There is one somewhat unusual treatment for BPH on the market. It involves botulinum toxin (Botox) injections directly into the prostate. This is injection of a poison, the same one that has become popular for dealing with facial wrinkles. Seventy-three percent out of a test group of patients with BPH reported a 30% improvement in urinary symptoms a year after the injections. Side effects are said to be minimal, but it is probably too soon to say whether results are long-lasting and there is no long-term downside risk. When used as a cosmetic treatment, the effects of Botox typically last about six months.

According to one theory, a sufficient level of water consumption is important for keeping prostate enlargement down. Apart from the fact that adequate hydration is important for health, there may be a causal relationship between the fact that thirst declines with age at around the same time as prostate enlargement occurs. If BPH could be prevented or cured with an adequate intake of water, what a simple cure that would be for a seemingly complex problem.

Tomatoes are rich in lycopene, especially when cooked. It's thought that lycopene may help in keeping prostate enlargement under control. I tend to think that it may help a little in conjunction with other remedies, but on its own I doubt that it will make a difference. A bit of sunshine is said to help too, thanks to its contribution of vitamin D (see chapter 14 on supplements).

CHAPTER FORTY-FOUR
WEIGHT WATCHING WORRIES

I was going to call this chapter 'Dieting' or 'Losing weight', but it seemed to me that this sent out the wrong signals. Yes, the worried well might include some men who are overweight, but probably not the obese. If you are obese, you might be worried – you should be worried – but you won't be well. That goes without saying, whether we're talking about liver damage, impotence, diabetes or a long list of other problems.

It has been said many times before. Yo-yo dieting doesn't work. Lose weight according to the latest fad diet – and that usually means losing weight fast – and you will not only put the lost weight back on again, but probably some more into the bargain. The reason is that the body's delicate weight control system, developed over more than a million years, will read diet as famine and overcompensate eventually in preparation for further dearth to come. Your body will actually put on weight – and for weight read fat – in preparation for the next food shortage. If you live in drought-stricken sub-Saharan Africa, that might be the best thing for your body. Chances are, however, that you do not live in sub-Saharan Africa and have more than adequate food supplies to hand.

So how do you lose weight and keep it off, assuming that you want to and need to? For a start, don't count calories – that's obsessive. Instead be roughly aware of how many calories you need and how many the food that you eat contains. With a little practice you should be able to estimate within about 15% how many calories such-and-such a food contains in a portion or, for example, 100 grams.

A growing number of people of both sexes are overweight or obese. The reasons – all lifestyle factors – have been covered over and over in the press: junk food, processed food, ready-made meals high in fat, lack of exercise, TV and computers, the decline of sport in schools, modern transport, child safety, school meals, even the abolition of National Service. The outcome is an army of young men who are overweight before they hit twenty and may well be obese by the time they reach forty.

Body Mass Index (BMI) is weight in kilos divided by height in metres squared. A score of 30 or over signals obesity, while a score over 25 and under 30 indicates an overweight problem. That Brad Pitt has a BMI of 26 (overweight) and Mike Tyson a BMI of 32 (obese) shows how, when looking at anyone who is lean, fit and muscular, the BMI can be misleading. The trouble is that in only looking at weight and height, it assumes that everyone of a given height or weight has the same body composition. However, it is probably fair to say that for 90% of the population, the BMI is a good indicator of whether there is a weight problem or not. A better indicator, though, is body fat measured by bioelectrical impedance analysis (BIA). A middle-aged man with a body fat level (as a percentage of total weight) in the 17% – 20% range is doing fine. From 21% to 23% he is a bit borderline, and over 23% he should probably work harder on his exercise and dietary routines. I would guess that Brad Pitt is probably somewhere around the 15% mark.

An increasingly popular way of telling whether you have a weight problem is to measure your waist (without cheating) and then measure your hips. The first measurement should be 90% of the second or less. It's sometimes said that for a man, the waist measurement should be 37" or less, but of course that can only be a rough guide, as men come in a variety of statures, and achieving 37" might be unreasonable if you are 7' tall. The reason why waist measurement is now thought to be so crucial is that fat around the abdomen is not like fat in the rest of the body. We're not talking about the subcutaneous fat under the skin around your middle. We're talking about the deep fat between your abdominal muscles and encircling your abdominal cavity. This visceral fat produces dangerous hormones and it's very hard to get rid of.

According to one survey, 43.9% of men are overweight and a further 22.7% are obese, based on BMI. Notwithstanding the weaknesses in BMI measurement, which give an overly high score in those who are fit and muscular, that's a total of 66.6% of the UK population who allegedly weigh more than they should. Many of these will fit the criteria for what has become known as the metabolic syndrome or syndrome X. This is a group of symptoms, any two of which predispose to diabetes. The metabolic syndrome is therefore said to be a pre-diabetic syndrome. The symptoms are: poor blood sugar control, raised cholesterol, raised blood triglycerides, high blood pressure, sticky blood (making clotting more likely) and excessive abdominal fat.

Metabolic syndrome might better be described as slow metabolic rate syndrome, because as we put on excess weight, this has the effect of slowing our metabolism (see chapter 26 on metabolism). When metabolism slows, we burn fewer calories. If we don't burn the calories we eat, they get stored in our fat cells and we put on weight. Therefore fighting the problems of weight gain is about speeding up metabolism. When you exercise, muscle mass increases, which speeds up the rate at which calories are burnt. Basal Metabolic Rate (BMR) is defined as the number of calories required to keep your basic bodily functions operational. These include blood circulation, breathing, the neural system, liver, kidneys, brain, heart and so on, even when you are asleep. This basal metabolism accounts for about 70% of the calories you burn. The higher your BMR, the more calories you will burn just to keep your body ticking over, irrespective of any physical activity during the day. The fitter you are and the lower your fat percentage, the higher your BMR. BMR is another way of looking at biological or metabolic age. The higher your BMR, the lower your metabolic age. Whether it is lower than your chronological age will depend on how fit you are.

Weight problems are linked to glucose and insulin – the less glucose we eat, the less insulin we need to produce to keep our sugar level under control. This is where the idea of the Glycaemic Index came from. Most sugary foods are 'fast release' in that they quickly lead to a high level of blood sugar. Fruit sugar (fructose) tends to be slow to medium release, but too much sugar and especially too much fruit juice can still raise insulin levels fairly fast. On the other hand slow release foods are carbohydrates that are safer to eat if you don't need that sudden surge of energy that fast release sugars give you. And slow release carbohydrates will therefore be less likely to be stored as fat. You may need to consult a GI book, though, to find out where a particular food lies on the GI Index. White rice is high (fast) on the list, for example, but basmati rice is low, as is rye bread, while bread made from wheat flour is high.

What you are doing by choosing foods low on the Glycaemic Index is selecting nourishment from slow release rather than fast release (or medium release) carbohydrates. (Remember, all sugars are carbohydrates). The object is too keep sugar and therefore insulin release down, and consequently limit fat storage, unless of course you are about to run a marathon and need fast release glucose for sustained energy, but in that situation there is no worry about surplus to requirement being stored in the form of fat.

Around 10% of the NHS budget goes on diabetes. Obesity has trebled in the UK in the last twenty years. Around 2 million people in the UK are known to have the disease and another million are thought to have it without being aware of the fact. It is calculated that those knowingly suffering from diabetes will rise to 4 million by 2014. Of those with diabetes, 90% have Type 2 diabetes (T2D) and 10% have Type 1 diabetes (T1D). The epidemic is in T2D, which is almost always associated with obesity (see chapter 15 on diabetes).

Diabetes isn't the only thing that weight problems can lead to. Being overweight is conducive to heart disease and strokes and to certain types of cancer. Being fat doesn't help your mood either, and people who are overweight or obese are more likely to suffer from mood disorders and depression in particular. That they generally die younger goes without saying. Here there is a contradiction, though, as there is a school of thought that says that fat people are happy-go-lucky and therefore less stressed than the rest of us.

It was thought for many years that heredity might play a part in obesity. There is still much speculation in this area, but one gene, called the apolipoprotein A5 gene (APOA5) has been identified as giving some immunity to obesity in the 13% of the population who have a particular variant of the gene. However, if those with the gene do manage to put on weight in the wrong places, they have more difficulty in getting rid of it than those who do not have the gene.

Other genes play a part in weight problems. One is called the FTO gene, which comes in two variants in all of us. If you get two copies of one variant, you are 70% more likely to be obese than if you inherited two copies of the other variant. If you got one copy of each variant, you have a 30% increased chance of obesity. An increased risk does not guarantee being overweight or obese – it just increases your propensity to have a weight problem. In time other genes that play a part in weight gain will almost certainly be found.

There has been much talk of a diet pill that will make it unnecessary to diet and exercise to lose weight. There have been quite a few false dawns, but one drug does seem to offer some promise, though so far it is only available on a private prescription. It comes from the realm of chemical metabolic engineering, as distinct from genetic metabolic engineering. The drug is rimonabant (trade name Acomplia). It claims to burn calories by tricking the body into believing it is being exercised when it isn't. A quarter of those in the trials lost 10% of their body weight in a year. It seemed like a fat person's dream come true – lose weight without having to bother about diet or exercise. Glucose control got better, cholesterol and triglyceride counts improved, including a significant improvement in 'good' (HDL) cholesterol.

How does rimonabant work? It blocks molecular receptors in the hypothalamus, the abdomen and the digestive tract, all of which have a role in regulating appetite, energy use, and fat and glucose metabolism. Cannabinoids, which play a key part in appetite and are the active ingredients in cannabis, are prevented from hooking up with their receptors. The result is that appetite is suppressed. It influences a chemical called anandamide, which has an impact on the brain (ananda means bliss in Hindi). But there may as yet be unwanted side effects to rimonabant. Release of the drug in the US has been delayed amid fears that it may increase the risk of suicide.

Doctors have been accused of being too ready to prescribe dugs for the obese rather than give them more chance to lose weight through exercise and good nutrition. Two thirds of all adults in the UK are obese or overweight, and the numbers have jumped 50% in the last decade. It has been calculated that unless the epidemic is halted, 90% of men will be obese by 2050. However, a government report paints an even more worrying picture, predicting that by 2025, 90% of men will be overweight and half of these will be obese. NHS expenditure linked to obesity is expected to grow sevenfold by 2050.

Two drugs that are prescribed are sibutramine (trade name Reductil) and orlistat (trade name Xenical). Sibutramine changes the chemical messages to the brain associated with food, while orlistat limits fat absorption. Both have side effects, which is why they should only be used as a last resort.

Leptin, a hormone produced by the body's fat cells, has been shown to play an important part in both appetite and satiety, and has therefore undergone considerable research in the hunt for a drug to control appetite. Research has found that a number of people lack leptin completely and as a result are unable to stop eating foods that excite their appetite. Treatment with leptin helped these people to stop overeating.

A hormone called pancreatic polypeptide (PP) is released from the small intestine when food is eaten. This signals to the brain that enough has been consumed and hunger pangs are then turned off. There is hope that injections of PP might help overweight and obese people to switch off their cravings for more food than their body needs.

Another natural approach to satiety is said to be found in eating pine nuts for their pinolenic acid, which has the ability to trigger the release of hormones announcing we are full even when we aren't. The risk, though, is that you could end up not getting enough calories because your brain always tells you that you are full before you have had as much to eat as your body requires. That's the problem with all satiety approaches to diet. It's said that pinolenic acid will soon be available in a range of foods such as yoghurts and salad dressings, but in the meantime you could eat a few handfuls of pine nuts each day. They are about 50% fat and along with other nuts, seeds and perhaps fish, could make a sizeable contribution to your daily fat quota.

Satiety itself now has an index: the Satiety Index. This isn't the same as the Glycaemic Index, but the idea is similar. In this case, foods high on the Index will leave you feeling full sooner and for longer – foods like potatoes, steak, muesli, oranges and bananas. Not surprisingly, foods that are low on this index tend to feature on most lists of junk food or food that is less healthy. This includes biscuits, white bread and corn-flakes, but also, perhaps surprisingly, cheese. Some findings are unexpected. Popcorn is high on this index. Note that the best foods to eat on either the Glycaemic or the Satiety Index are often the same – they will be high on the Satiety Index and low on the Glycaemic Index.

It's wrongly thought that dairy foods make you fatter. True, they might if you eat too much of them, but the fact is that they are not the villain they were once thought to be and the reason is their calcium content. When we don't get enough calcium our body tries to conserve the calcium we already have and this leads to the production of a hormone called calcitrol. This hormone encourages the body to store fat rather than burn it. When the body gets sufficient calcium it more readily burns fat and also makes it harder for itself to make and store new fat in the fat cells (adipocytes). With less calcitrol, the body can more easily trigger fat release into the blood stream so that it can be used for energy. Many people hold back on dairy because they think, wrongly, that they have a lactose (dairy sugar) intolerance.

The best dairy foods for the overweight are those high in calcium, or calcium-enriched, but which don't have too many calories. So it's still better to go for reduced fat versions. But if you are not trying to lose weight, you will still benefit from a diet with plenty of dairy. You could end up the same weight, but with more pounds made from protein (muscle) and fewer from fat. Calcium supplements are not a better option as they don't have the amino acids found in dairy foods that work together synergistically to build healthy bones and muscles.

Non-dairy foods that are a good source of calcium are tofu, sesame seeds, okra, spinach, sardines, tahini, dried figs and curly kale.

Women have traditionally been the main buyers of diet books, but more and more men have joined the hunt for an easy solution. Sadly there isn't one, but hope springs eternal and so thousands of books go on getting sold. Fad diets like the Scarsdale Diet, the Cambridge Diet and the Atkins Diet come and go and no doubt there will be many others that become as fashionable as these did. But you would be hard-pressed to find anyone, several years after trying any of these, who swore by them.

It isn't easy to lose weight and keep it off. I'm not talking about some-one who starts at 25 stone, goes to Weight Watchers, and reaches a sta-ble 14 stone a year later. While that person (and they are rare) will be less unhealthy for having shed 11 stone, their body will never be as fit as it would have been had they weighed 14 stone all along.

When you lose weight by dieting, much of the initial weight loss is from water, which makes up over half our body weight and is relatively heavy. Water is not a part of the make-up of fat – mostly it's held in our muscle tissue – so when you lose say 10 pounds of water, you lose no fat at all. And when you do lose fat, you do not lose fat cells. We are born with a finite number of fat cells and this is the number we have for life. When we get fat, these cells swell up and when we lose fat, they shrink. When they shrink they are just waiting, at the slightest sign of food or hint of famine, to swell up again in preparation for the next great dearth. Getting rid of surplus fat is an arduous task.

There are three kinds of weight loss pill, none of which I would rec-ommend, with the possible exception of rimonabant in extreme cases (see above). The first are fat blockers, the second are appetite suppres-sants and the third are herbal weight loss remedies. Only pills in the last group are likely to be relatively harmless. An example of a fat blocker is Alli, a fat blocker that has not been given the green light for over-the-counter sale, but is widely available on the web. Allegedly it produces 50% more weight loss than exercise and diet alone. The user is advised to exercise regularly and to eat no more than 15 grams of fat at any meal if they are to avoid diarrhoea. The trouble with fat blockers is that they prevent the body from utilizing dietary fat, and as fat carries minerals and vitamins, the body can be deprived of these essential micronutrients.

My advice is that you should only take drugs as a last resort, as all drugs tend to have side effects and what you gain on one front by taking them you may lose on another. In any case, most weight loss supple-ments simply do not work. You can lose fat surgically, but that has to be an act of desperation. However, there are more subtle suggestions, not for losing weight, but for not putting it on in the first place. Some people swear by the view that protein is more filling than fat or carbohydrate, therefore you can control your appetite and hence your weight by eating a protein-dominant diet. I have suggested elsewhere that 15% of calories from protein is about the right amount. I do not believe that suppressing appetite by going for a higher protein proportion will work. You might eat less as a result, and you might even control your weight this way, but at some cost, as your body fat percentage is likely to rise and with it your overall and your 'bad' LDL cholesterol count. Why? Because you are eating protein that is surplus to requirement and surplus protein gets stored as fat.

Recent studies have shown that men in particular put on extra weight around the middle – the familiar paunch or beer belly. Until not so long ago, it was assumed that this was fat like any other. Now we know otherwise. The visceral fat that gathers between and under the abdominal muscles and even around the lungs in extreme cases is a more dangerous fat, molecularly speaking, than the fat in the rest of the body. If your waist measurement is more than 90% of your chest measurement, you're in trouble. This new yardstick for revealing whether you are a candidate for a coronary event has proved extremely reliable since it was introduced. The trouble is that abdominal fat is the hardest kind of fat to get rid of.

You cannot get rid of fat in one particular part of the body only, though bodybuilders long believed that you could. When you lose fat, you lose it equally overall, except, seemingly, abdominal fat, which is extremely hard to lose once you have put it on. You might diet and exercise and think that because your waist measurement has come down, you have lost abdominal fat. But you will probably have lost less than you think, as what you will have lost above all is ordinary surface fat deposited between skin and abdominal muscles.

Women put weight on around their thighs and men put it on around their middles. Not only is it hard to lose abdominal fat, but it gets harder as you get older. Some men are born with a fast metabolism and are less likely to put on weight, no matter how much they eat. But most men have a slower metabolism that tends to get slower still with age. Then you burn fat more slowly and put on fat more easily. To maintain the same weight, or to lose weight, you have to put in more exercise and make more effort to eat well and less. Your appetite will tend to grow with age, at least in the years of middle age, and your ability to resist will get weaker. On the exercise front the news is even bleaker. As we age, we need ever more exercise to control our weight and our body fat ratio, but at the same time we naturally become less and less active.

Yet if we have the will to exercise hard, what happens is that we cannot, as we get older, sustain the same workouts as we could when younger – the same aerobic levels and the same weights for resistance training. Nor can we go hard at either for as long as we once could. We find it increasingly difficult to maintain muscle mass. We have to stop more frequently for a breather, and maybe we find that doing a 60 minute session is all we can manage when we would rather do 90 minutes. We find that we get tired more easily as we get older, we need more rest and sleep, especially after exercise, and our bodies need longer to recover before we are ready for more. I know from experience that after a hard workout I need nine hours sleep rather than eight. And sometimes I don't feel up to a full workout day after day. As for Sundays, that's my day of rest, and I do no exercise at all on Sundays. I don't even shave. There is a time to relax and rest and Sunday is it.

I've said that it is hard to lose weight and hard to maintain a given weight once you have lost weight. When I was 20, I was the same 6' 0.5" that I am now (no, you don't have to lose height as you age if you stay well and truly fit), but I was a fairly skinny 11 stone 3lbs. I had to put on weight to make the university discus team and I did this with weight training and drinking loads of whole milk mixed with a protein compound. The result was that I put on eight pounds in eight weeks, most of it muscle thanks to the intensity of the exercise and the undoubted fact that for me, as for most people, it is easier to put on weight than take it off. I have never been less than 11 stone 11 lbs since then. In fact I rapidly went up to 12 stone and stayed there for many years, just as I hovered around the 13 stone mark in my forties and fifties. Now I struggle to stay around the 13.5 stone mark and occasionally find myself pushing 14 stone.

What has happened over the 44 years since I was 11 stone 3 lb is that I have put on muscle and fat. I am fit for my age, but less fit than I would like to be. As one doctor said to me when I had my annual BUPA check-up, "You're fit, but you're not Sebastian Coe". I accept that there is no way I could be 12 stone again and maybe not even 13 stone. My body fat, at around the 17% mark, is good, but it was probably around 12% back when I was 20 years old. Is it a struggle to keep around the 13.5 stone mark? Definitely. What would my ideal be at my age (64)? I would say 12.5 stone with a body fat percentage of 15%. But I know that to get there I would have to exercise harder and longer than I do and would have to restrict my diet severely, though I'd still be able to eat what I do eat – just less of it.

So why don't I do that? For one thing, I would be worn out and therefore the effort would end up being counterproductive. My quality of life would get worse, not better, and probably I would have a shorter life ahead of me. I would be exhausted, living only to exercise, sleep and eat, and there has to be more to life. I would have to be on a calorie-restricted diet of no more than 1500 calories a day, whereas I currently eat about 2000 calories a day.

Tests with mice have shown that a severely restricted diet can lengthen life and there is an assumption that the same applies to men. However, no trials on humans have been tried to see if that holds true. I remember a magazine article a few years ago that showed a photo of a man who had taken a leap of faith and restricted his diet severely in order to increase his lifespan, hopefully by as much as the 40% achieved by the mice. The man was so thin that he looked like someone straight out of London Fashion Week. As I recall, he was on a diet of about 1200 calories a day. His eyes were sunk in his head and he looked about ten years older than he was. No one knows to what extent, if at all, restricting calories so drastically (and feeling permanently hungry, as the man admitted) really will lengthen your life. But even if it were true, there has to be a limit to how far most of us will go in compromising our quality of life, no matter what extension in years we may get from going down the route of a restricted diet, or for that matter doing too much exercise. (But see chapter 1 on ageing and chapters 3 and 14 on alcohol and supplements for a look at resveratrol supplementation, which is said to mimic the benefits of calorie restriction).

My advice is that you have a set of scales that gives your body fat as well as your weight, but don't become a slave to this and weigh yourself too often, and don't necessarily believe the body fat figure as such scales are notoriously inaccurate. Don't become obsessive. Obsessive men are hard to live with and obsession can lead to divorce. Newspaper articles keep reminding us that single men have shorter lives, which suggests, all else being equal, that divorce is best avoided or you could end up dying sooner rather than later.

I am not going to dwell on the subject of anorexia. While it is rare among men, it is even rarer among men in middle life. Paradoxically, it may haunt men in old age, but in this case is likely to be the result of a combination of poverty, depression, self- neglect and Alzheimer's disease, in which case it is not the same illness that afflicts thousands of teenage girls. However, it is worth touching on depression, as this is a deadly illness for many and can lead to years of misery if left untreated. Those who are depressed tend to neglect their diet and their need for exercise. Self-neglect can lead to diseases such as osteoporosis. From there it may only be a short step to a broken hip and death within months from a pulmonary embolism. In that way depression can kill. Osteoporosis is often thought of as a woman's disease, but it can affect men too. It can start in middle life and sometimes earlier. The best antidotes to osteoporosis are load-bearing exercise and a healthy diet.

What makes for an ideal weight? Your instinct and a look at yourself in the mirror should tell you roughly what your optimum weight should be. Take your build into account as well as your body fat percentage, which should be somewhere between 17% and 22%, though some tables will suggest that if you are over 60, this could rise to 18–24% or thereabouts. Women will typically have a higher range, since they carry more body fat than men.

If you do not yet have signs of a paunch around your middle, make sure that you don't develop one. If you are showing a bit of chub in the danger zone, you can only work on your overall body fat. The dangerous abdominal fat will go eventually if you persevere, but don't expect miracles overnight. It will be a long and hard battle, one for which most men don't have the willpower. The reward you get is not only a great-looking midriff, but more importantly the knowledge that you may have won a major battle in the war against cholesterol and heart disease.

Fat people who have had a heart attack live longer than others who have had a heart attack. Fat people have higher levels of cannabinoids, which encourage appetite, and these may be cardioprotective by dilating blood vessels, giving better circulation. Fat people also have lower blood platelet counts and thus may be at less risk of a clot. Fat people have a higher triglycerides count. This increases the risk of heart attack, but may reduce the incidence of cardiac arrhythmias. People on high fat diets are known to be more relaxed and unaggressive than those on a low fat diet. If we assume that those who eat a high fat diet are going to be fat, and being fat de-stresses, fat people may be less prone to a cardiac event than they would be if they were more stressed. However, being fat, they will still be more prone to heart problems than those who are not fat. A fat person who is depressed is likely to be stressed and is in the worst of all possible positions. If all that sounds confusing, it is. For fat people, there are pluses and minuses in being fat, but on balance it is better not to be fat if you want to avoid a heart attack.

Breakfast should be the biggest meal of the day and dinner the smallest. In between, according to some nutritionists, snacking is good, not bad, provided that total calories are limited and the right things are snacked on. This goes back to the idea that what was good for our cave-dwelling ancestors should be good for us, and in those days, it's doubtful if they ate three regular meals a day. Snacking can also control blood sugar levels better.

A fizzy drink called Enviga that contains extracts of green tea and caffeine is claimed to boost metabolic rate and help to burn calories. Nutritionists have expressed doubts about some of the weight-controlling claims made for this product, highlighting the fact that too much caffeine can cause heart arrhythmias in those susceptible. Caffeine can also lead to diarrhoea, dehydration, nausea, irritability and insomnia.

The idea that we should detox (fast) from time to time to rid the body of toxins is discredited by almost all serious nutritionists and weight researchers. The general consensus is that the body is well able to carry out its own cleansing, mainly through the lymphatic system, without the need for detox diets and similar fads.

It seems certain that by adopting a prehistoric caveman diet (called by some the Evo diet), we could all shed pounds. Whether most of us could stomach a lifetime of eating large piles of raw vegetables is doubtful. The fish, seeds, nuts and fruit might be more acceptable, however.

The obese are unlikely to be vegetarians. Eating red meat has been proven to increase muscular strength. However, it also increases the risk of cancer and heart disease. Iron and zinc, which come from meat, are hard to obtain from vegetable sources. On the other hand, vegetarians are known to live longer than meat eaters. My view is that healthy eaters who eat moderate amounts of lean meat and plenty of fruit and vegetables, organic fish and poultry are likely to live longer than the average vegetarian.

People who chew gum consume 10% fewer calories and have lower blood pressure. Since chewing gum mimics eating, it improves bowel function by causing the release of hormones which activate the digestive system. The best gum to chew is one containing xylitol, a natural sweetener derived from the bark of Scandinavian birch trees. It also improves the level of good bacteria in saliva and thus helps maintain oral health.

Fat people should avoid sugary foods as high blood sugar levels encourage the onset of Type 2 diabetes. Those who already have diabetes, or might have diabetes, should also avoid sugar as much as possible. However, sugar in the form of fructose (fruit sugar) is more acceptable as it has a low score on the Glycaemic Index. This means that it will only turn to fat slowly, if not burnt first as energy, and will only gradually cause blood sugar level to rise. This gives the pancreas time to respond and produce insulin.

A natural sweetener called agave nectar, available in health food shops, may soon be widespread in supermarket products. It comes in a liquid form from the same plant as tequila and is 25% sweeter than sugar. It's said to help burn fat and reduce sugar cravings. Being a fructose sweetener, rather than sucrose, it's low on the Glycaemic Index. It does not require insulin to break it down.

Eliminating fat from the diet completely can be dangerous. Fat helps the body to produce acetylcholine, which is important for memory and the proper functioning of the nervous and endocrine systems. It's also essential for the metabolism of the fat-soluble vitamins A, D, E and K. Little or no fat in the diet will lead to accelerated ageing.

The feel-good chemical in the brain when we eat is anandamine. Chocolate improves mood by slowing the breakdown of anandamine and prolonging feelings of wellbeing. However, chocolate contains sugar and despite the claim that some dark chocolates rich in cocoa solids are good for you as they contain plenty of anti-oxidants, the downside of the sugar content probably outweighs the upside of the anti-oxidants, although few chocoholics like to hear that. All chocolate is high in calories. Chocolate without sugar would taste bitter.

There are spreads and drinks on the market that will raise your 'good' (HDL) cholesterol level slightly. I think there are healthier ways of raising HDL – exercise for example. What the adverts won't tell you is how many calories there are in these spreads and drinks. There are a lot and you may have to eat or drink unacceptably large amounts of these products to get an HDL boost that is worthwhile. It's thought that around 80% of our cholesterol level, including HDL, is internally regulated and therefore not subject to dietary influence. Statin drugs influence internal regulation of cholesterol and therefore, like exercise, are a part of that 80% that is non-dietary.

There are 3,500 calories (kilocalories) to the pound. Therefore, all else being equal, if you burnt 2,000 calories a day and ate 1,500 calories a day for 14 weeks, you would lose a stone in weight in that time. In theory you could also lose that amount of weight by eating and burning 2,000 calories a day for 14 weeks, while additionally burning say 500 calories in an hour on a rowing machine each day. That's putting weight loss at its most basic, but as should be clear from what I have written above, it is far from being that simple. If you do set out to lose weight and would like the weight loss to come from your fat cells and not from protein (muscle) or water, try not to lose more than one pound per week.

Dietary carbohydrate is converted into glucose. Excess glucose is stored as saturated fat in the body's fat cells after conversion by the liver. The body can only store (in the liver) about 200 calories of glucose as glucose. Therefore carbs that are not immediately burnt as fuel for the body and not stored in the liver are turned to fat.

The average male produces about 1.5 litres of faeces a day – that's about 450 grams or just over one pound in weight. Stool frequency should be twice a day on a really healthy diet with lots of exercise. Exercise speeds up stool passage.

There is more downside than upside to fasting. The main risk is that the liver, which gets rid of impurities, will start to function less efficiently the longer you fast. There have been suggestions that fasting on alternate days causes fat cells to shrink. If this means that fat stores are burnt readily in preference to carbohydrate and protein, this is good news, but the problem is that I just don't believe it.

A report on obesity concluded that the problem was 23% down to environmental factors and 77% down to heredity. This doesn't mean that obesity is inevitable for some, it just means that they have to work harder to avoid it.

There is a battle going on between food manufacturers on the one hand and the Food Standards Agency (FSA) on the other over how best to warn consumers of the risks they take in buying food containing fat, sugar and salt. The 'traffic light' system has already been introduced voluntarily by several supermarket chains. As the name suggests, it highlights risk on the front of packaging, with different colours indicating the level of risk, red showing the highest level. However, a rival system based on Guideline Daily Amount (GDA) seems likely to prevail in the end, which is unfortunate, as it means that consumers have to understand the figures showing how much of GDA is contained per serving or per 100grams or per packet. The food manufacturers have opposed the traffic light system mainly because they fear it might be effective in reducing fat, sugar and salt consumption and this is exactly what they do not want. These three ingredients, two of which contribute to the obesity epidemic and one to cardiovascular disease, account for a good deal of food's tastiness and therefore their profit.

Another trick used by the food industry is to print dietary information on labels so small that it's difficult to decipher, especially if you need glasses to read and don't have them to hand in the supermarket. We can expect a lot more government and EU regulation of the food industry in the future in the battle against obesity. The food manufacturers want to go on giving consumers what they like rather than what is good for them. Expect trans fats to be banned soon.

Obesity is highest in homes where meals are no longer cooked with fresh ingredients, but come microwave-ready instead. Because ready-made meals and take-aways are now the norm at the lower end of the social scale, it's a fact that food expenditure is about the same at both ends of the scale if you exclude sit-down restaurants. At the top end of the scale meals are usually cooked at home from fresh ingredients, often organic, and while this has a cost to it, it costs no more to eat this way than to eat ready-made meals, often high in sugar, salt and fats, where the labour that goes into manufacture adds to the cost. The result is that healthy meals are eaten at the top end of the market and generally unhealthy meals at the bottom end, and the cost for each is about the same. So the argument that those who find themselves downmarket cannot afford to eat better looks rather weak.

Here are some useful numbers for measuring calories:

1 calorie = 1 kilocalorie

239 kilocalories (Kcal) = 100 kilojoules (KJ)

1000 kilojoules = 1 megajoule (MJ)

....

More Tips and Traps

In the UK we eat an average of 1.25 pounds of fruit and vegetables a day compared with the EU average which is 12% higher.

There's a theory that you can lose weight by eating more slowly. According to the theory, when we eat fast we eat too much before the message has got to our brain that we've eaten enough. By the time the message has got through we've already over-eaten.

Some men use amphetamines to lose weight. Amphetamine use without a prescription is illegal, and amphetamines are addictive and dangerous.

Acid reflux, which causes heartburn, is more prevalent the more overweight you are.

Saunas and Turkish baths are no use when it comes to weight loss as they only lead to water loss through perspiration, and this is likely to be made up from drinking afterwards.

Exercise raises glucose and serotonin levels in the brain, and adrenaline, nora-drenaline and dopamine levels in the blood. The combination of these is said to inhibit hunger pangs.

It's now thought that getting overall cholesterol level and 'bad' LDL cholesterol level down is more important than raising 'good' HDL cholesterol level as a proportion of total cholesterol.

On average, men burn about 70 calories an hour while they are sleeping.

CHAPTER FORTY-FIVE
WORK AND PLAY

A growing body of research shows that people who feel in charge of their lives – and their jobs in particular – are happier and live longer. This is why men who work for themselves or who are in charge at work and have plenty of independence and authority are less inclined to look forward to retirement, while men who view work as a chore, not a career, and see others as their masters usually cannot wait for retirement. If you are happy in your job and have lots of say in what you do and how you do it, you are (a) more likely to want to work beyond 65, and (b) more likely to live longer.

For some men, though, work is drudgery and they look forward to an easier life once they can give up the daily slog. For such men, retirement can come as a huge relief. The trouble is that unless it is properly planned and executed, it can be a disaster for health and happiness. There is no point in retiring unless it is to do something as rewarding or more rewarding than your job. And that is easier said than done. Doing nothing should not be an option unless you want to invite depression. One way to have a happy retirement is to do part-time work that is gratifying – work for a charity and help others. It's amazing how good you can feel. Better still, start a charity.

Some of the happiest people are those for whom their job is a calling rather than just a source of income. Professions like nursing, teaching and the clergy often attract people like this. They are carers in the so-called caring professions and, like working for a charity, these professions can produce a sense of satisfaction that comes from putting others first. The reward may be enhanced personal well-being and the better health that goes with a stronger immune system.

In America you will sometimes find people talking about their 'avocation', a word that suggests something that is the opposite of their job.

This tends to be a hobby, but is often something more than a hobby. It's often something that can be turned into an alternative occupation on retirement. I often like to say that you should work at your hobby for a living, and while this is not feasible for most people, it is for some. I collect antiquarian maps for a hobby, and it has crossed my mind that if and when I retire, I could become a map dealer, working at my hobby. Some people love gardening and might start a garden design business on retirement.

The important thing is to go from main job to a lesser occupation, whether or not it's one that makes money. After all, an occupation is only something that occupies your time, and unless you plan on watching TV with a beer in your hand, what you spend your time doing should be a major consideration when retirement age looms.

Retirement age, like the concept of retirement itself, is something pretty arbitrary. The law makes 65 (and eventually 68) the official retirement age for men, and many companies follow the law on this. But how productive you are at a given age raises the question of chronological versus biological age. There are plenty of examples of men still working actively in their eighties and nineties and even a few over the age of a hundred. Here's betting that continuing to work beyond the official retirement age has a lot to do with their longevity. A younger biological age keeps them going longer and the fact of work prolongs an already longer lifespan – provided that work is satisfying and even enjoyable, giving a sense of purpose and achievement. Here we are back to the idea of being in charge of your own life and destiny. You may be a one-man-band working for yourself, but if you work for a company, you don't have to be at the top of the tree to feel in charge – you just have to have plenty of autonomy or at least feel that you do (and in an enlightened company you should).

In the UK, the average man retires at the age of 63.8 years and lives for a further 12.4 years. Women on the other hand retire at 60.3 years and live for a further 21 years. The combination of longer longevity and earlier retirement for women therefore means that working women, on average, have 8.6 more years in retirement than men, though this gap is slowly narrowing.

What about the things you can do – work at – when you do retire from your job? Many people travel the world, and the older they are, the more secure they will feel if they take a cruise to see places. Retirees are now big business for the travel industry and a headache for the insurance business as medical claims rise exponentially when people over seventy travel to countries which only twenty years ago would have been considered too dangerous for all but youngsters in their twenties.

But the subject of retirement is perhaps more appropriate for men in later life rather than middle life. It is, however, important to start thinking about it many years in advance. For most men, that also means pension planning. Some men will be anxious and plan meticulously for their financial future, while others will take a more cavalier attitude to savings. There is no right or wrong way. Every individual is different. The important thing is not to be too obsessive. I know a couple who put themselves on a waiting list for a much respected retirement home while still in their forties. That would not be my way, but it was fine for them. For me the future is an adventure waiting to happen, rather like a trip to a Third World country, and half the fun is not planning in too much detail, though not planning at all would, I think, be foolish.

It's often said that you need to get the work-play balance right. The Americans are said to work too hard and the French not enough. Either way, we are brought up in the west with the idea that work is good for you, that it's the norm. So much so that we rarely stop to ask ourselves why we work. If we do ask, the answer seems obvious – we work to have a certain standard of living and to avoid making ourselves a burden on others or the state. That's our society as it has evolved under the influence of the Protestant work ethic. I'm old enough to remember the Fifties and Sixties, when we all thought we had never had it so good. Most of us were better off than the pre-war generation, but if you compare living standards fifty years ago with now, how things have changed. Yesterday's luxuries like cars and TV have become the norm. Consumerism has become the yardstick by which poverty is measured and we have had to invent the term 'relative poverty' to distinguish poverty in out society from poverty in say sub-Saharan Africa.

In the UK we have largely adopted the American ethos of 'work hard and play hard'. We work to live and to play, and we expect living and playing to cost money. Living and playing get more and more expensive, so we work harder and harder to cover the costs. The trouble is that working too hard, especially if you are not loving your job, can take a serious toll on your health. The contradiction is all too evident when you look at the numbers of men, usually in cities, who rush from work to the gym, then home to collapse in front of the TV with a drink. It's little wonder that sex within marriage is in steep decline. It's not just that many of us had plenty before we got married, it's also that now we work so hard, as do our wives and partners, we have no energy left for sex at the end of the day. Not a good recipe for a successful marriage.

Getting the balance between work and play is difficult. I can only tell you what works for me, but I have always been in the lucky position of being in charge of my own job and time. The important thing is to make time – spare time. One way I do this is by not having a mobile phone, except in the car for emergencies. Another way is to drive as little as possible and walk as much as possible. I do my best thinking while walking, so it's exercise and work of a sort at the same time. I avoid work meetings wherever possible, which means delegating to the right people. And I'm picky about social meetings, with family always coming first. But however you do it, the lesson is: make time, free up time to do your own thing, and when you do it, relax and do it slowly. You can see why the slow food movement came about. It isn't just about eating slowly and rejecting fast food. It's about making time for the here and now, living in the present instead of always rushing between the past and the future with no time left for you in between. It's about finding priorities in life beyond money and the need to rush that consumerism generates.

My tips when it comes to getting the work/play balance right are these: Throw away the mobile phone, or at least keep it in your car. Get a home gym to save time. In the winter, you'll find workouts much easier to face. Don't neglect your friends, but you don't have to drink a lot of alcohol to be social and have a good time. Take a holiday that will be relaxing, but not one where you lie on the beach all day soaking up ultraviolet rays. Holidays should be full of interest, and involve plenty of walking. If they are too stressful, rethink your plans. It's not for nothing that cruises suit older people less able to cope with the inevitable hassles of more conventional holidays.

Make the effort when it comes to looking after your relationship, and if you haven't got one, make the effort to get one. Take your partner to dinner now and then and treat her as someone special instead of taking her for granted. One of the fastest ways to shorten your life is to work too hard at the expense of your relationship. The damage this can do to your well-being, not to mention your partner's, can take years off your life. Some of life's great stressors, like moving house, losing loved ones and being made redundant may be inevitable, but divorce, in particular, is something to be avoided at all costs. The emotional, financial and physical cost can be enormous. Research has shown that men and women in a happy marriage have a higher level of antibodies to flu four weeks after getting a flu jab. In other words, a happy marriage may boost the immune system.

We take more and more holidays and some of us even take as many as half a dozen long weekends in Europe each year, with maybe a couple of long haul trips thrown in as well, and perhaps a UK trip or two. The trouble with travel is the stress it can cause. I have worked in the travel industry almost all my working life, as chairman of WEXAS, the travel club. As an insider I should know a lot about taking the stress out of travel. I have written two books on travel. I'm experienced at suggesting places to go and what to do when you get there. But I have never managed to master the stress-free holiday. I've told myself a hundred times that it comes down to attitude more than what you do and where you do it.

But I still get stressed when I travel. Checking in is a nightmare at Heathrow or Gatwick. Travelling in Business Class is better than Economy Class if you can afford it, and so is using airport lounges if you have access to them, but even so, as I get older, I find travel more and more stressful. I can stand back and see that this is partly me – I'm not as young as I was and that can make things that little bit more difficult. But I can also see that travel itself has changed over the years. People are ruder. Service has gone downhill. At the other end, in many countries, things are no better. And I'm not good at queuing at the best of times.

I don't get excited at having my passport stamped by a sullen bureaucrat jumped up in a uniform, even if I can understand where he or she is coming from. I'm not happy to check out of hotels where, as once happened in Poland, I am pursued out of a hotel costing £150 a night by the checkout clerk demanding, on the street, to know if I have taken anything from the mini-bar that morning.

I could fill pages with such stories. They are part of the joys of travel, and it's strange that years later, it's often the hassles we remember rather than the highlights of a trip. In fact I am experienced enough to see the funny side of such incidents, but they don't seem funny at the time and they certainly can be stressful. I am not saying don't travel – I am just saying that travel can be stressful and that the holidays that are meant to refresh after a hard time at work can often have the opposite effect unless we approach them in the right frame of mind.

Here are a few things that might perk up your life and your immune system at the same time, since happy people are known to have more immunity than unhappy people. Join a choir. Singing in a choir is a group activity and group activities bring on the endorphins and dopamine and raise your serotonin level. It's also good for your lungs and increases blood levels of oxytocin, the feel-good hormone more usually associated with chocolate and being in love. Laughing a lot has the same effect and laughter therapy is even available privately in some US clinics. It raises the pain threshold, helps you lose weight and allegedly can lessen the symptoms of Type 2 diabetes. It also helps people with rheumatoid arthritis by reducing the level of inflammatory chemicals in their blood.

Hobbies are good for your wellbeing. They moderate stress, boost the immune system, diminish depression and improve your mood. The more passionate you are about your hobby the better. When you are happier, for whatever reason – and laughter and a hobby are just two routes to happiness – your blood pressure falls and your immune system is strengthened.

Optimism is increasingly used as a measure of happiness and wellbeing by clinical psychologists. Those with a positive outlook are not only better at their jobs and generally more successful, they also tend to live longer. Most successful entrepreneurs are optimists. They have less atherosclerosis and are less likely to catch viruses, again suggesting a strong correlation between happiness and the immune system.

Do you need a life coach to tell you how to run your life? Life coaches, an American concept, have become popular in the UK in recent years. While I am in favour of personal trainers if you have the time and money, I feel that anyone who needs someone else to guide their life for them is lacking in the get-up-and-go that characterizes people who are happy and successful. If you need to hand over responsibility for the course of your life to another person, you may not be solving any of life's problems. In fact, you may be more in need of a psychotherapist than a life coach. I see life coaches as only one step removed from that other US phenomenon, the personal shopper. There are people who have the wish, not unnatural in all of us from time to time, to regress to childhood when everything was done for them and there was no personal responsibility, but when this wish is acted out by using money to hire others to do the most basic things for them, there is bound to be a feeling of helplessness that is the antithesis of being in total command of your own life. It's only when you truly feel in charge of your life that you are happy. This goes back to the idea that the happiest most successful people take responsibility for success and failure, while the unhappiest people, the pessimists, blame others for everything.

CHAPTER FORTY-SIX

EXTRA TIPS AND TRAPS
IN BRIEF

Hernia

There are many types of hernia. The term describes a condition in which part of your body intrudes into another part where it doesn't belong. The commonest type of hernia, and one which affects many men in middle life, is an inguinal hernia. This involves a part of the intestines protruding into an opening in the lower abdominal wall, which is made up of tendons and muscles. If the intestine is trapped there, the hernia is described as strangulated. An inguinal hernia may develop in either side (or both sides) of the groin over several years, and may be triggered in various ways, two of the commonest being lifting a heavy object, and straining to urinate in cases of benign prostatic hyperplasia (BPH) (see chapter 43 on the prostate). There may be discomfort or slight pain to start with. Assuming the problem has been identified early on, to rule out something more serious, it is probably wise to get treatment only when the pain becomes less tolerable. The normal treatment is with surgery, sometimes laser surgery, to insert a patch beneath the abdominal wall to block the opening creating the hernia. Stitches complete the operation, which is performed under local anaesthetic and may or may not involve an overnight stay in the hospital or clinic.

Also common is a sliding hiatus hernia, though this type of hernia is often left untreated permanently and correcting it with surgery tends to be unsatisfactory. Most men with a hiatus hernia will not even be aware that it is there. It's a hernia in which the upper part of the stomach protrudes up through the opening in the diaphragm between the stomach and the chest cavity. It's usually painless and the only likely sign that it is there may be acid reflux, especially at night, though even this may not be noticeable if it occurs only during sleep.

Fibromyalgia

This is a musculoskeletal disorder that doesn't normally respond to conventional painkillers. Now a treatment is available in the shape of a drug called Lyrica.

Stem Cell Research

This is a huge and growing research field. When we talk of stem cells we usually mean embryonic stem (ES) cells, which are cells that are able to divide, grow and mature into any one of the more than 220 different cell types in the body. This field of research has faced many ethical issues as, until recently, it has relied on using human foetal cells and cells from human eggs. Now a new type of stem cell called an induced pluripotent stem (IPS) cell can be generated using modified adult skin cells (fibroblasts) from the patient donor which can be reprogrammed to become any tissue type, thereby acting as though it were an embryonic stem cell, before being transplanted back, rather like 'spare parts', to the donor, with the bonus that there is little risk of rejection as the cells are not seen by the body's immune system as 'foreign'. However, this breakthrough still has a long way to go before it has practical application. The retroviral vectors used to manipulate the four genes targeted in this research risk triggering cancer tumours, and there is a known cancer link with one of the altered genes. One day, it is hoped, it will be possible to use stem cells to regenerate nerves and particularly the spinal nerves of paraplegics.

Parkinson's disease, Alzheimer's disease, rheumatism, motor neuron disease and diabetes are other areas where stem cell therapy is likely to prove useful, especially the testing of new drugs. Beyond that, there are dozens of diseases that may one day respond to stem cell therapy, as well as the potential for repair to human tissue that has been damaged.

Recently it was found that stem cell therapy was showing promise in regenerating tissue in hearts damaged by a heart attack and brains damaged by a stroke.

DNA Research

The battle is on to identify particular genes linked to particular diseases, now that we know that genes influence susceptibility to diseases and the way that the diseases progress. Every individual's genes are different, which means that one day it will be possible to tailor therapy to individual requirements.

One development in DNA therapy involves tuning specific genes on or off, and already drugs are being trialled for diabetic nerve damage (neuropathy), arterial disease and HIV. This will be followed by work on the brain cancer gliobastoma, and on single-gene diseases such as sickle-cell anaemia. The aim is to turn off damaging 'rogue' genes in some cases, and in others, to turn on protective genes. The process works by modifying gene activity using proteins called transcription factors. These can target specific genes in a form called a zinc-finger nuclease. For example, a drug designed around a zinc-finger nuclease can bind to the VEGF-A gene known to protect the nervous system, thereby reducing the pain and nerve damage associated with diabetic neuropathy.

DNA is also being used in the weight loss arena. The body size and shape of individuals varies widely, and about 600 genes are thought to be involved. So far seven of these have been identified, leading to clinics, mainly in the US, offering diet plans designed around how a particular individual expresses these genes. This new approach to weight loss has been given the name nutrigenomics. Essentially it's a branch of the wider field of personal genome analysis, which will become a major part of the screening scene in the next decade or so. The term 'gene screen' is likely to become a feature of the language of health and medicine.

Sixteen percent of the UK population have two copies of a variant of a gene called FTO (see chapter 44 on weight loss), making them 70% more likely to become obese. In other words, while what you eat and how much you exercise are important, they are not the whole story, which may come as some relief to those who are fat.

The GNB3 gene, one of the seven, controls insulin sensitivity, which in turn influences fat storage. Those with the gene may be able to lose weight on a low GI diet (see chapter 44 on weight loss). Those with the gene NPY are likely to feel constantly hungry and are advised to fight hunger pangs by snacking on vegetables, which is healthy and helps give a feeling of fullness. The Beta-3 gene has an influence on fat storage, especially in sedentary people, so those with the gene are advised to exercise more. One version of the gene called plasminogen inhibitor is linked to inflammation, and can cause a variety of problems in those who are overweight. Homocysteine, a metabolite of methionine (see chapter 41 on cardiovascular disease) is affected by the gene MTHFR. High levels of homocysteine are normally brought down by folic acid supplements.

It's clear that diet recommendations based on identifying particular genes is very much in its infancy. It would be an exaggeration to say that clinics offering personalised gene screens to arrive at diet plans are exploiting the gullible. However, my advice would be to wait a few more years until there is more science behind nutrigenomics.

Without delving into your genes, there are ways of telling whether the odds of putting on weight are stacked against you. These include: having an older mother; having a low birth weight; living near an industrial complex producing the pollutants organochlorines and organophosphates, which can activate dormant fat cells called preadipocytes; having central heating or air-conditioning at home or at work, since this will make you burn fewer calories without the effort to keep warm or cool down.

Cancer has been an area of intense DNA research for some years now, and in particular lung cancer, which kills more people worldwide than any other cancer. A gene called NKX2-1 has been found to have a strong link to lung cancer, and partly explains why some smokers never get cancer, while some non-smokers do. NKX2-1 appears to play a major role in the growth of cells in the lungs. A mutation in the gene, thereby causing cancer, will be targeted in the future with specific drugs, much as Herceptin is currently used to target breast cancers involving the gene known as Her-2. In time, the full genome of each of the 200 or so known types of cancer will be mapped, and drugs developed which take aim at the particular genes involved.

Following on from the mapping of the human genome, completed in 2003, the 1000 Genomes Project is underway to map the DNA of a test sample of at least 1000 volunteers from a wide range of ethnic groups with the objective of studying individual DNA variation and the extent to which this influences propensity to and the development of a variety of diseases. The results will cover at least one percent of the world's population. Some very rare and some very common genetic variants that link to certain diseases are already well explored. What this project will do is identify the broad range of variants in between. This will help to explain why some people are at risk of certain diseases while others are not, and point the way, in some cases, towards a treatment.

Pain

One of the goals of safe local anaesthesia is to find a painkiller (analgesic) which will make it possible to feel no pain while still being able to move. Such a painkiller would have widespread use in surgery, dentistry and childbirth. It might also be used to treat chronic itching. An experimental drug that shows promise is based on capsaicin, the hot ingredient in chilli peppers. It's combined with a drug called QX-314 that is given by injection. It blocks pain-sensitive nerves from signalling pain to the brain, without affecting other nerve pathways. QX-314, derived from lidocaine, is already used as a local anaesthetic. The addition of capsaicin results in only certain neural pathways being shut down, leaving others free to function.

Trials of supplements, drugs and surgical techniques

Throughout this book I have referred in various terms to trials, tests and research. In order to avoid making the book too technical, I have avoided giving references. I apologise in advance to my critics on this point. One thing I have learnt from researching this book is that most trials do not measure up to the gold standard that would be required for publication in journals like *Nature Medicine* and the *New England Journal of Medicine*. The standard trial is usually described as an RCT, which is a Randomised Controlled Trial. If we want to get more specific, we can say that a proper trial, at least where supplements and drugs are concerned, should be described as a randomised prospective placebo-controlled double-blind clinical trial.

If you explore the internet in search of validation for various supplements in the multi-billion dollar health market, you will find that there have been very few trials that meet the strictest criteria. Instead you will find a high proportion of dubious trial references, and even more dubious testimonials in support of various supplements that are for sale. The supplements themselves may or may not be what they purport to be – it's what is claimed for them that is more of a problem. The books on supplementation are not much better and generally contain a good deal of 'evidence' that has more to do with wishful thinking than science. Which is why the report in the ultra-respectable *New England Journal of Medicine* that Saw Palmetto did not work as a treatment for benign prostatic hyperplasia (BPH) (see chapter 43 on the prostate) made urologists worldwide sit up and take notice.

There are many good and mostly reliable reports on drug trials to be found on the Internet, and even many of those testing supplements are probably reliable. It's the usually long list of diseases that such and such a supplement may prevent or cure that leaves you wondering how anyone can actually know with such assurance. I have tried in this book to hedge around the viability of the supplements I mention (see chapter 14 on supplements), as I want to make it clear that currently the evidence for most is tenuous and supplements are best taken as a form of insurance and a preventive, rather than as a cure for a particular disease.

Trials for surgical techniques are a different matter, as I found out when I started looking at treatments for BPH, hiatus hernia and inguinal hernia, or even the treatment of angina, where the surgical choices are between bypass surgery and angioplasty. It seems that nowadays there is more than one surgical technique for a long lost of ailments. Knife or laser or heat treatment? Or ultrasound? Local or general anaesthetic? In-patient or out-patient surgery? Operate or wait and watch? Short-term, long-term or permanent outcome? Morbidity and mortality risk? Which drugs to use before and after? The good thing about trials of surgical techniques is that the outcome can usually be measured. With drugs and supplements, particularly as results might not be seen for years, the findings of trials are usually anything but absolute. I expect that in fifty years time, the picture may be a good deal clearer.

If you explore medical trials on the Internet, you will often come across the term meta-analysis. This is a substitute for a trial in an area of research where there have already been many trials. A meta-analysis looks at the results of a number of trials in the same area and attempts to provide conclusions that are a kind of 'average' of all the results. This form of analysis is now very common in medicine, where thousand of trials are ongoing at any one time.

Home testing kits

The Internet has changed the way we look at diseases, especially if we are among the worried well. Once doctors used to keep their patients in the dark, even writing prescriptions in a hand that was meant to be indecipherable to the common herd. Arguably this was one way in which doctors cultivated a certain mystique and rose to be such respected members of the community. Now that mystique has evaporated and so has some of the respect, though patient knowledge is only one factor involved.

Just as patients may turn to self-diagnosis using websites and books (and often get it wrong), they are also increasingly testing themselves at home for a growing list of complaints. There are now home testing kits available for meningitis, blood pressure, diabetes, heart rate and cholesterol level. Soon there will be home kits for liver function and HIV.

Parkinson's Disease

Parkinson's disease is known to be influenced by heredity in many cases, and there is a further likelihood of developing the condition if you were ever knocked unconscious – the more times the greater the likelihood. There is also evidence that exposure to herbicides and pesticides may increase the risk.

POST SCRIPT

Newspapers have their writers who prepare obituaries in advance for celebrities and the great and good. One of these writers noticed something the other day. A large number of the people he was writing about had something in common apart from their fame – they had undergone some tragic experience in their lives, often as children.

This makes you stop and think. It makes you think about what makes people famous or great. Talent helps, but so many people have greatness or celebrity thrust upon them, rather being born to it or having an undeniable talent. In other words they are either lucky or ambitious or both. I wonder about whether the great and the good live longer healthier lives, and how much their lives are influenced by talent, luck, ambition and birth. I feel sure that many of these people will have led unhappy lives, especially those who died young. A satisfying life is one which is relatively effortless. I don't mean by not working hard. I mean effortless because it is all about doing what comes naturally, rather than struggling for something that others might have. Life must have been easier in the days when there were no media to make people envious of what others had, and so people led contented lives without the material things that are now considered as the essentials of a normal life, or as something that is still a luxury, but might be achieved more by luck than effort.

The choice for the worried well is a hard one. I mean the choice of where to draw the line between healthy self-love and unhealthy narcissism, or to put that another way: the choice between acceptance of the health we have and the health we might have if we paid more attention to it. I think the answer varies for every individual. I started this book by saying that we should avoid extremes. I hope that the tips and traps I have described will help you decide where to draw your personal line.

USEFUL ORGANISATIONS AND WEBSITES

ALCOHOL

Alcohol in Moderation
www.aim-digest.com

Institute of Alcohol Studies
www.ias.org.uk

ALLERGY

British Allergy Foundation
www.allergyfoundation.com

ALTERNATIVE MEDICINE

National Center for
Complementary and Alternative
Medicine
www.nccam.nih.gov

ALZHEIMER'S DISEASE

Alzheimer's Disease Society
www.alzheimers.org.uk

ARTHRITIS

Arthritis Research Campaign
www.arc.org.uk

BACK PAIN

BackCare
www.backpain.org

CANCER

Imperial Cancer Research Fund
www.icnet.uk

Cancer Research UK
www.cancerresearch.gov

COUNSELLING AND PSYCHOTHERAPY

British Association for
Counselling and Psychotherapy
www.counselling.co.uk

DIABETES

Diabetes UK
www.diabetes.org.uk

HEALTH INFORMATION ONLINE

Bandolier
www.jr2.ox.ac.uk/bandolier

BBC Online Health and Fitness
www.bbc.co.uk/health

Best Treatments
www.besttreatments.co.uk

Centers for Disease Control and Prevention
www.cdc.gov

Cochrane Collaboration
www.cochrane.org

Cochrane Library
www.thecochranelibrary.com

Consumer Health Information Centre
www.chic.org.uk

EMBASE
www.EMBASE.com

e-med
www.e-med.co.uk

German Institute for Quality and Efficiency in Healthcare
www.informedhealthonline.com

Health on the Net Foundation
www.hon.ch

Medline
www.medline.cos.com

Medline Plus
www.nlm.nih.gov/medlineplus

National Institute for Health and Clinical Excellence (NICE)
www.nice.org.uk

Netdoctor
www.netdoctor.co.uk

Talk to a Doctor
www.talktoadoctor.co.uk

US National Library of Medicine and National Institutes of Health (Pubmed)
www.pubmed.gov

Washington University in St Louis School of Medicine
www.yourdiseaserisk.wustl.edu

DIAGNOSTIC SCREENING (Biochemistry)

The Doctor's Laboratory
www.tdlpathology.com

Biolab Medical Unit
www.biolab.co.uk

HCA International
www.hcainternational.com

DIETARY SUPPLEMENTS

British Supplement Information Service
www.bsis.org

Office of Dietary Supplements
http://ods.od.nih.gov

DRUG VERIFICATION AND VALIDATION

Healthy Skepticism
www.healthyskepticism.org

National Standard
www.nationalstandard.com

Royal Pharmaceutical Society of Great Britain
www.rpsgb.org

Medicines and Healthcare Products Regulatory Agency
www.mhra.gov.uk

EXERCISE

Human Kinetics
www.humankinetics.com

FOOD SAFETY

Food Standards Agency
www.food.gov.uk

Soil Association
www.soilassociation.org

Assured Food Standards
www.redtractor.org.uk

Marine Stewardship Council
www.msc.org

Freedom Food
www.freedomfood.co.uk

Vegan Society
www.vegansociety.com
Vegetarian Society
www.vegsoc.org

Fairtrade
www.fairtrade.org.uk

Lion Quality
www.britegg.co.uk

LEAF
www.leafuk.org

Organic Food federation
www.foodfed.com

HEART DISEASE

British Heart Foundation
www.bhf.org.uk

LUNG DISEASE

British Lung Foundation
www.lunguk.org

MEDICAL JOURNALS

Annals of Internal Medicine
www.annals.org

BMJ Best Treatments
www.besttreatments.bmj.com

BMJ Clinical Evidence
www.clinicalevidence.bmj.com

British Medical Journal
www.bmj.com

New England Journal of
Medicine
www.nejm.com

Journal of the American Medical
Association
www.jama.com

The Lancet
www.thelancet.com

MENTAL HEALTH

Mind
www.mind.org.uk

Rethink
www.rethink.org

Sane
www.sane.org.uk

NATIONAL HEALTH SERVICE and DEPARTMENT OF HEALTH

Department of Health
www.doh.gov.uk

NHS Choices
www.nhs.uk

National Health Service Direct
www.nhsdirect.nhs.uk

NHS National Library for
Health
www.library.nhs.uk

ONLINE HEALTH
RECORD STORAGE

www.healthvault.com

PATIENT
ORGANISATIONS

The Patients Association
www.patients-association.org.uk

Patient UK
www.patient.co.uk

DIPEx
www.dipex.org

POLLUTION

Chartered Institute of
Environmental Health
www.cieh.org

National Society for Clean Air
www.nsca.org.uk

PRIVATE HEALTHCARE
INFORMATION

Private Healthcare UK
www.privatehealth.co.uk

Harley Street Direct
www.harleystreet.com

PRIVATE DIAGNOSTIC
CLINICS

BUPA
www.bupa.com

BMI Healthcare
www.bmihealthcare.co.uk

European Scanning Centre
www.europeanscanning.com

Prescan
www.prescan.co.uk

Preventicum, London Centre of
Preventive Medicine
www.preventicum.co.uk

Quest Diagnostics
www.questdiagnostics.com

Nuffield Proactive Health
www.nuffieldproactivehealth.com

Medicentre
www.medicentre.co.uk

PROSTATE

Prostate Cancer Charity
www.prostate-cancer.org.uk

Association for International
Cancer Research
www.aicr.org.uk

Prostate UK
www.prostatecancertreatment.co.uk

RELATIONSHIPS

Relate
www.relate.org.uk

STRESS

The Stress Management Society
www.stress.org.uk

STROKE

The Stroke Association
www.stroke.org.uk

TEETH

British Dental Health
Foundation
www.dentalhealth.org.uk

TRAVEL OVERSEAS

Centers for Disease Control and
Prevention
www.cdc.gov/travel

Foreign and Commonwealth
Office
www.fco.gov.uk

Medical Advisory Service for
Travellers Abroad
www.masta.org

INDEX